D0929338

AGRICULTURAL FINANCE: SIXTH EDITION

HG
2051
U5
N4
1973

AGRICULTURAL FINANCE: SIXTH EDITION

AARON G. NELSON
Economic Research Service
United States Department of Agriculture

WARREN F. LEE
The Ohio State University

WILLIAM G. MURRAY
Iowa State University

88265

The Iowa State University Press, AMES

1 9 7 3

Library of Congress Cataloging in Publication Data

Nelson, Aaron Gustave, 1911–
    Agricultural finance.
    Includes bibliographies.
       1. Agricultural credit—United States.   2. Agricultural credit.
       3. Agriculture—Economic aspects.
I. Lee, Warren F., 1941–   joint author.
II. Murray, William Gordon, 1903–   joint author.
III. Title.
HG2051.U5N4 1973   332.7′1′0973   73–11112
ISBN 0–8138–0050–1

© 1941, 1947, 1953, 1960, 1967, 1973 The Iowa State University Press
Ames, Iowa 50010. All rights reserved

Composed and printed by
The Iowa State University Press

Sixth edition, 1973
Second printing, 1975
Third printing, 1976

CONTENTS

PART 3: FINANCIAL MARKETS AND AGRICULTURAL LENDING AGENCIES

PREFACE

THE sixth edition of *Agricultural Finance* is a major revision of the fifth edition (1967). This edition is organized in three parts. Part 1 emphasizes the principles of economics and finance as related to agricultural finance, Part 2 covers the financial management of the farm business, and Part 3 contains an analysis of financial markets and the lending institutions which serve the farming sector. *Agricultural Finance* is written primarily to serve as a textbook for undergraduate students; however, new material incorporated in the sixth edition should make this book suitable for advanced undergraduate and beginning graduate courses in agricultural finance as well. Updated lists of references for most chapters are provided to permit students to pursue areas of special interest in greater depth.

Part 1 contains an introductory chapter, a chapter on economic principles, and two new chapters—one covering the time value of money and one covering the theory of financial management.

In Part 2, the chapter on acquiring capital to farm has been expanded to include a more extensive coverage of partnerships, incorporation, and leasing. Material from the fifth edition on financial records has been updated and integrated into a three-chapter sequence covering the balance sheet, the income statement, and the cash flow statement. The subject of risk management has been expanded into a two-chapter sequence covering formal and informal insurance. Two new chapters, one dealing with retirement and another with estate transfer, have been added. Material from the fifth edition on interest rates and loan costs, loan repayment terms, the legal aspects of finance, and lenders' analysis and servicing of loans has been retained, with some revisions.

In Part 3 a new chapter has been added on the financial markets, and the chapter on monetary policy has been broadened to include a brief discussion of fiscal policy. These chapters are included to provide a basic understanding of the financial framework and operation of the financial system within which financial intermediaries serving agriculture operate. The chapter on financial intermediaries serving agriculture has been broadened to include equity capital in addition to credit. Material on lending institutions has been condensed somewhat to allow space for new material.

We gratefully acknowledge the suggestions and information given by a number of professional people who contributed to this work.

Gerald M. Burke, New Mexico State University; William McD. Herr, Southern Illinois University; Dana H. Myrick, Montana State University; Ewell P. Roy, Louisiana State University; Robert S. Smith, Cornell University; Robert C. Suter, Purdue University; and J. H. Yeager, Auburn University gave suggestions on the fifth edition which were used in planning the sixth edition.

John R. Brake, Michigan State University, reviewed most of the chapters in Parts 1 and 2 and provided numerous helpful suggestions. We are grateful to Professor H. B. Howell, Iowa State University, who furnished updated material for "Farm Business A" used in Chapters 7, 8, and 9. We also want to thank C. B. Baker and John A. Hopkin for granting us permission to use their work on farm firm growth in Chapter 4.

Gaylord E. Worden and his associates in the United States Department of Agriculture were, as always, helpful in providing data, charts, and material. Virden L. Harrison and Allen G. Smith reviewed Chapters 1 through 12 and provided many useful suggestions for improving the manuscript. Carson D. Evans and Forrest G. Warren furnished much of the data used to update the chapters on agricultural lenders. They also reviewed and gave comments on the chapters in Part 3.

Several people from the Department of Agricultural Economics and Rural Sociology, The Ohio State University, participated in this work. Norman Murray wrote the computer program used to generate the compound interest tables in the Appendix. Richard D. Duvick reviewed most of Parts 1 and 2 and offered many helpful suggestions. John E. Moore and Richard H. Baker reviewed Chapters 16 and 17. We owe a special thanks to David H. Boyne, department chairman, whose support and encouragement made this endeavor possible.

Emanuel Melichar, Federal Reserve System, and Ernest T. Baughman and associates, Federal Reserve Bank of Chicago, provided information and suggestions pertaining to monetary policy. Derl I. Derr and George W. Coleman, American Banker's Association; Kenneth J. Benda, Hartwick State Bank; and Warren R. Langfitt, Valley National Bank, provided material and suggestions for the chapter on commercial banks. Norvel W. Duncan, Kansas City Life Insurance Company; Vern A. Englehorn, Western Farm Management Company; George A. Fletcher, The Travelers Insurance Company; James O. Melton, The Mutual Life Insurance Company of New York; and Denzil C. Warden, Connecticut Mutual Life Insurance Company, reviewed fifth edition manuscript on insurance company farm loan policies and procedures and gave information and suggestions for updating this material. J. B. Ashcraft, Cities Service Company; P. C. Baichly, Monsanto Commercial Products Company; Carleton C. Dennis and R. J. Kutil, Agway Incorporated; C. E. Erickson, Cargill; D. G. Funk, International Harvester Company; and Dean E. McKee, Deere and Company, provided assistance, information, and suggestions on merchant-dealer-manufacturer financing.

Gene L. Swackhamer provided material and information on the Farm Credit System, reviewed the manuscript for Chapter 24, and gave suggested revisions. Nolan Kegley and others provided material on the Farmers Home Administration and reviewed the chapter from the viewpoint of accuracy.

The assistance of these and other individuals and organizations is sincerely appreciated and acknowledged. However, the authors alone are responsible for the material presented and the views expressed.

AARON G. NELSON

WARREN F. LEE

WILLIAM G. MURRAY

PART 1: PRINCIPLES OF AGRICULTURAL FINANCE

CHAPTER 1: NATURE AND SIGNIFICANCE OF AGRICULTURAL FINANCE

IN MODERN FARMING, as in any other business, the key to a satisfactory money income is a proper amount and combination of productive assets such as land, livestock, machinery, labor, and managerial talent. These productive assets are referred to as capital.[1] The amount of capital a farm operator controls, the terms and conditions under which it is obtained, and the way it is used determine, to a large degree, the level of income.

A knowledge of fundamental principles and analytical procedures facilitates obtaining control over capital and using it efficiently. The study of agricultural finance helps provide such knowledge. Economic analysis helps determine how much capital it will pay to allocate to alternative uses. Financial analysis relating to income, repayment capacity, and risk-bearing ability indicates the total amount of capital the farm business can safely use. Supplemental information pertaining to the legal aspects of borrowing, leasing, and contractual arrangements helps the farmer select the means of acquiring and controlling capital that will contribute most to his farming operation.

MEANING AND SCOPE OF AGRICULTURAL FINANCE. Agricultural finance is the economic study of the acquisition and use of capital in agriculture. It relates to both the macrofinance and microfinance aspects of the agricultural sector of the economy.

Macrofinance. Macrofinance pertains to financing agriculture in the aggregate. Since the total amount of capital in the economy is limited, macrofinance is concerned with (1) the amount of capital to be allocated to agriculture, (2) the terms and conditions under which it is made available, and (3) the way in which it is used in the aggregate sense of balanced production and economic efficiency. Mac-

---

1. The factors of production are often called land, labor, and capital, where capital refers to machinery, equipment, and other man-made factors. The broader definition of capital is adopted in this book, the term *capital* referring to all factors of production as well as to intangible capital such as money or currency, bonds, stocks, and other securities. This broad definition of capital can even be expanded to include *human capital* such as labor and management.

rofinance includes the study of the Federal Reserve System, private and government lending agencies, and the securities exchanges, all of which play a role in raising funds in the capital markets and allocating these funds to the various sectors in the economy and to the individual firms within these sectors.

Part 3 of this text deals with the specialized financial intermediaries that raise funds in the capital markets and channel these funds into the farming sector. An understanding of the lending procedures followed by agricultural lenders such as commercial banks, the Farmers Home Administration, Federal Land Banks, life insurance companies, Production Credit Associations, merchants and dealers, and others is an important part of macrofinance.

Microfinance. Microfinance refers to the financial management of the individual farm business.[2] The function of management is to make decisions in an environment of uncertainty to achieve the goals of the owner or owners of the business. The financial manager is responsible for performing financial analysis in order to make decisions on the acquisition, use, and protection of capital within his business as well as on the legal control of the business.

Financial analysis is concerned with keeping and analyzing financial records and other information needed to intelligently evaluate the past, present, and future financial position of the business. The balance sheet, the income statement, and the cash flow statement are the principal types of records employed by the financial manager in financial analysis.

The acquisition phase of financial management involves determining the sources of capital and the amount of capital to be obtained from each source. The commercial farm operator, or any business manager for that matter, really has only two basic sources of capital, namely, his own equity capital and someone else's capital. Equity capital includes the capital acquired through savings, gifts, inheritances, marriage, etc. Beyond these sources, the financial manager must gain control over outside sources of capital by means of borrowing, leasing, custom hiring, contract farming, and possibly acquiring outside equity capital through a partnership or by issuing shares of stock. To be successful, the financial manager must understand the consequences of using these various sources of capital on the profitability, risk, and rate of growth of his business.

Use of capital involves allocating a limited supply of capital among alternative uses within the business, between the business and

---

2. The term *farm* will be used to include both farm and ranch, and the term *farm management* will include ranch management unless otherwise indicated.

the household, and between present and future uses. Thus the financial manager must have a systematic method of evaluating investment alternatives.

Protection of capital involves evaluating the degree of risk and uncertainty associated with the business and utilizing various types of formal and informal insurance strategies to keep these risks within safe bounds. Holding reserves in the form of cash, investments, and unused borrowing capacity, diversification of enterprises, forward contracting, and hedging are examples of informal insurance. Formal insurance contracts such as life, medical, casualty, and liability insurance policies are also important in the protection of capital in the farm business.

Legal control of the business is closely related to the acquisition phase. Capital control relates to the legal arrangements through which resources are acquired, managed, used, and transferred. The financial manager must decide, for example, whether his business should be operated as a sole proprietorship, a partnership, or a corporation. He must be aware of the legal and other constraints on managerial flexibility associated with the various methods used to control resources. Finally, he must also insure that the ultimate transfer of his capital to new owners and managers can be carried out in an orderly manner.

SIGNIFICANCE OF AGRICULTURAL FINANCE. Tremendous strides in technology enabled United States farmers to increase agricultural production by over 40 percent between 1950 and 1970. The technological revolution of agriculture is a well-known phenomenon. Mechanization, improved varieties, modern chemical pesticides and fertilizers, and new production methods have all been combined to increase production per acre, per animal, and per man-hour of labor. /This technological revolution has brought about several significant changes in the structure of agriculture. These changes include (1) the substitution of physical capital for labor and the increased use of purchased inputs, (2) fewer and larger farming units, (3) the need for substantially more capital both in the aggregate and on a per farm basis, and (4) narrowing profit margins. In this section these trends are analyzed. The projections to 1980 give some indication of what the situation may be like at the end of this decade if present trends continue.

Substitution of Physical Capital for Labor. Figure 1.1 illustrates the trends in the use of selected resources in farming. The use of labor in farming has declined steadily because of mechanization and other forms of new technology. Figure 1.1 also indicates

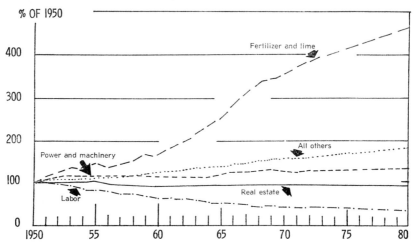

FIG. *1.1—Index of quantities of selected farm inputs used. (Data for 1950 to 1971 courtesy of ERS, USDA. Projections to 1980 are based on linear trend.)*

that the use of cropland remained virtually constant during the period 1950–70. By and large, inputs such as machinery, fertilizers, and chemical pesticides, which are being used in increasing amounts, are purchased from nonfarm sources. The growing use of purchased inputs (including many produced on other farms) compared to farm-produced inputs has created an increased demand for cash operating funds.

Fewer and Larger Farming Units. Greater investment in mechanical power and machinery not only facilitates handling more land but it also stimulates the farmer to acquire a larger acreage to spread his fixed costs in machinery and equipment. This pressure to expand has resulted in a rapid consolidation of smaller farms into larger units.

Figure 1.2 shows the trend in the number of farms by sales class in the United States for 1960 and 1970, with projected numbers to 1980. The total number of farms decreased from about 4 million to less than 3 million during the 1960s and the greatest decline in farm numbers occurred among the group of small farms with less than $10,000 annual sales of farm products. The number of farms with sales of $10,000 to $19,999 has remained fairly constant, while the number of farms with sales of more than $20,000 has been increasing rapidly. Food and fiber production in the United States is becoming more and more concentrated among a relatively small number of large firms. Approximately 20 percent of all farms have sales of $20,000 or more, but these larger farms account for nearly four-fifths of the total sales from the entire farming sector.

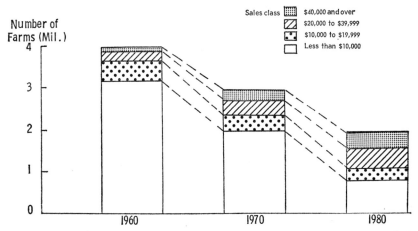

FIG. *1.2—Number of farms by value of sales class. (Data for 1960 and 1970 courtesy of ERS, USDA. Projections to 1980 are based on linear trend.)*

Growing Capital Requirements. The aggregate effect of increasing capital requirements is shown by the balance sheet of the farming sector, portrayed graphically in Figure 1.3. The balance sheet of the farming sector brings together the assets and liabilities of agriculture as though it were one large farm business.

Caution must be used in interpreting these balance sheet data. First, they are aggregates and, therefore, do not reflect the actual financial situations of the individual owner-operators, tenants, and

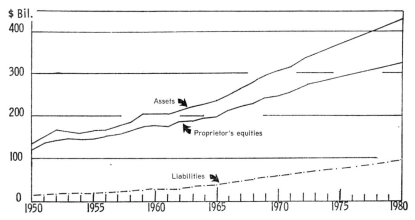

FIG. *1.3—Balance sheet of the farming sector. (Data for 1950 to 1972 courtesy of ERS, USDA. Projections to 1980 are based on linear trend.)*

landlords. Moreover, the data on the balance sheet do not permit full separation of the farm business and the farm household. Another characteristic of the balance sheet data is that assets are valued at current market prices. The valuation of farm assets at market prices makes farm-nonfarm comparisons difficult because comparable data for nonfarm industries are based on depreciated values, that is, on the *book value* or *cost basis* of the assets.

The balance sheet of the farming sector illustrates the steady increase in total capital requirements. Between 1950 and 1970 the total market value of all farm assets increased from $132.5 billion to $311.4 billion. Rising farm real estate values accounted for about 75 percent of this increase, the remainder coming from increases in the amounts and prices of nonreal-estate assets. Overall, inflation rather than real growth accounted for about 88 percent of the nearly $180 billion increase in farm assets that occurred during this period because, at the beginning of 1970, the total value of farm assets in 1947–49 prices was only $154.8 billion.

Total liabilities have also increased rapidly, both in absolute and relative amounts. In 1950 total liabilities were $12.4 billion, and the debt:asset ratio, a common measure of financial strength, was 9.4 percent. By 1970 total liabilities were $58.1 billion and the debt:asset ratio was 18.7 percent. At first glance, the debt:asset ratio in agriculture compares very favorably with the debt:asset ratio of approximately 40 percent reported for all manufacturing firms in the United States. However, the 40 percent ratio for manufacturing firms is based on the book value of assets. At the beginning of 1970, the estimated cost basis value of all farm assets was $185.0 billion and the corresponding debt:asset ratio was 31.4 percent, still not as high as the manufacturing sector ratio, but reasonably close.

The combination of the rapid growth in total capital requirements in agriculture and a steadily declining number of farms has produced an almost phenomenal growth in capital and credit requirements *per farm*. During the 1960s the market value of total assets per farm for all farms in the United States more than doubled, rising from about $51,500 to $104,800. In 1970 the largest 20 percent of all farms—those with total sales exceeding $20,000—had total assets of nearly $260,000 per farm. On the other side of the farm balance sheet, the debt load per farm for all farms in the United States more than tripled from about $6,000 to $19,600 during the 1960s. The average debt load for farms with total sales of $20,000 or more was over $50,000 per farm on January 1, 1970.

Although these aggregate figures tell us very little about the financial positions of individual farmers or the wide variations among types of farms, they clearly indicate that capital and credit requirements per farm are already high and they are growing rapidly. The

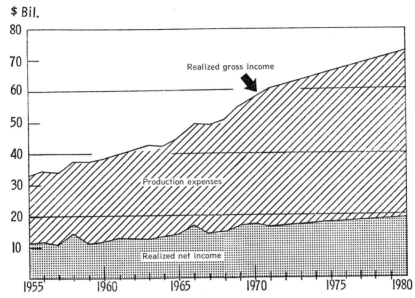

FIG. *1.4—Farm income components. (Data for 1955 to 1971 courtesy of ERS, USDA. Projections to 1980 are based on linear trend.)*

farm operator who hopes to become a part of the 20 percent of the farmers in the United States who produce about four-fifths of the agricultural output will, on the average, need to control about a quarter of a million dollars in productive assets. The rapid growth in total liabilities per farm indicates that borrowing is one method being used more extensively to gain control of additional resources. Many farm operators successfully carry much larger than average debt loads but there are definite limitations on the extent to which borrowing can be used to finance a business enterprise.

Narrowing Profit Margins. While aggregate capital and credit needs in the United States farming sector continue to increase, aggregate net income from farming has been rising very slowly. Figure 1.4 illustrates the well-known cost-price squeeze in agriculture. Gross income has been increasing but production costs have been rising even faster, so net income, as a percentage of gross income, has been constantly declining.

One might well ask how it is possible for an industry to support a rapidly increasing amount of debt with a slowly increasing net income. From 1950 to 1969, aggregate interest charges increased from $0.6 billion to $3.3 billion, respectively. Interest charges account for a major portion of the debt servicing needs, but they are included in the production expenses in Figure 1.4. Likewise, depreciation on capital items, which would correspond to principal payments on loans for depreciable capital, are also included in the production expenses. But the increased level of debt outstanding on farm real estate has brought about higher principal payments on this debt, and these must be paid from net income. About half the total amount of farm debt outstanding is classified as real estate debt.

One possible explanation of the ability of the farming sector to support this larger debt load is the increasing concentration of agricultural production among a relatively few large firms. Over half the total amount of farm debt outstanding is owed by farms with sales of $20,000 or more and it is reasonable to assume that the operators of these larger farms are better farm managers and thus are capable of carrying larger debt loads.

Nonfarm income is another factor that explains the farming sector's ability to carry more debt. Many farm operators and members of their families have full-time or part-time off-farm jobs. In the aggregate, farm operators and their families now derive about as much net income from nonfarm employment as they do from their farming operations, and part of this nonfarm income is available for farm debt repayment. Nonfarm income is an especially important source of funds among the farms with less than $10,000 annual sales.

Farm lenders have also played an important role in enabling the farming sector to utilize more borrowed capital. By continuously updating their policies and procedures for farm loan analysis and supervision, they have been able to lend more money with little, if any, sacrifice in the quality of their agricultural loan portfolios.

IMPLICATIONS OF THE CHANGING FINANCIAL STRUCTURE OF FARMING.

The technological revolution in agriculture is expected to continue into the foreseeable future. The structural changes accompanying this revolution—the substitution of capital for labor, fewer and larger farms, growing capital and credit requirements, and a rising ratio of farm production expenses to gross farm income—will also continue to occur. Although the exact magnitude of the changes in the structure of agriculture in the United States cannot be precisely estimated, the general trends are clear. The number of farms will continue to decline and those that remain will be larger. Aggregate capital and credit needs will continue to increase, and farm production, income, capital, and credit use will become increasingly concentrated among the larger firms. The owners and operators of the smaller farm firms will stay in business largely through their growing reliance on income from nonfarm sources.

These trends raise some important questions. First, can the institutions and individuals that supply farm credit continue to meet the challenge of providing for the financial needs of farmers? The total amount of farm credit outstanding has more than doubled during each 10-year period since 1950 and projections indicate that the 1980 farm debt load may be nearly twice as high as it was in 1970. If the projected growth in farm debt materializes, will some farm lenders find it increasingly difficult to perform their dual role of raising funds in the capital markets and rationing these funds among their farm borrowers? Some lenders, particularly smaller country banks, are too small to serve large farming operations effectively now.

Another perplexing question is, How can the individual farm operator cope with the rapidly rising capital requirements of his business? What combination of equity capital, credit, leasing, custom hiring, and contract farming will enable him to achieve a sufficiently large farm business, given the usual limitation of a fixed equity capital base? Can the family farm as we know it now survive as an economically viable entity in the face of the rapidly increasing capital requirements of farming?

Precise answers to such questions are elusive, but these and other issues are included in the area of agricultural finance. The remainder of Part 1 of this book develops the theoretical and conceptual framework of agricultural finance. Part 2 deals with the financial management of the modern commercial farm business, and Part 3 covers the characteristics of the principal suppliers of agricultural credit.

QUESTIONS AND PROBLEMS

1. Explain the meaning of macrofinance and microfinance as related to agricultural finance.
2. Discuss the reasons for the growing capital requirements in agriculture. Estimate the amounts of capital needed to start full-time farming in your area as a tenant. As an owner.
3. Compare the trends in the total amount of debt outstanding in the farming sector with total assets. With gross farm income. With net farm income.
4. Find figures showing farm real estate and nonreal-estate debt outstanding in your state for recent years. How do the trends in your state compare with the national trends? Discuss reasons for any significant differences.
5. Discuss whether the family farm will remain economically viable in view of the rapidly growing capital requirements of farming. Do you think that American agriculture will eventually be dominated by giant corporate farms?
6. What factors might tend to reduce the trend to fewer and larger farming operations?

REFERENCES

Baker, C. B., and Holcomb, J. M. "The Emerging Financial Problems in a Changing Agriculture." *Jour. Farm Econ.*, vol. 46, no. 5, Dec. 1964.

Baum, E. L.; Diesslin, H. G.; and Heady, E. O., eds. *Capital and Credit Needs in a Changing Agriculture.* Iowa State Univ. Press, Ames, 1961.

Benson, Richard A. *A Comparative Analysis of Financing Requirements of Selected Types of Farm Operations in the Eastern Corn Belt for 1980.* Unpublished Ph.D. thesis, Mich. State Univ., 1970.

Boyne, David H. *Changes in the Real Wealth Positions of Farm Operators, 1940–1960.* Mich. Agr. Exp. Sta. Tech. Bull. 294, 1964.

Brake, J. R., ed. *Emerging and Projected Trends Likely to Influence the Structure of Midwest Agriculture, 1970–1985.* Agr. Law Center, College of Law, Univ. of Iowa, June 1970.

———. *Future Capital and Credit Needs of Canadian Agriculture.* Dept. Agr. Econ., Univ. of Guelph, Publication A.E. 70/3, 1970.

———. "Impact of Structural Changes on Capital and Credit Needs." *Jour. Farm Econ.*, vol. 48, no. 5, Dec. 1966, pp. 1536–45.

Brimmer, Andrew F. "Central Banking and the Availability of Agricultural Credit." *Am. Jour. Agr. Econ.*, vol. 50, no. 2, May 1968, pp. 357–65.

Garlock, Fred L. *Farmers and Their Debts: The Role of Credit in the Farm Economy.* ERS, USDA, Agr. Econ. Rept. 93, June 1966.

Irwin, George D. "Three Myths about the Balance Sheet: The Changing Financial Structure of Farming." *Am. Jour. Agr. Econ.*, vol. 50, no. 5, Dec. 1968, pp. 1596–99.

Krause, Kenneth R., and Kyle, Leonard R. "Economic Factors Underlying the Incidence of Large Farming Units: The Current Situation and Probable Trends." *Am. Jour. Agr. Econ.*, vol. 52, no. 5, Dec. 1970, pp. 748–63.

Lee, John E. "Changes in the Financial Structure of the Farm Sector and the Implications for Research." *Am. Jour. Agr. Econ.*, vol. 50, no. 5, Dec. 1968, pp. 1552–63.

Melichar, Emanuel. "Farm Capital and Credit Projections to 1980." *Am. Jour. Agr. Econ.*, vol. 51, no. 5, Dec. 1969, pp. 1172–77.

North Central Extension Public Affairs Committee. *Corporation Farming: What Are the Issues?* North Central Workshop Proc., Univ. of Nebr., Dept. Agr. Econ. Rept. 53, 1969.

Ortel, Dennis D. *The Transfer of Large Farms.* Cornell Univ., Agr. Exp. Sta. Bull., A.E. Res. 180, 1965.

Saunders, A. D. *Financing Alaska's Farms.* Alaska Agr. Exp. Sta. Bull. 35, 1964.

Williams, Darwin. *A Financial Profile of Corn Belt Farms.* Mo. Agr. Exp. Sta. in cooperation with Farm Prod. Econ. Div., ERS, USDA, Spec. Rept. 134, July 1971.

CHAPTER 2: BASIC ECONOMIC PRINCIPLES INVOLVED IN FINANCE

ECONOMIC PRINCIPLES form a basis for making decisions relative to financing the farm business. They provide a framework for deciding the enterprises to be included in the business, the relative amounts of various factors of production to be employed in each enterprise, and the total amount of capital to be used in the business. A knowledge of economic principles also helps in comparing the various sources of finance and in determining the amount of capital to be utilized from each source.

These principles are not unique to finance or to any other particular aspect of the farm business. They are universally applicable in all aspects of management. Only the application varies.

The objective of this chapter is to review briefly the basic economic principles involved in finance. A few illustrations will be used to help clarify the principles. Their application and importance in financial analysis will become evident in the following chapters.

PRINCIPLE OF DIMINISHING RETURNS. The principle of diminishing returns is of prime importance in economic analysis.

The level to which a farmer should push yield per acre, marketing weight per animal, milk production per cow, and size of farm all revolve around this principle. It comprises the basis for the entire framework of marginal analysis, the most comprehensive and powerful tool in economics. Based on physical relationships, it has economic significance whenever the physical goods involved have value.

The principle of diminishing returns refers to the amount of additional output obtained as additional inputs of variable factors of production are added to a fixed amount of other factors. The principle may be expressed in its simplest form as follows: With the quantity of one factor of production held constant or fixed, the additional output derived from each additional unit of a variable factor declines after a certain level of variable factor use has been attained.

One Variable Factor. Fertilizer application in crop production provides a good illustration of the principle of diminishing returns.

This chapter is intended to provide an introduction to basic economic principles essential to an understanding of principles of finance. Students who have a good understanding of basic economic principles, including marginal analysis, may skip pages 13 to 29.

TABLE 2.1:   Grain Production Related to Various Levels of Fertilizer Application (Hypothetical data)

Inputs			Output: Grain Production	
Fixed factor	Variable factor: nitrogen fertilizer	Total	Average per unit of fertilizer	Additional per unit of fertilizer
	(no. of units)	*(cwt)*	*(cwt)*	*(cwt)*
1	0 (no nitrogen)	24		
				16
1	1 (20 lb)	40	40.0	
				10
1	2 (40 lb)	50	25.0	
				6
1	3 (60 lb)	56	18.7	
				3
1	4 (80 lb)	59	14.8	
				1
1	5 (100 lb)	60	12.0	
				0
1	6 (120 lb)	60	10.0	

Table 2.1 portrays grain production with various amounts of fertilizer applied to a bundle of fixed factors. The term *bundle* is used for the fixed factors (such as land, seed, labor, tractor fuel, and machine services) to emphasize that the proportions as well as the absolute quantities of these factors are held constant. As the amount of fertilizer applied is increased, *total* production increases, but at a decreasing (diminishing) rate. This is reflected in the decrease in additional production per unit of fertilizer added. The first unit of fertilizer applied increased production 16 hundredweight. However, the second unit applied increased production only 10 hundredweight. Additional (incremental) production associated with increased applications of fertilizer continued to decline until, finally, the sixth unit of fertilizer produced no increase in output.

More Than One Variable Factor. The degree to which production of a product per unit of input diminishes depends in large measure on the number of factors involved in producing the product—the number that are allowed to vary and the number that are fixed. The above example illustrates diminishing returns with only one variable factor and all others fixed. If greater amounts of other factors of production also were applied as more fertilizer were added, incremental grain production would decline less sharply. Assume, for example, applications of labor, power and machinery, herbicides, etc., were increased along with fertilizer. Total production likely would increase to a considerably greater extent; that is, additional production associated with successive applications of the bundle of variable inputs would not decline so much.

Constant Returns. Diminishing productivity usually occurs in per
   acre yields, per animal gains, or per animal production. However,
   many situations are found in agriculture where productivity is
constant, perhaps leading one to question the universal application
of the law of diminishing returns. Constant productivity may be possible under two circumstances:
1. Where there are no fixed resources and all factors of production
   are increased simultaneously. In our fertilizer example it was
   assumed a bundle of fixed resources—one acre of land and associated seed, labor, machinery services, and the like—was used. Grain
   production declined since, as fertilizer applications were increased,
   there was relatively less of the fixed factor with which the fertilizer
   could work, or combine, in the production process. If the resources that were assumed to be fixed had been increased along
   with fertilizer, the increase in production would have been at a
   constant rate. However, as the size of business grows, increasing
   all factors of production together becomes difficult, with the result
   that sooner or later diminishing returns become evident.
2. Where factors that are fixed have reserve or excess capacity. For
   example, livestock enterprises often can be expanded with existing
   facilities without adversely affecting the level of production. Excess capacity of the fixed improvements is sufficient to permit the
   expansion. Also, farmers buy or rent additional land to increase
   the size of their farming operation without any significant reduction in yields. In this example, as well as in the preceding one,
   there is sufficient excess or reserve managerial ability to facilitate
   the expansion. However, constant returns will be realized only
   so long as there is excess capacity in the fixed factors. When any
   one of the factors is fully utilized, further expansion of production
   will be accompanied by diminishing returns.

Diminishing Economic Returns. The principle of diminishing returns
   has economic significance since most of the factors of production
   and products produced have economic value. By converting the
physical data to monetary terms, diminishing economic returns are
portrayed. Comparing these returns with the costs involved provides
the basis for determining whether production is profitable and, if so,
the level of production that will maximize returns.

The fertilizer example discussed above is expanded in Table
2.2 to portray costs and returns in addition to the physical data. It
was estimated that the bundle of fixed factors cost $100 and that each
20-pound unit of fertilizer cost $2.50. The grain produced was priced
at $2.00 per hundredweight.

The total value of output (column 11) obviously increases at a
decreasing rate, the same as total physical output (column 7). Simi-

TABLE 2.2: Costs and Returns Related to Diminishing Returns in Grain Production (Hypothetical data)

Inputs		Cost of Inputs				Output			Value of Output			
Fixed factor	Variable factor: nitrogen	Fixed factor	Variable factor	Total cost	Added (marginal) cost	Total	Average per unit of fertilizer	Additional (marginal)	Per cwt	Total	Avg per unit of fertilizer	Additional (marginal)
(1)	(2)	(3)	(4)	(5)	(6)	(7)	(8)	(9)	(10)	(11)	(12)	(13)
	(no. of units)	(dol)	(dol)	(dol)	(dol)	(cwt)	(cwt)	(cwt)	(dol)	(dol)	(dol)	(dol)
1	0	100	0	100		24			2.00	48		
1	1	100	2.50	102.50	2.50	40	40.0	16	2.00	80	80.00	32
1	2	100	5.00	105.00	2.50	50	25.0	10	2.00	100	50.00	20
1	3	100	7.50	107.50	2.50	56	18.7	6	2.00	112	37.33	12
1	4	100	10.00	110.00	2.50	59	14.8	3	2.00	118	29.50	6
1	5	100	12.50	112.50	2.50	60	12.0	1	2.00	120	24.00	2
1	6	100	15.00	115.00	2.50	60	10.0	0	2.00	120	20.00	0

larly, value of the additional (marginal) output (column 13) follows the same pattern as the additional (marginal) physical output (column 9). Similar relationships prevail with constant returns.

Marginal Concepts. The term *marginal* is widely used in economics and should be clearly understood. It means the same as "added" or "additional," and also is used synonymously with "incremental."

With reference to inputs, marginal means the last unit of a factor of production or resource applied, and marginal factor cost refers to the cost of that input. For example, in Table 2.2 the marginal input is one unit of fertilizer, arbitrarily taken to be 20 pounds of nitrogen. The marginal factor cost is $2.50 (column 6).

With reference to output or products, marginal means the amount of product produced with the last unit of a factor or resource applied. For example, in Table 2.2 the marginal physical product is shown in column 9. The marginal physical product of the first unit of fertilizer applied is 16 hundredweight, the marginal physical product of the second unit of fertilizer is 10 hundredweight, and so on. The value of the marginal product, shown in column 13, is obtained by multiplying the marginal product by its price. The value of the marginal product is commonly referred to as *marginal returns*.

FIXED AND VARIABLE COST CONCEPTS. An understanding of the distinction between fixed and variable costs, together with the reasons for the difference, is essential in economic analysis. Profit maximization is determined by marginal analysis, an essential ingredient of which is variable costs. Thus one needs to be able to distinguish between fixed and variable costs, and to do this an understanding is needed of what makes costs variable or fixed. The problem is not simply one of setting up two lists, one of fixed costs and the other of variable costs. The classification is complicated by the fact that the same item of cost may be fixed under certain circumstances and variable under others.

Fixed Costs. Fixed costs, as the term indicates, are fixed; they are constant, not subject to change. They are the result of past commitments, of costs already "sunk," of overhead costs.

Costs ordinarily thought of as being fixed include property taxes, insurance on improvements, building depreciation, interest payments on farm real estate debt, cash rent, and the like. If a hired man is employed on an annual basis, his wage is a fixed cost. Depreciation on machinery is generally considered as a fixed cost on the basis that the machines usually become obsolete before they are worn out. Such costs are not influenced by what is produced or by the level of production.

Variable Costs. Variable costs, as the term indicates, vary with the level of production, and with what is produced. In contrast to fixed costs, they have not been sunk—management is free to determine whether or not the expense should be incurred.

Costs usually classified as variable include such input as seed, tractor fuel, fertilizer, repairs, and feed. Labor hired by the day or week as needed is a variable cost. Interest payments on operating loans usually are classified as a variable cost.

Influence of Time on the Nature of Costs. In the above example of fixed and variable costs, the classifications are arbitrary since costs that are fixed under certain circumstances are variable under others, and vice versa. Time is the culprit involved.

In the long run there are no fixed costs; all costs are variable. This concept may strike one as impossible at first, but a moment's reflection shows that it is feasible. Consider cash rent, for example. Once a cash lease has been signed, the farmer is obligated to pay the rent. When the farmer signs the lease, the payment specified becomes a fixed cost. However, it is fixed only for the term of the lease. When the lease expires, the farmer is free to determine whether or not he wants to rent the property again. Similarly, building depreciation is a fixed cost in the short run since it occurs regardless of whether or not the farmer uses the building. However, depreciation will occur only as long as the building lasts. When the building is gone, there are no sunk costs remaining. The farmer is free to make decisions that will best suit his production plans. Property taxes probably come closest to being a truly fixed cost since they are ever present. Moreover, since they are determined by society, the individual farmer has little control over them. However, in the long run taxes are subject to change, and they are changed as changes in the level of production and in products produced affect the assessed value of the resource.

All costs are variable in the long run since a sufficient period of time is involved so that each factor employed in production is completely used. Obviously, the period of time involved is not the same for all factors of production. The long run associated with each factor is the lifetime of the factor. Therefore, there are no sunk costs remaining at the end of a long-run period.

Since no sunk costs are involved, the long run also connotes managerial freedom to decide whether or not a cost should be incurred. Fixed costs stem from past commitments by management. For example, interest payments stem from a past commitment by management to borrow money. Building depreciation is the result of a past commitment by management to construct a building, which, in turn, gives rise to sunk costs until such time as the building is fully depreciated. The long run pertinent to each factor of production is that period required for all committed costs to be fully retired or expended, leaving management free of costs associated with past commitments.

A critical point in the distinction between fixed and variable costs is managerial freedom to determine whether or not a cost should be incurred. Whenever the manager does not have this choice, the funds already have been sunk and, therefore, the cost is fixed. Thus costs generally classified as variable become fixed as the production period progresses. For example, the cost of seed, fertilizer, tractor fuel, etc., are variable costs up to the time they are utilized. But once they have been applied in land preparation and growing the crop, they are fixed—they are sunk costs over which management has no control.

These concepts are of great significance in determining whether it will pay to produce and, if so, how far to go in use of variable factors.

WILL IT PAY TO PRODUCE? The usual objective in undertaking a business venture is to produce income at least sufficient to cover all costs. Over the long pull, both fixed and variable costs must be covered if the business is to be profitable. When this objective is realized, there is no question as to whether it will pay to produce. However, there is a question when gross income is less than the total of fixed and variable costs.

In the short run it will pay to produce whenever gross income is greater than variable costs. Since fixed costs do not change even though production is nil, one will be ahead financially by producing as long as sufficient income is forthcoming to cover costs related directly to producing the crop or product. When gross income is greater than the total of fixed and variable costs, the objective is to maximize profit by expanding production to the point where marginal factor costs are equal to marginal returns. When gross income exceeds variable costs but is insufficient to also cover fixed costs, losses are minimized by again applying the principle of marginal cost equals marginal return, that is, by using more resources until added factor costs equal added returns. These points will be further analyzed in the next section.

The fact that it will pay to produce if gross income is greater than variable costs can be illustrated by data for a 240-acre grain-livestock farm given in Table 2.3. The first column shows that gross income is sufficient to more than cover total costs, leaving net farm

TABLE 2.3:   Costs and Returns for a 240-Acre Grain-Livestock Farm with Three
Levels of Fertilizer Application (Hypothetical data)

	Costs and Returns with:		
Item	No fertilizer	40 lb of N per acre of corn	80 lb of N per acre of corn
	(dol)	*(dol)*	*(dol)*
Gross Income	31,565	33,350	33,785
Variable Costs			
Seed	325	325	325
Fuel and machine repairs	1,895	1,945	1,990
Hired labor, including prerequisites	885	960	985
Fertilizer	None	490	980
Crop supplies	995	995	995
Custom work	215	215	215
Livestock purchased	7,800	7,800	7,800
Other livestock expense	875	875	875
Feed purchased	4,420	4,420	4,420
Other	290	290	290
Total Variable	17,700	18,315	18,875
Fixed Costs			
Property taxes	1,230	1,230	1,230
Insurance	275	275	275
Interest	2,500	2,500	2,500
Building depreciation and repairs	875	875	875
Machinery and equipment depreciation	1,750	1,750	1,750
Other	475	475	475
Total Fixed	7,105	7,105	7,105
Total Costs	24,805	25,420	25,980
Net Income	6,760	7,930	7,805
Added Costs	. . .	615	560
Added Gross Income	. . .	1,785	435

income of $6,760. Thus it is profitable to operate the farm. But
would it be profitable if prices received for farm products were one-
third lower? Gross income would then be only $21,044, which is less
than total costs of $24,805. A net loss of $3,761 would be realized. It
would still pay to operate the farm, however. Gross income of $21,044
is $3,344 greater than variable costs, and this amount would cover part
of the fixed costs. Thus the farmer's loss would be minimized by operating the farm even though total costs were not covered.

HOW FAR WILL IT PAY TO EXPAND PRODUCTION? Once
a farmer has determined that production is profitable, the next
question is, How much in the way of resources will it pay to use?
The principle of marginal cost equals marginal return is the proper
measure to use in answering this question. Net income is at a maximum when

$$\text{Marginal Cost (MC)} = \text{Marginal Return (MR)}. \qquad (2.1)$$

Budgets for the 240-acre grain-livestock farm referred to in the preceding section (see Table 2.3) indicate that income from corn can be increased by adding commercial fertilizer. Applying 40 pounds of nitrogen added $615 to variable costs but increased gross income $1,785. Thus the budget analysis indicates it would be profitable to apply 40 pounds of nitrogen. The second 40 pounds of nitrogen applied per acre increased costs $560, but gross income increased only $435. Thus the analysis indicates it would not pay to apply the second 40-pound unit of fertilizer since the added cost was greater than the added return. The most profitable amount of fertilizer to apply probably would be somewhere between 40 and 80 pounds of nitrogen per acre.

The illustration of the principle of marginal cost equals marginal return just presented is based upon analysis of the whole farm. The analysis also can be applied to an individual enterprise or segment of the farm business by preparing a *partial* budget for the enterprise or part being studied. It also can be used to determine how far to go in applying variable inputs on a per acre, per cow, and per animal basis. As indicated above, the illustration presented in Table 2.2 assumes a bundle of fixed factors consisting of one acre of land and associated seed, labor, machinery services, and the like, to which were added varying amounts of commercial fertilizer. Marginal income (column 13) from the fourth unit of nitrogen applied was $6.00, which is greater than the marginal factor cost of $2.50 (column 6). Thus, adding the fourth unit of nitrogen increased net income. Marginal income from the fifth unit of fertilizer was only $2.00, however, which is less than the marginal factor cost of $2.50. Therefore, applying four units of fertilizer gave the highest profit per acre. Observe that net income per acre ($8.00) is at a maximum with this level of fertilizer application.

In the discussion of the principle of marginal cost equals marginal return given in the preceding paragraph, the approach was to add additional units of the variable factor until marginal returns had declined to the point where they were equal to the unit price of the factor. Another approach is to add additional units of the variable factor until marginal costs have risen to the point where they are equal to the price of the product. This approach is illustrated in Table 2.4, which is based upon the physical and cost data given in Table 2.2. Marginal cost per unit of output (column 6) is derived by dividing added costs by added production.

Keeping in mind that the price of grain produced was $2.00 per hundredweight (see Table 2.2, column 10), one finds that the principle of marginal cost equals marginal return indicates it will pay to

TABLE 2.4: Marginal and Average Costs per Unit of Output

Inputs of Nitrogen	Grain Output	Fixed Costs	Variable Costs	Total Costs	Marginal Costs per Unit of Output	Average Fixed Costs per Unit of Output	Average Variable Costs per Unit of Output	Average Total Costs per Unit of Output
(1)	(2)	(3)	(4)	(5)	(6)	(7)	(8)	(9)
(no.)	(cwt)	(dol)	(dol)	(dol)	(dol)	(dol)	(dol)	(dol)
0	24	100	0	100.00		4.17	0	4.17
1 (20 lb)	40	100	2.50	102.50	0.16	2.50	0.06	2.56
2 (40 lb)	50	100	5.00	105.00	0.25	2.00	0.10	2.10
3 (60 lb)	56	100	7.50	107.50	0.42	1.79	0.13	1.92
4 (80 lb)	59	100	10.00	110.00	0.83	1.69	0.17	1.86
5 (100 lb)	60	100	12.50	112.50	2.50	1.67	0.21	1.88
6 (120 lb)	60	100	15.00	115.00	Infinity	1.67	0.25	1.92

apply four 20-pound units of nitrogen. At this rate of application the marginal cost per unit of output is 83 cents, considerably less than the unit product price of $2.00. However, the added product produced with the fifth unit of nitrogen would cost $2.50 per hundredweight, 50 cents more than the price of the product. Thus returns are maximized by applying somewhere between 80 and 100 pounds of nitrogen, the same conclusion indicated by the former approach.

Note that the significant comparison involved in maximizing net income is marginal cost versus marginal return. Some people are misled by the value of average output, thinking that if average returns are greater than costs it will pay to produce the additional product. The error of this reasoning is demonstrated by the fifth application of fertilizer in Table 2.2. Average income is $24.00 (column 12), much more than the marginal cost of $2.50. However, as was pointed out above, adding the fifth unit of fertilizer actually reduced net income.

MINIMIZING COSTS. The principle of diminishing returns indicates how production or income will vary as additional resources are applied per acre, per animal, or per farm. It provides an analytical framework for determining whether it will pay to use a given bundle of resources in production and, if so, the amount of resources to use. However, nothing is said about the composition of the bundle of resources. What combination of fertilizer nutrients will be most economical? What combinations of machines and men will cost the least? How much protein supplement should be included in the livestock ration to be most economical? These are the types of questions with which we are concerned in this section. In each case the question is, In what proportions should two competing resources or practices be used in producing a given amount of product to maximize profit?

Diminishing Rates of Substitution. Consider first the situation in which diminishing rates of substitution are involved as one factor or practice is substituted for another with a given level of output. A diminishing rate of substitution occurs whenever addition of successive units of one factor replaces less and less of a second factor used in production of a product. For example, the initial application of protein in beef-fattening rations replaces a substantial amount of grain. However, the second unit added to the ration replaces less grain than the first, the third unit less than the second, and so on. Thus successive additions of protein replace less and less grain or, in other words, protein substitutes at a diminishing rate for grain in rations for fattening cattle. The problem is to determine the most profitable grain-protein supplement combination.

TABLE 2.5: Combinations of Variable Factors of Production, *A* and *B*, in Producing 1,000 Units of Product, *Y* (Hypothetical data)

Factor Combination	Factor *A*	Factor *B*	Marginal Rate of Substitution of *A* for *B**	Cost of Producing 1,000 Units of *Y* with		
				A @ $6 *B* @ $1	*A* @ $4 *B* @ $1	*A* @ $2.50 *B* @ $1.00
(1)	(2)	(3)	(4)	(5)	(6)	(7)
	(units)	*(units)*		*(dol)*	*(dol)*	*(dol)*
1	20	300		420.00	380.00	350.00
			7			
2	25	265		415.00	365.00	327.50
			5			
3	30	240		420.00	360.00	315.00
			4			
4	35	220		430.00	360.00	307.50
			3			
5	40	205		445.00	365.00	305.00
			2			
6	45	195		465.00	375.00	307.50
			1			
7	50	190		490.00	395.00	315.00

* Units of factor *B* replaced by 1 unit of factor *A* at the given level of production.

Analysis involved in solving the problem is illustrated in Table 2.5. It is assumed that 1,000 units of product *Y* are produced with factors *A* and *B*. The letter *Y* is used to represent any product produced under conditions of diminishing rates of substitution, and the letters *A* and *B* are used to represent two factors used in production of product *Y* that substitute for each other at diminishing rates. Beef production with protein and grain already has been indicated as an example. The quantity of Y produced remains constant at 1,000 units, while the quantities of the two factors required vary inversely; that is, the quantity of factor *A* increases, while the quantity of factor *B* decreases. In changing from factor combination (1) to factor combination (2), five units of factor *A* replace 35 units of factor *B*. At the other extreme, five units of factor *A* replace only five units of factor *B*. Thus a diminishing marginal rate of substitution of factor *A* for factor *B* is evident. The marginal rate of substitution for each of the factor combinations is shown in the fourth column.

The costs of producing 1,000 units of product *Y* with three sets of prices for factors *A* and *B* are given in columns 5, 6, and 7. With factor *A* priced at $6.00 and factor *B* at $1.00 per unit, costs are at a minimum with factor combination (2), that is, when 25 units of factor *A* and 265 units of factor *B* are used. Changing the price ratio changes the relative amounts of the factors it will pay to use, of course. With factor *A* priced at $4.00 and factor *B* at $1.00, costs are at a minimum somewhere between factor combinations (3) and (4). With factor *A* priced at \$2.50 and factor *B* at \$1.00, the least cost combination is realized by using 40 units of factor *A* and 205 units of factor *B* to produce the 1,000 units of product *Y*.

Costs are at a minimum when the factor substitution ratio is equal to the inverse of the price ratio. The substitution ratio is the number of units of the *replaced* factor divided by the number of units of the *added* factor. The price ratio is the price of the added factor divided by the price of the replaced factor. In algebraic form

$$\frac{\Delta A}{\Delta B} = \frac{Pb}{Pa} \tag{2.2}$$

where $\triangle A$ represents a small change in the amount of factor *A*, $\triangle B$ represents a small change in factor *B*, and *Pb* and *Pa* represent the prices per unit of factors *B* and *A*, respectively. If the substitution ratio is greater than the price ratio, costs can be reduced by using more of the added factor. On the other hand, if the substitution ratio is smaller than the price ratio, costs can be lowered by using less of the added factor. Costs are at a minimum when the cost of the factor replaced is equal to the cost of the factor added.

In applying this principle to the example given in Table 2.5, $\triangle A$ represents the change in factor *A*, which is five units in all cases. The changes in factor *B*, or $\triangle B$, can vary from 35 units to five units. With factor *A* priced at \$4.00 and factor *B* at \$1.00, we substitute the known quantities in the equation and solve for the unknown, $\triangle B$, as follows:

$$\frac{5}{\Delta B} = \frac{1}{4} \quad \text{or} \quad \Delta B = 20.$$

Thus costs are at a minimum somewhere between factor combinations (3) and (4). With the data given, this is as close as we can come to the optimum combination of factors.

Constant Rates of Substitution. Not all factors of production or practices substitute for one another at diminishing rates. In some cases the rate of substitution is constant. Use of machines versus manual labor illustrates this type of relationship. For example, two cotton pickers or two corn pickers will substitute for twice as many men as one picker. When constant substitution rates are involved, the problem of minimizing costs is simply one of determining which practice, or factor, is least expensive and using that in the production process. The one that is most economical ordinarily will be used exclusively, there being no reason to use a combination of the two.

COMBINING ENTERPRISES. The two preceding sections have dealt with the amount of resources it will pay to use in production (factor-product relationships) and the combination of factors that will be most economical (factor-factor relationships). In this section we are concerned with the third major problem facing managers: the combination of enterprises that will produce the greatest net income (product-product relationships). The objective is to outline concepts involved in combining enterprises and to present guiding principles that are helpful in making decisions.

The problem of combining enterprises arises primarily because of limitations on capital available. If capital were not limited, a farmer could expand his acreage and improvements as far as he wished. There would be no need to choose among enterprises. He could produce all the crops and livestock enterprises adapted to his area of operation and expand output of each to the point where marginal costs and returns were equal. Some farmers own or have access to large amounts of capital, running into millions of dollars, which permits them considerable flexibility. However, in most cases the amount of capital available limits the enterprise combinations that can be included in the farm business, and also their size.

The problem involved in combining enterprises depends in part on the interrelationships between enterprises, that is, whether they are independent, competitive, supplementary, or complementary. Under conditions of limited capital, few, if any, enterprises are completely independent. Primary concern is with the three latter enterprise relationships.

Competitive Enterprises. Competitive enterprises compete with each other for use of resources. This raises two questions: Which enterprises should be included in the business, and How large should each enterprise be? With limited resources, the number of enterprises that can be included will be limited and, since expansion of one enterprise will necessitate contraction of another, the sizes of the enterprises included will be limited.

Enterprises that compete for use of resources may substitute for each other either at increasing or at constant rates. The rate of substitution of one enterprise for another refers to the amount of one enterprise displaced as another is added to the business or as an existing enterprise is increased in size. Enterprises substitute at increasing rates when an increase in one requires larger and larger reductions in the other. They substitute at constant rates when a uniform increase in one requires a uniform reduction in the other. Increasing rates of substitution always occur when diminishing marginal productivity takes place in producing either or both of the two competing products. Constant rates of substitution always occur when

TABLE 2.6:   Combinations of Products Y_1 and Y_2 That Can Be Produced with Six Units of Factor X (Hypothetical data)

Product Combination	Product Y_1	Product Y_2	Marginal Rate of Substitution of Y_2 for Y_1*	Income with: $Py_1 = \$1$ $Py_2 = \$3$	Income with: $Py_1 = \$1$ $Py_2 = \$6$
(1)	(2)	(3)	(4)	(5)	(6)
	(units)	(units)		(dol)	(dol)
1	42	0		42	42
			0.33		
2	40	6		58	76
			0.80		
3	36	11		69	102
			1.50		
4	30	15		75	120
			3.00		
5	21	18		75	129
			5.00		
6	11	20		71	131
			11.00		
7	0	21		63	126

* $-\Delta Y_1/\Delta Y_2$; i.e., reduction in production of Y_1 associated with an increase of 1 unit in Y_2.

constant marginal productivity prevails in production of the products.

An example of two products substituting at increasing rates is given in Table 2.6. It is assumed that six units of resources are available that can be used to produce either product Y_1 or Y_2. One unit of resources produces 11 units of Y_1; the second unit of resources adds 10 units of product, making a total of 1; the third unit of resources adds nine units of product, making a total of 30; and so on until the sixth unit of resources adds two units of product, making a total of 42. Note that each successive unit of resources adds less to the total product; that is, diminishing marginal productivity takes place in producing product Y_1.

Diminishing marginal productivity also occurs when the six units of resources are used to produce Y_2. The first unit of resources produces six units, the second unit of resources adds five units, the third four units, and so on until the sixth unit of resources adds only one unit of product, making a total of 21.

The various combinations of products Y_1 and Y_2 that can be produced with the six units of resources are shown in columns 2 and 3. For example, 40 units of Y_1 and six units of Y_2 can be produced. If one more unit of resources is used in the Y_2 enterprise, production is increased to 11 units but production of Y_1 is reduced to 36 units.

The marginal rate of substitution of Y_2 for Y_1 is shown in column 4. In changing from product combination (1) to (2), the marginal rate of substitution is 0.33; that is, a reduction of two units of Y_1 releases sufficient resources to produce six units of Y_2. As additional resources are shifted, the sacrifice in production of Y_1 increases relative to the increase in Y_2, until 11 units of Y_1 are required to substitute for one unit of Y_2.

Determining the most profitable combination of enterprises depends upon the rate of substitution of one enterprise for another and the prices of the products. Again in Table 2.6, with Y_1 priced at $1.00 and Y_2 at $3.00, the highest income is realized by producing either 30 units of Y_1 and 15 units of Y_2 or 21 units of Y_1 and 18 units of Y_2. Profits are at a maximum somewhere between these two combinations. With Y_1 priced at $1.00 and Y_2 at $6.00, income is at a maximum when 11 units of Y_1 and 20 units of Y_2 are produced. Increasing the price of Y_2 relative to the price of Y_1 made it profitable to produce relatively more of Y_2.

With a fixed amount of resources, maximum income is obtained when the marginal rate of product substitution is equal to the inverse of the price ratio. In algebraic form

$$\frac{\Delta Y_1}{\Delta Y_2} = \frac{Py_2}{Py_1} \qquad (2.3)$$

where ΔY_1 represents a small change in the quantity of product Y_1, ΔY_2 represents a small change in the quantity of product Y_2, and Py_2 and Py_1 represent the prices of the two products.

Applying this principle to the situation portrayed in Table 2.6, ΔY_1 represents the change in production of Y_1 associated with a change (increase or decrease) of one unit in the amount of resources. ΔY_1 has a similar meaning with reference to production of Y_2. With Y_1 priced at $1.00 and Y_2 at $3.00, income is at a maximum where ΔY_1 is 9 and ΔY_2 is 3. Thus the marginal rate of product substitution is equal to the inverse price ratio, indicating as is evident in the table that the optimum combination of enterprises Y_1 and Y_2 is between product combinations (4) and (5).

When competitive enterprises substitute for each other at a constant rate, income generally is maximized by specializing in one enterprise and excluding the other. In such cases it is very infrequent that price and substitution ratios are equal. Thus it is unlikely that income can be maximized if both products are produced.

Supplementary Enterprises. Enterprises are supplementary when they jointly permit more complete use of resources than when only one enterprise is included in the business. Supplementarity arises due to existence of unused resources that are fixed as far as the farm is concerned but that are variable between enterprises. Supplementary enterprises do not compete with other enterprises for resources, neither do they contribute anything to other enterprises—such as is the case with complementary enterprises. A small garden or fruit orchard, a a small flock of sheep, and hogs following fattening cattle are examples of enterprises that are primarily supplementary enterprises on many farms.

Since truly supplementary enterprises have no relationship to other enterprises in the farm business, the discussion of enterprise relationships given above does not apply. The decision to be reached is whether the price of the product is sufficient to make production profitable.

Complementary Enterprises. Enterprises are complementary when one adds to the production of another. A complementary enterprise does not cause a sacrifice in production of another product as is the case with competitive enterprises. Neither does it stand alone as pure supplementary enterprises do. Given a fixed amount of resources, enterprises that are complementary will produce more product as a pair than the sum of their products produced independently. Alfalfa and grain production are examples of complementary enterprises. Alfalfa complements grain as a result of a by-product, nitrogen, which it produces.

Quite a number of complementary relationships exist in agriculture. Enterprises are never complementary over all possible combinations of the two, however. Complementarity always gives way to competition as one enterprise is expanded relative to the other.

Income is increased by resource combinations that encourage complementarity since a greater total product is produced. Price comparisons are not needed when allocation of resources between complementary enterprises is being considered. However, as soon as the complementary relationship gives way to a competitive relationship, price relationships become of immediate importance.

Choosing among Sources of Capital. The model for determining the minimum cost combination of factors of production is the appropriate model to use in determining the amount of capital to obtain from various sources. In applying this model, capital obtained from each source is considered as a different factor of production.

Capital obtained from one source substitutes for capital from another source on a dollar-for-dollar basis. In other words, the rate of substitution is constant. Under such circumstances, the problem is one of determining the most economical source of capital and obtaining the needed capital from that source. The problem is not quite that simple, however, due to (1) limitations on capital available from various sources, (2) increasing costs (monetary plus nonmonetary) of capital derived from a given source, and (3) "lumpiness" of capital acquired by renting. Capital available from savings or equity may be the most economical source, but the amount of such capital generally is limited. The rate of savings may be increased but only at a higher "cost." Similarly, the amount of capital that can be obtained by borrowing tends to be limited. Larger amounts may be obtained by using second mortgages, and the like, but again the cost is increased. Thus all the capital used in a business usually will not be obtained from one source. Several sources will be used, with the amount obtained from each being increased until the marginal cost of each source is equal and, in turn, equal to marginal returns from use of capital. Since nonmonetary costs are involved, the equality will be determined in terms of satisfaction rather than dollars.

ALLOCATION OF CAPITAL TO ALTERNATIVE USES. Allocation of capital to alternative uses involves both internal and external aspects of the farm business. Consideration here is directed to allocation of capital between the farm business and external competitors for funds: primarily the farm household and nonfarm business ventures. The capital being considered is owned capital (savings, gifts, inheritances, etc.) and current income received during a given period, say 1 year.

Farm Business versus Farm Household Use of Funds. The farm business and the farm household compete for funds in the same manner as do competitive enterprises. Pressure exerted by the farm business for more and more capital, together with interest of the family in expanding the size of business so as to increase income, effectively encourages allocation of capital to the business on most farms. On the other hand, a certain amount of funds is required for even minimum living standards, and farm people are becoming more comfort conscious. As a result, the farm household is becoming an increasingly keen competitor for available funds.

With limited capital (there would be no problem if capital were unlimited) a family must choose among alternatives in production and consumption. They must decide how much of their capital to invest in the farm business and how much to use for consumption. In other words, the question of farm business versus farm household use of funds is basically a question of determining the allocation of capital between savings and current consumption.

ALLOCATION POSSIBILITIES. During a period of time the family has a given amount of capital at its disposal. The family has the choice of spending this capital for current consumption or saving it for consumption at a later time, or of allocating part of it to each use. The model for determining the optimum allocation of capital between the two uses is portrayed in Figure 2.1.

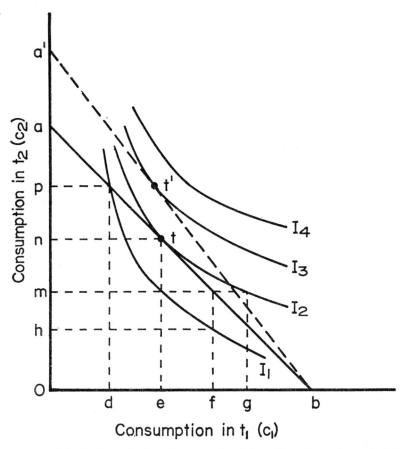

FIG. *2.1—Basic relationships involved in allocation of capital to consumption and savings.*

Consumption in the current time period t_1 is registered on the horizontal axis, and savings, or consumption in a later time period t_2, is measured on the vertical axis. The amount of capital available is represented by oa, which is equal to ob. The various alternatives for allocating capital between consumption in time period t_1 and in time period t_2 are indicated by the allocation possibility (isocapital) line ab. The family may go on a spending spree and spend all their capital ob in the current period. On the other hand, they might live very frugally and save their accumulated capital plus a part of their current income. Their savings for consumption in period t_2 would then approach oa. The allocation chosen by most families falls somewhere between these two extremes.

The optimum allocation of capital between current and future consumption depends upon the amount of satisfaction associated with each use. Thus satisfaction is the appropriate choice indicator to use in this case rather than product prices. The methodology outlined for analysis of product-product relationships may be applied; however, the indifference concept is used in place of prices.

INDIFFERENCE CONCEPT. The indifference concept may be illustrated by the indifference curves shown in Figure 2.1. Each of the indifference curves I_1, I_2, I_3, and I_4 is comprised of a continuous line of points, each point on a given indifference curve representing combinations of consumption in the current time period C_1, and consumption in a future time period (savings) C_2, which give equal satisfaction or utility. Thus od of C_1 and op of C_2, oe of C_1 and om of C_2, and of of C_1 and oh of C_2 each has the same utility to the farm family. It is a matter of indifference to the family which of the three combinations of C_1 and C_2 they have.

The indifference curves shown in Figure 2.1, being convex to the origin, indicate that an increasing amount of savings for consumption in t_2 (C_2) is needed to compensate for loss of each successive unit of current consumption (C_1). For example, a gain of hm in C_2 adds as much utility as is lost by a sacrifice of ef of C_1. However, if a second unit of C_1, de (equal to ef), is sacrificed, a larger amount of C_2, mp, is needed to replace it.

Indifference curves higher in the plane of a diagram represent higher levels of satisfaction. Thus indifference curve I_2 represents a higher level of satisfaction than indifference curve I_1. Similarly, indifference curve I_3 represents a higher level of satisfaction than curve I_2. For any indifference curve, all points represent the same level of satisfaction and the curves that constitute one person's, or one group's, indifference map never cross each other.

OPTIMUM ALLOCATION. The point of tangency t of allocation opportunity curve ab and indifference curve I_2 represents the optimum allocation of capital to current consumption and savings. Any other allocation of capital yields less total satisfaction (satisfaction from current consumption plus satisfaction from savings). An allocation of od dollars to current consumption and op dollars to savings would be possible, of course. However, this combination lies on indifference curve I_1, which indicates total satisfaction is less than at point t. In other words, by shifting some capital from savings to current consumption, the farmer could raise the level of total satisfaction to indifference curve I_2.

While total satisfaction would remain the same by shifting from point t to any other point on indifference curve I_2, such a shift is not possible with the amount of capital available. An allocation of om

dollars to C_2 and og dollars to C_1, for example, would produce the same level of total satisfaction as at point t. However, capital available is inadequate for such a combination. With *om* dollars allocated to C_2, only *of* dollars remain for C_1, *fg* dollars short of the amount required for total satisfaction to be equivalent to point t. It follows, therefore, that the optimum allocation of capital to current consumption and to savings is the one represented by point t. At this point

$$\frac{\Delta C_1}{\Delta C_2} = \frac{\Delta Sc_2}{\Delta Sc_1} \tag{2.4}$$

where ΔC_1 represents the marginal unit of capital allocated to current consumption, ΔC_2 represents the marginal unit of capital allocated to savings (consumption in time period t_2), and ΔSc_1 and ΔSc_2 represent the change in satisfaction the family derives from use of one unit of capital for current consumption and for savings. Or expressed in another form

$$\Delta C_1 \, \Delta Sc_1 = \Delta C_2 \, \Delta Sc_2 \tag{2.5}$$

which indicates the optimum allocation of capital to consumption and to savings is achieved when the satisfaction from the last (marginal) unit of capital allocated to consumption is equal to the satisfaction derived from an equivalent unit of capital allocated to savings.

EFFECT OF THE RATE OF RETURN. In the foregoing discussion nothing has been said about the effect of the rate of return on the rate of savings. A small amount may be saved when the return is low; in fact, people typically will save a minimum amount even if the monetary return is negative. But what happens to the rate of savings as the rate of return increases? Two opposing forces are at work. One force encourages extra savings since the rate of return is higher. Each dollar spent for current consumption is more expensive—hence, one is inclined to *substitute* extra savings for current consumption. However, working against this so-called substitution effect is the second force called the *income effect*.[1] With a higher rate of return one is better off and is likely to be inclined to spend more for current consumption. Thus the net effect of a change in the rate of return on the rate of savings depends upon which is the more powerful, the substitution effect or the income effect.

---

1. The income effect of an increase in the rate of return is defined as the tendency for a person to feel more affluent and able to afford more consumption goods. The related substitution effect is the tendency for a person to want to react to the higher cost of current consumption, due to the higher rate of return that must be foregone to enjoy current consumption, by substituting savings for the additional consumption goods that could be purchased with the higher return.

With most people of modest means, the substitution effect of a higher rate of return is assumed to outweigh the income effect. The rate of savings will, therefore, be positively correlated with the rate of return. As the rate of return increases, other things being equal, the amount saved will increase. This is true particularly of younger farmers who generally have great need for more capital in their business. Thus the rate of return anticipated on savings affects the allocation of capital between consumption and savings. This point may be illustrated by reference to Figure 2.1.

The distance aa' in Figure 2.1 represents the return expected on the capital oa that may be saved. Assuming this return is realized, capital available for consumption in time period t_2 will be the original capital saved plus the return realized, that is, oa plus aa' equals oa'. As a result, the allocation of capital between current consumption and savings will be based on curve $a'b$. Since we have assumed that the substitution effect is stronger than the income effect, the point of tangency t' is farther to the left than point t. In other words, a smaller amount of capital will be used for current consumption and a larger amount will be saved. The higher the anticipated rate of return on savings, the greater will be the shift of capital from current consumption to savings, and vice versa.

The amount of capital saved will depend to a large degree upon the nature (shape) of the indifference curves that, in turn, depends upon the goals of the family. Indifference curves that are more nearly horizontal than those portrayed in Figure 2.1 mean that the family has a relatively high preference for savings, and more capital, therefore, will be allocated to savings. Indifference curves that are steeper than those portrayed indicate the opposite result.

EFFECT OF TIME. Time also affects the allocation of capital to consumption and to savings. Savings grow over time when earnings they produce are allowed to accumulate. A $100 savings account at 5 percent interest, compounded annually, will grow to $127.63 in five years. On the other hand, the $127.63 five years in the future are not worth $127.63 today. The worth today depends upon the rate of discount. If discounted at 5 percent, the $127.63 five years from now are worth only $100 today.

It is evident that the effect of time on the allocation of capital to consumption and to savings depends upon the relationship of the rate of earnings on savings to the rate of discount on consumption in a future time period. If the rate of earnings is large relative to the rate of discount, time will serve to encourage savings. Under such circumstances line $a'b$ in Figure 2.1 will be considerably steeper than line ab. The point of tangency will be to the left of point t, indicating that relatively more capital will be allocated to savings. However, if the rate of earnings is less than the rate of discount, time will tend to discourage savings. Under such circumstances curve $a'b$ would fall below ab; that is, it would be flatter than line ab, with the result that the point of tangency in the indifference map would move to the right of point t, indicating relatively less capital would be saved.

The rate of discount varies from one person to another, and particularly from one age to another. Older people generally discount future consumption more than younger people. This fact, coupled with changes which age brings in goals and indifference curves, explains in large measure the pattern of consumption and savings. A young family with limited resources has great need for machinery, livestock, and the like. Earnings on capital invested in such items usually are relatively high. The rate of discount on future earnings usually is relatively low. Thus the margin between earnings and discount is large; that is, aa' in Figure 2.1 is relatively large. The line $a'b$ is relatively steep, causing the point of tangency to move to the left, indicating greater relative emphasis on savings. As the family accumulates capital and develops a farm unit that enables it to have a reasonably comfortable income, the rate earned on capital often declines. More machinery may be purchased than is actually needed because of the satisfaction it gives. Quality livestock may be acquired more for the boost they give to prestige and satisfaction than to income. As the family becomes older, goals continue to change not only with age but also with the level of income. The shape of their indifference curves may change (become steeper in Figure 2.1), indicating relatively less preference for savings. Similarly, their rate of discount of future consumption may increase and, along with a lower rate of earnings on savings, cause the line $a'b$ to fall below line ab in Figure 2.1. Thus with steeper indifference curves than those shown in Figure 2.1, and with line $a'b$ more nearly horizontal than line ab, the point of tangency would shift substantially to the right, indicating that relatively little capital would be allocated to savings. In fact, capital allocated to savings may be less than accumulated capital, that is, capital saved in earlier years, or inherited. In other words, the family may use some of its accumulated savings for current consumption. This is often reflected by run-down machinery, lack of improvements, limited attention to conservation, etc.

Farm Business versus Nonfarm Business Use of Funds. In the preceding section consideration has been directed to allocation of a given (limited) supply of capital between production (savings) and consumption. The problem considered in this section is the allocation of a given amount of capital used for production between farm and nonfarm business ventures. The problem is pertinent regardless of whether or not the farmer has surplus capital. The farmer who is short of capital for operating his farm must decide whether he could make more money (or derive more satisfaction) by using part or all of his capital in nonfarm business ventures. The farmer with surplus capital faces this same question plus the problem of whether the surplus capital will earn more or less in the farm business than in nonfarm business ventures. It is assumed that the farm business can be expanded to make use of the funds if that alternative is determined to be most profitable.

PRODUCTION POSSIBILITIES WITH INCREASING RATES OF SUBSTITUTION. The economic model for allocating capital between competing enterprises may be applied directly to this problem. Consider, for example, the situation portrayed in Table 2.7. A farmer has 10 units of capital available that he may use in the farm business, in enterprise Y_1, or in a nonfarm investment, enterprise Y_2. If the capital is used in enterprise Y_1, products shown in column 2 will be produced. A corresponding production function for enterprise Y_2 is shown in column 3. Production possibilities with the 10 units of capital are shown in columns 4 and 5. Since diminishing returns occur in the production function for Y_1, Y_2 substitutes for Y_1 at an increasing rate.

As shown earlier in the chapter (eq. 2.3), the most profitable combination of enterprises is when

$$\frac{\Delta Y_1}{\Delta Y_2} = \frac{Py_2}{Py_1}$$

with ΔY_1 representing a small change in output of product Y_1; ΔY_2, a small change in output of product Y_2; and Py_2 and Py_1 representing prices per unit of product. With Py_1 at $2.00 and Py_2 at $1.00, income is at a maximum when

$$\frac{\Delta Y_1}{\Delta Y_2} = 0.5$$

This solution may be confirmed by reference to column 7 of Table 2.7, which shows the maximum income of $106.40 falls between marginal rates of substitution 0.48 and 0.68. Thus the actual maximum income slightly exceeds $106.40—but with the units of capital given, this is as close as we can come. Maximum income is realized by allocating seven units of capital to the farm enterprise and three units of capital to the nonfarm enterprise.

In allocating capital between two enterprises, only variable costs of production are considered in determining the quantities of the two products to produce. Fixed costs of production are not involved. This fact is of considerable significance in allocation of capital. It means that relatively more capital will be allocated to established farm enterprises that can be expanded within the framework of existing

TABLE 2.7: Production Functions, Production Possibilities, Marginal Rate of Product Substitution, and Income under Increasing Rates of Substitution (Hypothetical data)

Inputs of Capital	Output		Production Possibilities with 10 Units of Capital		Marginal Rate of Substitution of Y_2 for Y_1 ($\Delta Y_1/\Delta Y_2$)	Income with Py_1 @ \$2 Py_2 @ \$1	Production Possibilities with 10 Units of Capital		Marginal Rate of Substitution of Y_2 for Y_3 ($\Delta Y_3/\Delta Y_2$)	Income with Py_3 @ \$2 Py_2 @ \$1
	Y_1	Y_2	Y_1	Y_2			Y_3	Y_2		
(1)	(2)	(3)	(4)	(5)	(6)	(7)	(8)	(9)	(10)	(11)
0	0	0	50.0	0		\$100.00	33.3	0		\$66.60
1	9.0	5.0	49.5	5.0	0.10	104.00	33.0	5.0	0.06	71.00
2	18.0	10.0	48.1	10.0	0.28	106.20	32.1	10.0	0.18	74.20
3	25.8	15.0	45.7	15.0	0.48	106.40	30.5	15.0	0.32	76.00
4	32.4	20.0	42.3	20.0	0.68	104.60	28.2	20.0	0.46	76.40
5	37.9	25.0	37.9	25.0	0.88	100.80	25.3	25.0	0.58	75.60
6	42.3	30.0	32.4	30.0	1.10	94.80	21.6	30.0	0.74	73.20
7	45.7	35.0	25.8	35.0	1.32	86.60	17.2	35.0	0.88	69.40
8	48.1	40.0	18.0	40.0	1.56	76.00	12.0	40.0	1.04	64.00
9	49.5	45.0	9.5	45.0	1.70	64.00	6.0	45.0	1.20	57.00
10	50.0	50.0	0	50.0	1.90	50.00	0	50.0	1.20	50.00

fixed costs than to nonfarm enterprises (investments) being considered. In nonfarm enterprises (investments) in which farmers usually invest (savings accounts, bonds, stocks, etc.), all costs are variable from the farmer's viewpoint. Income realized by the farmer on his investment is based upon income of the company after all costs—both fixed and variable—have been deducted from gross income. Thus the income per dollar of capital put in nonfarm investments tends to be relatively low compared with returns from capital used in established farm enterprises. This point can be illustrated by further reference to Table 2.7.

Enterprises Y_1 and Y_3 are assumed to be identical with the exception that Y_1 is an established enterprise whereas Y_3 is still in the planning stage; that is, no fixed costs have been incurred, all costs are variable. Variable costs for enterprise Y_1 are assumed to be two-thirds of total costs. Since variable costs for enterprise Y_3 equal total costs, variable costs for enterprise Y_1 are only two-thirds of variable costs for Y_3. As a result, output of enterprise Y_3 per unit of capital is only two-thirds of the output for enterprise Y_1. This relationship can be observed by comparing columns 4 and 8 in Table 2.7. As a result of the smaller output, enterprise Y_3 competes less favorably for capital than enterprise Y_1. With enterprises Y_1 and Y_2 competing for the 10 units of capital, the optimum allocation was 7 units to Y_1 and 3 units to Y_2. With enterprises Y_3 and Y_2 competing, only 6 units of capital are allocated to Y_3, with 4 units being allocated to Y_2.

Since substantial fixed costs are involved in agriculture, and since many farm businesses can expand substantially without a proportionate increase in fixed costs, agriculture is a strong contender for capital in the short run. In the long run, however, the situation is quite different. Since all costs are variable in the long run, production per unit of capital is relatively low on many farms. In some cases, income (output multiplied by price) is less than total costs (capital used in production of the output). When such a situation prevails it does not pay to invest more capital in the farm business. Income would be maximized by liquidating the business and investing the capital elsewhere.

PRODUCTION POSSIBILITIES WITH CONSTANT RATES OF SUBSTITUTION. The illustration presented in Table 2.7 and the related discussion pertain to a situation where an increasing marginal rate of product substitution occurs. When the farm and nonfarm products substitute at constant rates, the same principles apply, but it is unlikely that a combination of products will be produced. Production of one or the other of the products will be most profitable and, therefore, maximum returns will be realized by using all the capital available to produce that product.

QUESTIONS AND PROBLEMS

1. Explain the principle of diminishing returns.
2. Is the principle of diminishing returns a physical or economic law? Discuss.
3. Explain how increasing the number of factors of production that are permitted to vary affects diminishing returns.
4. Are "constant returns" possible? If so, doesn't this negate the principle of diminishing returns? Discuss.
5. Using the data in Table 2.2, prepare a chart or figure showing total output, average output, and additional (marginal) output.
6. Explain what is meant by the term *marginal*.
7. Distinguish between fixed and variable costs. What considerations may cause costs to change from fixed to variable and vice versa?
8. How can one determine whether or not it will pay to produce?
9. How can one determine how much to produce?
10. Using the data in Table 2.4, prepare a chart or figure showing the following costs per unit of output: marginal, average variable, average fixed, and average total costs. What is the relationship of average variable, average fixed, and average total costs per unit of output? What is the relationship between marginal costs per unit of output and average total costs per unit of output?
11. Theoretically, how can one determine whether or not his costs are as low as they should be?
12. Using data in Table 2.5, prepare a chart showing the combinations of factors *A* and *B* that can be used to produce 1,000 units of product. Using the prices given, show graphically the least cost combination of the two factors.
13. What is meant by diminishing marginal rate of substitution? What is its significance in economic analysis?
14. What guides do economic principles provide in combining enterprises? Explain.
15. Using the data in Table 2.6, prepare a chart showing the production functions for products Y_1 and Y_2. (Use the X axis for the six inputs of factor X and the Y axis for the amounts produced.) Prepare another chart showing the combinations of products Y_1 and Y_2 that can be produced with the six units of factor X. Using the product prices given, show graphically the optimum combination of the two enterprises.
16. Outline the principle involved:
    a. In inventorying the amount of capital available to the farm business.
    b. In choosing among various sources of capital.
17. Outline and explain the economic model a family may use in allocating capital to the farm business and the household.
18. Should farmers put any of their capital in nonfarm investments? Explain the economic principles involved.
19. Explain how fixed and variable costs influence the allocation of capital to farm business and nonfarm business investments.

20. Explain the effect of the rate of return on savings on allocation of capital.
21. Does time have an effect on the allocation of capital to consumption and to savings? Explain.

REFERENCES

Heady, Earl O. *Economics of Agricultural Production and Resource Use.* Prentice-Hall, Englewood Cliffs, N.J., 1952, Chap. 14.

Heady, E. O., Back, W. B., and Peterson, G. A. *Interdependence between the Farm Business and the Farm Household with Implications on Economic Efficiency.* Iowa Agr. Exp. Sta. Res. Bull. 398, June 1953.

Hesser, Leon F. "Conceptual Models of Capital Rationing among Farmers," *Jour. Farm Econ.,* vol. 42, no. 2, May 1960, pp. 325–34.

Hillman, C. H., and Steward, D. D. *Financial Management Practices of Farm Families in Southeastern Ohio Agriculture.* Ohio Agr. Exp. Sta. Res. Bull. 940, June 1963.

Irwin, G. D., and Baker, C. B. *Effects of Lender Decisions on Farm Financial Planning.* Ill. Agr. Exp. Sta. Bull. 688, Nov. 1962.

CHAPTER 3: INFLUENCE OF TIME ON COSTS AND RETURNS

IF YOU were to offer a friend a choice of two alternatives—a gift of $100 today or a gift of $100 at some future date, say one year from now—your friend would probably elect to receive the $100 today. His choice would demonstrate an important concept known as the *time value of money*. In its simplest terms, the time value of money concept is that a dollar now is worth more than the prospect of receiving a dollar at some future date.

Suppose that you offer the following two alternatives: a gift of $100 now or a gift of $105 one year from now. Your friend would find it more difficult to choose between these latter two alternatives because you have offered him a $5.00 compensation for waiting a year to receive the gift. His hesitation raises two questions: (1) Why is a dollar now worth more than a dollar at some future time? (2) How much greater is the value of a dollar now as opposed to the prospect of receiving a dollar in the future?

REASONS FOR THE TIME VALUE OF MONEY. There are three basic reasons for the almost universal preference of a dollar now over the prospect of receiving a dollar in the future.[1] The first is *uncertainty*. We live in an uncertain world, hence a dollar in hand today is a sure thing, while the promise of a dollar one year from now is uncertain. In the above example, your friend will be thinking of the many circumstances that might make it impossible for you to give him the $100 gift a year from now. If he thinks there is a reasonably high probability that you will not be able to grant him a gift a year from now, he will choose the $100 today over $105 a year from now. Thus the degree of uncertainty in part determines how much more a dollar is worth today.

The fact that everyone has *alternative uses for money* also explains the time value of money. Possibly your friend would prefer to receive the $100 gift now because he needs cash to buy something, pay off some bills, take a vacation, or whatever. Even if he does not

---

1. See Richard D. Aplin and George L. Casler, *Capital Investment Analysis: Using Discounted Cash Flows* (Columbus, Ohio: Grid, 1973), Chapter 3.

need the money now, he probably realizes that he can put it into a savings account or invest it and earn interest. The expected returns from alternative uses of money, whether they be monetary or non-monetary returns, also partially determine the time value of money. If your friend could earn more than 5 percent per annum in a savings account, for example, he would prefer $100 today over $105 a year from now.

Inflation is the third factor that accounts for the time value of money. The price level in the United States economy has risen almost continuously for several decades. Although the prospect of deflation cannot be ruled out entirely, everyone has become accustomed to the fact that today's dollar will, in all likelihood, have a lower purchasing power in the future. The gift of $105 in one year as opposed to $100 now usually will more than compensate for the inflation in the United States economy, although rates in excess of 5 percent have occurred within the past few years. Many countries are not as fortunate in this respect. Brazil, for example, experienced inflation rates in excess of 25 percent per year during much of the 1960s.

INTEREST. The time value of money is also important to lenders and investors and it helps to explain the important role played in the economy by interest. Interest is defined as the price paid for the use of money or capital. Interest compensates the supplier of money or capital for uncertainty, for alternative uses of his capital, and for the loss of purchasing power due to inflation.[2] Thus *interest represents the time value of money.* In addition, the interest rate must cover any explicit costs associated with the transfer of money from supplier to user. These explicit transfer costs would include expenses such as administration expense, collection costs, and bad debt losses in the case of loans, and brokerage commissions for the purchase and sale of securities.

Growth of a Cash Outlay. A cash outlay grows over time due to the compounding of interest charges or opportunity costs involved in using the capital. If $100 are put in a savings account with interest at 5 percent, compounded annually, it will increase, or grow, to $127.63 by the end of 5 years. The rate of growth of a cash outlay over time depends primarily on the interest rate. With interest at

---

2. Keynes suggested that interest compensates the supplier of money for parting with liquidity. This "liquidity preference" arises out of three motives—the transactions motive, the precautionary motive, and the speculative motive. See John M. Keynes, *The General Theory of Employment, Interest and Money* (New York: Harcourt, 1936), p. 167.

10 percent, compounded annually, $100.00 will grow to $161.05 at the end of 5 years, compared with $127.63 with interest at 5 percent. The frequency of compounding also influences the rate of growth; the more frequent the compounding, the faster the growth. With interest at 10 percent compounded semiannually, $100.00 will grow to $162.90 by the end of 5 years, compared with $161.05 when the interest was compounded annually.

Since costs grow as a result of interest or opportunity cost accumulations, the equation for compounding interest

$$S = s(1 + i)^n \tag{3.1}$$

may be used to show growth in a cash outlay. S represents the sum at the end of n periods; s, the amount that is invested for n periods; and i, the interest rate. Applying this equation to $1.00 invested at 5 percent interest compounded annually for 3 years, we have $S = 1(1.05)^3 = \$1.16$. Note that in this example "n periods" is 3 years, since interest is compounded annually. If interest had been compounded semiannually for 3 years, the annual interest rate would have been divided by 2 and n increased to 6, since 6 periods would have been involved.

The amount of 1 at compound interest is given in Appendix Table 1. As in the equation, the letter n at the top of the first column refers to the number of periods; and the numbers at the top of the other columns refer to the interest rate i applicable to the period being used. For example, when n refers to years, the annual interest rate should be used; when n refers to 3-month periods, i equals the annual interest rate divided by 4.

Discounting Income. Discounting income is the procedure whereby the present value of future income is determined. The concept is the converse of growth in value due to accrued interest. Thus, with interest at 5 percent, $1.00 today grows to $1.05 in a year and, conversely, $1.05 a year from now is worth only $1.00 today.

The present value of given income in a future year is derived by using the equation

$$V = \frac{I}{(1 + i)^n} \tag{3.2}$$

where V is present value, I is future income, i is the discount (or capitalization) rate, and n is the number of years before the income will be received. This is the equation to use when future income is discounted on an annual basis. If the income is discounted m times per year, i should be divided by m, and n multiplied by m.

This equation can be derived directly from Equation 3.1, given above, for compounding costs. Equation 3.1 was

$$S = s(1 + i)^n$$

Dividing both sides by $(1 + i)^n$ we have

$$\frac{S}{(1 + i)^n} = s \frac{(1 + i)^n}{(1 + i)^n} \tag{3.3}$$

or

$$s = \frac{S}{(1 + i)^n} \tag{3.4}$$

In Equation 3.1, s represented the principal sum invested, which is the unknown amount, V, in Equation 3.2. S represented the sum of the compounded costs, which in Equation 3.2 is the amount of income, I, to be received at the end of a future year. Thus Equations 3.2 and 3.4 are identical, the letters used having been changed to better represent the terminology.

Application of Equation 3.2 can be illustrated by determining the present value of $127.63 to be received at the end of 5 years, assuming the discount rate is 5 percent. (This odd amount is used since it is the end product of an example used above in compounding costs.) Substituting the known quantities in Equation 3.2 gives

$$V = \frac{\$127.63}{(1 + .05)^5}$$

$$V = \frac{\$127.63}{1.2763} = \$100$$

The present value of 1 at compound interest is given in Appendix Table 2. As in the equation, the letter n at the top of the first column refers to the number of years involved, and the numbers at the top of the other columns refer to the discount or capitalization rate i.

Using this table in solving the above example, first find the column headed with 5 percent, move down to n equals 5, and read 0.7835. This amount multiplied by $127.63 gives $100.00.

The present value of a sequence of annual incomes is given by the equation

$$V = \frac{I_1}{(1 + i)} + \frac{I_2}{(1 + i)^2} + \frac{I_3}{(1 + i)^3} + \cdots + \frac{I_n}{(1 + i)^n} \tag{3.5}$$

In this equation I represents annual (net) income, which may or may not be the same each year. When annual income varies from year to year, Equation 3.5 is used to compute present value. However, when annual income is constant and continues in perpetuity, Equation 3.5 may be reduced to

$$V = \frac{I}{i} \qquad (3.6)$$

The discount (capitalization) rate i has a very significant influence on present value. For example, a perpetual annual income of $100 discounted at 5 percent gives a present value of $2,000. Lowering the discount (capitalization) rate to 4 percent increases the present value to $2,500. Thus, in deriving and using the present value, one should always be cognizant of the importance of correctly estimating the discount (capitalization) rate. This rate should always reflect the opportunity cost of money and the degree of risk involved.

When the annual income is constant but does not continue in perpetuity, Equation 3.5 becomes:

$$V = I \frac{1 - (1 + i)^{-n}}{i} = I \frac{(1 + i)^n - 1}{i (1 + i)^n} \qquad (3.7)$$

A constant income stream that continues for a finite period is called an *annuity*. For example, a 3-year $100 annuity would be a constant annual income stream of $100 continuing for 3 years, with the $100 payments received *at the end of each year*. The present value of this annuity, discounted at 5 percent would be:

$$V = 100 \frac{(1.05)^3 - 1}{0.05 \, (1.05)^3}$$

$$V = 100 \frac{1.1576 - 1}{0.05 \, (1.1576)} = \$272.32$$

This same result could have been obtained by using Equation 3.5 and Appendix Table 2.

$$V = \frac{100}{1.05} + \frac{100}{(1.05)^2} + \frac{100}{(1.05)^3}$$

$$V = 95.24 + 90.70 + 86.38 = \$272.32$$

The use of Equations 3.5 and 3.7 to find the present value of a constant income stream continuing for a finite time period becomes rather tedious when n is large. The present value of an annuity of 1 is given in Appendix Table 4. The 5 percent column of Appendix Table 4 for $n = 3$ indicates that the present value of a 3-year 5 percent annuity of 1 is 2.7232. Multiplying the table value by $100 gives $272.32, the same answer that was obtained by using Equations 3.5 and 3.7.

SOME APPLICATIONS OF THE TIME VALUE OF MONEY CONCEPT. The equations in the preceding section are more than merely devices used to determine interest charges. Many decisions can be better evaluated through the use of these concepts, as the following examples illustrate.[3]

Value of a Bond. Bonds are debt obligations of corporations and of federal, state, or local governments. Large corporations and governments borrow money from the investing public by issuing bonds just as individuals and owners of small business concerns borrow money using notes, mortgages, and charge accounts. Bonds of major corporations are traded on the major securities exchanges; hence, the initial purchaser of a newly issued bond can generally convert his bond to cash any time he wishes because a new buyer can nearly always be found in the secondary market.

Consider the case of a retiring farmer who wants to invest some of his money in corporate bonds. The bonds in question have a $1,000 face value and pay a 5 percent interest rate. He knows that investments of similar quality are returning 7 percent per annum, that is, the time value of money is 7 percent. If these bonds mature 10 years from now, how much should he pay for the bonds so that his investment will yield 7 percent per annum?

The first step in solving this problem is to set up a diagram showing the income stream for this bond. Assuming that the issuing corporation pays interest on its bonds annually and that the retiring farmer will receive the first interest payment 1 year from the date of purchase, the income stream diagram would be

End of year:	0	1	2	3	4	5	6	7	8	9	10
Income:	0	$50	$50	$50	$50	$50	$50	$50	$50	$50	$50 +$1000

The use of a diagram helps to organize the problem in such a way that the income stream can be accurately portrayed. Bond valuation is simply a problem of finding the present value of a $50, 10-year annuity plus the present value of the $1,000 face value that will be received at the end of 10 years, using a discount rate of 7 percent.

The solution can be set up as in Table 3.1.

The retiring farmer can afford to pay $859.48 for each bond. Another interpretation is that if he does pay $859.48 for the bonds and holds them to maturity, his investment will yield exactly 7 percent per annum (compounded). If he pays less than $859.48, his rate

---

3. Methods of estimating the future cash flows for the examples in this section are not discussed. It is assumed that all cash flows are on an after-tax basis.

TABLE 3.1:   Estimating the Price of a Bond, Using the Present Value Method

Time (years)	Income Received at End of Year	Present Value Factor	Present Value of Income
1-10	$ 50	7.0236*	$351.18
10	1,000	0.5083†	508.30
Total Present Value = Bond Price =			$859.48

* From the 7 percent section of Appendix Table 4.
† From the 7 percent section of Appendix Table 2.

of return would exceed 7 percent but if he pays more than $859.48 his return would be less than 7 percent.

This example illustrates an important characteristic of bonds and other negotiable fixed income securities such as notes, mortgages, land contracts, and savings certificates. Their prices will fluctuate above or below the par or face value with variations in the market rate of interest. In this example, the bonds that the retiring farmer is purchasing probably sold at, or very close to, their par value when they were first issued. Since that time, the market rate of interest on investments of similar quality has risen from 5 percent to 7 percent; hence, the price of the bond dropped from $1,000 to approximately $860. The price of this bond would be listed in the financial pages of the newspaper at approximately 86, meaning that it is currently selling at 86 percent of its par value.

Fixed income investments such as bonds are generally believed to be very safe investments. Consider, however, the position of the investor who bought these bonds at par when the market rate of interest was 5 percent and then was forced to sell them after the market rate had risen to 7 percent. He would have lost approximately $140 on each $1,000 bond. On the other hand, the investor who buys bonds when interest rates are high may realize some capital gains if interest rates subsequently decline.

Valuation of Farm Real Estate. A related problem concerns investing in farm real estate. Consider the following investment in a small orchard. The property in question has 25 acres of young trees that will reach full production after 3 years. It is estimated that until the trees mature, the revenue will just cover expenses, but thereafter the net income will be $100 per acre for years 4 through 20. The property will be worth an estimated $200 per acre 20 years from now. If the prospective purchaser requires an 8 percent return on his investment, how much should he pay for the property?

This example is similar to the bond valuation problem, but the orchard investment is complicated by the fact that there is no net revenue until the end of the fourth year. Assuming that all payments are received at the ends of years 4 through 20, the income stream per acre is

End of year:	0	1	2	3	4	5	. . . . .	20
Income:	0	0	0	0	$100	$100	. . . . .	$100 +$200

Finding the present value of the $200 price at the end of 20 years is straightforward. The present value of 1 to be received at the end of 20 years when the discount rate is 8 percent is 0.2145 (from Appendix Table 2). This value multiplied by $200 gives $42.90. The discount factor for the deferred annuity is found by multiplying (the present value of 1 per annum, 17 years, 8 percent) $\times$ (the present value of 1, 3 years, 8 percent). This procedure gives a discount factor of 7.2407, which when multiplied by $100 gives $724.07.[4] Thus the present value of the income stream (the indicated purchase price of the orchard) is $724.07 + $42.90 = $766.97 per acre. It should be recognized that since all income and expenses were estimated a realistic range for the purchase price would be between $750 and $800 per acre. The solution to the orchard valuation problem is summarized in Table 3.2.

TABLE 3.2:   Estimating the Price of an Orchard Property, Using the Present Value Method

Time (years)	Income Received at End of Year	Present Value Factor	Present Value of Income
1– 3	$ 0	. . .	$ . . .
4–20	100	7.2407	724.07
20	200	0.2145	42.90
Total Present Value (Price per Acre) =			$766.97

Finding the Rate of Return on an Investment. The time value of money can also be used to calculate an unknown rate of return on a proposed investment. Consider the case of a farm operator who is contemplating an investment in some feed-handling facilities for his beef operation. He has estimated that this equipment will

---

4. In general, the discount factor for a deferred annuity can be found as follows: Find the present value factor of 1 per annum using $n =$ the total number of payments and multiplying this factor by the present value of 1, using $n =$ the number of years in which no payments are received. An alternate procedure is to use: (Present value of 1 per annum, $n =$ the year the final payment is received) — (Present value of 1 per annum, $n =$ one less than the year in which the first payment is received).

cost $40,000 and that the reduced labor costs and increased efficiency will add an estimated $6,000 per year to his net income for a 10-year period. There will be no salvage value from the equipment at the end of 10 years. He wants to know what rate of return this investment offers.

In this problem, the income stream and the initial investment are known and the discount rate must be found. This is done by finding the discount rate that equates the present value of the income stream with the initial investment outlay. Assuming that the added income is received at the end of each year and that the investment outlay is made now, the income stream diagram is

End of Year:	0	1	2	3	. . .	10
Income:	−$40,000	+$6,000	+$6,000	$+6,000 .	. .	+$6,000

Note that the initial investment outlay is represented as *negative income*. This problem can be solved by first setting up an equation with one unknown, the discount factor, which is represented in the equation as x percent.

$$\$6,000 \text{ (present value of 1 per annum, 10 years, } x\%) = \$40,000$$

$$\text{(present value of 1 per annum, 10 years, } x\%) = \frac{40,000}{\$\,6,000} = 6.6667$$

The interest rate that corresponds to the discount factor of 6.6667 for 10 years is found by looking across the $n = 10$ row in Appendix Table 4. The present value of 1 per annum is 6.7101 when the discount rate is 8 percent and 6.4177 when the discount rate is 9 percent. Interpolation between these two factors shows that the factor 6.6667 corresponds to a discount rate of approximately 8.1 percent.

The 8.1 percent rate of return offered by this investment is called the *internal rate of return* or the *yield* of the investment. If this farm operator can earn more than 8.1 percent on alternative investments, he should not install the feed-handling equipment (assuming, of course, that the degree of risk on his other investment alternatives is comparable). However, if other investment alternatives involving similar degrees of risk return less than 8.1 percent, the feed-handling facilities would be an acceptable investment.

The net present value method can also be used to determine whether the feed-handling facilities should be installed. The net present value of an investment is the present value of the net cash income minus the present value of the net cash outlay, using the opportunity cost of capital as the discount rate. A net present value of zero or greater indicates that the proposed investment alternative is acceptable.

If this farm operator requires a 9 percent return on invested capital, the net present value calculation would be

Time (years)	Income received at end of year	Present value factor	Present value of income
0	—$40,000	1.0000	—$40,000
1–10	6,000	6.4177	38,506

Net present value = —$ 1,494

Since the net present value is less than zero, this investment alternative would be unacceptable. If a discount rate of 8 percent had been used in the net present value calculations, the net present value would be +$261, indicating that the feed-handling facilities should be installed.

Sometimes it is desirable to express the results of the net present value method as a *benefit:cost ratio*. The benefit:cost ratio is the present value of the cash income divided by the present value of the cash outlay. A benefit:cost ratio of less than 1 indicates that the investment alternative should be rejected. In this example, the benefit:cost ratios for the 8 percent and 9 percent discount rates are 1.01 and 0.96, respectively.

The feed-handling equipment problem illustrates the relationship between the net present value method and the yield method of evaluating investment alternatives. Both methods incorporate the time value of money. In the net present value method, the opportunity cost of capital is specified in advance, whereas with the yield method, the yield of the investment is compared with the opportunity cost of capital after the calculations have been made. The yield (or internal rate of return) is defined as the discount rate that equates the present value of the net cash income with the cash outlay. In this example, if the 8.1 percent rate of return were used in the net present value calculations, the net present value would turn out to be (approximately) zero.

Since the yield method involves some rather complicated trial and error calculations, the net present value method is usually preferable. However, the yield method has one important advantage: the answer is expressed as a percentage rate of return instead of a dollar amount, and businessmen normally think in terms of the percentage rate of return on an investment.

SUMMARY. The time value of money is a very important and useful concept. A dollar today is worth more than the prospect of receiving a dollar at some future time because of uncertainty, alternative uses for money, and inflation. Interest is the price paid for the use of money or capital, and it compensates the investor for giving up liquidity.

Some applications of the time value of money were given in this chapter to acquaint the reader with the techniques of compounding and discounting income streams. Additional problems are given at the end of the chapter and further applications of the time value of money are presented in later chapters.

QUESTIONS AND PROBLEMS

1. Explain the reasons for the time value of money.
2. If $100 are left to accumulate in a savings account that pays 5 percent per annum, how much money would be in the account at the end of 3 years? 5 years? 15 years? Draw a graph of the growth in a sum of money over a 20-year period invested at compound interest rates of 5 percent, 8 percent, and 12 percent per annum.
3. Using a 7 percent opportunity cost of capital, calculate the present value of
   (a) A single payment of $1,000 received at the end of 8 years.
   (b) A payment of $1,000 received at the end of each year for 8 years.
   (c) A $1,000 perpetual income stream.
   (d) Eight annual payments of $1,000, the first payment to be received now.
4. A farmer earns a net income of $14,000 per year. If the rate of inflation is expected to be 3 percent per annum, how much will he have to be earning 10 years from now to enjoy the same level of living that the $14,000 income would provide today?
5. Look up some bond quotations in the financial pages of a newspaper. Calculate the amount an investor could afford to pay for these bonds using a 7 percent discount rate. Compare your estimated prices with the current selling prices for each of these bonds. What do your comparisons tell you about the rate of return being demanded by investors buying these bonds in today's market?
6. The manager of a small tomato-packing company is contemplating the purchase of new grading and sorting equipment. The equipment will cost $26,000 and the manager feels that it will result in reduced labor requirements and higher prices for the product. The labor savings and higher prices will add an estimated $4,800 per year to the company's net, after-tax income over a period of 8 years. At the end of its 8-year useful life, the equipment will have an estimated salvage value of $2,000.

   If the company's opportunity cost of capital is 10 percent, use the net present value method to determine whether or not this grading and sorting equipment should be purchased. Is the yield of this investment higher or lower than 10 percent?

7. A cash grain farmer wants to know whether he should buy his own combine or hire a custom operator to harvest his 300-acre crop. He can purchase a combine for $16,500 and it would have a $2,500 salvage value at the end of its 10-year useful life. The after-tax costs of labor, fuel, lubrication, repairs, insurance, storage, and other ownership costs would be $600 per year. He estimates that the after-tax cost of custom hiring will be $9 per acre.

   If this farmer's opportunity cost of capital is 9 percent, use the net present value method to determine whether he should buy the combine or hire a custom operator.

8. If the farmer in problem 7 had a 500-acre crop and the annual after-tax cash expenses of owning and operating the combine are $800 instead of $600, should he own or custom hire?

REFERENCES

Aplin, Richard D., and Casler, George L. *Capital Investment Analysis: Using Discounted Cash Flows.* Grid, Columbus, Ohio, 1973.

Bierman, Harold, Jr., and Smidt, Seymore. *The Capital Budgeting Decision,* 3rd ed. Macmillan, New York, 1971.

Erven, David E. *An Analysis of Alternative Capital Investment Evaluation Techniques with Adaptation of the Computer to the Net Present Value Method.* Unpublished M.S. thesis, Ohio State Univ., 1969.

Kent, Frederick C., and Kent, Maude E. *Compound Interest and Annuity Tables.* McGraw-Hill, New York, 1963.

Martin, James E. *The Real Cost of Investment Alternatives.* Dept. Agr. Econ., Okla. State Univ., May 1966.

Pasour, E. C., Jr.; Nichols, T. E., Jr.; and Bradford, G. L. *Applying Economic Principles in Replacing or Purchasing Agricultural Equipment.* Dept. Agr. Econ., N.C. State Univ., EIC-10, June 1969.

Walrath, Arthur, and Gibson, W. L., Jr. *The Evaluation of Investment Opportunities: Tools for Decisionmaking in Farming and Other Businesses.* ERS, USDA, in cooperation with Div. of Res., Va. Polytech. Inst., Agr. Handbook 349, Feb. 1968.

CHAPTER 4: THEORY OF FINANCIAL MANAGEMENT

THE FARMER who keeps a good set of books and pays his bills on time may be regarded by most people as a good financial manager. Indeed, it would be difficult to dispute this observation because failure to keep adequate records and being chronically late in meeting financial obligations are two symptoms of poor financial management. However, financial management involves much more than keeping books and paying bills. This chapter covers some of the more important concepts from the growing field of the theory of financial management.[1] The more applied aspects of the financial management of a farm business are covered in Part 2.

ECONOMIC ACTIVITIES OF A FIRM. A firm is a business organization that produces goods and/or services. The economic facets of a business may be classified as production, marketing, and financing activities. The management of the firm is responsible for making decisions on these three basic economic activities. Production activities require decisions on what products or services will be produced, how they will be produced, and how much of each will be produced. Marketing activities involve managerial decisions on matters such as the procurement of inputs and the pricing and distribution of output. Financing activities require management decisions on capital *acquisition* and capital *use*.

Obviously, the scope of the finance function overlaps with production and marketing activities. Decisions on what products will be produced and in what volume will, for example, determine the amount of capital that the business will need. The question of how products will be produced requires the evaluation of investment alternatives. Similarly, marketing and finance are interrelated because the selection of suppliers of inputs and marketing outlets for products is often dictated by the amounts and terms of available financing. While recognizing these interactions among production, marketing, and finance,

---

1. For a more detailed examination of the theory of financial management, see Ezra Solomon, *The Theory of Financial Management* (New York: Columbia University Press, 1963).

one should keep in mind that finance is concerned with capital acquisition and capital use.

GOAL OF FINANCIAL MANAGEMENT. The financial manager is responsible for recognizing and fulfilling the financial goals of the owner or owners of the firm. Admittedly, he must also be cognizant of the goals of everyone who may be associated with the firm, such as employees; customers; creditors; suppliers; federal, state, or local governments; and even society as a whole. Obviously, fulfilling the often conflicting goals of such a diverse group of people, not to mention himself, is a complex task for the financial manager. For this reason the theory of financial management assumes that the financial manager is primarily concerned with one goal—maximizing the *net present worth* of the future earnings of the owner(s) of the business. This concept differs somewhat from the traditional economic goal of profit maximization. In its simplest terms, profit maximization implies that the manager of a business will always try to maximize the difference between total revenue and total costs per unit of time. However, the goal of maximizing the net present worth of the earnings of the owners includes a consideration of not only the amount of the net earnings but the *timing* and *risk* of the earnings as well.

Consider, for example, the earnings streams of investment alternatives A and B listed in Table 4.1.

Investments A and B both require an initial outlay of $500 and both return $1,000 in net earnings over the four time periods. The profit maximization criterion would suggest that Investments A and B are equally desirable because both return an average of $250 per period on the $500 capital outlay. On the basis of the net present worth of the earnings, Investment A is superior to Investment B because Investment A returns a larger proportion of the earnings in the earlier time periods. Assuming that Investments A and B involve

TABLE 4.1: Income Streams for Investment A and Investment B (Hypothetical data)

Timing of Earnings	Investment A	Investment B
Initial Capital Outlay	—$500	—$500
Earnings at End of Period		
1	400	100
2	300	200
3	200	300
4	100	400

similar amounts of risk and that the opportunity cost of capital is
8 percent per annum, Investment A has a net present value of $359.81
while Investment B has a net present value of only $296.19.

Alternative courses of action can be differentiated by assigning a
higher discount rate to risky ventures. Consider investment alternatives C and D in Table 4.2.

TABLE 4.2:   Income Streams for Investment C and Investment D (Hypothetical
data)

Timing of Earnings	Investment C	Investment D
Initial Capital Outlay	—$200	—$200
Earnings at End of Period		
1	100	125
2	100	125
3	100	125
4	100	125

The profit maximization criteria would result in the selection
of Investment D, because for the same $200 capital outlay, Investment
D offers $25 additional returns per period. Suppose, however, that
Investment D is a very high-risk investment and that the financial
manager feels that he would need a 20 percent rate of return on Investment D compared to only 8 percent on Investment C. When the
income streams for C and D are discounted at 8 percent and 20 percent, respectively, Investment C has a net present worth of $131.21
while Investment D has a net present worth of only $123.59.

FINANCIAL IMPLICATIONS OF RISK. One of the functions of
financial management is to evaluate the returns and risks associated with alternate courses of action in the business. This evaluation of investment alternatives is the key to making correct decisions
on how capital should be used in the business.

Business Risk. Different investments involve varying amounts of risk.
This type of risk is called *business risk*. Business risk is the variation in net earnings arising out of the kinds of enterprises in
which the firm is engaged. Weather, disease, and price changes constitute business risk in agriculture. In Figure 4.1, the concept of business risk is illustrated for two hypothetical investment alternatives.
The probability distributions of the net earnings for Investments F
and G are illustrated.

Investment F offers a modal (or most frequent) return of $4,000
per year while Investment G offers a modal return of $6,000 per year.

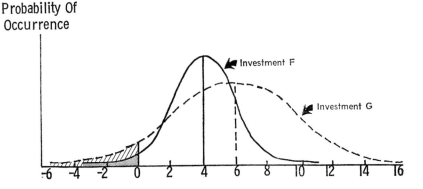

FIG. *4.1—An illustration of business risk.*

However, Investment G also involves a greater degree of risk. The probability of occurrence for any range of earnings per year is measured by the corresponding area under the curves. The probability that Investment F will yield negative returns is shown by the black shaded area under curve F to the left of the $0 point on the horizontal axis. The probability that the returns from Investment G will be less than $0 includes not only the black shaded area under curve F but also the cross-hatched area between curves F and G. In statistical terminology, the probability distribution of the earnings of Investment G has a higher *standard deviation,* the standard deviation being one commonly used measure of risk.

It must be pointed out that risk usually works both ways. It can be observed in Figure 4.1 that while Investment G has a higher probability of yielding negative returns, it also offers a higher probability of returns in excess of $6,000. Thus the choice between these two investments is not clear-cut. The profit maximization rule would indicate that Investment G is superior; however, some businessmen would prefer Investment F because it involves less risk. This choice is largely a subjective one, depending upon personal preferences for risk versus returns as well as on financial ability to carry the greater degree of risk involved. Returns in farming enterprises fluctuate from year to year because of yield variability, price changes, and many other factors that cause variations in revenue and expenses. Some farmers exhibit more *risk aversion* than others and prefer enterprises with lower average, but more stable, returns while others are willing to accept larger amounts of risk to achieve higher average incomes.

Financial Risk. Just as the evaluation of business risk and the earnings associated with alternative courses of action determines how capital should be used in the business, the evaluation of *financial* *risk* determines *how much* capital should be acquired. In Chapter 1 it was pointed out that the financial manager really has only two basic sources of capital, namely, his own equity capital and someone else's capital. The term *nonequity capital* is used to refer to borrowing, leasing, and other arrangements or contracts. Large corporations also have the alternative of raising additional equity capital by issuing new common stock. Generally speaking, raising new equity funds through a stock issue is not a relevant capital acquisition alternative for most farm businesses, although the trend to larger farm units may lead to the more widespread use of this practice in the future. Thus the use of additional capital in the typical farm business nearly always implies using additional nonequity financing with a fixed or given amount of owner equity.

The use of nonequity capital, whether it be acquired by borrowing, leasing, or some other contractual agreement, creates a fixed financial commitment in the form of principal, interest, rent, or other obligations.[2] This financial commitment to the supplier of nonequity capital results in *financial risk*. As leverage (the amount of nonequity capital relative to equity capital) increases, the financial commitment increases; hence, the risk increases. At the same time, as long as the rate of return on capital invested exceeds the cost of using nonequity capital, there is a gain from the use of leverage in the form of increased returns to the owner of the business.

Principle of Increasing Risk. The tendency for risk to increase at an increasing rate as the relative amount of nonequity capital used in a business increases is referred to as the principle of increasing risk. The way in which this principle works is illustrated by the hypothetical data in Table 4.3.

It is assumed that the operator of this farm business has $50,000 in equity capital and that he can borrow or lease additional capital at a cost of 6 percent of the amount borrowed or leased. He can use his $50,000 alone and operate a very small farm business or he can borrow or lease additional capital and operate a larger business. Columns 2, 3, 4, and 5 illustrate the situation with leverage ratios (nonequity capital ÷ equity capital) ranging from 0 to 2:1.

Consider first the situation portrayed in column 2 where the operator has full equity in his business. When a 12 percent return is earned on capital used in the business, the gross return is $6,000, and since there is no interest to pay, the earnings before taxes are $6,000.

---

2. The share lease that is widely used in agriculture involves committing a percentage share of total revenue. In this sense, share leasing has many of the attributes of outside equity financing because some of the risk is borne by the owner of the capital.

TABLE 4.3: Illustration of Principle of Increasing Risk (Hypothetical data)

Line	Item		Leverage = Nonequity Capital / Equity Capital			
		0	0.5	1	2
	(1)	(2)	(3)	(4)	(5)
1.	Equity capital used in business	$50,000	$50,000	$ 50,000	$ 50,000
2.	Nonequity capital used in business	0	25,000	50,000	100,000
3.	Total capital used in business	$50,000	$75,000	$100,000	$150,000
	Income when rate earned on investment is +12%				
4.	Gross returns on capital	$ 6,000	$ 9,000	$ 12,000	$ 18,000
5.	Cost of nonequity capital (6%)	0	1,500	3,000	6,000
6.	Pre-tax net return on capital used	$ 6,000	$ 7,500	$ 9,000	$ 12,000
7.	Income tax (20% of net return)*	1,200	1,500	1,800	2,400
8.	After-tax net return on capital used	$ 4,800	$ 6,000	$ 7,200	$ 9,600
9.	Rate earned on equity capital	9.6%	12.0%	14.4%	19.2%
	Income when rate earned on investment is −12%				
10.	Gross return on capital	($ 6,000)†	($ 9,000)	($ 12,000)	($ 18,000)
11.	Cost of nonequity capital	0	1,500	3,000	6,000
12.	Total return on capital used	($ 6,000)	($10,500)	($ 15,000)	($ 24,000)
13.	Rate of return on equity capital	(12%)	(21.0%)	(30.0%)	(48.0%)

* A constant tax rate of 20% of net income is used for all income levels. In an actual situation, the tax rate would increase with increasing income.
† Figures in parentheses are negative.

It is assumed that the income tax rate for this business is 20 percent of the net earnings; thus income taxes would amount to $1,200, leaving an after-tax income of $4,800—a 9.6 percent rate of return on the $50,000 equity. Similarly, there is a 12 percent loss on owner equity under adverse business conditions.

The situation changes, however, when nonequity capital is used. When $25,000 of nonequity capital are combined with the $50,000 in equity capital, and the rate of return on total capital is 12 percent, the after-tax rate of return on equity capital increases by 2.4 percent, from 9.6 percent to 12.0 percent, under favorable business conditions. Under adverse business conditions, the use of the $25,000 in nonequity financing increases the loss on owner equity from 12 percent to 21 percent—a net change of 9 percentage points from the all-equity situation. As the leverage ratio increases to 1:1, the owner of the business stands to earn 14.4 percent on his equity under favorable business conditions but he would lose 30 percent under adverse conditions. If he used $100,000 in nonequity capital, he could realize a 19.2 percent return on his equity, but he would stand to lose 48 percent.

The hypothetical data in Table 4.1 merit careful study because they illustrate the combined effects of business risk and financial risk. Business risk is reflected in Table 4.1 by comparing rows 9 and 13 for any given degree of leverage. Financial risk is illustrated by the increasing difference between the entries in rows 9 and 13 as leverage increases. Three things are evident from these figures: (1) as leverage increases, there is a tendency for the spread between possible gains and possible losses to increase; (2) with an equal percentage gain and loss on total capital used in the business, the magnitude of the loss is greater than the magnitude of the gain on owner equity; and (3) income taxes tend to reduce possible gains but they do not reduce possible losses, even though interest is a tax-deductible expense. This adverse tax effect occurs because the business is subject to income tax when it shows a profit, but it does not receive an income tax refund if it incurs losses.[3]

LEVERAGE AND FIRM GROWTH. In the preceding section, the effects of leverage on income were examined. As long as the marginal rate of return on capital exceeds the marginal cost of using nonequity capital, the owner of the business may increase the level of income with increased leverage. If he is able to reinvest some of this income in his business, save it, or use it to repay borrowed

---

3. In actual practice, losses can be carried forward to future years by using income averaging and other provisions of the Federal Tax Law.

capital, his net worth will increase over time. For example, if the $100,000 business portrayed in column 4 of Table 4.1 were to spend say, $5,400 out of the $7,200 after-tax income on consumption expenditures, the owner equity in the business would be increased by $1,800 or 3.6 percent on the $50,000 equity. This process of plowing back a portion of the earnings results in firm growth where *firm growth* is defined as an increase in owner equity. If, for example, the $1,800 is used to repay borrowed capital, the business portrayed in column 4 would have $51,800 in equity capital and $48,200 in nonequity capital at the end of the time period under consideration. Alternatively, he could also increase the total capital investment to $101,800 in which case he would have $50,000 in nonequity capital and $51,800 in equity capital.

Firm-Growth Equation. The process of farm firm growth has been described in terms of a mathematical model.[4] This model is very useful in understanding the combined effects on the rate of firm growth of return on capital investment, the cost of nonequity capital, leverage, taxes, and consumption.

The assumptions of the farm firm growth model are as follows:

1. The income tax rate on earnings remains constant for all income levels.[5]
2. The proportion of after-tax earnings used for consumption (or alternatively, the proportion of after-tax earnings reinvested) remains constant for all sizes of businesses.
3. The rate of return on total capital invested is constant for all sizes of businesses.
4. The cost per unit of nonequity financing is constant for all degrees of leverage and all sizes of businesses.

The following notation is used:

A is the total capital investment
E is the amount of owner equity
D is the amount of nonequity capital
r is the rate of return on total capital investment
i is the cost of nonequity financing
c is the proportion of after-tax income needed to meet farm family consumption
t is the income tax rate
L is leverage $= D/E$

---

4. See C. B. Baker and J. A. Hopkin, "Concepts of Finance Capital for a Capital-using Agriculture," *Am. Jour. Agr. Econ* 51 (Dec. 1969): 1055–64.
5. Under progressive income tax rates, the tax rate increases with increases in income. The assumption that the tax rate remains constant is used to simplify the analysis.

Following this notation, the gross earnings on total capital (before payment of interest and taxes) are equal to (rA) and the earnings after payment of interest but before income taxes are $(rA - iD)$.

If the income tax rate is t, the net after-tax earnings will be

$$(rA - iD) (1 - t)$$

The net after-tax income is the amount available for family consumption and reinvestment in the business. If the operator and his family use the proportion c of their after-tax income for consumption, the amount which can be reinvested in the business is

$$g = (rA - id) (1 - t) (1 - c) \tag{4.1}$$

Equation 4.1 can be illustrated using the data from Table 4.1, column 4, under favorable business conditions, where

$$A = \$100,000;\ E = \$50,000;\ D = \$50,000;\ r = 0.12;\ i = 0.06;\ \text{and}\ t = 0.20.$$

If he consumes \$5,400 out of his after-tax income of \$7,200, his average propensity to consume is 0.75, that is, c in Equation 4.1 is 0.75. Thus the increase in the owner equity of the business is

$$
\begin{aligned}
g &= [(0.12)\ (\$100,000) - (0.06)\ (\$50,000)]\ (1 - 0.20)\ (1 - 0.75) \\
&= [\$12,000 - \$3,000]\ (0.80)\ (0.25) \\
&= \$1,800
\end{aligned}
$$

Equation 4.1 can be modified to give the *rate of change* in owner equity, g', where $g' = g/E$. Dividing both sides of Equation 4.1 by E gives

$$\frac{g}{E} = g' = \left[\frac{rA}{E} - \frac{iD}{E} \right] (1 - t) (1 - c) \tag{4.2}$$

Since the sum of equity capital plus nonequity capital is equal to the total amount of capital used in the business, that is, $A = D + E$, Equation 4.2 becomes

$$g' = \left[r \left(\frac{D + E}{E} \right) - i \left(\frac{D}{E} \right) \right] (1 - t) (1 - c) \tag{4.3}$$

Since $L = D/E$, Equation 4.3 can be simplified to

$$g' = [L (r - i) + r] (1 - t) (1 - c) \tag{4.4}$$

Equation 4.4 can also be illustrated using the data from Table 4.1. The rate of growth in owner equity for column 4, with $c = 0.75$, would be

$$
\begin{aligned}
g' &= \left[\frac{\$50,000}{\$50,000}\ (0.12 - 0.06) + 0.12 \right] (1 - 0.2) (1 - 0.75) \\
&= 0.036 = 3.6 \text{ percent}
\end{aligned}
$$

Equation 4.4 can be used to estimate the rate of growth in owner equity for any combination of return on capital, cost of nonequity capital, tax rate, and consumption rate. Its primary usefulness, however, lies in the fact that it clearly shows the effects of these variables on the rate of firm growth.

Equation 4.4 shows that, other factors remaining constant, (1) increases in leverage L and/or the spread between the rate of return on invested capital and the cost of nonequity capital $(r - i)$ result in a more rapid rate of growth in owner equity, and vice versa, and (2) increases in the proportion of income used for consumption c and/or income tax rate t cause a reduction in the rate of growth in owner equity, and vice versa. Figure 4.2 illustrates the effect of leverage on the rate of firm growth for several levels of r, given specified rates for interest, taxes, and consumption.

Examination of the Assumptions of the Model. The static growth model implies that as long as the marginal rate of return on invested capital exceeds the marginal cost of nonequity financing it pays to increase leverage. However, examination of the basic assumptions of the model indicates why extremely high degrees of leverage are rarely observed in the real world.

The assumptions that the tax rate and the proportion of income consumed remain constant for all levels of income do not hold in the real world. Federal income tax rates are progressive, meaning that higher income levels are taxed at higher rates. Thus, as the size of the firm increases, the rate at which earnings are taxed will increase, and the gains from leverage will be reduced. At the same time, as net earnings increase, the typical farm family will probably consume a declining proportion of the farm income and reinvest a correspondingly larger share of the income in the business. The tendency for the marginal propensity to consume to decline as income increases would magnify the firm growth effects of leverage. Perhaps it would be reasonable to assume that increases in the income tax rate would be offset by decreases in the marginal propensity to consume and the expression $(1 - t)(1 - c)$ in Equation 4.4 would remain relatively constant as firm size increases.

The assumption that the rate of return on total capital invested is constant for all sizes of businesses is also unrealistic. It is more reasonable to expect the rate of return with capital use to be subject to the law of diminishing returns. Thus r in Equation 4.4 will eventually begin to decline once the business reaches a certain size. This ultimate decline in the rate of return on total capital invested would tend to reduce the rate of firm growth.

Finally, the assumption that the cost of nonequity financing remains constant as leverage increases is unrealistic. Lenders tend to

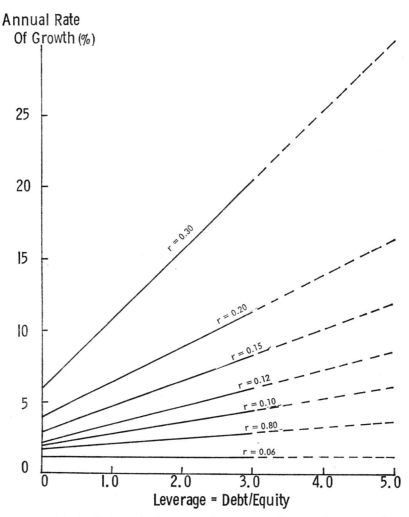

FIG. *4.2—Relationship between leverage and annual rate of firm growth. (Calculated from* g′ = [L (r − i) + r] (l − t) (l − c) *with* i, t, *and* c *specified as 0.06, 0.20, and 0.75, respectively.*

look with disfavor on extremely high degrees of leverage and react by increasing interest rates on loans or simply refusing to advance additional credit. This tendency for lenders to limit the amount of credit they will provide to the business is known as *external capital rationing.* At the same time, the operator of the business will also be reluctant to push the use of leverage to extremely high levels. For one thing, he recognizes that the degree of financial risk increases as leverage increases. He also recognizes that as he uses more credit there

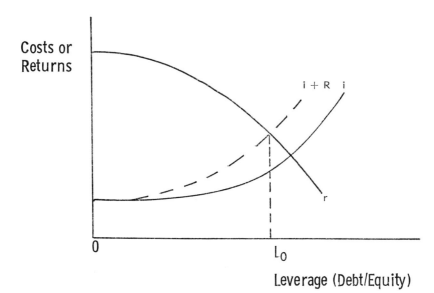

FIG. *4.3—Equilibrium in the use of leverage.*

will be less credit in reserve. Unused borrowing capacity constitutes a reserve much the same as cash or near cash assets and these reserves of unused credit are important to the manager of a business. This reluctance on the part of the businessman to use unlimited amounts of nonequity financing is called *internal capital rationing.*

The tendency for the rate of return on capital to decrease and for the cost of nonequity capital to increase with increasing amounts borrowed are illustrated in Figure 4.3. The curve labeled r shows the diminishing marginal productivity of capital as additional nonequity capital is combined with a fixed amount of equity capital. Curve i reflects external capital rationing—the tendency for the cost of nonequity financing to rise once the acceptable degree of leverage is exceeded. The curve $(i + R)$ shows the combined effects of internal and external capital rationing. In addition to the actual interest cost of nonequity financing, the operator of the business incurs costs in the form of increased financial risk and reduced credit reserves.

Conceptually at least, there is an optimum degree of leverage (point L_0 in Fig. 4.3), beyond which it does not pay to use additional nonequity capital. The gain from the use of leverage is maximized when the marginal rate of return on invested capital r is equal to the marginal cost of nonequity capital $(i + R)$. Observations on actual farm situations would show that farm operators and agricultural lenders or other suppliers of nonequity financing behave much as shown in Figure 4.3. Leverage varies widely among farm businesses but overall debt:equity ratios in excess of 3:1 are rarely encountered, and lenders carefully scrutinize cases where debt:equity ratios exceed 2:1.

SUMMARY. A firm is a business organization that produces goods and/or services. The financial manager of a firm is primarily responsible for maximizing the net present worth of the earnings of the owners of the firm. The net present worth criterion is used because it explicitly considers the fact that the owner or owners of the firm are concerned with both *earnings and risk* and not merely with maximizing profits.

The financial manager must be concerned with two kinds of risks—business risk and financial risk. Business risk is the variability in income associated with the type of business in which the firm is engaged. Financial risk is the increased chance of incurring losses as leverage increases. The combination of business risk and financial risk is described in the principle of increasing risk.

Other things being equal, profitable firms that use leverage will show more rapid rates of growth in owner equity than firms that use only equity capital. Strict adherence to this principle would imply that the more leverage, the better. However, rising tax rates, diminishing marginal returns on capital investment, and the rising marginal cost of nonequity financing caused by internal and external capital rationing all combine to restrict the use of leverage to generally accepted limits.

QUESTIONS AND PROBLEMS

1. Explain the differences between *maximizing profits* and *maximizing the net present value of the earnings* of the owners of a business.
2. Distinguish between the terms *business risk* and *financial risk*. Discuss how these two kinds of risk are combined in the principle of increasing risk.
3. What is the principle of increasing risk? Set up a hypothetical table such as Table 4.3 to illustrate the principle of increasing risk. Assume that total capital in the business remains constant and that equity declines. Do your illustration and the one in Table 4.3 support the same conclusion?
4. Using the firm-growth equation (Equation 4.4), compare the rates of growth of the four firms in Table 4.3, assuming favorable business conditions. Assume that the withdrawal rate for family consumption needs is 60 percent of after-tax earnings. What do your comparisons tell you about the relationship between leverage and the rate of firm growth?

5. Explain why internal capital rationing and external capital rationing limit the use of leverage to generally accepted levels, even though additional leverage may result in a more rapid rate of firm growth.
6. What do lenders and farmers in your area consider to be generally acceptable degrees of financial leverage?

REFERENCES

Baker, C. B., and Hopkin, J. A. "Concepts of Finance Capital for a Capital Using Agriculture." *Am. Jour. Agr. Econ.,* vol. 51, no. 5, Dec. 1969, pp. 1055–64.

Bodenhorn, Diran. "A Cash Flow Concept of Profit." *Jour. Finance,* vol. 19, no. 1, Mar. 1964, pp. 16–31.

Bostwick, Don. *Farm Financial Management Research: A Theoretical Analysis.* Farm Prod. Econ. Div., ERS, USDA, ERS-389, Nov. 1968.

———. "Financial Returns in Agriculture." *Am. Jour. Agr. Econ.,* vol. 51, no. 5, Aug. 1969, pp. 662–65.

———. "Returns to Farm Resources." *Am. Jour. Agr. Econ.,* vol. 51, no. 5, Dec. 1969, pp. 1528–35.

Brake, J. R. "Firm Growth Models Often Neglect Important Cash Withdrawals." *Am. Jour. Agr. Econ.,* vol. 50, no. 3, Aug. 1968, pp. 769–72.

Grossman, P. A., and Headley, J. C. *Yield and Income Variability for Major Crops in Illinois: A Basis for Farm Decisions.* Dept. Agr. Econ., Agr. Exp. Sta., Univ. of Ill., AERR 73, Feb. 1965.

Hall, Hollis D., and Walker, Odell, L. "An Economic Analysis of the Growth of Oklahoma Grade A Dairy Farms Using the Growth Simulation Technique." Okla. State Univ., AE-7012, Feb. 1970.

Harrison, Virden L. *Management Strategies and Decision Processes for the Growth of Farm Firms.* Unpublished Ph.D. thesis, Purdue Univ., Aug. 1970.

Solomon, Ezra. *The Theory of Financial Management.* Columbia Univ. Press, New York, 1953.

Stovall, John G. "Income Variation and Selection of Enterprises." *Jour. Farm Econ.,* vol. 48, no. 5, Dec. 1966, pp. 1575–79.

PART 2: FINANCIAL MANAGEMENT OF THE FARM BUSINESS

CHAPTER 5: FARM FINANCIAL MANAGEMENT

THE large and increasing amounts of capital required in agriculture, as outlined in Chapter 1, serve to emphasize the need for more attention to management of finances. When farms were smaller and fewer inputs were purchased, finances were relatively less important in the overall picture. However, as farms have developed into substantial businesses, a definite need has arisen for astute handling of financial affairs. Earnings of capital, both absolutely and in one use as compared to another, are crucial to the farm business since (1) capital requirements are extremely large and (2) a high proportion of gross income is required to pay for purchased inputs.

What is the role of the financial manager of a farm business? The theory of financial management covered in Chapter 4 suggests that the financial manager must consider the timing and risk of the earnings along with the amount of earnings. This chapter introduces Part 2 of the text, which covers the application of financial management.

Financial management and farm management are synonymous in many respects. This overlapping is natural since farm management is the primary activity, with financial management contributing to the overall management of the firm. Thus, while no attempt is made to explicitly differentiate financial management and farm management, the financial aspects of farm management are treated in somewhat more detail than is generally the case in farm management.

MANAGERIAL PROCESS. The manager's job is to make decisions in an environment of uncertainty. Managing a business in the utopian world of perfect knowledge would be a simple task, and perhaps even a dull task, because prices, yields, production costs, and profits would be known in advance. In the real world, however, no one knows exactly what the future will bring. Prices, yields, and costs may turn out to be higher or lower than expected. The institutional structure within which the business operates may change, bringing about new tax laws or new standards governing waste disposal and the use of pesticides. A serious auto accident, an illness in the family, or a lawsuit may completely alter the future course of a farm business. These and many other uncertainties that characterize the real world bring about the need for management.

The managerial process can be defined in terms of a step-by-step procedure:[1] (1) goal formulation, (2) problem recognition, (3) analysis, (4) decision making, (5) action, and (6) responsibility bearing. Thus the financial manager is responsible for formulating goals, recognizing and analyzing problems, making decisions, taking action, and accepting the responsibility for actions taken with regard to the financial affairs of the business. Aspects of financial management analyzed in this chapter are (1) goal formulation, (2) financial decisions, and (3) procedures that facilitate effective financial management.

DEFINING GOALS. Financial management is not an end in itself but a means of accomplishing goals or objectives. The first step in financial management, therefore, is to determine the goals. Individual and family goals grow out of needs and interests, past experiences, and values. Goals are the ends toward which individuals and families work.

Goal setting is a continuous process. In every family there are several goals, some of which may conflict. Thus, establishing goals involves weighing interests and needs and modifying either the goals or the methods of attaining them. Not all goals are equally important and some may be stepping stones to achieving subsequent or more ultimate goals.

Goals of the family may be classified into two groups: those involving consumption and those pertaining to production. Goals involving consumption relate to the home itself, its furnishings, food and clothing of the family, vacation, and the like. Goals pertaining to production involve the farm business and any nonfarm investments the farmer may own. Such goals relate to the size and type of farm to be operated, the type and quality of livestock, and the level of production to be achieved. We are concerned with the latter group of goals in this chapter.

Goals ordinarily define specific objectives. Some are immediately attainable and often imperative, others may be reached in months, while some may take years or perhaps a lifetime. The short-term goal may be to rent a farm; the intermediate goal, owner operation with the aid of considerable borrowed funds; the more distant goal, owner operation with a reasonably safe equity. An immediate goal may be a specific cropping system; the long-term goal may be to bring additional land into cultivation by drainage or irrigation, and to improve production through soil conservation, improved rotations,

---

1. See Lawrence A. Bradford and Glenn L. Johnson, *Farm Management Analysis* (New York: John Wiley & Sons, 1953), pp. 1–11.

and fertilization. The present ranch may accommodate 200 cows and appurtenant young stock; the long-term goal may call for expanding to a 500-cow unit.

Goals are important in financial management since they indicate investments that will be called for, expenses to be met, and income to be realized. Thus goals should be formulated with these things in mind. They should be sufficiently explicit and nonduplicating so that associated finances can be estimated. Timing of the goal should be recorded to indicate when funds will be needed for their fulfillment and/or when income will be forthcoming.

FINANCIAL DECISIONS. The financial manager is concerned mainly with the problems associated with capital acquisition and capital use in the business. Since capital acquisition and capital use are involved in virtually every phase of farm management, five questions that pertain specifically to the financial aspects of the business have been identified: (1) How much total capital should be employed? (2) Which sources of capital should be used? (3) How should the total capital be allocated among alternative uses? (4) What strategies for reducing risk and uncertainty should be used? (5) Under what form of legal organization should the business be operated? At first glance, these questions might appear to be once-in-a-lifetime decisions that pertain only to the beginning farmer; however, most farmers continually face these questions at virtually all stages of their careers.

Amount of Capital It Will Pay to Use. Consideration of the overall amount of capital it will pay to employ in the business usually is approached within a long-run planning framework. Most factors of production, therefore, are subject to modification. Management may be relatively fixed, but most commercial farmers have sufficient surplus ability to permit considerable expansion of the business before diminishing returns become serious. Under such circumstances, marginal returns decline very little with increased use of capital, while marginal costs gradually increase until they equal marginal returns.

The increase in marginal costs associated with the use of capital may arise from three sources: increased operating costs associated with the size of the unit, increased risk involved in using larger amounts of credit, and nonmonetary costs involved in acquiring and using capital. The long-run average cost curve concept indicates the relative level of costs associated with different sizes of farms. Theoretically, costs eventually will increase as the size of farm increases, due to inefficiencies associated with size, limitations of management, and the like. Quite a number of studies of the cost structures of various sizes of farms indicate, however, that increasing costs generally do not occur within the size of most commercial farms. While this generalization may not hold for all farms and farmers, it appears that relatively little of the increase in marginal costs typically is associated with size as such.[2] The increase in marginal costs associated with the use of larger amounts of capital stems primarily from risk aversion and nonmonetary costs involved in acquiring and using capital. These costs are responsible for internal capital rationing in the farm business.

Risk of loss of equity capital increases as the relative amount of borrowed capital used in a typical farm business increases. As the analysis of the principle of increasing risk covered in Chapter 4 shows, risk of loss of equity capital due to crop failure, low prices, or other adverse conditions—the possibility of loss of the farm business—generally limits the amount of credit used in the business to less than it would pay to use under conditions of perfect knowledge. Even when the consequences may not be so serious, using more credit often has adverse effects. Worry over not being able to meet the loan payments increases. The lender may ask more questions and require more information on the business.

For several reasons nonmonetary costs increase as the amount of capital acquired for use in the business increases. As the amount of capital saved in a given period increases, dissatisfaction or negative satisfaction associated with foregoing current consumption increases. More difficulty may be encountered in finding capital to rent or borrow. The cost of management may increase due to the added time, effort, and worry involved in managing a larger amount of capital.

Choosing among Sources of Capital. A basic requirement for developing farm financial plans is a general indication of how much capital is available. For example, Does the farmer have access to $50,000, $100,000, or $500,000? With this general indication, plans can then be developed for specific uses of the funds. The specific amount to be used will depend upon the profitability of using capital, the terms and conditions involved in acquiring capital, and the amount of risk the family can carry. These aspects of capital acquisition and utilization by the farm business are considered in some detail in subsequent chapters.

---

2. There is evidence that very large farming operations may realize larger profit margins because they are able to obtain quantity discounts for purchased inputs and higher prices for products. See Kenneth R. Krause and Leonard P. Kyle, "Economic Factors Underlying the Incidence of Large Farming Units: The Current Situation and Probable Trends," *Am. Jour. Agr. Econ.* 52 (Dec. 1970): 748–63.

Many farmers do not take an overall look at finances and, therefore, do not realize the amount of capital to which they have access. Two reasons probably are that (1) they have not investigated the various sources of capital, and (2) they have not developed a pattern of analysis to help them determine the amount of capital they should obtain from each source.

As was pointed out in Chapter 2, several sources of capital will normally be used. The cost of capital is an important consideration in choosing among sources of capital since interest rates, fees, and other costs do vary among lenders. The question of risk must also be considered when choosing sources of capital. The use of nonequity capital usually results in increased financial risk; however, some sources of nonequity capital involve more risk than others. For example, custom hiring may be more desirable than a long-term lease or ownership with borrowed capital because custom hiring does not result in a fixed, long-term financial obligation. The sources of capital available, together with an analysis of the advantages and disadvantages of each, are discussed in the next chapter.

Allocation of Capital to Alternative Uses. With limited capital (there would be no problem if capital were unlimited) the financial manager continually faces the task of deciding among competing uses of funds. The limited supply of capital must be allocated among alternative uses in production, between production and consumption, and between present and future use.

The basic economic principles covered in Chapter 2 and the concept of the time value of money that was introduced in Chapter 3 provide a basis for analyzing problems in capital allocation. At this point, it would be advisable to review the following principles that relate to capital allocation:

1. With a fixed amount of resources, maximum income is obtained when the marginal rate of substitution is equal to the inverse of the price ratio.
2. Costs are at a minimum when the factor substitution ratio is equal to the inverse of the price ratio.
3. The optimum allocation of capital to consumption and to savings is achieved when the satisfaction from the last (marginal) unit of capital allocated to consumption is equal to the satisfaction derived from an equivalent unit of capital allocated to savings.
4. A dollar received now is worth more than the prospect of receiving a dollar at some future date.

Risk Management. Risk management is the use of formal and informal insurance strategies to keep risk and uncertainty within tolerable bounds. Insurance always involves a cost, thus the subject of risk management could be treated within the general framework of capital allocation. However, since dealing with risk and uncertainty is an integral part of the management function, the analysis of insurance is treated separately in this text. The basic question confronting the financial manager is, Which types of insurance should be employed and how much money should be spent on each? Insurance needs vary widely according to the individual's financial and personal goals. A young farm family with a heavy debt load, for example, cannot assume as much risk and uncertainty as an established farmer in a strong equity position. The topic of risk management is treated in detail in Chapters 12 and 13.

Selecting the Appropriate Legal Organization. Farm businesses have been traditionally organized as sole proprietorships. In recent years, however, growing capital requirements with the associated problems of raising funds and transferring resources from one generation to the next have brought about a significant increase in the use of partnerships and corporations. According to the United States Census of Agriculture, there were 1.73 million commercial farms (that is, farms with sales of $2,500 or more) in 1969. Nearly 1.5 million of these farms were individual or family owned, 221,535 were partnerships, 21,513 were corporations, and 10,070 were classified as "other." Among the corporate farms, 19,716 had 10 or fewer shareholders and only 1,797 had more than 10 shareholders, indicating that most farm corporations are probably closely held family farm corporations. Comparable data for earlier years are not available but there are indications that the relative importance of both corporations and partnerships is growing rapidly.

The trend toward more partnerships and corporations has raised a controversial social issue. The fear that larger farming units will eventually take over and replace the family farm has prompted some states to pass legislation prohibiting farm corporations or limiting the extent of their operations. Our concern here is not with the social issue but rather with the fact that choosing the legal organization is vitally important to financial success in farming. The wrong choice can lead to problems such as lack of management continuity between generations, lack of capital for expansion and growth, and unnecessarily high income and estate taxes.

PROCEDURES THAT FACILITATE EFFECTIVE FINANCIAL MANAGEMENT.
The analysis phase of management is an information-gathering process. To be effective, the financial manager must possess a great deal of general knowledge about the economic environment in which he operates and he needs very detailed

information about his business in particular. He must also have an organized procedure for recognizing and solving financial problems.

General Knowledge Requirements. The financial manager should keep up-to-date on the economic environment in which he operates. He should be aware of the prices of inputs and outputs and he should try to determine their probable future trends. Synthetic substitutes for natural fibers and changes in import-export regulations are examples of factors that can have adverse or favorable financial effects on the individual farm business. Changes in the legal and institutional environment are also important to the financial manager. He must be familiar with the legal rights and obligations of borrowers, lenders, tenants, landlords, and owners of real and personal property. He should also be aware of laws governing the distribution of property after one's death.

Keeping up with the changing environment requires a great deal of time, but the consequences of failing to do so can be serious. Subsequent chapters provide some of the general information needed by the financial manager, but regular study of newspapers, farm magazines, extension service publications, and other sources of information is important.

Farm Records. Records of the farm business should be kept and used as an integral part of good business and tax management. On commercial farms, farm records are practically a necessity for income tax purposes and if properly designed will contribute materially to financial management. Records should provide the following information as a minimum:

1. A complete annual inventory of assets and liabilities in sufficient detail and with adequate description to make them understandable. The number and description of livestock; items of machinery; method of depreciation; names, addresses, and explanation of accounts receivable and payable will be helpful.
2. A complete listing and description of income and expense items during the year, preferably by enterprise. This part of the record should also show production, purchases, births, debt payments, funds borrowed, and the like, to permit bringing the inventory up-to-date.
3. A summary of cash flows and an analysis of each enterprise in the farm business for use in management decisions and for tax purposes.

These basic records provide the detailed information needed for effective financial management. Knowledge of the past financial progress and the present financial position of the business is extremely useful in planning for the future. They also measure financial strength in terms of *liquidity* and *solvency*. Liquidity is the ability to meet financial commitments, such as loan payments, accounts with suppliers, payroll, and family living needs, on schedule. Solvency describes the extent to which debts would be covered if the business were forced into liquidation. Because of the importance of farm records, three chapters are devoted to this subject.

Financial Plans. Establishment of goals has limited merit unless these goals are organized and coordinated in financial plans for the farm business. It has been said that "when we fail to plan, we plan to fail." When we fail to plan, almost certainly some of our most valued goals go begging because available funds will have been spent on the less important goals. Plans serve as guides in achieving goals in farming, as blueprints and specifications serve as guides in the engineering and construction fields.

A minimum of two basic financial plans should be made: a short-time plan or budget covering the period immediately ahead—year, quarter, or whatever period is most pertinent—and a long-time plan. These two basic plans should be supplemented with other plans as necessary to provide a well-organized basis for achieving goals. For example, if a major purchase is contemplated, a special analysis might be helpful in determining the influence of the outlay on the business and farm family. Moreover, the basic short-term and long-term plans should be rebuilt or revised from time to time to keep them up-to-date.

Building financial plans is not a simple task. While they need not be made a matter of drudgery, creating more dissatisfaction than satisfaction, plans must be based upon a sound foundation and proper business procedures to provide reliable guidance for decisions.

Home Business Office. A business office in the home facilitates keeping adequate records and knowing where documents can be found when they are needed. An office provides a place to work on business affairs; to keep records up-to-date; and to file bills, important papers, checks, and the like. Readily replaceable business papers and those currently used can be kept in the home business office. However, important records, papers, and documents such as wills, leases, mortgages, stock certificates, bonds, and insurance policies are best kept in a safe-deposit box or fireproof safe. The duplicate copy of income tax reports should be kept for at least 5 years.

A record, in duplicate, should be made of all important documents telling where they are kept. One copy should be kept with the documents in the safe-deposit box, and the duplicate can be maintained in the business center at home for handy reference.

QUESTIONS AND PROBLEMS

1. Outline the steps in the managerial process. Discuss these steps as they might pertain to a major financial decision such as buying a farm.
2. Explain the relationship between setting financial goals and making financial plans.
3. List the five major decisions that the financial manager faces. Outline a general approach for dealing with each of these major decisions.
4. Describe the business procedures which will facilitate effective financial management. To what extent do you feel farmers in your area are following effective business procedures?

REFERENCES

Bradford, Lawrence A., and Johnson, Glenn L. *Farm Management Analysis.* John Wiley & Sons, 1953.

Coffman, George W. *Corporations with Farming Operations.* ERS, USDA, Agr. Econ. Rept. 209, June 1971.

Heady, Earl O. *Economics of Agricultural Production and Resource Use.* Prentice-Hall, Englewood Cliffs, N.J., 1952, Chap. 14.

Hesser, Leon F. "Conceptual Models of Capital Rationing among Farmers." *Jour. Farm Econ.,* vol. 42, no. 2, May 1960, pp. 325–34.

Hillman, C. H., and Steward, D. D. *Financial Management Practices of Farm Families in Southeastern Ohio Agriculture.* Ohio Agr. Exp. Sta. Res. Bull. 940, June 1963.

Irwin, G. D., and Baker, C. B. *Effects of Lender Decisions on Farm Financial Planning.* Ill. Agr. Exp. Sta. Bull. 688, Nov. 1962.

Krause, Kenneth R. "Application of the Financial Management Function in the Family Size Farm Firm." *Am. Jour. Agr. Econ.,* vol. 51, no. 5, Dec. 1969, pp. 1536–42.

Krause, Kenneth R., and Kyle, Leonard R. "Economic Factors Underlying the Incidence of Large-scale Farming Units: The Current Situation and Probable Trends." *Am. Jour. Agr. Econ.,* vol. 52, no. 5, Dec. 1970, pp. 748–63.

Raup, Philip M. "Economies and Diseconomies of Large-scale Agriculture." *Am. Jour. Agr. Econ.,* vol. 51, no. 5, Dec. 1969, pp. 1274–83.

Smith, Frank J., Jr., and Cooper, Ken. *The Financial Management of Agribusiness Firms.* Univ. of Minn. Agr. Ext. Serv., in cooperation with USDA Fed. Ext. Serv., Div. of Marketing and Utilization Sciences, Spec. Rept. 26, Sept. 1967.

Technical Committee for NC-32. *Family Financial Security.* North Central Regional Res. Publ. 131, Iowa Agr. Exp. Sta., Spec. Rept. 36, Mar. 1964.

CHAPTER 6: ACQUIRING CAPITAL TO FARM

DATA GIVEN in Chapter 1 indicate the large capital requirements of a farm business. The question then arises, Where can the needed capital be acquired?

It has been pointed out previously that there are two basic sources of capital—equity and nonequity. However, many widely used sources of capital fall somewhere in between these two extremes. The sources of capital in farming listed below represent a continuum between pure equity and pure debt financing.

1. Savings
2. Gifts and inheritances
3. Outside equity capital
4. Leasing
5. Contract production
6. Borrowing

SAVINGS. Capital accumulated through savings (defined as net worth, less gifts and inheritances) forms the foundation of the farm financial structure. Except for gifts and inheritances, savings provide the backbone for farm and ranch capital. Savings provide not only capital, as such, but risk-bearing ability (reserves) and demonstrated capacity to earn and save, two very essential components of a strong credit rating.

Farming is big business and big business requires a large amount of capital and a sound financial foundation and framework that savings alone can provide. Few people who are unable to save will be successful in commercial farming. The farmer is the one to whom profit derived from farming accrues and, therefore, he must stand the risk of loss. Funds are also needed for sickness, education, and other family uses. Savings must be accumulated by the successful farm family to provide a financial base for all such purposes.

Accumulating any amount of savings takes time for most people. Living standards tend to be upgraded as income increases, which leaves little for savings. However, it is surprising how rapidly wisely invested savings grow. Even a small amount saved regularly produces a surprisingly large sum in a fairly short period. For example, an investment of $100 per month at 6 percent per annum will amount to nearly $7,000 at the end of 5 years.

GIFTS AND INHERITANCES. Because of the dominance of the family farm, much of the owner equity capital in agriculture today has been acquired through gifts and inheritances from the previous generation of farm operators. These two methods of acquiring capital are distinctly different as far as the timing of the receipt of the capital is concerned. However, they are closely related in that gifts to prospective heirs usually result in a substantial reduction in estate taxes and probate costs. The legal and tax aspects of the intergeneration transfer of capital are covered in more detail in Chapters 16 and 17. In this chapter, we merely want to identify this important means of acquiring capital.

Gifts and inheritances have provided many farm families with the equity base needed to finance a successful business. The obvious disadvantage is that gifts and inheritances are often not received when they are needed most. Since the average life expectancy in the United States is over 70 years, young farmers may not receive substantial amounts of capital through inheritance from parents and/or other relatives in the early stages of their careers.

Another disadvantage is that gifts and inheritances often come with strings attached. Some farmers transfer property to heirs subject to a life interest on behalf of the surviving spouse. Gifts may be made with either implicit or explicit restrictions on managerial control, which can sometimes seriously impair the progress of the young farmer.

ACQUIRING OUTSIDE EQUITY CAPITAL. There are several methods of bringing someone else's equity capital into the farm business. One of the commonest examples is the case where older farmers furnish capital to younger family members through some combination of gifts, loans, leasing, shared ownership, partnership, incorporation, or some other type of formal or informal agreement. Although these arrangements are usually made among members of the same family, two or more unrelated individuals can and often do pool their equity in a farm business.

When a farmer departs from the sole proprietorship form of business organization to bring in additional capital, he should recognize that in addition to sharing profits he must be willing to share managerial responsibilities. Generally, the participants in a business venture should share profits in direct proportion to their respective contributions of labor, management, and capital. Failure to recognize this basic rule is almost certain to result in an unsatisfactory arrangement.

There are several other essentials of a successful partnership or other business organization involving two or more persons. The *goals* of all participants, including their spouses, should be compatible. They should be capable of getting along together and respecting each other's judgment. The business must be large enough to provide an adequate living for all parties. Good records, sound farm management, and common sense in the handling of money will help to avoid disagreement. Finally, a written agreement will prevent misunderstanding.

Legal Aspects of Partnerships. In forming partnerships the partners should know and understand what is involved and give proper attention to legal aspects. Each person entering into a partnership assumes considerable responsibility for actions of the other partners. In the case of a general partnership, any one partner may sell property of the partnership, make contracts for the business, and create partnership debts without consent of other partners. Moreover, each partner has unlimited liability for suits against the partnership.

Usually these things are relatively unimportant in father-and-son partnerships, but provision should be made for handling eventualities—perhaps as one way of insuring that difficulties will not arise. Since laws governing partnerships vary from state to state, a qualified attorney should be employed to help prepare the partnership agreement, incorporating proper safeguards. Adequate insurance should be carried to cover insurable liability claims against the partnership.

Death of either partner automatically terminates a general partnership. This possibility should be recognized and the method of dissolving the partnership in such event should be included in the agreement. Some partnership agreements include a "buy and sell" clause that specifies the terms under which the remaining partners can take over in the event one partner should die or withdraw from the business.

A special form of partnership called a *limited partnership* enables one or more of the partners to invest capital in the business without assuming management responsibilities. The liability of limited partners is restricted to their capital investment and they may not participate in the management of the business. At least one of the partners in a limited partnership must be a general partner with unlimited liability and the partnership must be written in compliance with state or local laws. The death or voluntary withdrawal of a limited partner from the business does not result in dissolution of the partnership, as is the case for general partnerships. Comparatively few family farms are organized as limited partnerships, although they may be useful under certain circumstances. For example, a family member who is interested in investing in the business but does not wish to assume managerial responsibilities could be accommodated in a limited partnership. A few large farms are organized as limited partnerships and some of their equity capital is acquired by selling limited partnership interests in the public securities markets.

Acquiring Equity Capital through Incorporation. Forming a corporation provides another method of acquiring capital to farm. A corporation is a legal entity authorized by state law and is capable of doing business, making contracts, borrowing money, and the like, the same as an individual proprietor. The procedure for forming a corporation is outlined in the law and should be followed exactly. For this and other reasons, services of a qualified lawyer are essential for incorporating a business.

Individuals who form a corporation are its owners and are issued certificates representing shares to show the interest each holds in the corporate assets. The shareholders elect directors to represent them in business policy and management decisions. The directors in turn employ officers who operate the business according to policy established by the directors.

Generally speaking, incorporation is a possibility in any business of reasonable size. Many family farms are large enough to at least consider incorporating. In general, however, only larger farms have found incorporation advantageous. Two reasons were the relatively high federal income tax rates on corporate income and double taxation of dividends. Revision of federal tax laws in 1958 largely removed these impediments, however, opening the door for greater use of corporations by commercial family farms. This tax law revision is covered in Subchapter S of the Internal Revenue Code and corporations organized under the provisions of this law are called "Subchapter S" or "pseudo" corporations.

When a corporation is formed to operate a farm business, it takes the place of the farmer as owner and operator. An individual may manage and operate the farm similar to any farmer, but he does so as an employee of the corporation, not as an individual entrepreneur.

A corporation provides a means by which a group of individuals may pool their funds and operate a business. Members of a family may organize a corporation to operate the home farm and to facilitate its transfer to a son or a son-in-law without disrupting the business. Other individuals may also form a corporation to carry on a farming operation. For example, two or more families with inadequate capital to farm efficiently on an individual basis may use the assets they do have to advantage by pooling them in a farm corporation.

In addition to serving as a means of obtaining capital, incorporation of the farm business may serve to hold the unit together and permit continuity of operation from one generation to the next. This feature assumes added importance as the size of business increases. Should one shareholder of an incorporated business die or decide to sell out, there is no need to break up the business, as in a general partnership. The stock may merely be transferred to a new owner. This ability to transfer ownership of undivided interests provides an easy means for children and others to buy into a farm business. It also facilitates estate planning by permitting parents to divide and transfer estates without reorganizing the business.

Some fringe benefits may be obtained through incorporation, with advantages in terms of benefits and taxes. Since social security benefits are based upon earnings of individuals it may be advantageous for a farm operator to receive a constant salary even though the income of the corporation may fluctuate from year to year. The availability of profit-sharing and pension plans may favor the corporate form of business in some instances. For example, with a qualified pension plan, some corporate profits can be used to provide retirement income for employees even though they are stockholders. The corporation pays no tax on earnings applied to the pension plan, and the employee is taxed only when he receives the retirement benefits. Somewhat similar benefits accrue from medical insurance plans, employee death benefits, and group life insurance.

There are some problems or disadvantages associated with incorporating a farm business that should be carefully and thoroughly considered. For example, unless proper safeguards are included in the legal framework the business may not be managed in the best interests of minority stockholders. Some expenses are involved in incorporating, and a corporation may pay certain annual fees and taxes that are not required of other types of business organizations. Furthermore, some time and expense are involved in maintaining records of the corporation and in filing the corporate tax returns. Annual meetings must be held, directors and officers elected, and an annual report of the business filed with the secretary of state.

A purported advantage of the corporation from the standpoint of capital acquisition is that the owners (stockholders) have limited liability, that is, the shareholders cannot be held personally liable for debt obligations or other responsibilities of the corporation. As a practical matter, however, the limited liability feature of the corporation does not hold for most closely held family farm corporations. First, most lenders require that corporate officers (usually the owners in farm corporations) personally endorse all loans, thereby making them liable for the debt. Furthermore, lenders tend to look more closely at loan applications from farming corporations because of the limited liability aspect; thus the corporate form of organization may in fact be a disadvantage as far as capital acquisition is concerned.

Public Offerings of Corporate Securities. Most farm partnerships and corporations are formed for the purpose of pooling equity capital supplied by family members or a small group of unrelated individuals. However, some large agricultural corporations have used public offerings of securities such as common and preferred stock, general partnership interests, limited partnership interests, and certificates representing herds of breeding livestock to raise equity capital.

Normally, a public offering should be considered only if a large amount of equity capital is needed. A public offering is a rather complicated procedure that requires the assistance of an investment banker, an underwriter, an accountant, and an attorney.[1] Obtaining equity capital with a public offering may be expensive, particularly if the offering is relatively small. Selling additional shares may dilute the earnings of shares already outstanding. A public offering usually extends voting rights to outsiders who, in some cases, may eventually take over control of the business. Moreover, publicly held corporations cannot be organized under Subchapter S of the Internal Revenue Code. Thus the business may be subject to higher income taxes if shares are sold to the public. The annual reports of a public corporation are more widely distributed, thus becoming public information, which may be undesirable.

LEASING. A lease is essentially a capital transfer agreement that gives the *lessee* (user) control over assets owned by the *lessor* for a specific period of time for an agreed-upon payment (usually referred to as *rent*).

Leasing Real Estate Capital. Leasing is a common way of obtaining control of additional real estate capital for farming. Of the 2.7 million farms reported in the *1969 United States Census of Agriculture*, 13 percent were operated by tenants, and nearly 672,000 farms—about 25 percent of the total—were part-owner farms.

Real estate leases are usually classified according to the kind of rent paid. Most of them fall into three general groups: the crop-share

---

1. For a more complete discussion of public stock offerings, see John A. Hopkin, "Some Basic Issues in Going Places," a paper presented to the symposium *Going Public—Finding the Facts for the Agribusinessman*, Boulder. Colo., June 15, 1970.

lease, the livestock-share lease, and the cash lease. With share leases, a share of the crop or livestock production is paid to the landlord as rent. With a cash lease, rent agreed upon is paid in cash. The various types of leases may be combined or otherwise modified in renting a farm. A common method is to give a share of the grain crops as rent and pay cash for hay and pasture.

The crop-share lease is the commonest type of rental arrangement in the United States, and farms operated on this basis are found in all parts of the nation. With the crop-share lease, the landlord usually provides the land and improvements and pays related taxes and other expenses, while the tenant pays most of the operating expenses and furnishes power, machinery, labor, and livestock. Some expenses such as seed and fertilizer may be shared with the landlord. Crops produced are shared as agreed upon in the lease.

Farms rented with a livestock-share lease are found almost exclusively in the Corn Belt and some adjacent states. The tenant and landlord customarily share both crop and livestock production, as well as some of the expenses. The landlord usually furnishes the land, buildings, and other improvements; the tenant and landlord commonly own the livestock jointly and share the annual expenses of crop and livestock production. The livestock is most often owned on a 50–50 basis, and expenses and income are shared in the same proportions.

Cash leases are used most frequently in areas where yields are relatively stable and where production involves a relatively small amount of risk and uncertainty. They also are frequently used for part-time or residential farms. With cash leasing arrangements, the landlord is paid a specified cash payment and usually furnishes the land, buildings, and other improvements. The tenant furnishes all other items required for production, including labor, machinery, livestock, and operating expenses. The entire production of crops and livestock belongs to the tenant.

The concepts of cash and share rent are sometimes combined in what is called standing rent. A fixed rent is agreed upon but in place of cash, payment is made in a fixed measure of products, such as one-third bale of cotton, 25 bushels of corn, or 10 bushels of wheat. The dollar amount of rent the landlord receives varies with the price of the product, as it would with share rent, but the amount of product he will receive is known in advance. Thus the landlord has greater security in years of low yield, while the tenant makes more profit in years of high yield.

There are a number of advantages and disadvantages to leasing, as there are with all methods of obtaining capital. The advantages for the tenant include the possibility of obtaining control of a large amount of capital with relatively little risk, the possible benefit from landlord managerial assistance, and the possibility of having a more nearly adequate farm unit that will facilitate efficient production. On the other hand, when one leases a farm, uncertainty of tenure is involved, living accommodations and farm improvements frequently are inadequate, rental arrangements may not contribute to efficient maximum production, and the cash or share rent must be paid. This rent must compensate the landlord for taxes and any other assessments on the property, maintenance, depreciation, improvements, a competitive or opportunity return on investment, and the risk and uncertainty associated with his investment. Thus, while the tenant avoids these costs and responsibilities by renting, he pays someone else to assume them. Another disadvantage of leasing instead of owning real estate is that any capital gains resulting from inflation in land values accrue to the landlord.

Many of the disadvantages of share leasing can be avoided if the landlord and tenant use a written lease agreement that is equitable to both parties. An equitable lease is one in which the income received by both parties is proportional to their respective contributions. The contributions that should be included are interest on investment, taxes, depreciation, repairs, insurance, labor, management, and variable production costs such as seed, fertilizer, chemicals, feed, fuel, etc. Table 6.1 illustrates the procedure for calculating and separating the contributions of the landlord and tenant. Variations of this form may be used, depending upon the individual situation.

After the shares have been estimated as shown in Table 6.1, the parties can then enter a bargaining process to arrive at a final agreement. If land available for leasing is in short supply, for example, the tenant may be willing to accept a somewhat lower share than the contributions would indicate. Nevertheless, the complete listing of all contributions indicates those areas where they can reasonably bargain with each other to arrive at a mutually satisfactory agreement.

Machinery Leasing. Outright purchase, often with the use of borrowed capital, has been the traditional method of acquiring control over farm machinery. However, the rapidly rising investment in nonreal-estate assets, as shown in Chapter 1, has prompted many farm operators to consider leasing as an alternative to ownership of farm equipment.

Equipment leases are classified mainly on the basis of the term of the contract and the services provided. An *operating lease* is a short-term contract—the term ranging anywhere from a few hours to two or three growing seasons. Under an operating lease the farm operator leases the equipment by the hour, day, week, month, or year. Normally the lessor is responsible for insurance, taxes, and major repairs and the lessee covers variable operating expenses such as fuel,

TABLE 6.1: Example of How the Contributions of Tenant and Landlord Can Be Calculated and Used As a Basis for Dividing Income on a Crop-Share Rented Farm

Contribution	Tenant			Landlord		
	Value	Rate	Value of annual contrib.	Value	Rate	Value of annual contrib.
Land and Buildings						
1. Interest (4–6% of valuation)				$128,000	5%	$ 6,400
2. Real estate tax						1,280
Buildings, Water Systems, Fences, and Other Permanent Improvements*						
3. Depreciation (2–4% of replacement value)				$ 30,000	3%	$ 900
4. Repair (1–2% of replacement value)					1½%	450
5. Insurance						225
Power and Machinery†						
6. Interest at 6–8% of (new cost plus salvage value) ÷ 2 $\frac{(30,000 + 3,000)}{2}$		7½%	$ 1,238			
7. Depreciation (10–14% of replacement cost less salvage value)		12½%	3,375			
8. Repair (3% of new cost)			900			
9. Insurance			120			
10. Personal property tax			185			
Labor and Management†						
11. Operator 8 mo, 500/mo			$ 4,000			
12. Family help 1 mo, 300/mo			300			
13. Hired labor			600			
14. Management (10% of gross income)‡			2,512			
Other Operating Expenses						
15. Seed			$ 840			
16. Fertilizer			1,800			
17. Pesticides and misc. supplies			800			
18. Total			$16,670			$11,893
19. Percent of contributions by each			58.4%			41.6%

SOURCE: Adapted from Philip A. Henderson, *Is Your Lease Fair?* NCR Ext. Publ. 9, 1969, p. 5.
* Include building costs only to the extent that they are actually used in the crop enterprise.
† Include only that portion attributable to crop production on this farm.
‡ The division of management responsibilities will vary from situation to situation.

lubricants, and routine maintenance; however, there are many variations of the operating lease. *Custom hiring,* for example, is an operating lease arrangement whereby the owner of the equipment furnishes the machine operator in addition to covering all operating expenses. A *full service lease* is an operating lease contract under which the lessor assumes total responsibility for all repairs and maintenance costs.

The *financial lease,* in contrast to the operating lease, is a longer-term contract under which the lessor essentially provides financing to the lessee. Usually the lessee is responsible for all repairs and maintenance just as he would be if he had purchased the equipment outright. Thus the financial lease is very similar to an outright purchase using borrowed capital with the lease payments corresponding to loan payments; however, the down payment under the financial lease is considerably lower and, under a true lease, title to the equipment remains with the lessor upon expiration of the contract.

The Internal Revenue Service has frequently ruled that some so-called lease contracts are really loans because title to the equipment is transferred to the lessee at the end of the term of the contract for a nominal sum of money. The distinction between a true lease and a loan has important tax implications. Rental payments under a true lease are tax deductible whereas only the "interest" portion of the "loan" payments and depreciation are deductible if the lessee obtains title without fully compensating the lessor for the salvage value at the end of the term of the contract.

There are several possible advantages of leasing equipment. Leasing eliminates or minimizes the down payment usually associated with purchasing, thereby freeing limited capital for alternative uses. Beginning farmers who are short on capital often find that leasing some of their machinery is a good way to stretch limited resources. Leasing is often a more desirable way to acquire highly specialized equipment because the lessor assumes the risk of obsolescence. Many lease contracts can be terminated by the lessee on relatively short notice, thus providing flexibility in the type and size of equipment used.

Leasing may be less expensive than ownership. Many fixed costs such as insurance, taxes, storage, and interest on investment are avoided. Under most operating leases, major repairs and sometimes minor ones are paid by the lessor. Custom hiring has the additional advantage of avoiding the cost of labor for the machine operator.

Under some circumstances, financial leasing may be cheaper than ownership on an *after-tax* basis. The full amount of any rental payments on qualifying leases can be treated as a tax-deductible expense. With ownership, only depreciation and the interest actually paid on loans used to buy the equipment are deductible. Of course, operating and maintenance costs are also deductible, but, as was pointed out earlier, these would normally be the same for either alternative.

Leasing, as compared with ownership using borrowed capital, often eliminates many of the responsibilities associated with ownership. Depending on the contract, the lessor is responsible for paying insurance premiums and taxes. He must also take care of title documents and other red tape arising from ownership. The time involved in selecting equipment and bargaining over price may be reduced with leasing.

Despite its advantages, leasing machinery is not always better than ownership. Ownership offers more complete control over the machinery, since all decisions are made by the owner. He is free to select the exact type and size of machine he wants and he can sell or trade anytime it seems desirable.

Ownership of equipment is often less expensive than leasing. If the machine is used to capacity and has a high residual value, ownership may cost much less than leasing. Writing off of depreciation expenses and interest payments on loans used to buy the machine may give ownership a tax advantage over leasing.

One of the most important disadvantages of operating leases, such as custom hiring, is that the machine may not be available when needed. Crop losses arising from delayed harvest can be very costly. Furthermore, the quality of work done by a custom operator may be inferior.

A clear understanding of the lease agreement by both parties will eliminate many of the potential disadvantages of equipment leasing. Generally a written lease agreement should be used, although a formal written contract is normally not used for custom hiring and other short-term operating leases.

Livestock Leasing. The typical livestock-share lease contract mentioned previously in this chapter usually covers land and buildings as well as livestock. In recent years, however, livestock leasing has become an increasingly popular method of acquiring capital in farming. Typically, basic herd livestock such as dairy cows, beef cows, and sows are being leased on a cash or share basis.

The terms of livestock leases vary widely and, due to their limited use, standard rental rates and other terms have not been well established. In one instance that we know of, a farmer leases dairy cows for a cash rent that ranges from $7.00 to $10.00 per month, depending on the quality of the animals. The lessor retains title to the cows and he receives the salvage value when they are culled from the lessee's herd. In addition, the lessor owns all heifer calves. The lessee receives all income from sales of milk and bull calves. Normally the lessor assumes fixed costs such as depreciation, taxes, and return on investment and the lessee pays variable costs such as feed, housing, veterinary services, and labor.

Dairy cow leasing arrangements are attractive to younger farmers who have limited capital to invest. Also, leasing enables the lessee to use all his facilities for mature cows while the lessor raises the heifers. In many cases, the lessor is an older farmer who no longer wants to milk cows. Leasing permits him to use his facilities for young stock and still derive some income from mature cows.

In many livestock leasing arrangements the lessor may not be a farmer at all. In the case of beef cow leasing, for example, nonfarm investors purchase beef cows through a broker and the broker in turn arranges a lease with a rancher. Beef cow leasing enables the rancher to stretch limited financial resources and the nonfarm investor usually earns a good return on his capital because of certain tax advantages associated with livestock ownership.[2]

Livestock leasing shares many of the disadvantages of equipment and real estate leasing. It may be more expensive than outright ownership as a means of controlling capital and the lessor retains a certain degree of control over the animals. As with any leasing arrangement, the benefits and costs must be carefully evaluated and a written agreement should be used.

CONTRACT FARMING. An increasing amount of the capital used in the farming sector is being furnished by farm input suppliers, processors, and distributors under various types of producer contracts. The linking of two or more stages in the chain of production is referred to as *vertical coordination.* At the one extreme is *vertical integration,* which refers to the case where two or more firms are merged into one ownership and management unit.[3] At the other end of the vertical coordination spectrum are the traditional open-market arrangements that link the farm firm with input suppliers and output purchasers. The degree of vertical coordination in agriculture generally falls between these extremes but usually involves varying degrees of financing for the farming operation. Therefore, contract farming is a way for a farmer to obtain additional capital with which to work.

---

2. Much of the income from breeding livestock is in the form of capital gains that are taxed at half the rate applicable to ordinary income up to a maximum rate of 25 percent. These capital gains provisions are the basis for "tax-loss farming" that is attractive to wealthy investors who are in high tax brackets.

3. The term *vertical integration* is commonly used to refer to any contractual arrangement linking the farm firm with input suppliers, processors, or wholesalers. The technically correct definition of vertical integration is adhered to in this section.

Contract production is not new in agriculture. Contracts of various types have been used for a long time with cannery crops, sugarbeets, broilers, and the like. However, vertical integration, where the supplier, processor, or distributor takes over the farm production operation and stacks it on top of his normal function, is relatively new.

Types of Forward Contracts. When the traditional open market form of market coordination fails (a) to provide the needed market outlet for input suppliers or (b) to provide farm products of the proper specifications at reasonable prices for marketing firms, one of three basic types of forward contracts may be used. The *market specification contract,* as the name implies, is an agreement under which farm inputs or products will be exchanged at some specified future date at an agreed-upon price (or basis for calculating the price). Market specification contracts are commonly used for fruit and vegetable crops grown for the processed market. In the case of tomatoes, for example, growers enter a contract with the processor before the growing season begins. This contract specifies the acreage that is to be grown, the price per ton, and in some instances, the delivery schedule. *Production-management contracts* provide the same features as do market specification contracts but in addition the farmer receives technical advice and management services from the input supplier or processor. In the case of cannery crops, for example, the processor may specify seed varieties, fertilizer application rates, and other cultural practices such as plant spacing, cultivation, and harvesting dates.

Market specification and production-management contracts typically do not provide any financing per se; however, they do have financial implications for the farmer, because lenders tend to look more favorably on a loan application if marketing arrangements are guaranteed by a producer contract.

Under *resource-providing contracts* the farmer receives financing from the marketing firm as well as a guaranteed market outlet and production-management assistance. Most of the producer contracts in the broiler industry are resource-providing contracts. The feed company usually provides short-term financing for feed delivered to the farm. Similarly, either the feed company or the processor will furnish the baby chicks. In some cases, the processor or the feed company may provide longer-term financing to erect buildings and buy equipment. As a general rule, the degrees of risk and managerial control assumed by the feed company and the processor vary proportionately with the amount of financing they furnish.

As is the case with any method of acquiring capital, contracting has its strengths and weaknesses. Perhaps the most important advantage is the financing that the farmer receives both directly from the contracting firms and indirectly through other lenders who are more assured of loan repayment when a contract is in existence. Often, many of the production and marketing risks are shared by the farmer and the contracting firm instead of being borne entirely by the farmer. In addition to financial help, the farmer usually receives managerial advice and technical assistance such as production scheduling, high quality breeding stock and seed varieties, fertilizer recommendations, veterinary services, custom-blended feed, the latest equipment, and other supplies and services that would not otherwise be available.

Contracting usually leads to better coordination of the production and marketing phases, thereby resulting in higher profits and reduced risk for both farmers and contracting firms. Moreover the consumer often receives a better quality product at lower prices, the case of chicken broilers being only one example.

Perhaps the most obvious disadvantage of contract production is the loss of managerial control. Under some contracts the farmer may become little more than a hired hand. The farmer may also have to accept lower net returns to compensate the contracting firm for providing financing and sharing production and marketing risks. Sometimes contracting may cause a farmer to become overextended because of the ease with which financing can be obtained. Finally the farmer loses the opportunity to gamble on the market, therefore, he will not benefit from higher market prices.

BORROWING. Borrowing constitutes the remaining method farmers use to acquire capital; this has been left until last to facilitate linking this discussion with the treatment of credit in subsequent chapters. Moreover, since most of the rest of the book is devoted to various phases of use and acquisition of credit, this section is limited to a brief discussion of the meaning of borrowing and of credit as a source of capital. It also includes reasons sometimes put forth against borrowing, and advantages that can be realized by using credit.

The word *borrow* means to receive something with the understanding that it or its equivalent will be returned as agreed upon. Stated another way, borrowing means the ability to command capital or services currently for a promise to repay at some future time. In terms of money, borrowing involves obtaining a certain amount of funds to be repaid as specified in the note.

The word *credit* comes from the Latin word *credo* meaning *I believe*. Hence, credit is based upon confidence. When one borrows money, the loan is based upon confidence in the future solvency of the person and in his repaying the loan as per agreement. In this sense credit means ability to command the capital of another in return for a promise to pay at some specified time in the future.

While credit has a somewhat technical meaning of its own, it is used in financial circles and writings as meaning about the same as borrowing. This synonymous usage probably has come about for convenience sake. The word *credit* is short and easy to use. Holding strictly to technical meanings often involves using two words rather than one. For example, a phrase might read "use of borrowed funds." It is somewhat more convenient to say "use of credit."

Borrowing probably ranks next to saving or using one's own capital as a means of obtaining capital to farm. Few commercial farmers operate without using credit. Some have adequate finances of their own but use credit at times throughout the year rather than disrupt investment programs or other use of owned capital.

Using credit as a means of obtaining control of resources is similar in some respects to leasing. When funds are obtained by borrowing, interest is paid for use of capital; while, with a lease, rent is paid for use of the capital. Both borrowing and renting involve employment of capital for a period of time. However, the use of credit permits greater flexibility than renting. Credit can be used to acquire any type of resource or service needed by the farmer, while renting usually is employed to acquire fewer types of resources, the commonest being farm real estate. Credit permits acquiring varying amounts of a resource according to the needs of the farmer, while renting tends to involve fixed amounts or blocks of resources, such as a piece of land or a whole farm.

Borrowing involves more risk of losing owned capital than does renting. With renting, the maximum payment that can be demanded is the share or cash rent; this is somewhat comparable with the interest payment on borrowed funds. With share rental arrangements, the payment is automatically cut in case of low production or prices. With borrowing, however, the payment generally includes in addition to a fixed interest charge, part or all of the principal borrowed. If the principal is lost, the borrower may have to liquidate some of his own capital to repay the loan.

Except for special cases, some property or assets must be owned before a loan can be obtained. Since most lenders do not loan their own money, laws or regulations under which they operate require them to obtain the borrower's pledge of security or collateral for a loan. Usually the security is some specific property that can be sold to liquidate the loan if it is not repaid as per agreement. Where the loan is not large and where the individual has a good credit rating, only the borrower's signature may be required. In such cases the borrower, in effect, pledges all his assets as security. The general intent of the law and regulations is that security pledged be adequate to repay the loan even if it must be sold under unfavorable circumstances. Since most loans that break down do so under unfavorable circumstances, this provision seems reasonable.

Classification of Credit. There are two main purposes for which farmers borrow money: for business and for consumption. We are concerned here with business credit. However, there are many different types or uses of business credit, and a proper classification will facilitate communication and also financial analysis. Unfortunately, no one classification is completely satisfactory for all purposes. Therefore, four primary classifications are summarized here.

In the *time classification,* credit is classified in three groups—short, intermediate, and long—according to the term of the loan. The following general classification is customary, together with the further division into monthly, seasonal, and annual loans.

1. Short-term credit (production credit)
   a. Monthly (0–3 months)
   b. Seasonal (3–9 months)
   c. Annual (9 months–1 year)
2. Intermediate-term credit (1–5 years or 1–10 years)
3. Long-term credit (real estate credit)

Long-term loans fall definitely into a separate grouping, being as the name implies, credit extended on real estate security for periods longer than 1 year—usually 10 to 30 years or more, depending on the terms offered by the mortgage lender. An equally specific classification is not possible, however, for short-term and intermediate-term credit.

Intermediate credit is usually defined as credit extended for purposes that will provide full payment, not in one season, but in several seasons. The term intermediate credit has been used to designate those loans maturing in a year but renewed from year to year if the security and the income of the borrower warranted. Loans on dairy herds, beef cattle herds, improvements, and machinery come in this category.

Such an overlapping in classifying short-term and intermediate credit makes for confusion, as the following example will illustrate. A farmer raising crops borrowed $5,000 each year to finance his crop expenses. A livestock farmer borrowed $5,000 on his herd, renewing the note each year when it came due. The short-term loan to the crop farmer enabled him to produce a cotton crop, while the intermediate-term loan on the beef cattle herd enabled the livestock farmer to produce a crop of beef calves each year. It may be argued that the crop loan was a separate transaction each year while the livestock loan was continuous over several years. But each farmer had to have the $5,000 to finance his business, year after year, the only important difference being that the cotton farmer needed the credit a few months of the year while the livestock farmer needed it the entire year. This is a difference largely of degree, depending on the number of months required to raise crops or produce livestock.

A bona fide intermediate loan is one used for investments that mature over a period longer than a year. Orchards, livestock, equipment, drainage or irrigation systems, and machinery are good examples of investments in this intermediate category.

The distinction between short-term, intermediate-term, and long-term credit coincides with a difference in loan purpose. Short-term loans are generally used for the production of farm crops and livestock; intermediate-term loans are generally for working-capital assets like machinery; and long-term loans are frequently for the purchase of a farm. A classification of credit according to purpose brings out this close relationship between time and purpose.

The *purpose classification* appears to be the easiest to understand because each loan is labeled according to the use made of the proceeds. This classification generally groups loans according to the purpose of the loan, with subclasses based upon specific uses of the funds. Among the common uses made of credit, the following are the most important:

1. Production loans (short-term and intermediate-term loans) to
   a. Buy seed, feed, and fertilizer
   b. Pay operating expenses
   c. Buy feeder livestock
   d. Carry or buy range livestock
   e. Buy dairy cattle
   f. Buy machinery—equipment or tractor
   g. Finance commodity storage
   h. Refinance any one or a combination of the above
2. Real estate loans (long-term loans) to
   a. Purchase a farm
   b. Purchase additional land
   c. Finance buildings, drainage, irrigation, and other improvements
   d. Refinance any one or a combination of the above
3. Farmer cooperative borrowing to
   a. Pay operating expenses
   b. Finance patrons
   c. Finance commodity storage
   d. Finance buildings, equipment, or real estate purchase
   e. Refinance any one of above

The purpose classification has the advantage of facilitating analysis to determine the profitability of a specific loan if other records essential to such an analysis are kept. It also gives information on which loans are for investment purposes and which are for operating credit. Long-term loans for purchase of land usually are primarily for investment since the land is not used up in the production process. On the other hand, funds put into operation of the farm are used up in one or a few years. Production expenses, such as for seed, are completely used in one year, while a tractor lasts for several years. These things are important from the viewpoint of using credit since they influence the repayment capacity of farmers. Where items are used up in the production process, their value enters the gross cash farm income flow, assuming operations are profitable, and are available to apply on repayment of the loan. If funds are used to buy a tractor that lasts for 10 years, for example, the depreciation expense enters the cash income flow over the 10-year period and can be used to apply on the tractor loan. In contrast, where investments are not used up there is no depreciation and only the return on the investment enters the cash flow, with the result that principal payments on loans thus invested must be taken from net income or savings. This limits the amount of debt a farm family can incur for investment purposes.

The *security classification* of credit provides a third classification often used. The two major classifications are secured and unsecured loans, as the following indicates.

1. Secured loans
   a. Short-term and intermediate-term loans
      (1) Loans secured by tangible personal property (stored crops, livestock, machinery, equipment, etc.)
      (2) Loans secured by intangible personal property (government bonds, stocks, life insurance policies, etc.)
      (3) Warehouse receipt loans
      (4) Conditional sales contracts
   b. Long-term loans
      (1) Real estate mortgage loans
      (2) Land contracts
2. Unsecured loans

Short-term and intermediate-term loans may be either secured or unsecured. When secured, they usually are secured by movable property such as machinery and livestock under the provisions of the Uniform Commercial Code, which is discussed in Chapter 14. Long-term loans generally are secured by a mortgage on real estate. When the term *farm-mortgage loans* or *debt* is used (as it frequently is in USDA publications) it generally refers to loans secured by farm real estate.

Purchase contracts (conditional sales contracts and land contracts) are essentially a method of securing credit, although legally they differ significantly from loans. In the case of a loan, ownership of the property passes to the borrower, whereas with purchase contracts, title to the property remains with the seller, to be delivered at some future date or upon payment of a specified sum. The legal aspects of credit are discussed in more detail in Chapter 14.

The *lender classification* of credit is frequently used because the policies of lenders vary greatly. Quite often this classification is used in conjunction with the time grouping, as the following summary classification illustrates.

1. Short-term and intermediate-term (nonreal-estate) loans
   a. Commercial banks
   b. Production Credit Associations
   c. Other financing institutions, discounting with Federal Intermediate Credit Banks
   d. Farmers Home Administration
   e. Commodity Credit Corporation
   f. Merchants and dealers
   g. Individuals and others
2. Long-term (real estate) loans
   a. Commercial banks
   b. Insurance companies
   c. Federal Land Banks
   d. Farmers Home Administration
   e. Individuals and others

This type of classification is used in the latter part of the text in the discussion of lenders.

Advantages of Borrowing. The use of credit has definite advantages. The people who own land and have funds to lend are often not operating farmers. The capital-owning group is made up of older people, retired farmers, widows, endowment funds, estates, banks, and insurance companies, as well as more wealthy individuals with money to lend. These various agencies and individuals are in no sense operating farmers. Operating farmers, fitted by training, experience, and age to carry on crop and livestock production, sometimes do not have the necessary capital required to operate a farm. The competent young farmer between the ages of 20 and 35 with a family to support may have everything needed for farming except enough capital. The individuals who have capital, on the other hand, oftentimes do not have the physical ability, training, desire, and experience that the young farmer has. Thus the two are interdependent. Indeed, the cooperation of the management and capital owned by these two groups makes for successful farming; either alone would fail.

Leasing is an alternative to ownership, using borrowed capital, but livestock, equipment, and operating expenses are capital items not as easily adapted to the leasing process as are land and buildings. Owners of livestock and equipment find it difficult and costly to provide the supervision necessary to lease these items to others. It is still more difficult for the farmer to make arrangements for the payment of operating expenses such as seed, taxes, labor, and fertilizer unless he has savings or uses credit. The landlord frequently is willing to take a share of the crop in payment for the use of his land, but the laborer must be paid in cash weekly, biweekly, or monthly. Thus it is evident that renting or hiring does not always provide a satisfactory substitute for the use of credit.

Credit makes it possible for farmers to take advantage of new machines, good seed, fertilizer, livestock, and labor, all of which enable the farmer to organize and operate a larger and more profitable business.

Disadvantages of Borrowing. The primary disadvantage of borrowing is the risk of loss associated with use of credit. One never borrows money with the expectation that a loss will be sustained. A reputable lender never makes a loan that he thinks will result in loss. However, farming is a risky business, and using credit may be disastrous unless the borrower has the risk-bearing ability needed to withstand adversity.

Closely related to the risk disadvantage is the problem of meeting payments as they come due. Loan proceeds are used in the business and cash may not always be available to meet loan payments. In fact, loan proceeds used to buy land never are available to repay the loan; payments must be made from net income.

A third problem involved in using credit is determining whether or not it will pay to borrow. Borrowing involves repaying not only the principal but also the interest charged for use of the funds. The borrower will be at a disadvantage unless, by using the credit, net income is increased at least enough to cover the interest on the loan. Each of these three points—risk, repayment of loans, and income related to use of credit—is considered in some detail in the following chapters.

COMBINING SOURCES OF CAPITAL. Savings, gifts, and inheritances constitute the equity capital in a farm business. This equity capital base can be supplemented with outside equity through a partnership, incorporation, or other agreement. Nonequity financing (leasing, producer contracts, and borrowing) can be used to supplement the equity capital base.

Many modern commercial farms use several sources of capital simultaneously. The resulting combination of methods of financing the business leads to some rather complex situations in which it becomes difficult to identify the "farmer."

Consider the case of the large commercial feedlots that now account for a major portion of the total beef production in the nation. It has been estimated that a 30,000-head feedlot, for example, requires a total capital investment of about $9 million. This total figure is broken down as follows: real estate and equipment, $1.2 million; feed inventories and operating costs, $0.3 million; cattle, $7.5 million.[4] Many of these feedlots are incorporated and corporate stock is issued to provide the equity base to finance the real estate and equipment. Borrowed capital is used extensively to finance the balance of the investment in real estate, equipment, feed and operating expenses, and cattle. In many cases, some or all of the cattle are fed commercially for outside investors on a custom basis.

Rice growing provides another example of the complexity of financing arrangements in agriculture. It is not uncommon for rice growers to lease all or part of their land from one or more landowners and all or part of the rice acre allotment from one or more other parties. In addition, rice growers use some combination of borrowing and/or custom hiring to finance operating expenses and machinery services.[5]

Complex financing arrangements are not restricted to any particular areas of the United States as they once were. Many Midwest crop and livestock farms are owned by one party and leased by a second individual who, in turn, may hire one or more other people to provide a complete package of machinery services on a custom-hire basis. Hog men in several states have formed feeder pig cooperatives to supply their demand for quality feeder pigs. The members of these coops supply the equity capital and may borrow the balance from a Bank for Cooperatives and other lenders. This capital is used to finance the construction of farrowing facilities and breeding stock. Members receive a proportion of the feeder pigs based on the number of shares they own.[6]

---

4. See Raymond J. Doll, "Cattle Feeding in the Tenth District: Financing," *Monthly Review*, Fed. Res. Bank of Kansas City, July–Aug. 1970, pp. 11–18.

5. J. Bruce Hottel, "Tenure as Related to the Growth of the Farm Firm," discussion paper, Annual Meeting of W-104 Regional Project on Firm Growth, San Francisco, June 22–23, 1971.

6. See "Feeder Pig Production, Cooperative Style," *Successful Farming*, May 1971.

SUMMARY. There are dozens of other examples of complex financing arrangements in agriculture. The concept of a farmer as a person who owns all of his land, livestock, and equipment outright and borrows a small amount each year to finance his operating expenses is becoming outdated. The need for large amounts of capital per farm and the accompanying need to spread the risk among several suppliers of capital has led to innovative combinations of all six sources of capital discussed in this chapter.

QUESTIONS AND PROBLEMS

1. Name the six basic methods of acquiring capital to farm. Discuss the differences between equity and debt financing as they pertain to capital acquisition.
2. Discuss the advantages and disadvantages of partnerships and incorporation as means of acquiring equity capital to farm. Do the laws in your state prohibit or restrict farm corporations?
3. List the essential conditions for a successful family farm agreement.
4. Talk with farmers in your area who have formed partnerships and corporations. If possible, study their partnership agreements or corporate charters.
5. Discuss the types of real estate leases commonly used. Which type is most prevalent in your area?
6. Explain how to draw up a fair-share lease for a crop or crop and livestock farm.
7. List the advantages and disadvantages of leasing livestock and farm machinery. Under what circumstances is ownership likely to be less expensive than leasing?
8. Explain why contract production is becoming more commonplace in agriculture. What are the disadvantages of contract production from the farmer's viewpoint?
9. Outline the four major classifications of credit and discuss the use of each.
10. Discuss the advantages and disadvantages of credit as a means of acquiring capital to farm.
11. To what extent are farmers in your state combining the six sources of capital discussed in this chapter? Explain why several sources of capital are used by many farmers.

REFERENCES

Bailey, Warren R., and Lee, John E. "The New Frontiers of Finance." *Contours of Change*. The Yearbook of Agriculture, USDA, 1970, pp. 10–19.
Becker, Manning, and Nelson, Gene A. "Investment Analysis: A Case Study of the Machinery Buy or Lease Decision." A paper presented at Agr. Clinic of Oregon Bankers Assoc., Dept. Agr. Econ., Oreg. State Univ., Dec. 1970.

Carman, Hoy F. "Income Tax Planning for Farmers." *Am. Jour. Agr. Econ.*, vol. 51, no. 5, Dec. 1969, pp. 1543–47.

———. "Tax Shelters in Agriculture: An Example for Beef Breeding Herds." *Am. Jour. Agr. Econ.*, vol. 50, no. 5, Dec. 1968, pp. 1591–95.

Connor, Larry J., and Benjamin, Gary L. "Farm Machinery: Renting and Leasing in Michigan." *Mich. Farm Econ.*, no. 310, Dept. Agr. Econ., Mich. State Univ., Nov. 1968.

Corty, Floyd L., *Leasing Farm Land for Rice Production*. Dept. Agr. Econ., La. State Univ., Agr. Exp. Sta., Res. Rept. 383, Sept. 1968.

Dennistown, R. M.; Nodland, T. R.; and Hasbargen, P. R. *Leasing Farm Machinery*. Dept. Agr. Econ., Univ. of Minn., Rept. 291, July 1967.

Epperson, James E., and Bell, Sidney C. *Getting Established in Farming with Special Reference to Credit*. Auburn Univ., Agr. Exp. Sta. Bull. 400, Apr. 1970.

Frick, George E., and Christensen, Robert L. *Base-Incentive Cow Rental Contract*. Univ. of N.H., Coop. Ext. Serv. Circ. 388, May 1967.

Harris, Marshall, and Massey, Dean T. *Vertical Coordination via Contract Farming*. USDA, Misc. Publ. 1073, Mar. 1968.

Hasbargen, Paul, ed. *Corporate Farming*. Dept. Agr. Econ., Univ. of Minn., Staff Paper P 70-7, May 1970.

Hayenga, Marvin L., et al. *Vertical Coordination in the Pork Industry*. Agr. Econ. Rept. 194, Dept. Agr. Econ., Mich. State Univ., in cooperation with Farm Prod. Econ. Div., ERS, USDA, Feb. 1972.

Henderson, Philip A. *Is Your Lease Fair?* NCR Ext. Publ. 9, 1969.

Hill, E. B. *Father-Son Farming Agreements: Some Important and Troublesome Features*. Mich. State Univ., Agr. Exp. Sta., Res. Dept. No. 56, 1966.

Hopkin, John A. *The Corporation as an Effective Form of Business Organization for the Family-Oriented Agricultural Farm*. Texas A&M Univ., Jan. 1971.

———. *Leasing versus Cash Purchase versus Credit Purchase of Depreciable Assets*. Dept. Agr. Econ., Univ. of Ill., AET-7-69, Dec. 1969.

Hunt, James E., and Shaudys, E. T. *Farm Equipment Leasing*. Ohio Agr. Res. & Dev. Center, Res. Circ. 170, June 1969.

Irwin, George D., and Smith, Lawrence N. "Machinery Leasing: Perspective and Prospects." *Agr. Finance Rev.*, vol. 33, Farm Prod. Econ. Div., ERS, USDA, July 1972, pp. 42–47.

Johnson, Jerome E. *Suggestions on Father and Son Farming Agreements*. N.Dak. State Univ., Agr. Exp. Sta. Bull. 457, Sept. 1965.

Levi, Donald R. *Agricultural Law*. Lucas Bros. Pub., Columbia, Mo., 1971, Chapter 10.

Luckham, W. R. *Guidelines for Equitable Egg Production Contracts*. Va. Polytech. Inst., Ext. Publ. 303, Sept. 1969.

Mighell, Ronald L., and Jones, Lawrence A. *Vertical Coordination in Agriculture*. Agr. Econ., ERS, USDA, Rept. 19, 1963.

NCR Farm Management Extension Committee. *The Farm Corporation: What It Is, How It Works, How It Is Taxed*. NCR Ext. Publ. 11, revised 1973.

Scofield, William H. "Nonfarm Equity Capital in Agriculture." *Agr. Finance Rev.*, vol. 33, Farm Prod. Econ. Div., ERS, USDA, July 1972, pp. 36–41.

USDA, ERS, Farm Prod. Econ. Div. *Farm Corporations and Their Income Tax Treatment*. Proceedings of a seminar, Mar. 1970.

CHAPTER 7: FINANCIAL ANALYSIS OF THE FARM BUSINESS: THE BALANCE SHEET

FINANCIAL ANALYSIS involves maintaining and using records and other information needed to measure the financial performance of the business. A farmer cannot possibly make intelligent decisions on the allocation and use of capital unless he possesses adequate information regarding the past and current financial condition of his operation. Some astute farmers glean considerable information from observation coupled with income and expense transactions involved in operating the business. However, as the size of farm increases, the technological revolution progresses, and cash expenses consume an increasingly large part of gross income, management needs more adequate records properly summarized and analyzed to provide a reliable basis for judgment in managerial decisions.

The most widely used financial statements are the *balance sheet*, the *income statement*, and the *cash flow statement*. In this and the two chapters that follow, these three important sources of financial information are illustrated, using actual data from a 240-acre hog-beef fattening farm located in the Corn Belt, referred to as Farm Business A. Mr. A, the owner and operator of the farm, is rated as an average hog-cattle manager, and somewhat above average in operating efficiency. He began farming as a tenant operator in the late 1950s and purchased his own farm on a land contract in 1962. As our analysis of this farm business will show, Mr. A has shown steady financial progress since 1959.

BALANCE SHEET. The *balance sheet,* otherwise known as a *net worth statement,* is a summary of the assets and liabilities of the business, together with a statement of the *owner's equity* or *net worth.* Its primary function is to measure the financial solvency of the business; that is, it shows the margin by which debt obligations would be covered if the business were terminated and all assets were sold. The balance sheet is a comparatively simple statement and has come into common usage in the business world. Lenders usually obtain a statement as a part of every loan application and keep on file an up-to-date statement of the financial condition of each borrower. Financial statements also are used by farmers in record keeping and in making out income tax reports, and may be used by landlords in interviewing prospective tenants.

101

The balance sheet has two characteristics that should be kept clearly in mind:

1. It always refers to a specific date or point in time.
2. It always is divided into three parts:
   a. The assets or value of things owned
   b. The debts owed
   c. The difference between these two, which is the owner's equity (or deficit if debts exceed assets)

It is this last item, the owner's equity or deficit, that makes the statement balance.

It is important to note that the balance sheet shows only assets *owned* and debts *owed*. To the extent that leased capital is also employed in the business, the balance sheet does not completely reflect the total size of the business, nor does it usually show the financial obligations associated with leases used to acquire real estate or non-real-estate capital.

The record of Farm Business A will be used as an aid in studying the balance sheet and in developing the ratio analysis of financial strength. The record covers the period 1959–72, although comparatively little information is available from 1959 to 1965. These data give an opportunity to observe changes that occurred over time and how these changes are involved in the analysis. A balance sheet for Farm Business A as of January 1, 1959, in its simplest form, is shown in Table 7.1.

The first point to observe in a balance sheet is the date. A balance sheet represents a snapshot of the business at just one instant of time, in this example at the close of business on December 31, 1958, and the beginning of business on January 1, 1959. Since the ending of one year is the beginning of the next, the instant of time is midnight on December 31. The statement given does not hold for the end of the day on January 2 because Farmer A may have sold a load of grain during the day to a neighbor. Obviously this

TABLE 7.1:   Farm Business A—Balance Sheet as of January 1, 1959

Assets		Liabilities and Owner Equity	
Cash	$ 206	Accounts payable	$ 142
Grain	3,624	Notes	12,982
Hay	982		
Livestock	6,052		
Machinery	8,042	Owner equity	5,782
TOTAL	$18,906	TOTAL	$18,906

transaction would affect the balance sheet. It is important, therefore, that the balance sheet be recognized for what it is—*a statement of the financial position of the farm business as of a certain date.* A snapshot is a good analogy because a balance sheet is a picture of the business at the time, and only at the time, the picture is taken. The income and cash flow statements, which will be covered in the next two chapters, are more like moving pictures that show what happens through a period of time.

The form shown is the conventional one used in accounting; the assets or items owned on January 1, 1959, are listed on the left side of the statement. The total of these assets as shown is $18,906. Supposedly this is the sum for which Farmer A could have sold his farm business at that time, given a reasonable amount of time. On the right side of the statement are the debts owed, totaling $13,124. The difference between the assets and debts outstanding is $5,782, which represents the owner's equity, or net worth, of Farmer A in his business. It is the amount of net worth, not assets, that indicates the solvency of the borrower. A farmer may be operating a farm business with assets of $100,000, but if he has debts of $80,000, his net worth is only $20,000.

The question is often raised as to why the net worth figure is placed on the liabilities side of the statement. It is placed there to show that the owner, like other creditors, has a claim against the business equal to the net worth figure. The balance sheet shows the inventory value of property owned, and the difference between the value of property owned and total debts outstanding is called the equity, or net worth. Thus the assets are the first consideration. After they are valued, the people and businesses who have given Farmer A credit are allotted a portion of the assets equal to their total loans, and the remainder of the assets are considered as belonging without qualification to Farmer A. If the assets were sold, the creditors would come first and Farmer A would get what was left, which would be more or less than the net worth, depending on whether the assets actually sold for more or less than they were valued on the balance sheet. An allowance would have to be made for any costs associated with selling assets such as realty commissions, auctioneer's fees, and capital gains taxes. So the net worth actually is a liability of the business, for the business owes that amount to the owner, just as it owes stated amounts to the lenders.

When the amount of debt outstanding is greater than the value of assets, the difference is called the *net deficit* and the farmer is insolvent to that extent. A net deficit is placed on the assets side of the balance sheet because it represents the shortage of assets. Thus, when the assets, or the shortage of assets, are added, they will equal the total liabilities and the two sides of the balance sheet really balance.

TABLE 7.2:   Farm Business A—Balance Sheet as of January 1, 1960

Assets		Liabilities and Owner Equity	
Current		Current	
		Account payable, hardware	
		store	$ 167
Cash	$ 262	Account payable, tractor	
Corn, 3,550 bu	3,443	fuel	95
Soybeans, 561 bu	1,122	Note at bank, feeder cattle	4,100
Hay, alfalfa, 67 tons	1,006	Note at bank, feed	3,291
Hogs, market, 87 head	1,394	Total	$ 7,653
Sows, 12 head	380		
Feeding cattle, 36 head	4,178		
Poultry	140	Intermediate	
Total	$11,925		
		Loan from father, unsecured	$ 5,220
Intermediate			
Truck and auto (farm		Long-term	
share)	$ 1,150		
Machinery and equipment	7,023	(None)	
Total	$ 8,173		
		Owner equity	$ 7,225
Fixed			
(None)			
TOTAL	$20,098	TOTAL	$20,098

Assets are usually listed according to the ease with which they may be converted into cash, beginning with cash on hand and ending, as in the examples, with land and buildings, which are difficult to sell on short notice. The listing may be in the abbreviated form as in Table 7.1, but it is desirable to divide the assets into current assets, such as cash and livestock; intermediate assets, such as machinery; and fixed assets, such as land.

Debts are listed either in the order of their length of term or in the order of the assets to which they apply, as for example, livestock, machinery, and real estate loans, in the order named. The balance sheet of January 1, 1960, shown in Table 7.2, illustrates the grouping of assets and liabilities.

Classifying assets and liabilities as current, intermediate, and fixed (or long term) contributes to analysis of the liquidity of the business. This point is considered in detail later in the chapter.

NEED FOR PHYSICAL DATA. Information conveyed by balance sheets and analysis of such information are severely limited if physical data are not given in the statements to aid in interpreting the values. For example, the balance sheet shown in Table 7.1 shows grain valued at $3,624 but no information is given as to the kind or amount of grain on hand. The value exceeds the value of corn in the balance sheet for January 1, 1960, but there is no indication as to whether the quantity increased or decreased from the beginning to the end of the year. Similarly, no information is given in the balance sheet for January 1, 1959, on the kind or numbers of livestock on hand. The total value is approximately the same as on January 1, 1960. But without physical data in the January 1, 1959, balance sheet, one does not know whether the values are similar because the numbers and weights were similar, or whether a change occurred in numbers and weights, and also in unit prices.

A similar problem is involved when real estate comprises part of the assets of a balance sheet. The value of real estate shown in the balance sheet may not change from one year to the next, but without physical data a lender unfamiliar with the situation would not know whether the acreage had changed. He might assume that the same acreage was involved, but he could not be sure. Or perhaps the value of real estate may be $14,000 higher at the end than at the beginning of the year, as was the case in 1971 for Farm Business A. Was more acreage added or was the value per acre increased? Without physical data one does not know.

A detailed balance sheet that makes it possible to separate changes in the financial condition of the borrower according to whether they are caused by value changes or by changes in the physical inventory is essential if a complete and accurate analysis is to be made of the financial condition of the farm business. The balance sheets for January 1, 1960, shown in Table 7.2, and those for January 1, 1971, and January 1, 1972, given later in Tables 7.4 and 7.5, are presented in more detailed form to show both the physical numbers and value data needed to make an analysis of the condition of the business. Information on quality and weight also is needed and might well be included in the statement, particularly for market livestock such as hogs and feeding cattle. Information of this type to supplement that given in the balance sheet may be obtained by personal inspection of the property.

VALUATION DIFFICULTIES. The need to show physical as well as value data in the balance sheet is primarily due to difficulties in valuation of the assets. This difficulty increases progressively from the liquid to the fixed assets. Cash, government bonds, grain on hand, and livestock ready to sell are easy to value on a current market price basis. Breeding stock and machinery cannot so easily be converted into cash and, consequently, are valued with more difficulty. Land is the most difficult of all to value because it is infrequently sold, is not standardized in quality, and is sold only after considerable effort is expended to obtain a buyer who is interested in the farm. Unfortunately the land value item on the balance sheet for a farm business is usually the largest, a fact that makes interpretation of land value figures extremely important in balance sheet analysis. For example, a modest increase of $25 per acre for a 240-acre farm would cause an increase of $6,000 in fixed assets. This might well overshadow any other changes that occurred in the balance sheet.

Accuracy in valuing assets can only be approximated and must be defined with reference to some period for which the values are expected to hold good. It is possible to value corn, hay, cotton, hogs, and wool according to the market price on the day specified in the balance sheet. With land, and other nonliquid assets that are much more difficult to value, a good practice to follow is to value them on a realistic basis. One way to do this is to enter them at cost less depreciation, or *book value*. Another way is to use an accurate market value if it can be estimated from sales of similar property in the area.

Valuing at cost or book value is a good rule but it is not entirely satisfactory. It leads to some strange situations, especially when one farm is compared with another. For example, one farmer may have bought his farm in 1950 for $40,000. After allowance for depreciation and improvements, it may be valued, using the book value method, at $45,000 in 1970. A second farmer may have bought a similar farm in 1970 and paid $75,000. Other things being equal, the second farmer would show a total asset figure $30,000 greater than the first farmer.

When land values rise over long periods of time, as they have done over the past three decades in the United States, it is desirable to make adjustments periodically in balance sheet values to keep them in line with realistic current values. The values used should be sufficiently below the market value to allow for the realtor's commission and other expenses incurred if the farm were to be sold. Adjusting values periodically facilitates analysis of the equity and liquidity position of the business as well as the rate earned on equity capital and on assets managed. Thus the balance sheet will portray a realistic picture of the business that would be an advantage in submitting an application for a loan.

TREND ANALYSIS. A balance sheet as of a given time may not give a representative picture of the financial situation, due to unusual forces affecting production or prices at the time. Thus it is desirable to have a series of balance sheets for a business to provide a representative financial picture and also to show trends in the financial structure of the business. These are reasons why lenders make a practice of obtaining a current balance sheet with each loan application and renewal.

While balance sheets for Farm Business A were not available for all years, those for January 1, 1960, and 1966 through 1972 provide considerable information on trends which occurred during that period of time. The balance sheets for 1965 through 1970 are summarized in Table 7.3 and the balance sheets for 1971 and 1972 are given in Tables 7.4 and 7.5, respectively. Farmer A made good financial progress during this period, as shown by a comparison of the balance sheets. One major change reflected by the balance sheets is the addition of a farm that is reflected in the balance sheet for the first time on January 1, 1965. The balance sheets show that this farm was purchased sometime between January 1, 1960, and January 1, 1965, but they do not indicate the time. If annual balance sheets were available, the year could be identified, but still the time within the year would be unknown. This point is made to reemphasize that the balance sheet does not provide a record of what goes on during the year. As indicated above, it only shows the situation at a given time.

Owner's equity of Farm Business A increased from $7,225 January 1, 1960, to $27,778 January 1, 1965, jumped to $53,268 on January 1, 1966, and then increased to $101,896 on January 1, 1972. The increase in owner's equity of $20,553 from January 1, 1960 to January 1, 1965, may be considered on first thought to represent financial progress from farm income over the 5-year period. However, Mr. A and his wife inherited $14,000 that they used to help buy their farm in 1962. Thus not more than $6,553 of the increase in owner's equity can be attributed to farm income, and perhaps some of that came from nonfarm sources. While a comparison of two balance sheets in time gives an indication of financial progress over the period, information as to sources of the financial progress must be ascertained from the income statement and other records showing funds added to or withdrawn from the business.

The $18,392 increase in owner's equity between January 1, 1971, and January 1, 1972, deserves further consideration. As indicated by comparing the January 1, 1971, and 1972 balance sheets, $14,000 of this increase resulted from an increase in the value of the real estate. The farm had been valued at $442 per acre since 1967 and the increase to $500 per acre was made to reflect a more realistic market value for the farm at the beginning of 1972. If we disregard the increase in the land value, the increase in net worth between January 1, 1971, and January 1, 1972, was only $4,392. A similar upward revaluation of the real estate accounted for some of the $25,490 increase in net worth between January 1, 1965, and January 1, 1966.

Further examination of Tables 7.4 and 7.5 reveals that there

TABLE 7.3: Farm Business A—Comparative Balance Sheets as of January 1, 1965–70

	1965	1966	1967	1968	1969	1970
ASSETS						
Current						
Cash & bank						
balance	$ 506	$ 400	$ 560	$ 730	$ 640	$ 970
Corn	7,140	6,400	9,600	7,380	6,150	9,750
Soybeans	...	1,890	1,625	2,860	3,400	2,760
Hay	1,188	1,260	1,000	1,200	600	500
Hogs, market	5,147	9,250	10,430	7,900	10,500	11,600
Feeding cattle	7,000	15,200	13,700	22,400	24,100	25,800
Total	$ 20,981	$ 34,400	$ 36,915	$ 42,470	$ 45,750	$ 51,380
Intermediate						
Machinery, truck,						
auto	6,520	6,246	13,018	11,338	13,334	15,332
Fixed						
Real estate,						
240 acres with						
buildings	84,000*	96,000†	106,000	106,000	106,000	106,000
TOTAL ASSETS	$111,501	$136,646	$155,933	$159,808	$165,084	$172,712
LIABILITIES & OWNER EQUITY						
Current						
Accounts pay-						
able	$ 118	$ 301	$ 415	$ 155	$ 534	$ 803
Note for feeders	6,106	9,875	16,730	21,000	23,000	25,000
Operating note	3,179	1,282	4,400	3,080	2,667	3,157
Total	$ 9,403	$ 11,458	$ 21,545	$ 24,235	$ 26,201	$ 28,960
Intermediate						
Loan from father	5,220	5,220	8,000	8,000	8,000	8,000
Long-term						
Real estate						
contract	69,100	66,700	64,300	61,900	59,500	57,100
TOTAL LIABILITIES	$ 83,723	$ 83,378	$ 93,845	$ 94,135	$ 93,701	$ 94,060
OWNER EQUITY	27,778	53,268	62,088	65,673	71,383	78,652
TOTAL LIABILITIES & OWNER EQUITY	$111,501	$136,646	$155,933	$159,808	$165,084	$172,712
Change in Owner Equity from Previous Year	$	$ 25,490	$ 8,820	$ 3,585	$ 5,710	$ 7,269

* Real estate value increase reflects added improvements, in this case a new house.

† Real estate value increased to better reflect current market value.

108

TABLE 7.4: Farm Business A—Balance Sheet as of January 1, 1971

Assets			Liabilities and Owner Equity		
Current			**Current**		
Cash	$	1,340	Accounts payable	$	1,222
Corn, 7,488 bu		9,360	Note at bank, feeder cattle		28,000
Soybeans, 1,400 bu		3,640	Note at bank, feed		2,470
Hay, alfalfa, 30 tons		600	Total	$	31,692
Hogs, market, 364 head		7,900			
Feeding cattle, 148 head		32,100	**Intermediate**		
Total	$	54,940	Loan from father,		
			unsecured	$	4,000
Intermediate			**Long-term**		
Truck, auto, farm			Real estate contract	$	54,700
machinery	$	12,956	Total liabilities	$	90,392
Fixed					
Real estate, 240 acres	$106,000		Owner equity*		$83,504
TOTAL	$173,896		TOTAL		$173,896

* Gain due to change in inventory value of real estate is $12,000 over purchase price plus cost of improvements added.

TABLE 7.5: Farm Business A—Balance Sheet as of January 1, 1972

Assets			Liabilities and Owner Equity		
Current			**Current**		
Cash	$	1,270	Accounts payable	$	978
Corn, 7,750 bu		7,750	Note at bank, feeder cattle		15,300
Soybeans, 2,000 bu		5,600	Note at bank, open		3,265
Hay, alfalfa, 30 tons		600	Total	$	19,543
Hogs, market, 442 head		12,600			
Feeding cattle, 75 head		16,900	**Intermediate**		
Total	$	44,720	Loan from father,		
			unsecured	$	2,000
Intermediate			**Long-term**		
Truck, auto, farm			Real estate contract	$	52,300
machinery	$	11,019	Total liabilities	$	73,843
Fixed					
Real estate, 240 acres	$120,000		Owner equity*		$101,896
TOTAL	$175,739		TOTAL		$175,739

* Gain due to change in inventory value of real estate is $26,000 over purchase price plus cost of improvements added.

was a $10,220 decrease in current assets between January 1 and December 31, 1971. Most of the decrease is accounted for by the decrease in the number of feeding cattle from 148 to 75 head. The value of corn on hand also dropped even though the physical quantity changed very little because Mr. A valued his corn 25 cents per bushel lower on January 1, 1972. Decreases in the value of feeding cattle and corn on hand were only partially offset by increases in inventories of market hogs and soybeans.

The $10,220 decrease in current assets was accompanied by a $1,937 decrease in intermediate farm assets, which reflects depreciation as well as sales and purchases of machinery. Thus the total decrease in current and intermediate term assets was $12,157. This decrease in assets might possibly be viewed with some concern; however, such fluctuations are fairly typical of feeder livestock enterprises. Furthermore, Farmer A reduced his total liabilities by $16,549 between January 1, 1971, and January 1, 1972. The net result of a $12,157 decrease in nonreal-estate assets and a $16,549 decrease in total liabilities gives the $4,392 increase in net worth, not counting the increase in land value.

RATIO AND COMPARATIVE ANALYSIS. A number of ratios are used to provide additional information on financial progress beyond that given by the absolute dollar values given in the balance sheet. Balance sheet ratios put all sizes of business on the same basis. For example, a net worth of $100,000 would be relatively high if total assets were $150,000 but very low if total assets were $500,000. The usefulness of such ratios depends to a considerable degree on availability of a reliable basis for comparison, to enable one to judge whether the ratio for a particular farm is good, fair, or poor. However, this factor is not as critical with balance sheet ratios as with income statement ratios since balance sheet ratios have more significance in and of themselves. Moreover, budget analysis can be used in connection with the ratios to test pertinent financial relationships.

A classic measure of financial condition used in balance sheet analysis is the current ratio, which indicates the extent to which current assets, if liquidated, would cover current debts outstanding.

$$\frac{\text{Total current assets}}{\text{Total current debt}} = \text{Current ratio} \qquad (7.1)$$

The first line in Table 7.6 shows the trend in the current ratio for Farm Business A. On January 1, 1972, Farm Business A had $2.29 of current assets for each dollar of current debt. The current position was somewhat erratic between 1960 and 1972 but this be-

TABLE 7.6: Farm Business A—Balance Sheet Ratios, January 1, 1960–72

Ratio	How Calculated	1960	1965	1966	1967	1968	1969	1970	1971	1972
Current	$\dfrac{\text{Current assets}}{\text{Current debt}}$	1.55	2.62	3.09	1.71	1.75	1.75	1.77	1.73	2.29
Intermediate	$\dfrac{\text{Cur.} + \text{int. assets}}{\text{Cur.} + \text{int. debt}}$	1.56	1.88	2.62	1.69	1.67	1.73	1.91	1.90	2.59
Net Capital	$\dfrac{\text{Total assets}}{\text{Total debt}}$	1.56	1.33	1.70	1.66	1.70	1.76	1.84	1.92	2.38
Debt:Equity	$\dfrac{\text{Total debt}}{\text{Owner equity}}$	1.78	3.01	1.42	1.51	1.43	1.31	1.20	1.08	0.72
Equity:Value	$\dfrac{\text{Owner equity}}{\text{Total assets}}$	0.36	0.25	0.41	0.40	0.41	0.43	0.46	0.48	0.58

havior is also typical of feeder livestock enterprises. The average current ratio over the 9 years shown in Table 7.6 was 2.03. Standards as to what is a good or minimum acceptable current ratio are rather difficult to establish. This is also true to some degree for all balance sheet ratios. In general, any sudden decrease in the current ratio, or a steady downward trend, should be investigated.

Since current assets include those normally turned into cash within 1 year, the current ratio in effect reflects liquidity within 1 year's time. If this period is too long, the quick ratio, also referred to as the "acid test" ratio, may be used. It is used to reflect the adequacy of cash, accounts receivable, and marketable securities (bonds, stocks, etc.) to cover all current liabilities.

Another measure of current liquidity relates current debt to owner's equity. The reasoning back of this ratio is that owner's equity reflects ability to pay off current debts either by use of current assets or by borrowing. A business may show a very poor current ratio, but if the operator has a high net worth, the financial position of the business may be relatively secure. However, for this ratio to be meaningful, the owner's equity must be in a sufficiently liquid state so it could be used either directly or indirectly to meet the current debts.

The intermediate ratio is used to reflect the intermediate liquidity position of the business in much the same way as the current ratio is used in the short-run situation.

$$\frac{\text{Total current and intermediate assets}}{\text{Total current and intermediate debt}} = \text{Intermediate ratio} \quad (7.2)$$

Over an intermediate period of time, both current and intermediate assets will be converted into cash in the normal operation of the business. The ratio reflects the likelihood that cash derived in this process will be adequate to cover debt payments coming due during the same period of time. The intermediate ratio for Farm Business A was 1.56 on January 1, 1960, 1.88 on January 1, 1965, and 2.59 on January 1, 1972. The intermediate ratio appears adequate for the size and type of business operated by Farmer A because it is unlikely that the value of the current and intermediate assets would decrease either due to physical losses or price declines to that point where they would not cover current and intermediate debts. The relatively steady increase over a period of time in the ratio is a favorable sign. An upward trend in the ratio adds risk-bearing ability in the use of intermediate credit.

The long-run liquidity position of a business is indicated by the net capital ratio.

$$\frac{\text{Total assets}}{\text{Total debt}} = \text{Net capital ratio} \quad (7.3)$$

This ratio is probably the most important measure of the overall *solvency* position of the business because it reflects the likelihood that the sale of all assets of the business would produce sufficient cash to cover all debt outstanding. The ratio for Farm Business A was 1.56 on January 1, 1960, 1.33 on January 1, 1965, and 2.38 on January 1, 1972. Since Mr. A was a tenant farmer in 1960, no real estate was involved in his net capital ratio at that time. Purchase of a farm on contract naturally reduced his ratio. The upward trend in the net capital ratio in Table 7.6 reflects Mr. A's steady financial progress.

The net capital ratio is considered a long-run concept since real estate is involved. However, since good land is not converted into cash through the production process, as are other assets, the period involved is really the time required to sell the farm. Thus the time period concept involved in the net capital ratio differs from that involved in the intermediate and current ratios.

Another overall measure of liquidity commonly used is the ratio of total debt to owner's equity.

$$\frac{\text{Total debt}}{\text{Owner's equity}} = \text{Debt:equity ratio} \qquad (7.4)$$

This ratio for Farm Business A was 1.78 on January 1, 1960, 3.01 on January 1, 1965, and 0.72 on January 1, 1972. In other words, on January 1, 1972, Mr. A's debts were 0.72 times his equity in the farm business. This was a much smaller ratio than on January 1, 1965. Purchase of the farm on contract in 1962 was partly responsible for the relatively high ratio in 1965 compared to 1960. Relatively large real estate debt incurred by use of purchase contracts may cause a farmer's debt:equity ratio to be high. But this should not be interpreted as meaning that real estate debt will always cause a high debt: equity ratio. Conventional mortgage loans on real estate usually do not run much over 70 percent of the value, and periodic payments may gradually reduce this percentage. It is not uncommon for relatively larger loans to be made on chattel property.

Equity is often related to the value of assets. The ratio is

$$\frac{\text{Owner's equity}}{\text{Value of assets}} = \text{Equity:value ratio} \qquad (7.5)$$

The ratio of equity to value for Farm Business A was 0.36 on January 1, 1960, 0.25 on January 1, 1965, and 0.58 on January 1, 1972. The drop in the ratio from 1960 to 1965 was caused by purchase of the farm on contract. The improvement in the ratio from 1965 to 1972 shows the increased strength in the financial structure of the business.

While the equity:value ratio may be used to reflect the overall situation, it is more commonly used to depict owner's equity in an individual item. Reference to the amount or percent paid down in purchase of an asset reflects the ratio of owner's equity to value of the asset.

Equities of less than 25 percent are usually scrutinized with extreme care by lenders. But this figure is by no means a strict borderline. A 20 percent equity position for a well-managed farm business may be safer than a 60 percent equity in a business where the management is questionable. The types of assets involved also have a bearing on the size of the ratio that may be considered safe.

The ratios of current assets to current debts, of intermediate assets to intermediate debts, and of fixed assets to long-term debts are often used as a simple test to determine whether debts are properly distributed among current, intermediate, and long-term obligations. In 1972 the current ratio for Farm Business A was 2.29, the ratio of intermediate assets to intermediate debts was 5.51, and the ratio of fixed assets to long-term debts was 2.29. Mr. A's debts are reasonably well distributed among short, intermediate, and long-term loans. However, the current ratio could be increased somewhat by shifting some short-term loans to intermediate-term loans if payments on the short-term portion are too high.

Since the basic balance sheet relationship is total assets = (total debt) + (owner's equity), the equity:value ratio, the debt:equity ratio, and the net capital ratio are alternative ways of expressing the overall leverage position of the business. Thus, as Table 7.6 illustrates, a decreasing debt:equity ratio is equivalent to increasing net capital and equity:value ratios.

SUMMARY. A balance sheet shows assets, debts outstanding, and owner equity as of a specific date. The primary purpose of the balance sheet is to measure the solvency of the business, that is, the extent to which outstanding debt obligations would be covered if the assets of the business were liquidated. A trend analysis over a period of several years is needed to show the changing financial structure of the business. If the balance sheet is to accurately reflect the financial position of a business, the assets must be valued realistically, and in most farming operations, the valuation of real estate and other fixed assets is troublesome.

The balance sheet analysis for Farm Business A indicates that Mr. A made very favorable financial progress between 1959 and 1972. His net worth increased from $5,782 to $101,896, although as the note at the bottom of the January 1, 1972, balance sheet indicates, $26,000 of this increase in owner equity were due to periodic increases in the value of his real estate due to land price inflation. Also, as was noted earlier, Mr. A and his wife inherited $14,000 in 1962. Thus, of the $96,114 total increase in owner equity between 1959 and 1972, $56,114 were actually *earned* from farm and possibly nonfarm income, and $40,000 were due to the inheritance and increasing land values.

The analysis of Mr. A's balance sheet points out one weak point: it provides only very limited information about the *sources* of financial progress. The analysis of Mr. A's income and cash flow statements in the next two chapters will reveal more about his financial progress.

QUESTIONS AND PROBLEMS

1. Discuss the meaning of owner equity, or net worth; of net deficit. Explain how each is derived.
2. How may balance sheets be used by borrowers in deciding how much to borrow? By lenders in deciding how much to lend?
3. Compare the balance sheets for Farm Business A, given in this chapter, with balance sheets for a large corporation and a commercial bank. Discuss any similarities and differences.
4. Assume that you are a farm lender and that Mr. A has asked you for an additional loan of $75,000 to expand his operation so that he and his son can form a family farm partnership. Would you be willing to loan Mr. A and his son this additional amount, based on past financial progress?
5. Discuss how the balance sheet ratios discussed in this chapter would differ for an owner-operated farm and a tenant-operated farm. Would there be differences among feeder livestock farms, crop farms, and dairy farms?

REFERENCES

Duft, Ken D. *Financial Ratio Analysis: An Aid to Agribusiness Management.* Wash. State Univ., Coop. Ext. Serv., reprinted May 1969.

Smith, Frank J., and Cooper, Ken. *The Financial Management of Agribusiness Firms.* Univ. of Minn., Agr. Ext. Serv., Spec. Rept. 26, 1967.

CHAPTER 8: FINANCIAL ANALYSIS OF THE FARM BUSINESS: THE INCOME STATEMENT

THE *income statement* is one important measure of financial liquidity. *Liquidity* is the ability of an ongoing business to meet financial obligations, such as debt payments, rent, payroll, and family living needs, on schedule. Thus the income statement reveals the success or failure of a farm business over time. The cash flow statement, covered in the next chapter, supplements the income statement by showing where funds come from and where they are used.

We are concerned with an understanding of the income statement and related analyses to determine the information it will provide on costs and returns associated with use of varying amounts of capital in the farm business. How can this statement be organized and summarized to give the needed information? What information will it provide for determining how much credit it will pay to use? These are the types of questions considered in this chapter.

Preparation and analysis of an income statement for a typical farm business is a straightforward, simple, single-entry accounting process involving the listing of receipts and expenditures in general categories. However, it may appear to be a complex and involved undertaking due to the wide range of activities included in the farm business. Most of the problems encountered in determining the income of a large corporate business are found on a smaller scale in computing income of a farm business. Consequently one needs to have a clear understanding of what an income statement is, the information needed to prepare an income statement, and the way in which it is summarized. The discussion that follows is illustrated by the income statements for Farm Business A, the 240-acre hog-beef fattening farm in the Corn Belt introduced in Chapter 7.

INCOME STATEMENT. An *income statement,* also called a *profit and loss statement,* is a summary of receipts and gains during a specified period, usually a year, less expenses and losses during the same period, with a net income or a net loss as a result. It is a measure of output and input in terms of values.

Receipts. Receipts are derived from sales of crops, livestock, and livestock products during the year, and also from government payments and miscellaneous sources. On Mr. A's farm, income

TABLE 8.1:   Farm Business A—Income Statement for Year 1971

Receipts			
Livestock sales:			
Cattle, fat	$49,662		
Hogs	16,040		
Total		$65,702	
Crop sales		8,126	
Government payments		2,728	
Miscellaneous income		95	
Gross cash receipts			$76,651
Increase (decrease) in current inventory			(10,150)
			$66,501
Less: Livestock purchased		$19,484	
Feed purchased		13,478	$32,962
Gross income			$33,539
Operating Expenses			
Machinery and power		$ 4,491	
Hired labor		876	
Livestock		438	
Seed, fertilizer. etc.		4,208	
Interest on operating loans		1,578	
Miscellaneous		247	
Total operating expenses			$11,838
Net Operating Income			$21,701
Fixed Expenses			
Taxes, property		$ 2,829	
Interest on intermediate & long-term debt		2,290	
Repairs and insurance on improvements		1,023	
Depreciation on intermediate assets		2,641	
Depreciation on fixed assets		981	
Total fixed expenses			$ 9,764
Net Farm Income			$11,937

from these sources totaled $76,651 in 1971 (see Table 8.1). Any farm products used in the home should be valued and also included in receipts.

The objective in the receipts section of the income statement is to show as accurately as feasible the gross production of the farm, in dollars, during the year. This facilitates comparison of a given farm with other similar farms in the area from a management point of view. It also facilitates analyzing the trend of income on the given farm over a period of years. Therefore, recognition should be given to changes in the inventory value of livestock, crops, and other liquid assets during the year. The procedure of adjusting cash receipts for inventory changes to determine gross income is called the *accrual* method of accounting. While relatively few farmers use the accrual basis to report income for income tax purposes, a recognition of inventory changes is very important in analyzing the financial performance of a business. As was noted in the previous chapter, the value of Mr. A's current inventory (excluding cash on hand) was $10,150 lower December 31, 1971, than a year earlier. Thus this amount was subtracted from his gross cash receipts.

The sum of total receipts plus changes in inventories for farms with large purchases of feeder livestock and feed naturally overstates the income actually produced on the farm. It is customary, therefore, to correct this overstatement by deducting purchases of livestock and feed (as is "cost of goods sold" in conventional double-entry accounting) to obtain *gross income*. Mr. A's purchases of livestock totaled $19,484 and feed bought amounted to $13,478. These amounts deducted from $66,501 left a gross income of $33,539 for the year.

For purposes of financial analysis, receipts from the sale of capital assets such as real estate or machinery are generally not considered as income since such income is not really produced or earned during the period. However, for income tax purposes, income is adjusted for any *capital gains* (or losses) resulting from the sale of capital items. A capital gain, for example, would be realized if the amount received from the sale of a capital item exceeds its depreciated or book value.

Expenses. All expenses or costs involved in the operation of the business during the period covered by the income statement should be included in the income statement. Thus all operating and fixed expenses are included. However, capital expenditures to purchase fixed and working assets such as real estate, machinery, milk cows, and breeding stock are excluded since such items usually are used in the business for several years. The depreciation on these items that occurs during the period covered by the income statement is an expense, however, and should be included.

Operating, or variable costs, and fixed costs are shown separately in Table 8.1. As was pointed out in Chapter 2, operating costs such as seed, fertilizer, and fuel vary with the level of production. Fixed costs such as depreciation, taxes, insurance, and interest on intermediate and long-term debt remain relatively constant regardless of the level of production. The reason for separating fixed and variable costs in the income statement will become apparent later in this chapter.

Net Income. Three net income (or loss) figures are useful in analysis of the business: net cash income, net operating income, and net farm income. *Net cash income* equals cash receipts less cash expenses during the period covered by the statement, excluding purchases and sales of capital assets. The primary usefulness of the net cash income figure is in connection with analysis of cash flow. It also is useful in preparing income tax returns when the return is made on the cash basis. Further consideration is given to net cash income in the following section.

Net operating income is computed by subtracting operating expenses from gross income. Mr. A's net operating income was $21,701 in 1971 (see Table 8.1). This measure of income facilitates comparison of farms with different fixed cost structures such as different amounts of mortgage debt and different depreciation schedules. It also facilitates comparing income from operations on the same farm over a period of years even though fixed costs change, due to changes in mortgage indebtedness, etc.

Net farm income is computed by deducting fixed costs from net operating income. Mr. A's net farm income amounted to $11,937 in 1971. Net farm income represents the income accruing to operator and family labor, management, and equity capital. Of the three measures of income, it is perhaps the most useful. It represents more nearly than the other two measures of income the true net income of the business during the period covered by the income statement. Provided the data used in its preparation are accurate and realistic, net farm income approximates the amount available for family living, income taxes, and savings. Principal payments on debts, which are not already accounted for in expenses, such as loans incurred to purchase land, must also be paid out of net income.

When the income statement provides the detailed information needed for analysis, it may be somewhat complicated. However, keeping the basic objective and structure of the income statement in mind materially facilitates understanding how it should be set up and interpreted. The primary objective is to show the income produced and expenses involved in the operation of the business during the period covered by the statement, together with the net income (or loss) that is realized. Thus the income statement is basically comprised of three parts: receipts, expenses, and net income. Within this framework details are added to provide needed information. For example, the analysis presented in the latter part of the chapter makes specific use of gross income, total operating expenses, total fixed expenses, etc. Therefore, these details have been included in the income statement for Farm Business A. The final form and content of the income statement depend to a large degree upon the information that is needed.

TREND OF RECEIPTS, EXPENSES, AND NET INCOME. A
record of receipts, expenses, and net income over a period of years is invaluable in analyzing a farm business. An income state-

TABLE 8.2: Receipts, Expenses, and Income Summary of Farm A, 1960–71

	1960-65 Average*	1966	1967	1968	1969	1970	1971
				(dollars)			
Cash Receipts							
Cattle, fat	12,844	25,132	23,743	39,058	45,739	44,063	49,662
Hogs	12,744	17,297	20,275	11,659	12,088	16,214	16,040
Crops	2,254	4,871	4,967	7,133	6,015	5,031	8,126
Government payments	2,401	5,241	2,882	4,547	4,819	3,804	2,728
Miscellaneous	993	493	1,279	1,722	922	414	95
Total	31,236	53,034	53,146	64,119	69,583	69,526	76,651
Cash Expenses							
Machinery and power	2,387	2,579	3,450	3,594	3,944	4,158	4,491
Hired labor	144	435	63	710	406	1,333	876
Livestock	453	340	306	497	392	592	438
Seed, fertilizer, etc.	1,277	1,940	3,497	2,723	3,257	3,904	4,208
Feed purchases	4,997	10,802	7,369	8,514	12,045	10,171	13,478
Livestock purchased	10,635	11,933	24,082	24,459	26,319	30,199	19,484
Miscellaneous operating	787	106	157	95	211	430	247
Taxes, property	933	1,711	1,805	1,816	1,938	2,595	2,829
Interest	2,276	3,209	3,223	3,487	4,286	3,722	3,868
Repairs and insurance on improvements	219	695	1,669	1,115	1,403	1,989	1,023
Total	24,108	33,750	45,621	47,010	54,201	59,093	50,942
Net Cash Income	7,128	19,284	7,525	17,109	15,382	10,433	25,709
Increase (Decrease) in Current Inventory	5,162	2,496	5,815	2,900	5,361	3,142	(10,150)
Depreciation							
Intermediate assets	1,274	2,073	1,680	2,040	2,284	2,573	2,641
Improvements	853	999	981	1,389	981	981	981
Net Farm Income	10,163	18,708	10,679	16,580	17,478	10,021	11,937

* Prior to 1963 Mr. A was a tenant farmer.

ment for only 1 year may be misleading, especially where income is highly variable. This point may be illustrated by the record for Farm Business A given in Table 8.2. The average net farm income over the 12-year period 1960–71 was $13,652; however, it varied from a low of $4,505 in 1960 (when Mr. A was a tenant operator) to a high of $26,787 in 1965. Income statements for either of these 2 unusual years considered alone would have been very misleading.

The trend of receipts, expenses, and net income over time is significant in financial analysis. Mr. A's net farm income, while somewhat erratic, as is often the case with the feeder livestock enterprises, was generally stable to slightly upward over the 12-year period shown in Table 8.2. Although physical data are lacking, one might speculate that low hog prices and high feed prices in 1970–71 accounted in part for Mr. A's lower net farm income during the last 2 years shown in Table 8.2. Compare net cash income and net farm income. For the 12-year period 1960–71, net farm income for Farm Business A averaged $13,652 and net cash income averaged $14,653. Wide differences occurred in individual years, however. In 1962, for example, net farm income was $10,139 while net cash income was only $2,079. The reverse relationship may also occur. In 1971, net cash income was $25,709 while net farm income was only $11,937. Such differences are of considerable significance in repayment capacity, as will be shown in the next chapter.

INVENTORY ADJUSTMENTS. Reference was made above to the inventory adjustments that are made in arriving at gross income.

A similar adjustment, as well as an adjustment for depreciation, is made in deriving net farm income from net cash income. In other words, net cash income plus (minus) the increase (decrease) in the current inventory, less depreciation on intermediate and fixed assets, gives net farm income.[1]

Obviously, inventory adjustments are of paramount importance

---

1. Provided depreciation of intermediate assets and fixed improvements is included as an expense (a desirable accounting procedure), adjustments are not needed in the inventory value of these items in computing net farm income. If an increase (decrease) is made in the inventory value of land due to an increase (decrease) in the price level of land, the resulting increase (decrease) in owner equity is appropriately considered the same as a cash addition to (withdrawal from) the business. Such a change is not reflected in net farm income. On the other hand, if an increase is made in the inventory value of land due to an improvement in its productivity as a result of farming methods and conservation practices that are not depreciated, the increased value is appropriately reflected in net farm income, assuming the costs involved have been included in farm expenses. The same would be true if a reduction was made in the inventory value of land due to deterioration of productivity as a result of farming practices.

if a reliable net farm income figure is to be obtained. However, constant danger of misrepresentation exists. Increases or decreases in inventory values from the beginning to the end of the year are caused by changes in both *quantities* and *prices*. Changes in quantities usually do not cause major problems, except possibly where quality or weight per unit or per head changes. But changes in prices may cause distortions in the income picture, giving an incorrect impression of the farmer's ability to produce income. These points can be clarified by reference to the 1971 beginning and ending inventory of current assets of Farm Business A, which follows.

January 1, 1971		December 31, 1971	
Corn, 7,488 bu	$ 9,360	Corn, 7,750 bu	$ 7,750
Soybeans, 1,400 bu	3,640	Soybeans, 2,000 bu	5,600
Alfalfa hay, 30 tons	600	Alfalfa hay, 30 tons	600
Hogs, market, 364 head	7,900	Hogs, market, 442 head	12,600
Feeding cattle, 148 head	32,100	Feeding cattle, 75 head	16,900
Total	$53,600	Total	$43,450

Farmer A used different unit values for his corn, soybeans, and livestock at the beginning and end of 1971. His corn was valued at $1.25 per bushel at the beginning of the year and $1.00 per bushel at year end. The value of soybeans was increased from $2.60 per bushel on January 1 to $2.80 per bushel on December 31. Although one might question this procedure, the fact that the corn price was reduced significantly would suggest that Mr. A was being realistic in his price adjustments. The 25-cent per bushel reduction in the value of his corn in effect resulted in a loss of $1,937.50 (7,750 × $0.25) while the 20-cent per bushel increase in soybean prices resulted in a gain of $400 (2,000 × $0.20).

The per head values of market hogs and feeding cattle were both adjusted upward between January 1 and December 31, 1971. However, these adjustments cannot be entirely attributed to price changes because the quality and/or weights of the animals on hand may have been different. Again, we can probably assume that Mr. A used realistic prices to value his livestock inventories.

FINANCIAL TESTS—RATIOS. Analysis of pertinent financial relationships in the income statement provides information concerning performance of the farm business in addition to that obtained directly by income statement analysis. Without a basis for comparison, such as a summary of like relationships for similar farms in the area or similar information for the subject farm over a period of years, such ratios have little value. However, when a basis for comparison is available, pertinent comparisons provide valuable information. Progressive lenders generally use financial tests of various kinds in loan analysis. Working with a large number of farmers, they are in a position to develop ratio standards, formally or otherwise, to provide the basis for comparison needed to effectively use this type of information. In many states the Cooperative Extension Service also offers a farm records analysis that usually includes average ratios for various types and sizes of farms.

Income statement ratios can be divided into two categories: those that relate expenses to gross income and those that relate income to capital investment. Six of the commoner ratios are shown in Table 8.3, covering the period 1966–71 for Farm Business A.

Expense:Income Ratios. Expense:income ratios are used to measure the input:output efficiency of the business; that is, they measure the margin by which the value of total production exceeds production costs. To more accurately reflect the value of production, and to permit comparisons among different types of farms, expense:income ratios should be adjusted for purchased feed and feeder livestock.

The *operating ratio,* as the name implies, relates variable costs to gross income.

$$\text{Operating ratio} = \frac{\text{Total operating expenses}}{\text{Gross income}} \qquad (8.1)$$

In 1971 Farm Business A had total operating expenses of $11,838 and a gross income of $33,539, giving an operating ratio of 0.35. In other words, total operating expenses amounted to 35 cents per dollar of gross income. Over the 6-year period shown in Table 8.3, the average operating ratio was 0.28.

The fixed ratio relates fixed expenses to gross income.

$$\text{Fixed ratio} = \frac{\text{Fixed expenses}}{\text{Gross income}} \qquad (8.2)$$

In 1971 Farm Business A had total fixed expenses of $9,764 which, when divided by the gross income of $33,539, gives a fixed ratio of 0.29. In other words, fixed or overhead expenses such as property taxes, insurance, depreciation, and interest on intermediate and long-term debts amounted to 29 cents per dollar of gross income. The average fixed ratio between 1966 and 1971 was 0.29.

The operating and fixed ratios comprise the gross ratio.

$$\text{Gross ratio} = \frac{\text{Total expenses}}{\text{Gross income}} \qquad (8.3)$$

In 1971 operating expenses amounted to 35 cents per dollar of gross income and fixed expenses amounted to 29 cents per dollar of gross income, giving a gross ratio of 0.64, or 64 cents per dollar of gross income. Alternatively, net farm income in 1971 amounted to about 36 cents per dollar of gross income.

The three expense:gross ratios for Farm Business A indicate that

TABLE 8.3: Farm Business A—Income Statement Ratios, 1966–71

Ratio	How Calculated		1966	1967	1968	1969	1970	1971
Expense:Income Ratios*								
Operating ratio	$\dfrac{\text{Total operating expenses}}{\text{Gross income}}$		0.17	0.28	0.24	0.26	0.36	0.35
Fixed ratio	$\dfrac{\text{Fixed expenses}}{\text{Gross income}}$		0.26	0.33	0.27	0.26	0.33	0.29
Gross ratio	$\dfrac{\text{Total expenses}}{\text{Gross income}}$		0.43	0.61	0.51	0.52	0.69	0.64
Income:Investment Ratios								
Capital turnover	$\dfrac{\text{Gross income}\dagger}{\text{Average capital investment}}$		0.38	0.37	0.41	0.44	0.42	0.38
Rate of return on capital‡	$\dfrac{\text{Return to total investment}}{\text{Average capital investment}}$	× 100	9.5%	3.7%	7.4%	8.2%	3.3%	4.5%
Rate of return on equity‡	$\dfrac{\text{Return to equity}}{\text{Average net worth}}$	× 100	18.6%	4.2%	12.5%	12.6%	2.5%	4.2%

* All interest charges included in fixed expenses.
† Not adjusted for purchased feeder livestock and feed.
‡ Based on an unpaid operator and family labor and management allowance of $8,000 per year.

Mr. A is an efficient farm operator. With gross income and expenses adjusted for purchased feeder livestock and feed, his average operating ratio for the 6 years shown in Table 8.3 was 0.28 and the average fixed ratio was 0.29, giving an average 6-year gross ratio of 0.57. In other words, for each dollar of gross income, Mr. A received 43 cents in net farm income. It appears that Mr. A is the type of manager who watches his expenses very carefully. The upward trend in the gross ratio, particularly in 1970–71, may have been caused, as was suggested earlier, by unfavorable market prices for hogs and feed grains.

Income:Investment Ratios. Income:investment ratios are used to indicate the efficiency with which capital is being employed in the business. The capital turnover ratio is commonly used as a quick appraisal of capital use efficiency.

$$\text{Capital turnover} = \frac{\text{Gross income}}{\text{Average capital investment}} \qquad (8.4)$$

The unadjusted gross income figure is used purposely in the capital turnover because feeder livestock and purchased feed inventories are part of capital investment; thus gross income, which is not adjusted for "cost of goods sold," is the appropriate income figure to use.

The average capital investment figure is the average of beginning-of-year and end-of-year total assets. On January 1, 1971, Farm Business A had total assets of $173,896 and on December 31, 1971, total assets were $175,739, including the $14,000 increase in land value. The average of the January 1 and December 31, 1971, total asset figures is $174,818, which is probably a reasonable estimate of the average capital investment throughout 1971. The unadjusted gross income for 1971 was $66,501; thus the capital turnover ratio was 0.38. In other words, for each dollar of capital invested, Farm Business A generated 38 cents in gross income in 1971. Throughout the period 1966–71, Farm Business A generated an average of 40 cents for each dollar of capital invested.

The rate of return on investment is obtained by dividing net return to capital by average total assets for the year.

$$\text{Rate of return on investment} = \frac{\text{Net return to capital}}{\text{Average capital investment}} \qquad (8.5)$$

Net return to total capital used in the business is derived from net farm income by (1) adding back interest paid and (2) subtracting out an allowance for unpaid operator and family labor and for management. The calculations for Farm Business A for 1971 are as follows:

Net farm income	$11,937
Plus: Interest paid during year	3,868
	$15,805
Less: Allowance for operator and family labor and management	8,000
Return to total capital	$ 7,805

Relating the return to capital to the average amount of capital invested in the business in 1971 ($174,818) gives a 4.5 percent return on investment.

The return to owner equity may be obtained by subtracting a wage for operator and family labor and for management from net farm income. Using the figures given above for 1971, the return to Mr. A's equity capital was $3,937. Average owner equity during 1971 was $92,700. Thus the rate of return on equity capital was 4.2 percent.

Two cautions should be observed in interpreting rates of return on capital. First, since deductions from net farm income for operator and family labor and for management return are imputed from farm wage rates and professional farm management fees in the area, they may be either higher or lower than if they were established in the market. In the case of Farm Business A, the unpaid labor and management allowance was rather arbitrarily set at $8,000. Second, the rate of return indicated by 1 year's operation may be misleading. As was pointed out above, an income statement for only 1 year may be misleading. Since the rate of return on capital is based directly on the income statement, the rate of return for only 1 year may not portray a reliable picture. Table 8.3 shows the variation in rates of return on total investment and owner equity over the period 1966–71. The average rate of return on total investment for the 6-year period was 6.1 percent, ranging from a low of 3.3 percent in 1970 to a high of 9.5 percent in 1966. Average return on equity over the 6 years was 9.1 percent and varied from a low of 2.5 percent in 1970 to a high of 18.6 percent in 1966.

The rates of return on total investment and owner equity for Farm Business A deserve further analysis. First, the rate of return on invested capital, as calculated in Table 8.3 may seem low compared to nonfarm investment opportunities such as stocks, bonds, or even savings accounts. It should be recognized that capital gains on real estate and other assets were not included in the rate of return calculations. If, for example, the net farm income included say a 3 percent price increase in his farm real estate for 1971, his return on total investment would be about 6.5 percent instead of 4.5 percent and his return on equity would be about 7.9 percent instead of 4.2 percent. We do not suggest that capital gain on assets be explicitly included in rate of return figures. Nevertheless, capital gains, particularly in farm real estate, have been a very real source of income to most farmers in the United States since the late 1930s.

A second point illustrated by the rates of return on capital for Farm Business A is that the return to owner equity over time should generally be higher and much more variable than the rate of return on total investment. This result is logical because the equity capital in any business receives the residual income remaining after all other factors have been paid. This residual income will normally be quite variable from year to year. It is reasonable, therefore, that the equity capital should receive a higher average rate of return over time to compensate for the added risk.

MANAGEMENT FACTORS. Various measures of efficiency other than those related directly to the income statement may be used to indicate the income-producing ability of a farm business. Several of the most commonly used measures are shown in Table 8.4. Data are given for Farm Business A, together with the averages for a group of similar farms in the area.

Management Return. Management return is derived from net farm income by deducting a wage for operator and family labor and a return on equity capital used in the business. Using 1971 data for Farm Business A we have

	Net farm income		$11,937
Less:	Operator and family labor	$6,000	
	Interest on equity capital		
	(92,700 avg for 1971 @ 6%)	5,562	11,562
	Management return		$ 375

It will be observed that management return is derived from net farm income by following a procedure similar to that used in computing the return on capital. Similar cautions to those noted there also should be observed. First, the amount deducted for operator and family labor is estimated on the basis of wage rates for farm labor in the area. The objective is to deduct an amount that would have to be paid hired labor to do the work, exclusive of management and supervision, performed by the operator and his family. Similarly, the objective in arriving at interest on equity capital is to estimate the opportunity return the operator could realize by investing his capital elsewhere, that is, the amount he could earn, say, by putting his money in nonfarm investments. Since both of these amounts are estimates, they may be higher or lower than if they were established in the marketplace. Second, management return for 1 year alone may be misleading as is evident from data in Table 8.4. Management return for several years should be considered in appraising the capability of the operation.

Comparison of Mr. A's management return with the management return for other farmers operating similar farms in the area provides a basis for comparison in rating Mr. A's relative performance as a manager. On the basis of the 6 years, 1966–71, Mr. A's management return averaged $3,845 compared with the area average of

TABLE 8.4: Efficiency Factor Data for Farm A and Area Average, 1966–71

	1966		1967		1968		1969		1970		1971		Six-year Avg	
	Farm A	Area Average	Farm A	Area Average	Farm A	Area Average	Farm A	Area Average	Farm A	Area Average	Farm A	Area Average	Farm A	Area Average
Management Return (dol)	9,247	7,638	846	(951)	6,468	752	6,977	1,207	(844)	(850)	375	1,407	3,845	1,534
Corn Yield (bu)	100	107	97	104	100	102	126	111	110	110	125	114	110	108
Gross Value of Crops per Rotated Acre (dol)	102	104	86	91	88	80	95	92	102	108	109	106	97	97
Livestock Income per $100 Feed Fed (dol)	159	147	134	131	171	154	161	177	146	134	138	150	152	149
Gross Income per Man-Year (dol)	30,272	27,370	27,510	22,090	29,182	24,320	33,770	29,800	29,800	28,900	28,897	43,658	29,905	29,356
Gross Income per $1.00 Expense (dol)	2.33	2.19	1.63	1.53	1.95	1.67	1.91	1.74	1.45	1.62	1.55	1.60	1.80	1.73
Machinery and Power Cost per Crop Acre (dol)	21.84	28.55	23.64	30.06	25.61	30.62	27.93	36.15	30.18	32.53	32.42	30.03	26.94	31.32

NOTE: Figures in parentheses are negative.

$1,534. Comparison of individual years shows that Mr. A's management return was above the average 5 years and below the average 1 year. Thus it appears Mr. A's managerial ability, as reflected by management returns, is above average for farmers in the area.

Crop Yields and Value. Crop yields provide another indication of a farmer's management ability. Corn yields obtained by Mr. A are about average for the area in which he operates. There is an indication that his corn yields are improving over time relative to the area average.

Gross value of crops per rotated acre provides a composite picture of crop production. Mr. A also compares favorably in this respect with the average of other farmers whose records were available in the area.

Livestock Income. Livestock income per $100 of feed fed is a measure of management efficiency in livestock production. It is preferable to analyze livestock enterprises individually. However, it is not always possible or economically feasible to keep the necessary records. In such cases, a composite picture of livestock income related to the cost of feed fed is used to portray the overall picture.

Mr. A's record indicates that in 4 of the 6 years his livestock returns per $100 of feed fed were above the average of other farmers with records in the area. Livestock returns are a function of the combination of livestock enterprises on the farm, of feeding efficiency, and of the price paid for livestock bought and the price received for livestock sold. Thus a farmer may be an effective manager in terms of physical efficiency, but ineffective in terms of marketing efficiency. The latter often is most critical. Information is not available for Farmer A, but the lower returns for 1970–71 lend additional support to the conclusion that market prices of feed and livestock were a factor.

Gross Income per Man. Gross income per man-year is a measure of efficiency in the use of labor. With the cost of labor continually increasing, this measure of efficiency is becoming increasingly important. The level of gross income per man-year will vary with the type of farm and the type of enterprise. The ratio naturally will be much lower for labor-intensive enterprises than for labor-extensive enterprises. The ratio is also influenced by the amount of machinery and equipment and other resources available. Other things being equal, gross income per man is higher when resources are ample than when they are restricted or inadequate. However, providing machinery, equipment, and other resources for use with labor costs money. The objective is to obtain a balance among the various factors of production. Mr. A appears to measure up fairly well to the area average in gross income produced per man in the 1966–71 period.

Gross Income per $1.00 Expense. Gross income per dollar of expense (another expression of the gross ratio discussed above) is an overall measure of efficiency in use of resources. Other things being equal, a high ratio indicates a high net income. However, it should be kept in mind that efficiency measures reflect only output relative to input and give no recognition to volume. A moderate level of efficiency, coupled with a large volume of business, may produce more net income than a high level of efficiency and low volume. Both efficiency and volume should be considered in management decisions. In all but 2 years of the 1966–71 period, Mr. A's gross income per dollar of expense was above the average of other similar farmers with records in the area.

Machinery and Power Cost. Machinery and power cost per crop acre is an important management factor since machinery and power comprise an important cost item that needs to be watched. Machinery and power costs tend to be high on many farms because the farmer has more machinery than is needed.

Mr. A's machinery and power costs per crop acre are low compared with the average of other similar farms with records in the area. He was below the average in 5 out of the 6 years, and substantially below in some. Again, there is evidence that Mr. A is the type of farmer who watches his expenses very carefully.

APPRAISAL OF INCOME STATEMENT DATA. The income statement gives a good picture of a farm business. When statements are available for several years, they indicate trends that are very valuable in financial analysis. If statements for other similar farms in the area are available, one can obtain a good picture of how the subject farm ranks on various financial and management factors.

It is important to recognize the limitations of the income statement as a source of data. First, some accounting entries such as inventory changes and allowances for unpaid labor and management cannot be precisely determined. Also, the income statement covers the whole farm business. Enterprise records may be needed to supplement the income statement. Nevertheless, the income statement is one of the best tools available for use in analyzing the business. Moreover, it provides valuable data for use in budget analysis to determine whether or not additional capital can be profitably employed in the business.

QUESTIONS AND PROBLEMS

1. What is an income statement? What does an income statement measure?
2. What are the three basic parts of an income statement?
3. Why is it desirable to measure trends in receipts, expenses, and net income?
4. How are the following items handled in an income statement: purchased feeder livestock and feed, changes in inventories, family living expenses, income taxes, interest paid on loans, principal payments on loans?
5. Outline and explain six financial ratios that may be used in analyzing the income of a farm business.
6. A farm business has total assets = $100,000; return on investment = 12 percent; total debt outstanding = $60,000; interest charges on debt = $4,800. Calculate the rate of return on owner equity. If the allowance for operator and family labor and management is $8,000, calculate net farm income.
7. Discuss the use of management factors in evaluating a farm business. What management factors are most important in analyzing farms in your area?
8. Examine published income statements for a large corporation in a nonfarm business and compare them with the income statement discussed in this chapter.

CHAPTER 9: FINANCIAL ANALYSIS OF THE FARM BUSINESS: THE CASH FLOW STATEMENT

THE *cash flow statement,* also known as a *sources and uses of funds* or *flow of funds* statement, summarizes all cash transactions affecting the business during a given period of time such as a month, quarter, or year. The balance sheet and income statement covered in the two previous chapters are important tools for measuring the financial position and progress of the business. However, many farm lenders have experienced situations where a borrower has a good balance sheet and a high net farm income, but is constantly slow in meeting his financial obligations. In many cases this rather perplexing situation can be diagnosed and resolved by analyzing the cash flow of the business. Even in the absence of a financial problem, a cash flow budget will aid in predicting sources and uses of funds just as plans for crop and livestock programs help to predict requirements for labor, materials, feed, and shelter. A dairyman with a herd of 100 milk cows would be in rather serious difficulty if he used up all his roughage 2 or 3 months before his next forage crops could be harvested. He would find it necessary to buy forage, perhaps when prices are at their seasonal high, or sell some of his dairy breeding stock. Similarly, he would also be in serious difficulty if he did not have enough cash on hand to pay his taxes, hired help, or meet his loan payments on their due dates. Failure to meet financial obligations in a timely manner would have an unfavorable effect on his credit rating and general reputation in the community.

CASH FLOW STATEMENT. The income statement, covered in the previous chapter, forms the starting point of the cash flow statement; however, the cash flow and income statements differ in their treatment of several important accounting entries.

A complete cash flow statement will include several nonfarm items such as income taxes, nonfarm income, and living expenses. Cash withdrawals for management salary and stock dividends would correspond to family living expenses in an incorporated farm business. The cash flow statement also gives a more complete accounting of debt transactions by showing principal payments and proceeds of new loans, whereas the income statement shows only interest payments. The cash flow statement more fully reflects purchases and sales of capital items such as breeding livestock, machinery, and real estate. Expenses associated with capital items are shown on the income statement as a relatively constant annual depreciation allowance. However, the full amount of any capital sales or purchases is shown in the cash flow statement covering the period in which they occur.

Annual Sources and Uses of Funds. Table 9.1 summarizes the sources and uses of funds for Farm Business A for the period 1966–71.

The first point to note is that total cash *inflows* (or sources of cash) are equal to total cash *outflows* (or uses of cash). An "after the fact" cash flow statement, or one covering past years' operations, should always balance, and a cash flow budget for the future should be planned to balance. Obviously, cash flow budgeting is a much easier task if several years of data are available, as is the case for Farm Business A.

A closer examination of the cash flow summary for 1971 in Table 9.1 will illustrate the major characteristics of the cash flow and show its relationship to the balance sheet and income statement. Cash farm receipts and cash farm operating expenses were taken directly from the income statement in Table 8.1. The $1,340 cash on hand on January 1, 1971, a source of cash for the year, and the $1,270 cash on hand on December 31, 1971, a use of cash, appear in the January 1, 1971 and 1972, balance sheets shown in Tables 7.4 and 7.5. As was noted in Chapter 7, Mr. A paid off (or renewed) the $31,692 in current debts which were outstanding on January 1, 1971, as well as $4,400 of his intermediate and long-term debts. During 1971 Mr. A took out new current loans (or renewed existing ones) totaling $19,543, which was the amount of current liabilities outstanding on December 31. No intermediate or long-term loans were added in 1971. These debt transactions can also be observed by comparing the January 1971 and 1972 balance sheets in Chapter 7.

Capital assets transactions for 1971 were relatively small. Mr. A sold (or traded in) machinery and equipment worth $74 and purchased machinery and equipment worth $778, giving net capital purchases (purchases minus sales or items traded in) of $704. Contrast this with the $3,622 depreciation allowance for 1971, as shown in the 1971 income statement in Table 8.1. In 1966 net capital purchases were $8,845 (excluding a $10,000 expenditure for a new home), while the depreciation allowance for 1966 was only $2,127. This wide variation in net capital asset transactions, compared to the relatively stable annual allowance for depreciation, illustrates why net income is not always a valid indicator of the financial liquidity of a business. Over time, depreciation and net capital expenditures should approximately

TABLE 9.1: Farm Business A—Sources and Uses of Funds, 1966-71

	1966	1967	1968	1969	1970	1971
CASH INFLOWS						
Cash farm receipts	$53,034	$53,146	$64,119	$69,583	$ 69,526	$76,651
Capital sales:						
Breeding livestock	...	...	...	...	...	...
Machinery and equipment	1,128	425	96	535	240	74
Land and buildings	...	...	...	...	...	...
Beginning cash balance	400	560	730	640	970	1,340
Loan proceeds: current	21,545	24,235	26,201	28,960	31,692	19,543
intermediate & long-term	2,780	...	...	...	...	...
Nonfarm cash income						
Other						
TOTAL CASH INFLOWS	$78,887	$78,366	$91,146	$99,718	$102,428	$97,608
CASH OUTFLOWS						
Cash farm operating expenses	$33,750	$45,621	$47,010	$54,201	$ 59,093	$50,942
Capital and purchases:						
Breeding livestock						
Machinery and equipment	9,973	425	1,632	4,817	437	778
Land and buildings	10,000	...	2,500	...	...	...
Ending cash balance	560	730	640	970	1,340	1,270
Principal payments on debt:						
Current debt	11,458	21,545	24,235	26,201	28,960	31,692
Intermediate & long-term debt	2,400	2,400	2,400	2,400	6,400	4,400
Family living expenses & personal savings	7,500	7,100	9,800	8,910	5,050	7,200
Income and social security tax	3,246	545	2,929	2,219	1,148	1,326
Other						
TOTAL CASH OUTFLOWS	$78,887	$78,366	$91,146	$99,718	$102,428	$97,608

balance out. In the case of Farm Business A, net machinery purchases averaged $2,610 per year between 1966 and 1971 and the average annual depreciation allowance on machinery was $2,215. In a rapidly expanding farm business, net capital expenditures will normally exceed depreciation allowances by a wide margin and a cash flow projection should be used to supplement the income statement as a measure of financial liquidity.

The cash flow summary in Table 9.1 illustrates the importance of allowing for family living and income taxes, which, incidentally, are first-priority items to be covered. In 1971 these two cash outflows accounted for $8,526 and over the 6-year period they ranged from a low of $6,198 to a high of $12,729. Failure to allow for these two major uses of cash could lead to rather serious liquidity problems.

Seasonal Cash Flow Patterns. The annual cash flow statements in Table 9.1 tell us a great deal about Farm Business A. However, a yearly cash flow statement neglects the seasonal variation in sources and uses of funds. A farm business may show a favorable cash position for an entire year but there may be extended periods during the year when uses exceed sources of funds, necessitating the use of short-term credit and reserves of cash to smooth out the fluctuations. Mr. A keeps the bimonthly cash flow record shown in Table 9.2, although monthly, quarterly, or semiannual records may be used, depending upon the size and type of the business.

The figures in the right-hand column of lines 1 through 20 in Table 9.2 are from the 1971 income statement. Line 20 illustrates the seasonal variation in cash receipts and expenditures. Although net cash income for 1971 was $25,709, cash operating expenses exceeded cash receipts during the March–April and May–June periods. Net cash operating deficits, together with capital expenditures, family living expenses, and income taxes, resulted in total cash deficits (lines 33 and 36) of $7,427 in March–April and $4,731 in May–June, and $2,026 in November–December.

A closer examination of lines 34 through 41 will illustrate how Mr. A used cash on hand and current loans to offset the March–June cash deficit. On March 1 he had $1,460 cash on hand. By April 30 the cash balance was $843, indicating that Mr. A used $617 in cash to partially finance the $7,427 deficit in March–April. The remaining $6,810 needed to cover the deficit came from current loans from his bank and/or current accounts with suppliers. Hence his current loan balance increased from $27,905 on March 1 to $34,715 on April 30.

The cash deficit for the May–June period was $4,731. In addition Mr. A increased his cash on hand from $843 to $936, an increase of $93, and he made payments of $483 on his current debt. The sum of the cash deficit, $4,731, the increase in cash, $93, and the $483

TABLE 9.2: Farm Business A—Bimonthly Cash Flow Summary, 1971

	Jan.-Feb.	Mar.-April	May-June	July-Aug.	Sept.-Oct.	Nov.-Dec.	Total 1971
1. Cash Receipts							
2. Cattle, fat	$ ...	$ ...	$ ...	$19,614	$30,048	$ ...	$49,662
3. Hogs	4,176	2,969	1,352	...	3,241	4,302	16,040
4. Crops	3,792	...	...	...	1,632	2,702	8,126
5. Government payments	...	...	502	2,226	...	...	2,728
6. Miscellaneous	...	...	...	...	...	95	95
7. Total	7,968	2,969	1,854	21,840	34,921	7,099	76,651
8. Cash Expenses							
9. Machinery and power	672	708	409	850	891	961	4,491
10. Hired labor	...	...	...	263	613	...	876
11. Livestock	109	114	42	19	102	52	438
12. Seed, fertilizer, etc.	...	...	2,610	272	474	852	4,208
13. Feed purchases	2,126	1,977	2,294	3,104	2,657	1,320	13,478
14. Livestock purchased	...	2,601	...	...	16,883	...	19,484
15. Miscellaneous operating	50	50	30	30	50	37	247
16. Taxes, property	...	1,415	...	...	1,414	...	2,829
17. Repairs & insurance on improv.	...	301	...	294	313	115	1,023
18. Interest	104	...	...	1,100	476	2,188	3,868
19. Total	3,061	7,166	5,385	5,932	23,873	5,525	50,942
20. Net Cash Income (Deficit)	4,907	(4,197)	(3,531)	15,908	11,048	1,574	25,709
21. Capital Sales							
22. Breeding livestock	$ ...	$ ...	$ ...	$ ...	$ ...	$ ...	$ ...
23. Machinery and equipment	...	74	...	...	...	...	74
24. Real estate & improvements	...	...	...	...	...	...	...
25. Nonfarm Cash Income	...	...	...	...	...	...	...
26. Capital Expenditures							

TABLE 9.2 (cont.)

	Jan.–Feb.	Mar.–April	May–June	July–Aug.	Sept.–Oct.	Nov.–Dec.	Total 1971
27. Breeding livestock	…	…	…	…	…	…	…
28. Machinery & equipment	…	778	…	…	…	…	778
29. Real estate & improvements	…	…	…	…	…	…	…
30. Principal Payments on Intermediate & Long-term Loans	…	…	…	…	2,000	2,400	4,400
31. Family Living Expense	1,000	1,200	1,200	1,300	1,300	1,200	7,200
32. Income Taxes	…	1,326	…	…	…	…	1,326
33. Cash Surplus (Deficit)*	3,907	(7,427)	(4,731)	14,608	7,748	(2,026)	12,079
34. Effect on Cash & Current Loans							
35. Beginning cash balance	1,340	1,460	843	936	1,132	1,354	1,340
36. Cash surplus (deficit)*	3,907	(7,427)	(4,731)	14,608	7,748	(2,026)	12,079
37. Beginning current loan bal.	31,692	27,905	34,715	39,589	25,127	17,601	31,692
38. Current loan obtained	526	6,810	5,307	1,264	860	2,887	19,543
39. Payment on current loan	4,313	0	483	15,676	8,386	945	31,692
40. Ending current loan bal.	27,905	34,715	39,539	25,127	17,601	19,543	19,543
41. Ending cash balance	1,460	843	936	1,132	1,354	1,270	1,270

NOTE: Figures in parentheses are negative.
* Lines 20, 22, 23, 24, 25—lines 27, 28, 29, 30, 31, 32.

137

current debt payment is $5,307, which was financed by new current loans taken out during May and June. As a result, his current debt outstanding increased from $34,715 on May 1 to $39,539 on June 30.

A similar analysis of the July–August and September–October periods will show how Mr. A used net operating cash surpluses that resulted from cattle sales to reduce his current loans balance from $39,539 to $17,601 and to increase cash on hand from $936 to $1,354. The $2,026 cash deficit in November–December was financed by an $84 reduction in cash on hand and a $1,942 net increase in current loans outstanding. The $1,942 net increase in loans outstanding resulted from payments on current loans of $945 plus taking out new loans totaling $2,887.

The seasonal cash flow pattern for Farm Business A illustrates the importance of having a ready reserve of cash and unused credit to smooth out cash surplus and cash deficit periods. In a business like Mr. A's, cash operating receipts and expenses tend to be concentrated during certain months, and periods when sources of cash are high rarely coincide with periods when uses of cash are high and vice versa. Table 9.2 illustrates the almost continuous process of borrowing and repaying current loans and open accounts with suppliers. The alert reader will notice that lines 38 and 39 in Table 9.2 do not add up to the 1971 totals. The sum of the bimonthly columns for line 38 is $17,654, or $1,899 lower than the 1971 total of $19,543. Similarly, the sum of the bimonthly columns for line 39 is $29,803, which is also $1,899 lower than the 1971 total of $31,692. This apparent discrepancy arises because in the process of borrowing and repaying current loans, Mr. A left $1,899 of the January 1, 1971, current loan balance unpaid (or $1,899 of the original balance was renewed). To prove that there was not an actual discrepancy, one can sum the beginning current loan balance ($31,692) plus new loans taken out ($17,654) and deduct payments on current loans ($29,803) to obtain the December 31, 1971, current liabilities figure, $19,543.

CASH FLOW BUDGETING. The primary usefulness of detailed cash flow records such as those shown in Tables 9.1 and 9.2 is to aid in *projecting* or *budgeting* sources and uses of cash for the coming year, or perhaps several years. There are two levels of cash flow budgeting: the seasonal budget and the annual or longer-run budget. Cash flow budgeting can be a time-consuming project, so the amount of detail should be consistent with the need for such records. In general, cash flow budgeting is recommended for (1) beginning farmers, (2) established farmers who are contemplating a major expansion or other change in their operation, (3) farmers who are carrying a relatively heavy debt load, and (4) farmers who have high-risk enterprises, or enterprises that produce wide seasonal variations in cash receipts and expenses.

Seasonal Cash Flow Budgeting. A projection of monthly, bimonthly, or quarterly sources and uses of funds will often result in a significant reduction in interest charges on short-term loans by facilitating the use of a budgeted loan or line of credit. A budgeted loan, such as the one illustrated in Table 9.3, has three primary advantages:

1. It provides an opportunity for the lender and the borrower to review and analyze the entire business operation together. In this analysis the lender has an opportunity to study the business and the farmer, and to determine how the financing institution might be of great assistance. The farmer has an opportunity to discuss various aspects of the business and of financing with the lender. Together they can analyze the amount of capital that can be profitably and safely used, and where it should be used within the business.
2. A budgeted loan provides assurance that funds will be available to carry out business operations. With a budgeted loan the lender gives an overall commitment of funds that the financing institution will provide during a given period. Without such an assurance the farmer may be unable to obtain credit to carry out plans under way.
3. A budgeted loan usually is more economical than a series of individual loans or one single payment loan for the entire amount. Interest is paid only for the period the funds are used, and repayment of a portion of the loan can be made at any time surplus cash is available. In the example of a budgeted loan given in Table 9.3, interest savings were $698.06 compared with an annual single payment loan.

A seasonal cash flow budget may also reduce interest charges by reducing the amount of short-term borrowing needed. The bi-monthly record for Farm Business A shown in Table 9.2 indicates that net operating income (line 20) tends to be relatively high in the July 1 to October 31 period. Assuming that this pattern is fairly consistent from year to year, Mr. A could reduce his need for short-term credit by arranging to have annual or semiannual expenditures such as payments on intermediate and long-term loans, capital expenditures, and insurance premiums fall due between July 1 and October 31. A monthly cash flow record would enable Mr. A to determine more precisely an optimum payment schedule for these expenses.

TABLE 9.3: Example of a Budgeted Loan (Hypothetical farm data)

Date	Purpose of Advance or Source of Repayment	Amount Advanced	Principal Repayment	Balance Outstanding	Days Outstanding	Interest Accrued @ 7½%
January 10	Purchased livestock	$ 6,000				
	Labor	500				
	Fertilizer	1,500				
	Interest on mortgage	1,750				
		$ 9,750		$ 9,750	85	$170.24
April 5	Seed	$ 1,250				
	Fuel	1,250				
		$ 2,500		12,250	71	178.70
June 15	Feed	$ 1,500				
	Fencing & bldg. repairs	1,750				
	Interest on mortgage	1,750				
		$ 5,000		17,250	5	17.72
June 20	Sale of hogs		$ 7,000	10,250	56	117.93
August 15	Taxes	$ 1,250		11,500	21	49.62
Sept. 5	Labor	1,500		13,000	96	256.43
Dec. 10	Sale of corn		7,500	5,500	10	11.30
Dec. 20	Sale of hogs		5,500*	...	...	
	TOTALS	$20,000	$20,000*			$801.94

* Also paid $801.94 interest. If the whole $20,000 had been borrowed for the entire year, the interest would have been $1,500 instead of the $801.94 actually paid on the budgeted loan.

The usefulness of a seasonal cash flow budget goes beyond the actual planning of short-term credit. The projection of cash surplus and deficit periods will help to eliminate unprofitable practices such as the forced or premature sales of livestock and crops to meet financial obligations. Anticipation of cash surplus periods will also help to reduce idle cash balances. Some farming enterprises generate wide seasonal fluctuations in cash receipts and there may be periods of 2 to 3 months or more when otherwise idle cash and checking account balances could be profitably invested in short-term nonfarm investments such as savings certificates and government or corporate securities. If $10,000 can be invested at $5\frac{1}{2}$ percent, it will earn nearly $46.00 per month, which over time would represent a significant amount of money.

Annual Cash Flow Budgeting. Obviously, the projected sources and uses of funds for a farm business must balance on a yearly basis if the business is to remain solvent; thus annual cash flow projections for a year or two in advance are just as important as a seasonal budget. An annual cash flow budget can be summarized as shown in Table 9.1 or the right hand column of Table 9.2.

The annual cash flow budget is particularly important if the farmer is just getting started or if significant changes are being made in the business. The heavy capital expenditures involved in starting or expanding a farm business must be incurred immediately, but it usually takes 2 or 3 years before operating receipts and expenses reach projected levels. This problem is well documented in a study of 20 Michigan dairy farmers who had carried out major expansions in their operations.[1] Interviews with these 20 farmers and their lenders revealed that many experienced one or more of the following problems:

1. Net income was much less than expected because crop yields and milk production per cow decreased, particularly during the early phases of the expansion.
2. Capital expenditures for buildings, machinery, and breeding stock, as well as increases in operating expenses, were generally underestimated, with the result that credit needs were underestimated.
3. Because of the difficulty in forecasting income and expenses, loan repayment schedules were out of balance with repayment capacity. Some of the farmers were forced to use several sources of credit to keep going.
4. Overall management ability did not increase proportionately with increases in the size of the operations.

---

1. Richard A. Benson and John R. Brake, *Financing Expansion to Large-Scale Dairy Farming*, Res. Rept. 76, Agr. Exp. Sta., Mich. State Univ., East Lansing, 1969.

Most farm lenders would agree that the expansion problems of these 20 Michigan dairymen are often encountered in any new or expanding farm business. In many cases carefully prepared annual cash flow budgets will help to avoid these problems. Conservative estimates of sources of cash and realistic projections of capital purchases and operating expenses will enable the farmer and his lender to accurately project credit needs and set up a repayment schedule that is in line with repayment capacity.

SOLVING CASH FLOW PROBLEMS. The cash flow analysis may indicate that sources of cash are not adequate to cover uses of cash. In this situation the entire business should be analyzed to determine ways of increasing cash inflows and reducing cash outflows.

Possibilities for substantially increasing cash inflows are sometimes limited. Operating receipts can sometimes be increased through higher crop yields and improved livestock production efficiency such as higher milk production per cow or more rapid rates of gain and better feed conversion in meat animal production. In many smaller farming operations, the use of surplus family labor to generate nonfarm income is a method of increasing cash inflows.

Cash outflows can be reduced by eliminating or reducing some operating expenses and by keeping capital expenditures, particularly machinery and equipment, in line with the size of the business. The tendency to overinvest in capital items is a common cause of financial difficulty.

Possibilities for reducing family living expenses and income taxes should be investigated. Farm families are entitled to a level of living equal to that enjoyed by their nonfarm counterparts; however, unnecessary expenditures on luxuries will only compound financial problems.

Income tax management is becoming more important as the size of the average farming operation increases. A full explanation of the tax laws as they apply to the farm business would occupy an entire book in itself. We can merely point out that careful tax management, perhaps with the assistance of a professional farm tax consultant, will usually reduce income taxes substantially. Some farmers pay hundreds of dollars more in income taxes than they need to because they fail to take advantage of the many ways of reducing taxes or deferring the payment of taxes to future years.[2] Alternatively, a farmer would

---

2. An excellent discussion of the more important ways of reducing federal income taxes is found in Donald R. Levi, *Agricultural Law,* Lucas Bros., Columbia, Mo., 1971, Chap. 8.

not want to underpay his taxes. Careful tax management can avoid this pitfall as well.

Selection of the appropriate loan repayment period is one of the most powerful tools for managing the cash flow of a business. Reference to Tables 9.1 and 9.2 reveals that new loan proceeds and principal and interest payments on short-term, intermediate-term, and long-term loans represent major sources and uses of funds in Farm Business A.

At first thought it may appear that if a loan is profitable it could be repaid without difficulty. The type of assets purchased with borrowed funds influences the amount of indebtedness that can be carried. Assets that are paid for from *gross* income in effect pay for themselves. Loans for such purposes may be termed *self-liquidating* loans if the repayment period coincides with the period in which the assets are used up in the business. Other assets must be paid for from *net* income, and loans made to acquire such assets are *not* self-liquidating. Repayment capacity as related to each of these types of assets is discussed in the following sections.

Repayment of Self-liquidating Loans. A self-liquidating loan is one made to an individual, corporation, or other business entity operating a profitable business for acquiring goods or services that are expended or used up in the production process. The goods may be expended or used up completely in one production period or they may be used for a number of years. Seed for annual crops is an example of the former; machinery and improvements are examples of the latter.

Assuming normal production and profitable farm operation, funds used to acquire goods and services that are expended in the production process are recouped as part of gross cash income when farm products are sold. For example, consider Farm Business M, assumed to be earning a 6 percent return on capital over and above all other variable and fixed costs, including management. Assume further that Farmer M borrows $10,000 at 6 percent annual interest to buy feed for hogs, and that the hogs are sold 4 months later. The $10,000 plus $200 interest will be received as a part of the gross income from the sale of the hogs. Hence, $10,200 of gross income will be available to repay the $10,000 feed loan plus $200 interest. Therefore, as this example illustrates, loans for operating expenses are self-liquidating, providing the business is paying its way. Similarly, the original capital investment in intermediate assets, such as machinery and breeding stock, and in improvements, such as buildings, is returned to the operator over a period of years as part of gross income. If loan repayment is scheduled to coincide with return of the original capital investment, loans for such purposes also are self-liquidating. However, repayment of loans for intermediate-term purposes usually is scheduled at a somewhat faster rate than the rate of depreciation and, therefore, such loans are only partially self-liquidating.

As indicated by these examples, loans that are self-liquidating are those for purchase of goods and services that depreciate, or are used up, in the production process. The original investment or purchase price, or wage paid in the case of labor, becomes a part of gross income as the products they have been used to produce are sold. Therefore, it is evident that such loans are paid from gross income and *as long as the business is profitable* funds will be available to repay the loans. The fact that the business must be profitable is emphasized, since if such is not the case, the self-liquidating loan turns into one that is not self-liquidating. When this occurs, repayment becomes even more difficult than with the usual farm loan that is not self-liquidating, since the resources acquired with the credit have been lost, thereby reducing the earning capacity of the operator.

Repayment of Loans That Are Not Self-liquidating. A loan that is *not* self-liquidating is one made to acquire goods that are not expended or used up in the production process. A loan to purchase good land (which does not erode or otherwise deteriorate as it is used in production) is an example of a loan that is not self-liquidating. The concept involved can be illustrated by further reference to Farm Business M referred to in the preceding section. Assume that Farmer M borrows $100,000 at 6 percent annual interest to buy good land. Since capital in Farm Business M was assumed to earn a 6 percent return, the $100,000 invested in land will produce $6,000 of gross income annually, just enough to pay the interest. Hence, there is no gross income to use for repayment of the $100,000 loan, as was the case when a $10,000 loan was used to buy hog feed. Thus a loan for purchasing land is not self-liquidating. It may contribute indirectly to repayment capacity by enabling the farmer to produce more net income than would be possible without use of the resources. But the land is not gradually used up in the production process. It does not depreciate and thereby become a part of the gross cash flow available to meet principal payments on the loan. Instead, good land continues as a perpetual resource to be used again and again in the production process. Since it is not used up—does not become a part of the commodities which are sold—it only produces an "annual rent" or interest on investment. As equity increases, the amount of annual rent required for interest payments gradually declines and net income gradually increases, thereby somewhat increasing repayment capacity.

How then are loans that are not self-liquidating to be repaid?

They must be paid from net cash income. By deducting estimated living expenses and taxes from net cash income, an indication is obtained as to the amount of cash that will be available for debt payments. Note that loan payments are subservient to minimum living expenses and taxes. The lender can expect nothing by way of repayment until these two prior claims have been satisfied.

In general, then, loan repayment terms should be coordinated with the use made of the loan proceeds and with the amount of cash available for debt servicing. For self-liquidating loans, the repayment period should range anywhere from a few months to as long as 10 years, depending upon how quickly the assets involved are used up in the production process. The repayment period for loans that are not self-liquidating should be as least 20 years. Some lenders write real estate loans for as long as 30 to 40 years, and some leave part of the loan on a perpetual basis by setting up a repayment plan that retires only part of the original principal.

The selection of loan repayment terms will be covered in some detail in Chapter 11. However, an example at this point will illustrate the effect of the repayment term on cash outflow. Consider a $1,000, 7 percent loan to be repaid in equal annual installments that, over the total repayment term, will retire both principal and interest. If the loan is repaid in 1 year, the single payment would be $1,070. The approximate annual payments for some representative longer repayment periods would be 3 years, $381.10; 5 years, $243.90; 10 years, $142.40; 20 years, $94.40; 30 years, $80.60. These loan payments were obtained by multiplying entries in the 7 percent column of Appendix Table 3 by $1,000. The entries in Appendix Table 3 are rounded to four decimal places; thus the estimated payments may differ from the exact payment by a few cents. The effect of using a 20-year term instead of a 5-year term is a reduction in the annual payment of about $149.50 for each $1,000 borrowed. On a $50,000 loan, the difference would be $7,475, enough to cover the annual living costs for some farm families.

The foregoing would suggest that financial liquidity can be significantly improved by using longer loan repayment terms. The problem of too much short-term and intermediate-term debt can often be solved by refinancing the entire debt load over a longer term using long-term assets as collateral. Normally, loans can be repaid at a faster rate than is called for in the loan contract by *prepaying,* that is, by applying additional payments on the principal when surplus funds are available. However, some lenders charge a prepayment penalty to cover the fixed costs of making and servicing a loan that is repaid much sooner than was specified in the original contract. Also, prepayments normally do not reduce the payments due in succeeding years. Instead, the total payments called for in the original loan contract are applied to the reduced principal balance outstanding. Thus the loan will be completely repaid in a shorter period of time. The prepayment provisions of any loan contract should be fully investigated before the loan is taken out. There are some lenders, it is important to note, who accept reserve payments that bear the same interest as the mortgage loan. These reserves are kept for use in a year when the borrower may have difficulty in paying both interest and principal. In this way the borrower is able to use the surplus in good years to meet the deficits in poor years, and not accelerate the final due date on his loan.

SUMMARY. Financial liquidity is the ability of the ongoing business to meet financial obligations in an orderly manner. A cash flow record of past years' operations, together with realistic projections of annual and seasonal sources and uses of funds, is a valuable tool in analyzing the liquidity position of the business.

Minor cash flow problems can usually be solved by maintaining a high level of operating receipts and by keeping operating and capital expenditures in line with the size of the business. Tailoring loan repayment terms to the purpose of the loan and to the level of net income is probably the most important tool in cash flow management.

QUESTIONS AND PROBLEMS
1. Explain the purpose of a cash flow statement. Discuss the differences between an income statement and a cash flow statement.
2. How are the following items handled in a cash flow statement: depreciation, income taxes, family living expenses, interest payments on debt, principal payments on debt, nonfarm income, new loans taken out?
3. What is the usefulness of a budgeted loan for the lender? For the borrower?
4. Discuss the circumstances under which a lender should ask for an annual cash flow budget. A seasonal or monthly cash flow budget.
5. Outline the possibilities for solving cash flow problems in a farm business.
6. Contrast self-liquidating and nonself-liquidating loans as they relate to repayment capacity.

REFERENCES
Falls, S. D. "Farm Firm Debt Capacity: An Empirical Study of Northeastern Ohio Dairy Farms." Unpublished M.S. thesis, Ohio State Univ., 1972.

Mueller, Allan G. "Flow of Funds Analysis in Farm Financial Management."
    Jour. Farm Econ., Aug. 1966, pp. 661–67.
Wehrly, J. S., and Atkinson, J. H. *Debt Loan Capacity of Farms.* Purdue
    Univ., Agr. Exp. Sta. Res. Bull. 780, 1964.
Wirth, M. E., and Brake, John R. *The Michigan Farm Credit Panel: Cash
    Flows and Use of Credit, 1961.* Mich. Agr. Exp. Sta. Res. Rept. 8, 1961.

CHAPTER 10: INTEREST RATE TERMINOLOGY AND CALCULATION

THE COST of capital plays an important role in both allocation of capital within the business and in determining the amount of credit that can be profitably employed. Thus an understanding is needed of the factors that influence interest rates, methods used in figuring interest costs, and other costs in addition to interest that may be encountered in obtaining credit.

FACTORS INVOLVED IN THE INTEREST RATE. Interest is the price paid for use of money or capital; the interest rate is the ratio of the interest to the capital involved. Interest usually is considered to include payment for three things:

1. Pure interest, such as the rate paid on government bonds where there is a minimum of risk or other costs involved. Authorities differ somewhat in their views regarding pure interest. Classical economists viewed pure interest as representing the productivity of real capital. However, from the monetary approach, pure interest is the cost of forbearance or delaying the use of money. A similar view was held by Keynes who considered interest to be "the reward for parting with liquidity for a specified period."[1] With this dual meaning of pure interest, some economists have chosen to consider nonliquidity as a separate factor from pure interest in explaining the interest rate. According to this view, the longer the term of the loan, the greater the nonliquidity. Thus the nonliquidity part of the interest rate would be higher on long-term than on short-term loans.
2. Risk of losing the money loaned. If the risk is high, the interest rate is also high. Lenders, as a rule, compete actively for large loans in low-risk territory. High-risk areas are avoided by lending agencies that are looking for relatively safe loans. These agencies are willing to lend on farm mortgages at 7 percent in the Corn

---

1. John M. Keynes, *The General Theory of Employment, Interest and Money* (New York: Harcourt, 1936), p. 167.

Belt rather than loan at 9 percent in the drouth sections of the Great Plains.

3. Management and associated costs in making and servicing a loan. This aspect of interest involves both size and term of loan. Overhead costs often run about as high on a small loan as on a large loan. Or, put another way, management and servicing costs per dollar loaned typically run much higher on small than on large loans. As a result, the interest rate on small loans typically is higher than on large loans. Two real estate loans of unequal size, one of $10,000 and the other of $1,000, will illustrate this point. The two farm owners may be operating in the same territory, one with a large, highly productive farm and the other with an unproductive farm having a high percentage of pasture. The applications for the loans, which will be filled out by the lender or his agent, will require the same amount of time for both borrowers. The appraisal, determination of the amount to lend, the making out of loan papers, and closing or completion of the loan will require the same amount of time and expense. Finally, the collection of interest, and any correspondence or trips to the farm in regard to collections will be about the same for both farms. It is possible, of course, to charge each farmer a flat amount for application, appraisal, collection, and general supervision expense in addition to the interest charge. But in any event the cost of making the $10,000 loan is not much greater than that for making the $1,000 loan. If the fixed overhead, exclusive of risk, averages $20 annually for each loan, and the cost of funds to the lender is 5 percent, the lender will need 5.2 percent to break even on the $10,000 loan and the 7 percent to break even on the $1,000 loan. The situation is similar for long-term versus short-term loans. Initial overhead costs of making the loan are about as high for short-term as for long-term loans. Moreover, short-term loans with frequent payments (such as monthly installment loans) involve much more service expense (accounting, etc.), and sometimes more management, than longer-term loans with only one or two payments per year. This is a primary reason that interest rates on short-term loans usually are higher than on long-term loans.

Demand for money and the supply of money in the economy have an important influence on interest rates. When product demand and associated income are expected to be high, demand for capital to expand production strengthens. With limited capital available in the economy, interest rates tend to rise under such circumstances, with the result that people tend to save more. The increased supply of capital that is generated is loaned to business firms, which facilitates expanding production. When production has increased sufficiently to supply the demand for products, the demand for capital subsides and interest rates tend to level off or decline. Thus, as this simplified example illustrates, the forces of demand and supply operate in the money market to determine an equilibrium interest rate in much the same way that demand and supply operate in any competitive market to establish an equilibrium price.

While interest rates are subject to economic laws, they are also influenced to a great degree by man-made laws and policy. Monetary phenomena play a very significant role in the economy today, much more than formerly. The interest rate is, to a degree, a monetary phenomenon as evidenced by policy and operations of the Federal Reserve System and the central banks in other countries. Thus monetary measures are used to cause changes in the money supply and in interest rates needed to bring about desired changes in the economy. The way in which this is accomplished is outlined in a later chapter dealing with commercial banks and the Federal Reserve System.

There are a number of different ways in which interest may be computed, depending upon the terms of the loan and the policy of the lender. The method used makes a difference in the actual rate paid. Thus to make an intelligent decision on whether it will pay to use credit and, if so, on where and how much to borrow, a borrower needs to understand the various methods of charging interest.

Terminology from the mathematics of finance field will be used in the discussion of methods of charging interest. This terminology is well defined and consistently used in literature on mathematics of finance, which contributes to understanding the concepts involved. On the other hand, the student of finance should be aware of what appears to be another set of terminology used in the consumer finance field. This can be confusing since a number of the same terms are used in the two sets of terminology but with different meanings. Terminology long in use and in publications in the mathematics of finance field appears to have been misapplied as consumer credit developed. This hypothesis is supported by the fact that terms are used in consumer credit literature without being clearly defined or explained. As a result, the terminology is not consistently used from one publication to another. Thus it appears desirable to use terminology as defined in mathematics of finance.[2]

Simple Interest. Simple interest is the product of the principal, the time in years, and the annual rate of interest. For example, the interest on $1,200 for 1 year with the rate of interest at 6 percent

2. John R. Brake, *Interest Rate Terminology and Calculation,* Agr. Econ. Rept. 13, Mich. State Univ., East Lansing, Mar. 1966, pp. 3–4.

per annum equals $72.

With simple interest, the amount of interest is computed on the principal for the entire period of the loan. Only one payment of interest is made when the loan matures. Thus simple interest is suitable for only short periods of time, usually 1 year or less.[3]

When simple interest is computed for part of a year, the time in years is a fraction, the numerator being the term of the loan in days and the denominator the days in a year. When 365 days (366 days in a leap year) are used in the denominator of the fraction, the amount is called *exact* simple interest. For example, with a 60-day loan, using a fraction of 60 ÷ 365 (366 in a leap year) gives the exact amount of interest on the loan. When 360 days are used in the denominator of the fraction, the amount is called *ordinary* simple interest. Thus, with a 60-day loan, using a fraction of 60 ÷ 360 gives the ordinary simple interest due on the loan.

The 360 days are usually used in computing simple interest by commercial lenders due to the ease of computation. The number 360 has 22 factors (2, 3, 4, 5, 6, 8, 9, 10, 12, 15, 18, 20, 24, 30, 36, 40, 45, 60, 72, 90, 120, and 180) whereas 365 has only two (5 and 73) and 366 only three (2, 3, and 61). Thus computations can be performed more easily by using 360 than by using 365 or 366.

Since 360 is smaller than 365 (366), ordinary simple interest is always slightly greater than exact simple interest. Lenders also prefer ordinary simple interest for this reason.

Compound Interest. Compound interest is involved in saving or in use of credit whenever interest is paid more than once during the period involved. For example, compound interest is involved when interest is paid two, four, twelve, or n times per year on a savings account or on a loan. With this type of situation, interest paid for one period, either in cash or by adding it to one's account, is said to be *converted* to principal, or *compounded*. The interval between successive conversions is called the *conversion period*. The total amount due at the end of a conversion period is called the *compound amount*. *Compound interest* is the difference between the compound amount and the beginning principal. The *compound interest rate* is the rate per conversion period that is charged on the outstanding balance for that period; that is, the compound interest divided by the outstanding balance.

Compound interest is usually thought of in relation to growth of an investment. This subject was discussed in some detail in Chapter 3. However, compound interest has similar significance in use of credit. Borrowing is, of course, the converse of saving and, therefore,

---

3. It should be noted that simple interest does not correctly describe the nominal rate, as usage often implies. The nominal rate will be defined later.

TABLE 10.1:   Illustration of Compound Interest on a $100 Installment Loan with Interest at 1 Percent per Month

| Period | Beginning Balance | Interest | Periodic Installment | | | Ending Balance |
			Total	Interest	Principal	
1	$100.0000	$1.0000	$0	$0	$0	$101.0000
2	101.0000	1.0100	0	0	0	102.0100
3	102.0100	1.0201	0	0	0	103.0301
4	103.0301	1.0303	0	0	0	104.0604
5	104.0603	1.0406	0	0	0	105.1010
6	105.1006	1.0510	0	0	0	106.1520
7	106.1516	1.0615	0	0	0	107.2135
8	107.2131	1.0721	0	0	0	108.2856
9	108.2851	1.0829	0	0	0	109.3685
10	109.3679	1.0937	0	0	0	110.4622
11	110.4616	1.1046	0	0	0	111.5668
12	111.5662	1.1157	0	0	0	112.6825

both are affected by the same principles.

The similarity of the effect of compound interest on borrowing and saving can be demonstrated, as suggested by Brake,[4] by use of an example such as is presented in Table 10.1. An installment loan of $100 with interest at 1 percent per month is assumed. It is assumed that no installment payments are made during the year so the results can be readily checked against Appendix Table 1, which shows the amount of 1 at compound interest.

At the end of the first period (month) the interest due is $1.00 (see Table 10.1). Since no payment is made, the interest is converted to principal, making the ending balance $101.00. Interest for the second period is increased, therefore, to $1.01, which in turn is converted to principal, making the ending balance $102.01. This process continues each month and at the end of the year the compound amount is $112.68. Thus the compound interest for the year is $12.68, 68 cents more than with 12 percent simple interest.

Now compare Table 10.1 with Appendix Table 1. The balance at the end of the first period given in Table 10.1 is $101.00. The comparable figure in Appendix Table 1 is found by moving down the column headed *n* to 1 and across to the column headed 1%. Since the appendix table is set up on the basis of $1.00, the figures in the body of the table must be multiplied by 100 to make them comparable with those in Table 10.1. Multiplying $1.01 by 100 gives $101.00, the same as the ending balance for period 1 in Table 10.1. Similarly, the balance at the end of period 12 given in Table 10.1 is $112.68. Moving

4. Brake, p. 23.

down column n in Appendix Table 1 to 12 and across to 1% we find 1.1268 which when multiplied by 100 gives $112.68, the same as the ending balance for period 12 in Table 10.1. Since the compound amount of a $100 loan is the same as the amount of $100 saved at compound interest, it is evident that compounding interest has the same effect when money is borrowed as when it is saved.

The effect of compound interest involved in installment loans is the same regardless of whether the interest is converted to principal periodically, as in the above example, or whether it is paid at the end of each period. This point may be illustrated by comparing two $1,200 loans, each with a quoted annual rate of 6 percent. Interest is payable annually on loan No. 1 and semiannually on loan No. 2. Thus interest payments each year on the two loans are as follows:

	Loan No. 1	Loan No. 2
Interest paid end of 6 months	0	$36
Interest paid end of year	$72	36
Total	$72	$72

Obviously, the dollar amount of interest paid on the two loans is the same—$72. However, half the interest on loan No. 2 was paid at midyear. Therefore, borrower No. 2 did not have use of the $36 in his business the last 6 months of the year as did borrower No. 1. Since he was borrowing money at 6 percent interest, paying the $36 at midyear cost borrower No. 2, in effect, $1.08 more than borrower No. 1. In other words, compounding the interest semiannually on loan No. 2 increased the interest cost by $1.08.

In the above example, borrower No. 2 paid $36 interest semi-annually on his $1,200 loan with a quoted annual rate of 6 percent. The $36 may be obtained by *converting* the quoted annual rate of 6 percent to 3 percent semiannually. In other words, the 6 percent annual rate may be *compounded* semiannually and used to find the amount of semiannual interest. Such a periodic rate (rate per period) is referred to as the *compound rate,* the *true rate,* and the *actuarial rate.* The three terms are synonymous. Thus the *true* interest rate is the interest rate applied to the principal each payment period. Therefore, an annual rate can be correctly referred to as a true rate only when payments are made on an annual basis. This point should be given special attention since the term *true rate* is often incorrectly used in writings pertaining to interest.

Nominal and Effective Rates of Interest. When interest is paid two or more times per year, the quoted annual rate is called the *nominal annual rate,* which is usually shortened to the nominal rate. Thus, if a loan is payable semiannually and the quoted annual

rate is 6 percent, the true rate is 3 percent, and the nominal rate is
6 percent. When rates are quoted on a periodic basis, the nominal
rate represents the periodic rates converted to an annual basis. For
example, if the true interest rate is $\frac{1}{2}$ percent per month, the nominal
rate is 6 percent.

As indicated in the discussion of compound interest, when interest is converted more than once per year, the compound interest
is greater than when it is compounded annually. For example, with
$100 invested for 1 year at 6 percent, compounded annually, the ac-
tual interest earned is $6.00. However, if the quoted rate is com-
pounded semiannually, the actual interest earned is $6.09. Thus, be-
cause of the effect of compounding, the actual rate earned is 6.09
percent while the nominal rate is 6.0 percent. The rate of interest
actually earned in a year is called the *effective annual rate* of interest.
The effective rate is obtained by compounding the true rate for a
period of 1 year.

When the true rate is compounded more than once a year the
result is an effective annual rate that is larger than the nominal rate.
The two rates are equivalent, however, since they produce the same
amount of interest. Thus a nominal rate of 6 percent compounded
semiannually is equivalent to an effective rate of 6.09 percent.

The degree to which the effective rate exceeds the nominal rate
depends upon the level of the interest rate and the frequency of conversion. The difference between the two rates is relatively small at
low levels (assuming the same number of conversions of interest to
principal per year) but increases as the rate increases. With a nominal
rate of 6 percent, the difference is 0.09 percentage points (the effective
rate is 6.09 percent) when the conversion is semiannual, approximately
0.136 percentage points when conversion is quarterly, approximately
0.168 percentage points when conversion is monthly, and approximately 0.183 percentage points when conversion is daily.[5] Thus, while
the nominal rate provides a fairly good basis for comparing loans,
the effective rate provides a more precise basis.

Discounted Loans. A lender sometimes will make what is called a
discounted loan in which the interest is deducted from the principal at the time the loan is made. For example, a lender may
make a $1,200 loan for 1 year discounted at 6 percent. The borrower
would receive $1,128 ($1,200 minus 6 percent) and would pay the
lender $1,200 at the end of the year. The 6 percent rate in this case
is called the *discount interest rate*. Thus, in computing the actual
amount of interest to be paid, the discount interest rate is applied

---

5. H. E. Stelson, *Mathematics of Finance* (Princeton, N.J.: D. Van Nostrand, 1963), p. 34.

to the maturity value of the loan, that is, the value of the note. In contrast, simple interest is figured on the principal—$1,128 in the example. As a result, the simple interest rate on a given discounted loan is always higher than the discount interest rate.

Add-on Interest. With the usual short-term installment plan loan, interest is calculated on the beginning balance and then added to the principal to obtain the amount to be repaid in equal periodic installments. For example, a lender may make a $1,200 installment plan loan to be repaid in 12 equal monthly payments. If he uses a 6 percent rate, he would add $72 to the $1,200, and the payments would be $106 per month. In this example the 6 percent rate used by the lender is correctly referred to as a 6 percent *add-on interest rate*.

It should be noted that an add-on interest rate is not a nominal rate. As indicated above, a nominal rate is figured on the principal balance outstanding, with recognition being given to periodic principal payments. In contrast, the add-on rate is applied to the initial principal, disregarding principal payments that are made periodically throughout the term of the loan.

DETERMINING THE NOMINAL INTEREST RATE. As indicated by the preceding discussion, interest is charged in many different ways, and the method used has a significant influence on the amount of interest paid and on the interest rate on a loan. Interest paid on a discounted loan is greater, other things being equal, than with compound interest. Large differences prevail among various types of installment plan loans. On one type the interest charged is computed on an annual basis on the outstanding balance. On a second type an annual rate is used, but it is applied on the original principal, with no reduction being made for payments on the principal during the year. The amount of interest on the second type of installment plan loan is about twice the amount paid on the first type. Hence, with different types of loans and methods of charging interest, it is difficult to make comparisons. The objective of this section is to present material that will aid in finding the nominal rate that is being charged.

Equal Payment, Regularly Timed Loans. There are a number of methods for determining the approximate nominal interest rate on installment plan loans when payments are equal and regularly timed. Three of these are considered here. Some are more accurate than others and, in general, the methods that give the greatest accuracy tend to be the most complex. Thus the degree of accuracy desired should be considered in selecting the method to use.

CONSTANT RATIO EQUATION. The constant ratio equation can be used to approximate the nominal interest rate when the other terms are known. It is as follows:

$$\frac{2In}{Bt(n + 1)} = \text{Approximate nominal interest rate} \qquad (10.1)$$

where I is the interest or finance charge, n is the number of periodic payments required to liquidate the loan, B is the beginning principal (face amount) of the loan, and t is the term of the loan in years. Use of this equation may be illustrated by the example in the discussion of add-on interest. The principal was $1,200, the finance charges were $72, the number of payments was 12, and the term of the loan was 1 year. We, therefore, have

$$\frac{(2)(72)(12)}{(1,200)(1)(12 + 1)} = 11.08 \text{ percent}$$

The constant ratio equation is based on the assumption that the ratio of principal to interest in each periodic payment is the same as the ratio of the initial principal to the total interest or finance charge.[6] The assumption is not in accord with the facts, however, since with an even-payment installment plan loan the interest portion of each periodic payment gradually decreases and the principal portion gradually increases. Moreover, the longer the term of a loan, the greater the error in the assumption upon which the constant ratio equation is based. Therefore, Equation 10.1 gives only an approximation of the nominal interest rate, and a relatively poor one at that, particularly for long-term loans. The rate obtained is usually a little larger than the actual nominal rate.

STELSON EQUATION. A more accurate equation than the one just discussed has been presented by Stelson:

$$\frac{2Im}{n(B + a)} = \frac{2I}{t(B + a)} = \text{Approximate nominal interest rate}$$

$$(10.2)[7]$$

6. Ibid., p. 201.
7. Ibid., p. 76. The m was added by John R. Brake to put the interest rate on a nominal basis. See Brake, p. 16.

where m is the number of payment periods per year, a is the amount of each periodic payment, I is the interest or finance charge, n is the number of periodic payments required to liquidate the loan, B is the beginning principal, and t is the term of the loan in years. Using our add-on interest example, B is \$1,200, I is \$72, m is 12, n is 12, t is 1, and a is \$106. Therefore,

$$\frac{(2)(72)(12)}{(12)(1,200 + 106)} = \frac{(2)(72)}{(1)(1,200 + 106)} = 11.03 \text{ percent}$$

According to Stelson, Equation 10.2 will always give a closer approximation to the nominal interest rate than the constant ratio equation.[8] The rate will be on the high side except when n is very small.

DIRECT RATIO EQUATION. While somewhat more complex, the direct ratio equation gives a very close approximation to the nominal interest rate.[9] The equation is as follows:

$$\frac{6Im}{3B(n + 1) + (n - 1)I} = \text{Approximate nominal interest rate}$$

$$(10.3)[10]$$

where I is the interest or finance charge, m is the number of periodic payments per year, B is the beginning principal, and n is the number of periodic payments required to liquidate the loan.

Applying this equation to our add-on interest example, we have

$$\frac{(6)(72)(12)}{(3)(1200)(12 + 1) + (12 - 1)(72)} = 10.89 \text{ percent}$$

The direct ratio equation assumes that the amount of interest in each installment is distributed according to the sum of digits. For example, in a 12-month installment loan the first installment is assumed to include $12/78$ of the total interest, the second installment $11/78$ of the total interest, and so on until the last installment includes only $1/78$ of the total interest charged on the loan. The approximate nominal interest obtained by using the direct ratio equation is always very slightly too small.

---

8. Ibid., p. 76.
9. Ibid., p. 78.
10. Brake, p. 17. A similar equation is given by Stelson, p. 79.

A modification of the direct ratio equation

$$\frac{2I}{B(n + 1)} \left[\frac{3B(n + 1) + (2n + 1)I}{3B(n + 1) + (2n + 1)I} \right] m = \text{Approximate nominal interest rate}$$

$$(10.4)[11]$$

gives a very accurate approximation of the nominal interest rate. The nominal rate derived by use of this equation is, however, very slightly large. Applying Equation 10.4 to our add-on interest example gives an approximate nominal rate of 10.90 percent.

Comparing the approximate nominal interest rates for our add-on installment plan loan derived by use of the methods outlined above provides an indication of the relative accuracy of the equations. The rates were:

The constant ratio equation	11.08 percent
The Stelson equation	11.03 percent
The direct ratio equation	10.89 percent
The direct ratio equation, modified	10.90 percent

The nominal rate is actually 10.90 percent.

Equal Payment, Irregularly Timed Loans. With some installment plan loans, payments are equal and regularly timed except for the last. The last payment is regularly timed, but the amount may be more or less than the preceding payments. In such cases the Stelson equation can be used to calculate the approximate nominal interest rate by letting a represent the amount of the last payment.[12]

A more accurate equation, corresponding to Equation 10.3, which also may be used, is:

$$\frac{6Im}{3n(B + a) + I(n - 4)} = \text{Approximate nominal interest rate}$$

$$(10.5)[13]$$

where I refers to the interest or finance charge, m is the number of periodic payments per year, n is the number of periodic payments required to liquidate the loan, B is the beginning principal, and a is used to represent the last payment.

Some installment plan loans are set up so that payments do not commence immediately. For example, on a monthly installment loan, payments may not start until the third month. In such cases the fol-

---

11. Stelson, p. 79. I have added m to the equation to put the rate on a nominal basis.
12. Ibid., p. 77.
13. Ibid., p. 79.

lowing equation may be used to obtain the approximate nominal interest rate:

$$\frac{2I}{(t + F)(B + a)} = \text{Approximate nominal interest rate} \quad (10.6)[14]$$

I is the total interest or finance charge, t is the term of the loan in years, F is the proportion of the year that elapses before payments start, B is the beginning principal of the loan, and a is the amount of the periodic payment.

When payments on an installment loan follow a specified but irregular schedule, the following equation will give an approximation of the nominal interest rate:

$$\frac{12In}{BS} = \text{Approximate nominal interest rate} \quad (10.7)[15]$$

I, n, and B are used as defined above and S represents the sum of the numbers of those months in the future when payments are to be made.

Unequal Payment, Irregularly Timed Loans. If a loan is repaid in unequal and irregularly timed installments, the nominal interest rate cannot be very closely approximated with a formula.[16] Consider the case where the payments on a $2,000 loan are as follows: $610 in 4 months; $610 in 12 months; $510 in 18 months; and $510 in 24 months. The *equivalent balance* method can be used to estimate the nominal interest rate in simpler cases; however, in more complex cases, a completer program offers the only feasible method of accurately estimating the nominal rate.

First, assume that the total interest or finance charge, $240, is divided equally among the four installments. Thus each installment is regarded as a separate loan payment consisting of $60 interest. Under this assumption the principal payments would be $550 in 4 months; $550 in 12 months; $450 in 18 months; and $450 in 24 months. These four *separate loans* can be converted to an annual equivalent balance as follows:

The $550 repaid in 4 months is equivalent to $4/12 \times \$550 = \$183.33$ outstanding for 1 year.
The $550 repaid in 12 months is equivalent to $550 outstanding for 1 year.
The $450 repaid in 18 months is equivalent to $18/12 \times \$450 = \$675$ outstanding for 1 year.
The $450 repaid in 24 months is equivalent to $24/12 \times \$450 = \$900$ outstanding for 1 year.

---

14. Brake, p. 19.
15. Ibid., p. 20.
16. Ibid., p. 21.

Summing the annual equivalents gives $183.33 + $550.00 + $675.00 + $900.00 = $2,308.33 for 1 year. Dividing this into the $240 total interest charge gives an estimated nominal interest rate of 10.4 percent. The assumption that the total interest charges are evenly distributed among all payments is essentially a constant ratio approach; hence the equivalent balance method provides an approximation which tends to be on the high side.

Carrying Charges and Fees. Instead of interest as such, some time payment plans involve carrying charges that are added to the balance due. Carrying charges are often called by other names, such as time differential payments and credit or finance charges. In some cases inspection fees and sales commissions include some carrying charges. The carrying charge may take the form of a smaller discount or an addition to the purchase price. If a percentage rate is used, it will be applied to the face amount of the loan rather than to the unpaid balance. Where carrying charges are involved, the cost of credit is almost always greater than where a loan is secured from a commercial bank, the Production Credit Association, or other conventional lender.

A carrying charge might well be considered a red flag calling for careful consideration and study of costs involved. An example will illustrate the cost of such credit. Assume you are going to trade your old tractor on a new one costing $2,250. The allowance on the old tractor is $1,000, leaving $1,250. A carrying charge of $125 is added, making a balance due of $1,375. Principal payments of $687.50 are due at the end of 6 months and of 12 months. Substituting these figures in Equation 10.2, given above, gives

$$\frac{(2)(125)(2)}{(2)(1250 + 687.50)} = \frac{500}{3875} = 12.9 \text{ percent}$$

as the approximate nominal rate of interest.

Occasionally interest is charged in addition to the carrying charge. In such cases interest usually is charged on the face amount of the loan plus the carrying charge, with the result that the actual interest charge is very high.

To figure the cost of credit, it is necessary to include, in addition to the interest, all fees and charges. The actual cost of a 5 percent loan may be higher than that of a 7 percent loan because of the heavy fees and charges on the first loan. Application fees, inspection fees, and other loan charges may easily amount to as much as the interest on a small loan for a short period. For example, loan fees and charges of $7.50 on a 5 percent loan of $300 for 4 months are more than the interest. In consequence, comparisons of loans on a cost basis should always be made after all charges have been figured.

Many short-term and some intermediate-term loans are repaid on an "open" basis. In the case of open account credit provided by merchants and dealers, for example, the borrower is usually billed every 30 days, at which time the outstanding balance on the account is due. Usually there is no specific charge for this type of credit unless it runs for more than 30 days. Accounts outstanding for more than 30 days may be subject to an interest charge, such as $1\frac{1}{2}$ percent per month. Alternatively, there may be a "discount" for customers who pay within a certain period of time following the billing date. The terms might be quoted as "2/10/net 30," which means that there will be a 2 percent discount if the account is paid within 10 days, otherwise the balance (or net amount) is due in full within 30 days.

Very often the interest charges on extended charge accounts are very high. A $1\frac{1}{2}$ percent per month finance charge is equivalent to a nominal rate of at least 18 percent per year, the exact rate depending upon whether the monthly percentage finance charge is calculated on the balance outstanding *before or after* payments on the account are deducted. A borrower who passes up the discount when the terms are "2/10/net 30" would be paying a nominal rate of approximately 37.2 percent.[17]

Payment of insurance premiums on a semiannual, quarterly, or monthly basis also involves "interest" charges that are much higher than might be expected. Suppose, for example, that an insurance premium can be paid semiannually with a semiannual premium equal to 52 percent of the annual premium. The approximate nominal rate of interest on this "loan" would be 16.7 percent.[18]

Commissions and Other Loan Requirements. Commissions may be either a flat fee or a fixed percentage of the principal. The fixed percentage commission by itself is economically unsound, yet it is the traditional and common method. Federally sponsored agencies have been eliminating the fixed percentage plan, but it is still commoner than it should be. The chief argument in favor of this method is that it is the easiest and simplest method of paying the individual

---

17. Suppose the account balance is $100. The borrower could retire the loan by paying $98 by the 10th day or $100 between the 10th and 30th days. Thus he would be paying a $2 interest charge on a $98 loan outstanding for *at the most* 20 days. The approximate nominal rate would be $2/98 \times 365/20 \times 100 = 37.2\%$.

18. Consider a $100 annual premium. The first $52 semiannual installment would be paid in advance, leaving a "loan" balance of $48 oustanding for 6 months. The approximate nominal rate of interest would be $4/48 \times 12/6 \times 100 = 16.7\%$.

or firm for negotiating a loan. But a flat charge of so much a loan would be more equitable because most of the expenses in handling a loan have little relation to the size of the loan.

If a flat charge of $50 a loan were made, the negotiator of a loan would get as much for making the $1,000 loan as for making the $10,000 loan. As far as the mechanics involved in making the loan are concerned, this equal compensation would be justified. At least it would be a more reasonable method than paying 1 percent commission that would amount to only $10 on the one loan and $100 on the other loan. On the percentage basis there is an incentive not only to spend all the effort on the high value farms, but to encourage farmers in all instances to increase their askings because the larger the loan the larger the commission.

A combination of a flat charge and a percentage commission has some advantages over either method by itself. A small charge provides compensation for the loan expenses that do not vary with the amount involved, while a small percentage commission provides compensation for any added expenses, risk, and responsibility that increase with the size of the loan. A flat charge of $25 and a commission of one-fourth of 1 percent would allow a commission of $27.50 on a $1,000 loan and $50 on a $10,000 loan.

Minimum deposit requirements are still another factor accounting for differences in interest charges. If a bank specifies that $200 out of a $1,000 loan must be maintained on deposit, only $800 is used, and the interest should be figured as a percentage of $800, not of $1,000. In effect, however, such requirements are closely allied to service charges that are imposed by banks to compensate the bank for handling checks.

Production Credit Associations and Federal Land Banks do not have minimum deposit requirements as such but they do require their borrowers to purchase stock equal to 5 percent of the amount of the loan. Associations in need of additional equity capital can require stock purchases as high as 10 percent of the amount of the loan. The net effect of a 5 percent stock purchase requirement is that the borrower actually has the use of only 95 percent of the total amount borrowed. Suppose, for example, that a farmer wants to borrow $1,000 for 1 year. Since the stock purchase is generally rounded up to the nearest $5 unit, his total loan would be $1,055 and if the interest rate is 8 percent, he would owe $1,055 × 1.08 = $1,139.40 at the end of the year. He would receive a credit of $55.00 (plus any dividends declared) for his stock when the loan is repaid, thus he would repay $1,084.40, including principal and interest, and the effective rate of interest on his loan would be 8.44 percent. If he received a dividend on his stock, the effective rate of interest would be slightly lower. If the dividend rate on the stock is the same as that paid on the loan, there is then no extra charge involved in buying the stock. If the dividend is higher, which is not likely, then the interest rate paid on the loan is reduced by this excess of dividend over interest.

TRUTH IN LENDING. The foregoing suggests that calculating the nominal interest rate on a loan can be a rather complex procedure requiring specialized knowledge of a formula or other method of computation.

The fact that many borrowers (and some lenders for that matter) cannot accurately estimate nominal interest rates led to passage of Public Law 90-321, 90th Congress, 5.5, May 1968, titled the *Consumer Protection Act.* Title I of this act is referred to as the *Truth in Lending Act.* Truth in Lending is administered by the Federal Reserve Board and the specific provisions are defined in Regulation Z.

Truth in Lending applies to practically all credit extended to individuals and farmers that involves a finance charge or is repayable in more than four installments. Credit extended to nonfarm business and government units, nonreal-estate loans over $25,000 to individuals, and credit from registered brokers to purchase stocks, bonds, and other securities are exempt. Some agricultural organizations such as corporations, trusts, and cooperatives are also exempt.

The act requires lenders to state their total finance charges in dollar and annual percentage terms. Interest costs and any other charges that would not be required if the borrower had paid cash, such as creditor life insurance, must also be included in the finance charges and in the annual percentage rate. The act specifies that the dollar amount and annual percentage rate must appear in bold type on the loan contract. The act also provides a "cooling off" period for some real estate loan contracts. With the exception of first-mortgage loans made for the purpose of buying homes, borrowers have up to 3 business days to cancel any loan contract involving their residences as collateral.

Figure 10.1 shows the disclosure statement used by one lender to fulfill the lending law for their installment loans. In the example illustrated, $1,016.13 were borrowed for 3 years at 8 percent add-on interest, repayable in 36 monthly installments of $35.00. Thus the total finance charge was $35.00 × 36 minus $1,016.13, or $243.87. Regulation Z requires lenders to use the *actuarial method* to calculate the annual percentage rate on installment loans; hence the 14.55 annual percentage rate shown in Figure 10.1 is essentially the nominal rate discussed earlier. The Stelson equation (10.2) gives an estimated nominal rate of 15.47 percent and the direct-ratio equation (10.3) gives an estimate of 14.47 percent.

Truth in Lending does not set maximum interest rates that can

TRUTH IN LENDING DISCLOSURE RECORD

Date: 1/15/73

Borrower(s): J. Borrower

Recording Fee	Amount Financed	Closing Fee	FINANCE CHARGE	Total of Payments	ANNUAL PERCENTAGE RATE
	$1,016.13		$243.87	$1,260.00	14.55

Payment Schedule

____36____ installments of $ _35.00_ each due on the same day of each consecutive month beginning ___February 15___ , 19 _73_ , or as follows: _____

In the event of prepayment of the entire balance due, the interest charged thereon will be rebated according to the Rule of 78's. The unearned portion of interest shall be computed after subtracting a minimum charge of $10.00. Amounts less than $1.00 will not be refunded.

All payments received by bank more than 10 days after the due date thereof shall be assessed liquidated damages at the rate of 5¢ per dollar of payment due, not to exceed $3.00.

This credit is:

[ ]   UNSECURED

NOTE: Property given to secure any other obligation to bank, either previous to this credit or in the future, shall also be used to secure this obligation.

[X]   SECURED BY A SECURITY AGREEMENT COVERING:

[ ]   All household goods, furniture, fixtures, appliances and all other personal property now owned or hereafter acquired by the borrowers.

[X]   Other: Previous or future advances are secured by the property given as security for this loan.

Property insurance covering the above collateral is required. You may choose the company through which this insurance is to be obtained.

IF THIS LOAN IS AT LEAST PARTIALLY SECURED BY REAL PROPERTY, SEE SPECIAL NOTICE OF RESCISSION RIGHTS.

I hereby acknowledge receipt of a complete copy of this document.

_____
Borrower

FIG. *10.1—A Truth in Lending disclosure record.*

be charged nor does it require accurate disclosure of the nominal annual interest rate on revolving charge accounts.[19] To date, insurance companies have not been required to disclose finance charges associ-

19. As Consumer's Union has pointed out, the nominal rate of interest on a $1\frac{1}{2}\%$ per month revolving charge account can run much higher than 18% per annum if the finance charge is calculated as a percentage of the balance outstanding before payments on the account have been deducted. See Consumer's Union, *Consumer Reports, Buying Guide Issue,* 1972, pp. 383–85.

ated with their premium payment plans. Nevertheless, the act has eliminated many of the abuses of consumer and agricultural credit by informing borrowers of the actual interest rates being charged, thereby permitting them to make more accurate cost comparisons when shopping for credit.

QUESTIONS AND PROBLEMS

1. Define interest. What factors are involved in interest rates?
2. Define and compare simple interest and compound interest.
3. Explain and compare compound interest rate, true interest rate, actuarial interest rate, nominal interest rate, effective interest rate, discount interest rate, and add-on interest rate.
4. A farmer borrows $1,200 at 8 percent add-on interest. Use one of the formulae given in this chapter to estimate the nominal interest rate if the loan is repaid in 36 monthly installments; 24 monthly installments; 12 monthly installments; 8 quarterly installments. From your answers, observe the effects of the length of the repayment term and the payment interval on the nominal interest rate.
5. Redo problem 4, using a $1,200, 8 percent discount loan. Compare the nominal interest rates for otherwise similar add-on and discount loans.
6. Estimate the nominal interest rate for a borrower who pays accounts with a supplier 30 days after delivery when the terms are "2/15/n30."
7. An annual auto insurance premium of $200 can be paid in cash at the beginning of the year or in 10 monthly installments of $21 each, with the first $21 installment due in advance. Use one of the formulae from this chapter to estimate the nominal interest rate on this loan.
8. A $1,000 "8 percent" loan was repaid as follows: $420 at the end of 3 months, $220 at the end of 6 months, $320 at the end of 9 months, and $120 at the end of 12 months. Use the procedure for unequal and irregularly timed payments given in this chapter to estimate the nominal interest rate on this loan.
9. A farmer needs a $100,000 loan for 1 year to finance his operating expenses. His banker will lend him the money at 7½ percent per annum but he must keep 20 percent of his loan balance on deposit in a 4 percent savings account (that is, he will have to borrow a total of $125,000 to have the use of $100,000). If the principal and interest are repaid at the end of the year, calculate the nominal interest rate on this loan.
10. Discuss the merits of Truth-in-Lending legislation. Do you think that farm loans should be exempt from Truth in Lending as are most nonfarm business loans?

REFERENCES

Botts, Ralph R. *Farmers' Handbook of Financial Calculations and Physical Measurements.* Farm Prod. Econ. Div., ERS, USDA, Handbook 230, 1962.

Brake, John R. *Interest Rate Terminology and Calculation.* Dept. Agr. Econ., Mich. State Univ., Rept. 13, 1966.

Cissell, Robert, and Cissell, Helen. *Mathematics of Finance.* Houghton Mifflin, Boston, 1956.

Clonty, Ralph C., Jr. *Truth-in-Lending Manual.* Hanover Lamont, Boston, 1970.

Dewey, John. "The Geometry of Capital and Interest: A Suggested Simplification." *Am. Econ. Rev.,* Mar. 1963, pp. 134–39.

Federal Reserve Bank of Chicago. "Regulation Z: Truth-in-Lending." *Business Conditions,* Apr. 1969, pp. 11–15.

Gilson, J. C. *The Cost of Credit.* Univ. of Manitoba, Agr. Econ. Bull. 3, 1961.

Neifeld, M. R. *Neifeld's Guide to Installment Computations.* Mack Publ., Easton, Pa., 1951.

Stelson, Hugh E. *Mathematics of Finance.* D. Van Nostrand, Princeton, N.J., 1957.

Trefftz, K. L., and Hills, E. J. *Mathematics of Business, Accounting, and Finance.* Harper and Brothers, New York, 1956.

CHAPTER 11: LOAN REPAYMENT TERMS

REPAYMENT TERMS are usually set forth in the note or mortgage signed by the borrower when the loan is obtained. When a note or mortgage is not involved, the terms of the loan may be evidenced by the customary credit policy of the lender such as the policy of a farm supply dealer in handling charge accounts. From the standpoint of repayment capacity, the term of the loan and timing of the schedule of payments are of primary importance.

As the preceding chapter on finding interest rates indicates, there are numerous ways of repaying short-term loans, depending upon the policy of the lender and the needs of the borrower. However, most intermediate-term loans and nearly all long-term loans are repaid according to one of three basic methods: the *single payment plan, partial payment plan,* or *fully amortized.*

SINGLE PAYMENT LOANS. The single payment or lump sum payment loan calls for payment of the entire loan on the expiration of the term. Historically, the traditional farm mortgage loan was a 5-year single payment loan. The borrower paid the interest each year, and every 5 years he extended, renewed, refinanced, or repaid the loan. Usually the loan was renewed or refinanced for a larger or smaller amount according to the losses or profits of the borrower during the preceding 5 years. Every 5 years the borrower not only had to find a new lender, if the previous one wanted his money, but even with extensions and renewals, he usually had another commission to pay.

With improvements made in credit service to agriculture, the 5-year single payment loan gradually gave way to longer and modified end payment plans. A partial payment loan has become common, particularly among life insurance companies.

PARTIAL PAYMENT LOANS. The partial payment loan is a single payment loan with small fixed principal payments or installments each year during the repayment term of the loan. Principal payments made each year are not large enough to completely repay the loan, with the result that a fairly large amount, sometimes referred to as a *balloon* payment, is due at the end of the loan term.

A typical loan of this kind would be an $80,000 loan for a 20-year term with interest at 7 percent annually on the outstanding balance, and with principal payments of $2,000 per year. The first year the borrower would pay $5,600 of interest and $2,000 of the principal or $7,600; the second year, $5,460 of interest and $2,000 of the principal or $7,460, and so on. In the twentieth year he would pay $2,940 of interest and $2,000 of the principal or $4,940. With this payment schedule, one-half the principal will have been repaid in installments, so when the loan comes due in 20 years, the balloon payment would be $40,000. Although there are many varieties of the partial payment plan, the main provisions found in most of them are similar to those outlined.

AMORTIZATION LOANS. The amortization plan is a more extensive application of the partial payment plan. Amortization, strictly speaking, means killing by degrees, which may be interpreted as repaying the loan by a series of installments. Farm loans are customarily repaid in annual or semiannual installments while quarterly or monthly plans are more commonly used for consumer installment loans. Since computers are now widely used to calculate payments for any interest rate–repayment period combination, any period can be used that is agreeable to both the lender and borrower. Each installment is made up of principal and interest. The interest portion is just adequate to cover the interest due on the outstanding balance of the loan. The excess of each payment over the interest for the period is the amount by which the principal is reduced. The amount of this principal payment is the amortization. Two amortization plans, the even payment and the decreasing payment, along with the single payment plan, are illustrated in Table 11.1.

Decreasing Payment Plan. The decreasing payment plan provides for fixed principal payments and declining interest payments on the outstanding balance, and the payments continue until the loan is completely repaid. The difference between this type and the even payment plan is that the total payments decrease each time. Where the borrower is able to pay the higher initial installments this decreasing payment type is especially well suited. It has the advantage of being easier to understand at any point of time during the existence of the loan because the borrower can visualize quickly the effect that his annual principal payment has on the outstanding balance. In addition, there is a psychological advantage in the reduction of the total annual payments; it gives the borrower a definite sense of progress to have each payment lower than the previous one.

TABLE 11.1: Three Methods of Repaying a $1,000, 8 Percent Loan in Ten Annual Payments

| | Amortized | | | | | | | | Nonamortized | | | |
| | Level payment | | | | Decreasing payment | | | | Single payment | | | |
End of year	Total payment	Principal	Interest	Loan balance after payment	Total payment	Principal	Interest	Loan balance after payment	Total payment	Principal	Interest	Loan balance after payment
0	$ ...	$ ...	$ ...	$1,000.00	$ ...	$ ...	$ ...	$1,000.00	$ ...	$ ...	$ ...	$1,000.00
1	149.03	69.03	80.00	930.97	180	100	80	900.00	80	0	80	1,000.00
2	149.03	74.55	74.48	856.42	172	100	72	800.00	80	0	80	1,000.00
3	149.03	80.52	68.51	775.90	164	100	64	700.00	80	0	80	1,000.00
4	149.03	86.96	62.07	688.94	156	100	56	600.00	80	0	80	1,000.00
5	149.03	93.91	55.12	595.03	148	100	48	500.00	80	0	80	1,000.00
6	149.03	101.43	47.60	493.60	140	100	40	400.00	80	0	80	1,000.00
7	149.03	109.54	39.49	384.06	132	100	32	300.00	80	0	80	1,000.00
8	149.03	118.31	30.72	265.75	124	100	24	200.00	80	0	80	1,000.00
9	149.03	127.77	21.26	137.98	116	100	16	100.00	80	0	80	1,000.00
10	149.03	137.98	11.05	0.00	108	100	8	0.00	1,080	1,000	80	0.00
Totals	$1,490.30	$1,000.00	$490.30	$ ...	$1,440	$1,000	$440	$ ...	$1,800	$1,000	$800	$ ...

Even Payment Plan. The even payment plan of amortization, illustrated in Table 11.1, calls for equal payments each year with a larger proportion of each succeeding payment representing principal and a smaller amount representing interest. On a $1,000 loan with interest at 8 percent annually, written for a 10-year term on an even payment amortization basis, the annual installment is $149.03. The first payment is divided between interest of $80 and principal of $69.03. On the next payment, however, the amount of interest due is less because the outstanding balance is less. The interest of $74.48 is 8 percent of $930.97 for a 1-year period. Since the interest payment is less, the principal payment is more because the total payment is always the same under the even payment plan.

The equation for calculating the annual payment on an even payment plan loan is

$$P = B \, \frac{1}{a_{\overline{n}|i}} \tag{11.1[1]}$$

where P represents the amount of the annual payment (installment), B the face amount of the loan, n the number of years for which the loan is written, and i the annual interest rate. The symbol $\frac{1}{a_{\overline{n}|i}}$ represents the annuity that 1 will purchase for n years with an annual interest rate i. In terms of loan amortization, the symbol represents the annual total payment (installment) per dollar borrowed, for n years, with annual interest at rate i. Values for the symbol $\frac{1}{a_{\overline{n}|i}}$ are given in Appendix Table 3. To use the table, find the number of years for which the loan is written in the column headed n and move across the table to the column headed by the interest rate for the loan. The values in Appendix Table 3 have been rounded to 4 places, thus they only approximate the values of $\frac{1}{a_{\overline{n}|i}}$.

We are now ready to use Equation 11.1 to compute the annual installment for the loan referred to in Table 11.1. Substituting the appropriate figures in the equation, we have

$$P = 1,000 \times 0.1490$$

$P = 149.00$; which is 3 cents lower than the value shown in Table 11.1 because of the use of the rounded values in Appendix Table 3.

---

1. Justin H. Moore, *Handbook of Financial Mathematics* (Englewood Cliffs, N.J.: Prentice-Hall, 1929), p. 169.

The 0.1490 is found in Appendix Table 3 by moving down the column headed n to 10 and across to the column headed 8 percent.

Equation 11.1 is not flexible enough to cover situations where payments are made more than once each year. When a loan is amortized by means of more frequent payments, the following equation may be used:

$$\frac{P}{m} = B \, \frac{1}{a_{\overline{nm}|\frac{i}{m}}} \qquad (11.2)$$

In this equation the terms have the same representations as in Equation 11.1 and, in addition, m represents the number of payments of principal and interest per year (and also the number of times the interest is compounded per year) and i represents the nominal annual interest rate.

If the loan referred to in Table 11.1 were amortized on a semi-annual basis rather than on an annual basis, the appropriate figures substituted in Equation 11.2 would give:

$$\frac{P}{2} = 1,000 \, \frac{1}{a_{\overline{10 \times 2}|\frac{0.08}{2}}}$$

$$\frac{P}{2} = 1,000 \, \frac{1}{a_{\overline{20}|0.04}}$$

$$\frac{P}{2} = 1,000 \times 0.0736$$

$$\frac{P}{2} = 73.60, \text{ the semiannual payment.}$$

The semiannual installment would be $73.60 compared with the annual installment of $149.03. The total payment per year is lower with the semiannual payment plan due to the more frequent payment of interest. A reasonably close *estimate* of semiannual, quarterly, or monthly payments can be obtained by dividing the values in Appendix Table 3 by 2, 4, or 12, respectively. However, the estimate obtained using this method will always be slightly higher than that given by Equation 11.2. For the loan illustrated in Table 11.1, the estimated semiannual payment would be $1,000 \times 0.1490 \div 2 =$ $74.50, 90 cents higher than the exact answer given by Equation 11.2.

As Table 11.1 shows, the total dollar amount of interest paid over the 10 years is highest for the single payment plan because the borrower has the use of the $1,000 principal for the full 10 years. The present value method can be used to verify that the borrower pays exactly 8 percent per annum under all three repayment plans.

---

2. Ibid., p. 344.

The present value of the total payments under the level payment plan is:

$$149.03 \times a_{\overline{10}|8} = 149.03 \times 6.7101 = 1000.01$$

The value for $a_{\overline{10}|8}$ was obtained from Appendix Table 4.

The present value of the total payments under the single payment loan is found by discounting at 8 percent a 10-year $80 annuity (the interest payments) and adding the result to the present value of the $1,000 loan principal that the lender would receive at the end of 10 years. The present value of the interest payments is:

$$80 \times a_{\overline{10}|8} = 80 \times 6.7101 = 536.81$$

The present value of the $1,000 principal payment is:

$$1,000 \times \frac{1}{(1.08)^{10}} = 1,000 \times 0.4632 = 463.20$$

The value for $\dfrac{1}{(1.08)^{10}}$ was obtained from Appendix Table 2. Thus the present value of the total payments on the single payment plan is $536.81 + 463.20 = \$1,000.01$.

With the decreasing payment plan, each payment must be discounted separately using the values for $\dfrac{1}{(1+i)^n}$ from the 8 percent column of Appendix Table 2:

$$\frac{180}{(1.08)^1} + \frac{172}{(1.08)^2} + \frac{164}{(1.08)^3} + \cdots + \frac{108}{(1.08)^{10}}$$

$$= 180 \, (0.9259) + 172 \, (0.8573) + 164 \, (0.7983) + \cdots + 108 \, (0.4632)$$

$$= 999.90$$

The use of four-place tables causes the answers to be slightly different from the expected $1,000; however, the fact that the present value of the total payments for all three loans is approximately $1,000 does verify that the borrower would pay a nominal interest rate of 8 percent, regardless of which repayment plan is used.

VARIABLE OR FLEXIBLE PAYMENT LOANS. Loans that call for payments of interest or principal, or both, which are scheduled to fluctuate with crop yields or income, are designated as variable or flexible payment loans. The development of the variable payment loan was stimulated by the difficulties that lending agencies experienced with fixed payment mortgages of all types in areas where annual income fluctuations have been exceedingly wide. Very few, if any, lenders in the United States now offer a formal variable payment plan. Most lenders, of course, will adjust or defer loan payments when net farm income drops severely due to weather, disease, low prices, and the like. However, basing all loan payments on some index of prices, yields, or income has not been entirely successful.

The chief obstacle in the development of the variable payment mortgage loan has been in finding a satisfactory basis to which the variable payments may be adjusted. The suggestions thus far have centered on four factors:

1. Prices of farm products
2. Crop yields
3. Rental shares
4. Farm income

The *prices of products* plan provides for payments on principal or interest, or both, varying with a certain price index. The mortgage carries a definite term of years, interest rate, and schedule of principal payments, as for example, a 20-year term at 7½ percent with principal payments of 1 percent each year. But annual payments as specified in the plan are required only if the index of prices received by farmers for their products is around a certain normal level, for example, 100. If the price index is 120, the interest payment remains the same, but the principal payment increases. If the index drops to 70, not only is the principal payment omitted but a certain part of the interest due is postponed or added to the principal of the mortgage. This plan fails to work satisfactorily in areas where yields fluctuate. In such areas the plan may be worse than a fixed payment type because a drouth may send the price index up and call for a higher payment than if the yield is up to normal.

The *crop yields* plan of adapting the payments to crop yields, although not entirely satisfactory, has more in its favor. Payments are scheduled as in the previous plan, with variations in the regular plan if there are large fluctuations in crop yields. If wheat yields of 20 bushels per acre are normal, the payment is regular. If the wheat yield increases to 25 bushels, the principal payment is increased a definite prearranged amount. If, on the other hand, the wheat yield is only 12 bushels, the principal payment is waived and the interest payment reduced according to a schedule, and the unpaid interest extended or added to the principal. However, if yields only are used as a base, the plan does not work well for borrowers when yields are high and prices extremely low, or for lenders when yields are low and prices extremely high. To meet this objection the rental share plan is suggested.

The *rental share* plan is based on crop yields. In essence, the borrower turns over to the lender the share of the crop that he would give to a landlord as rent for the farm. The lender sells this crop share and applies the proceeds first on the interest and the remainder, if any, on the principal. The borrower pays more than a tenant because he agrees to pay the taxes, keep up the buildings, and pay the fire and extended coverage insurance premiums. The borrower is given the privilege of making additional payments on the principal on interest-paying dates. The main advantage of this plan is that the borrower sets aside a portion of the crop at harvest to be applied directly to his mortgage obligation. If he wants to feed this crop to his livestock, he must buy it from the lender. This plan results in a clear-cut division of the crop, with the lender obtaining all that the farmer can well afford to offer because the farmer is giving the lender as much as a tenant would give a landlord and, in addition, is paying the taxes and keeping up the improvements. Another favorable feature is the ease with which this plan is explained and administered. Most farmers are familiar with rental terms and readily recognize that a lender is entitled to the landlord's share. A final advantage is that this plan adjusts for both yield and price variations; if the yield or price is out of line, the lender makes the adjustment through the sale of the share that the borrower turns over.

The rental share plan, however, is not adapted to farms that specialize in livestock or have such a wide variety of crops that the computation of a crop return index or rental share is especially difficult. For such diversified farms the income plan has been suggested.

The *farm income* plan provides for payments adjusted to the farmer's net income. In theory this plan is ideal in that the payments are in line with what the farmer can pay. If crop yields or livestock returns are low, the income is low and the payments reduced accordingly, but if the reverse situation occurs, income is high and the payments are increased. But this ideal adjustment can be stated only in general terms. When a specific farm is considered, a multitude of questions arise. Should family living expenses be allowed as farm expenses and, if so, what limit, if any, should be placed on these expenses? What allowance, if any, should be made for poor management; if a farmer does not take good care of his crops or livestock, will his payment be reduced because he has done a poor job? What assistance will be given the farmer in keeping and summarizing the detailed records necessary to make this plan work, and who will pay the extra cost of the record-keeping supervision? These questions make the actual working out of this plan a formidable undertaking. The Farmers Home Administration offered a variable payment plan of this type with their farm ownership loans for a period of years. The plan worked fairly well in this instance since farm ownership loans are made only to a select and carefully supervised group of farmers. However, in recent years the Farmers Home Administration has abandoned this plan in favor of optional and reserve payments.

OPTIONAL PAYMENT PLANS. The *optional payment* provision,
an opportunity to make payments on the principal in addition to
the regular payments at any time or at any interest-paying date,
is a great convenience to the borrower. If the borrower is permitted to
refinance at a lower rate when interest rates decline, he saves a substantial amount on his annual interest bill. It is a great advantage,
too, if he can apply extra income from a good year on the principal
of his loan instead of allowing his funds to lie idle or investing at a
low rate.

The optional payment privilege, however, has some disadvantages
to the lender. It makes a loan less satisfactory because it may be paid
at any time unless certain limitations are specified. A common limitation is to specify that optional payments may not be made until 2, 3,
or 5 years have expired, which protects the lender against having the
loan paid soon after it is made, in which event the lender may lose if
he has borne the expense of negotiating the loan. This difficulty may
be avoided if a small charge is agreed upon as compensation to the
lender if the loan is repaid within the 2-, 3-, or 5-year period after the
loan is made. Another limitation is to specify that payments made
be in amounts of $100 or multiples of this amount, and also that
optional payments may be made only on interest-paying dates. These
last limitations simplify the handling of optional payments. An unusual limitation that enables a lender to hold a loan for the entire
period is to grant the borrower the option of paying one-half or less,
but never more than one-half, of the unpaid balance at any interest-
paying date. According to this plan, the borrower can never pay the
loan entirely until it comes due. Another type of optional payment
is to allow principal payments at any interest-paying date up to
some fraction, such as one-fifth or one-fourth, of the original principal, provided the funds are derived from farm income. Restriction
of the payment to farm income prevents lending agencies from taking
loans away from each other.

RESERVE PAYMENTS. *Reserve* or *future payments* allow the borrower to make advance payments that are held in reserve to
apply at a future date when hardships of one kind or another
may make it difficult or impossible for the borrower to pay his interest
and principal installment. The lender generally agrees to pay the
same interest on the advance payment as is charged on the loan so
the farmer does not lose any interest on the transaction.

Such a plan has a special advantage for maximum loans in areas
where income is highly variable. If a farmer in such an area had a
highly successful year and reduced his mortgage by an extra $1,000,

he still might have trouble the following year meeting his loan payment should he have a crop failure or some other calamity that reduced his income. On the other hand, if he placed this extra $1,000 in the reserve fund it would be earning interest at the mortgage rate and be available for use in a year when he could not otherwise make his interest and principal payment.

One difficulty lenders have experienced with reserve or future payment funds is that they are not built by the borrowers who need them. Farmers who build such reserves tend to be the ones who can meet payments from other sources even in difficult times. The borrower who has limited risk-bearing ability in other ways tends also to forego building a reserve fund to help carry his loan payments in low income years.

OTHER PAYMENT PLANS. Various other repayment plans, primarily combinations of provisions already outlined, have been developed by lenders to meet needs of borrowers. One plan provides for initial deferment of principal payments for up to 5 years. This provision permits the borrower to concentrate on repayment of short-term debts and on accumulation of working capital. While the mortgage lender does not gain added security by principal payments during this period, he does benefit by the stronger current and intermediate capital position developed by the borrower.

Another plan used by some lenders provides for discontinuance of principal payments when the loan has been reduced to a certain level. After the loan has been paid down to a certain level it is carried as a single payment loan. This plan recognizes that a conservative perpetual debt might well be carried on good farm real estate. It also leaves the farmer free to choose whether or not he should continue to save to accumulate equity in real estate.

With the long repayment terms now available on mortgage loans, the options of deferring principal payments during the early years of a loan or carrying all or part of the loan as perpetual debt are of little advantage to the borrower. The annual payment on an $80,000, 35-year, 8 percent loan under the even payment amortization plan would be about $6,864. Deferring the principal payment would reduce the total payment by only $464, a relatively small reduction for a loan of this size.

VARIABLE INTEREST RATES. Fluctuations in the market rates of interest constitute a risk for both borrowers and lenders. If rates rise after a long-term loan is made, the lender may incur a loss, while a subsequent decline in interest rates tends to hurt borrowers. To counteract the risk of fluctuating market rates some lenders have adopted variable interest rate plans that allow for changes in the interest rates on their loans with changes in money market rates. Production Credit Associations and Federal Land Banks adjust their interest rates according to changes in the average cost of raising money through the sale of debentures and bonds. Other lenders base changes in their loan rates on money market rates such as the prime interest rate charged by large commercial banks or yields on securities such as commercial paper, treasury bills, or corporate bonds.

Given the general upward trend in interest rates since the late 1940s, variable interest rate loans are obviously appealing to lenders. However, borrowers also benefit from variable interest rates. When interest rates reached historically high levels in 1970, many borrowers had to pay interest rates of up to 10 percent, and some paid more. Those who borrowed from a lender who had a variable interest rate plan saw the interest rates on their loans decline to between 6½ and 7½ percent as market rates declined during late 1971 and 1972.

SUMMARY. Repayment ability can be significantly enhanced by making certain that the *amount* and *timing* of loan payments are tailored to the purpose of the loan and to the amount of income available to meet the payments. The three basic repayment plans are *single payment loans, partial payment loans,* and *amortization loans.* Amortization loans are repaid according to either a level, or even, payment plan or a decreasing payment plan.

Despite the range of repayment plans now available, fluctuations in net farm income sometimes make it difficult to meet loan payments. Attempts by lenders to base loan payments directly on some index of prices, yields, or net income have not been widely used. However, optional payment plans and reserve payment plans have made it easier for many borrowers to adjust loan payments to their net income. Variable interest rate loans, a relatively recent innovation by some farm lenders, have largely removed the risk of changing market interest rates.

QUESTIONS AND PROBLEMS
1. Describe the three basic loan repayment plans. Under what circumstances would each of these plans be suitable?
2. Use Equation 11.1 and Appendix Table 3 to calculate the payments for a $1,000, 8 percent, level payment amortization loan according to the following terms: 2 annual payments; 5 annual payments; 10 annual payments; 4 semiannual payments; 10 semiannual payments; 16 quarterly payments.

3. Draw a graph showing the principal balance outstanding for years 1 through 10 for each of the three repayment plans shown in Table 11.1. Discuss how this graph explains why the dollar amount of interest paid over the 10-year term varies among the three repayment plans.

4. Using Equation 11.1 and Appendix Table 3, draw a graph showing the decline in the annual payments on a $1,000, 8 percent, level payment loan as the repayment period goes from 1 year to 40 years. Notice how the curve showing the annual payments declines rapidly at first, then flattens out as it approaches a straight line at $80. What does your graph suggest regarding the advantage of a perpetual loan over a 35-year or 40-year level payment amortization loan?

5. Why are variable or flexible payment plans suggested? What are the chief obstacles in developing a satisfactory variable payment plan?

6. Explain the difference between optional payments and reserve payments.

7. Get opinions on variable interest rate loans from farmers and lenders in your area. Do you think variable interest rate loans will become commoner in the future?

CHAPTER 12: RISK MANAGEMENT: INFORMAL INSURANCE

TWO KINDS of risk must be considered. *Business* risk is the variation in income resulting from the type of business the firm is engaged in. *Financial* risk is the probability of incurring relatively greater losses as the proportion of borrowed capital relative to equity capital increases. The combined effects of business risk and financial risk are embodied in the principle of increasing risk. This chapter and the following one deal with the many kinds of business risks associated with farming and with strategies for reducing these risks to manageable levels.[1]

IMPORTANCE OF RISK MANAGEMENT. Since the future is not known with certainty, there is a need for risk-bearing ability to offset fluctuations that might occur in expenses and income and to compensate for errors in judgment regarding returns and repayment capacity in use of credit. Considering how much one should borrow (from a risk-bearing viewpoint) has been likened to loading a truck.

> One would be foolish to load a truck to the point where an axle would break if a wheel hit a chuckhole in the road. A farm family would be equally unwise to take on a credit load to the point where they would go "broke" if adversity hit. Just as some highways have more holes than others, some areas and types of farming involve greater hazards and risk than others. Farmers in high-risk areas or with high-risk enterprises should take on a lighter debt load in relation to their equity than those in stable areas or in a type of farming where fluctuations in income are relatively small.[2]

Risk-bearing ability provides the last line of defense in the use of credit. If a promising venture proves to be unprofitable, risk-bearing ability must shoulder the load. If a farmer borrows funds for operating expenses and because of risk and uncertainty—such as natural hazards and low prices—income is inadequate to cover them, his

---

1. No distinction is made in this book between risk and uncertainty except as is evident from the discussion.
2. Based upon Aaron G. Nelson, *Credit as a Tool for the Agricultural Producer,* North Central Regional Publ. 4; and Great Plains Agr. Council Publ. 15, 1957, p. 10.

repayment capacity from current income also becomes inadequate and the load is shifted to risk-bearing ability.[3]

TYPES OF RISK AND UNCERTAINTY IN AGRICULTURE.

As indicated by the above discussion, conditions that make it necessary for a farmer to have risk-bearing ability as one basis for use of credit stem from fluctuations in income and expenses and from risk and uncertainty in operation of the farm business and household. Fluctuations that make risk-bearing ability necessary stem from five different kinds of change or uncertainty.

Production Uncertainty. Production uncertainty is a very important factor contributing to the need for risk-bearing ability in the use of credit. Production uncertainty is caused by variations in weather and by things such as disease, insects, and other biological pests. Production uncertainty is concentrated particularly in those areas where weather is unstable. For example, precipitation varies widely from year to year and period to period in parts of the Great Plains.[4] These areas have come to be known as high-risk areas because of their great variability of production. Wide swings in yields around a relatively low average create great uncertainty in production. With relatively low average yields—12 to 14 bushels for wheat in some areas—net income is low after costs of operation have been met. Under such conditions, below-average yields do not merely mean lower net income, as may be the case in higher income areas. When yields are low, income is inadequate to cover costs and, as a result, cash deficits accumulate.

The risk would not be so great if a poor year were followed by one that was average or above average. However, 2 or more years of drouth often occur together. Drouth periods sometimes extend for 5 to 10 years. Such conditions create extreme risk and explain why the area has become known as a high-risk area.

Other areas than the Great Plains and other crops than wheat suffer from natural hazards. Fruit orchards, for instance, have a highly variable production record. Disease and adverse weather conditions, including freezes, windstorms, and hail, often have a marked effect on production. A farmer in the Middle West may lose a crop because of chinch bugs, hail, drouth, corn blight, or excessive moisture. Farmers along rivers may be flooded. Boll weevils, floods, and excessive moisture may destroy the cotton farmer's crop.

---

3. Ibid., p. 10.
4. States usually included in the Great Plains are North Dakota, South Dakota, Nebraska, Kansas, Oklahoma, Texas, Montana, Wyoming, Colorado, and New Mexico.

Other hazards affect livestock production. Death losses from disease and adverse weather conditions are common. Hog losses from cholera or dairy herd losses from tuberculosis may strike an individual farmer unusually hard. Losses from bad weather conditions at farrowing, calving, or lambing time also affect production.

Crops, livestock, and improvements are subject to damage from windstorms, fire, and lightning. A tornado sweeping through a farm area may destroy almost everything in its path. Such losses may severely retard or reduce production and add materially to expenses as well.

In brief, natural hazards in all types of production are great and make extension and use of credit a risky business. These factors need to be given full recognition in consideration of risk-bearing ability.

Price Uncertainty. Closely associated with weather and other natural hazards that influence risk-bearing ability is the risk of price decline that the borrower and lender must face. The connection between natural hazards and price risk is evident if the analysis includes gross farm income, the resultant of yield multiplied by price. It is desirable, however, to treat these two causal factors separately in order to recognize their individual importance. In the aggregate, low levels of production are generally associated with higher prices; however, this generalization may not hold for the individual farmer.

Price uncertainty always has been a major consideration in farming. Many forces cause prices to fluctuate, such as the level of national prosperity, production of other farmers, and changes in consumer tastes. Prices change from week to week, from month to month, from year to year, and from period to period, and since credit is used for varying lengths of time on most farms, all these fluctuations contribute to uncertainty.

Considerable attention has been devoted to the problem of fluctuations in crop, livestock, and livestock product prices. As a result, government price support programs have been introduced for a number of crops and products. These have helped reduce price uncertainty, but input and product price fluctuations are still part of farming. A number of crops, livestock, and livestock products are not included in the price support programs. Moreover, fluctuations in farm product prices have added significance today due to the relatively narrow margin of net return involved in farming. With the advance of the technological revolution, more of the inputs involved in production are purchased. Some aspects of production formerly performed on the farm have been transferred to the processor. Competition and volume production have reduced the farmer's share of the consumer's dollar in most cases. The combined effect of such forces is that today a high proportion of gross income is required to cover purchased inputs. As a result, the farmer is particularly vulnerable to fluctuations in farm input and product prices.

The effect of product price fluctuation on farmers may be severe. It is not uncommon for wheat prices to fluctuate 25 cents per bushel from one year to the next. If a farmer had 500 acres, with an average yield of 20 bushels per acre, a 25 cent drop in price would mean a reduction in income of $2,500. If financing had been arranged on the basis of the higher price, such a drop in income might put the loan in jeopardy. Similarly, hog prices sometimes drop as much as $5 per hundredweight from one year to the next. On 200 market hogs weighing 225 pounds each, such a drop in price would mean a reduction in income of $2,250. Here, again, such a cut in income might well cause problems if a loan had been obtained on the basis of the higher price.

The more risky the enterprise the greater the risk is of loss due to price uncertainty. Cattle fattening is a relatively risky venture and large losses are not uncommon. Many farmers lost $50 to $75 per head in the 1963–64 feeding season and many hog farmers incurred serious losses due to a combination of low hog prices and high feed prices in 1970–71.

Short-term price fluctuations comprise an important aspect of risk-bearing ability for short-term use of credit. Long-term fluctuations should also be considered in use of long-term credit. A long-term downward trend in the price of a farm product should be recognized in analysis of returns and repayment capacity. The longer the term, however, the greater is the chance for error in judgment. Thus allowance should be made for risk-bearing ability to cover errors of judgment in returns and repayment capacity as well as the short-term deviations of commodity prices from the average.

Technological Uncertainty. Another type of uncertainty arises from new techniques or methods of production. New crop varieties, fertilizer mixtures, feed combinations, models of machines, and the like, are continually being developed by research workers and business concerns. While these new developments usually are based on approved experimental procedures, the results realized may be different from expected on a given farm. For example, a new crop variety may have been tested, experimentally, for a 3-year period and promise a 5-bushel yield increase. However, for various reasons, a given farmer may realize no increase in yield. This type of technological uncertainty may force the farmer to use his risk-bearing ability if the new practice does not work out as anticipated.

Another type of technological uncertainty relates to the rapidity of technological change. A new method may be adopted, but a still better method may follow close behind, making the investment in the new method somewhat obsolete. The first mechanical tomato harvesters were soon made obsolete by improved models; the same was true of cotton pickers, combines, and corn pickers. In such cases a substantial portion of the value of a machine disappears as soon as the new model comes on the market, and risk-bearing ability is needed to stand the loss.

A third type of uncertainty associated with technological change stems from the possibility of being left behind by not adopting new technological developments and adjusting the business to make full use of them. Many farmers who, a decade or so ago, had sufficient earning capacity and risk-bearing ability to use credit successfully now have become questionable credit risks. They have been slow to adopt new and improved practices and are operating the same size of unit as formerly.

Uncertainty Caused by Actions of Other Businesses and People. The course of action that will be followed by firms and people with whom the farmer does business causes a fourth type of uncertainty. If the farmer acquires part of his capital by renting, for example, the future action of his landlord creates uncertainty. The landlord may decide to increase the rent, rent to his brother-in-law, or sell the farm. If such things should occur, they might reduce the tenant's earning capacity and thereby curtail his risk-bearing ability. Similarly, if the farmer obtains part of his capital by borrowing, uncertainty may be caused by not knowing just what the lender will do. Customary financial arrangements allow some leeway for future negotiations or adjustments and the attitude of the lender at some point of time in the future may have an important bearing upon success of a farm venture. Government farm programs and various types of public action, such as taking of land for highways, or the passage of strict pollution control regulations, all create a question as to what the future holds. Actions of businesses and people such as these create uncertainty in varying degrees, which must be considered in analyzing risk-bearing ability.

Another type of uncertainty that results from interaction with other people is the possibility of a lawsuit. An auto accident caused by an animal that strays onto a public road, or an injury to a hired worker, are only two examples of situations in which the farm operator may be held legally liable for damages suffered by others. Farmers are especially vulnerable to large liability claims because their assets are highly visible. Land, buildings, livestock, and machinery are generally indicative of wealth. Thus damage claims against farmers tend to be high because of this perceived ability to pay. This tendency exists notwithstanding the fact that many farmers are heavily indebted and, therefore, are not as wealthy as appearances would indicate.

Uncertainty Caused by Sickness, Injury, and Death. No one knows what the future health of family members will be—when a serious illness may occur or when death will take some of the family members who are important in the business operation of the farm. Medical and hospital expense caused by a major illness may be substantial. When the farm operator is incapacitated, income suffers from loss of his labor and management in the business, and if he should die, a prime asset of the business is lost. Uncertainty arising from family health is of major importance in the farm business and should be fully recognized in considering risk-bearing ability.

STRATEGIES FOR REDUCING RISK AND UNCERTAINTY.

From the preceding section, it is apparent that financial success in farming is heavily dependent upon the ability of the manager to reduce risk and uncertainty or to improve his risk-bearing ability. Obviously risk and uncertainty cannot be totally eliminated. However, many sources of risk and uncertainty can be reduced and there are several strategies for improving one's ability to withstand adverse business conditions.

Formal and Informal Insurance. The financial consequences of many adverse events such as loss of life, medical expenses, auto accidents, casualty losses, and weather damage can be reduced by using formal insurance plans. That is, a policy can be purchased from an insurance company to cover all or part of any expected losses. Formal insurance is discussed in the next chapter. There are also informal arrangements discussed below that can be used to reduce risk and uncertainty. Both kinds of insurance carry a payoff in the form of reducing risk and uncertainty or minimizing the consequences of adverse events. Also, both kinds of insurance involve a monetary cost to the insured. In the case of formal insurance, this monetary cost is represented by premium payments. Informal insurance strategies nearly always result in foregone income.

INFORMAL INSURANCE STRATEGIES

Reserves. One way of reducing the consequences of adverse events is to carry reserves. The cost of holding reserves is the difference between the rate of return earned on reserves and the rate of return offered by alternative investment opportunities in the business. Most people carry reserves of cash or savings for a "rainy day." The rainy day in farming might include small everyday occurrences such as an equipment breakdown or it might be a more serious event such as crop failure or a severe price decline. Farmers carry other things in reserve besides cash and savings. Most livestock farmers hold carryover feed supplies to protect themselves against low crop yields and/or high prices for purchased feeds. Also, many farmers buy larger items of machinery and equipment than might be needed in an average year to protect against crop losses in unusually wet planting and harvesting seasons.

Reserve borrowing capacity is another very important form of protection against risk and uncertainty. In fact, most rational businessmen hold low amounts of cash or near cash reserves in comparison to the amount of unused credit because the cost of unused credit is lower than the cost of holding cash or savings. Suppose, for example, that money invested in the farm business offers a return of 15 percent per annum, that reserve funds held in a savings account earn 5 percent, and that money can be borrowed at 8 percent. The cost of holding cash reserves is the difference between the rate earned on the savings account and the rate that could be earned in the business, or 10 percent. The cost of holding credit in reserve is the rate of return earned in the business (15 percent) minus the cost of borrowing money (8 percent), or 7 percent.

This example also suggests that the cost of holding cash reserves can be reduced by making certain that these funds are invested in high-yielding investment alternatives. Only a minimum amount of reserve funds should be held as cash. Most should be kept in savings accounts or invested in short-term securities that can be liquidated on relatively short notice. The cost of holding credit in reserve can also be minimized by borrowing from low cost sources of credit and holding higher cost sources in reserve.

Hedging. As noted earlier, fluctuations in commodity prices can virtually wipe out a farmer's profit margin even though he may be a very efficient producer. Thus many producers, as well as processors and wholesalers of agricultural commodities, use the futures markets to hedge against price changes. The futures markets allow buyers and sellers to establish now the prices of products they intend to buy or sell on some future date. Many agricultural products, including corn, soybeans, broilers, cattle, eggs, hogs, orange juice, cotton, and potatoes, are traded in the commodity futures markets.

The technicalities of hedging are somewhat complicated; however, a simple example will illustrate the basic concepts. Suppose a corn grower observes in July that the price of December corn futures is $1.25, a price that will enable him to make a profit on his anticipated 20,000-bushel crop that year. Rather than taking a chance on having to sell his corn at a much lower price after harvest, he can "lock in" a price close to $1.25 per bushel by hedging. The transactions for this hedge might be as follows:

Date	Cash Market Transaction (per bu)	Futures Market Transaction (per bu)
July 1—*sell* 20,000 bu Dec. futures contract		+$1.25
Nov. 15—*sell* 20,000 bu corn for cash	$1.10	
—*buy* 20,000 bu Dec. futures contract		— 1.13
Difference		+$ .12
commissions, interest, and other costs		.01
Net difference		+$ .11

The farmer hedged his 20,000-bushel crop by *selling* December corn futures on July 1. On November 15, he *sold* his harvested corn for only $1.10. However, he purchased December corn futures on November 15 for $1.13, thereby fulfilling his futures contract at a net profit of 11 cents per bushel. The resulting price per bushel was the $1.10 cash price plus the 11 cents per bushel profit on the futures transaction, or $1.21.

It should be noted that hedging works because cash prices and futures prices tend to fluctuate together and the difference between them narrows as the contract month approaches. In this case cash prices dropped to $1.10 and the price of December futures dropped to $1.13 in mid-November. Thus effective hedging requires a knowledge of the probable basis—the difference between the cash price and the futures price. Transportation costs, storage costs, and other technical factors account for this basis.

It should also be recognized that hedging essentially eliminates any chance to gain from an increase in market prices. If, in the above example, the cash price of corn on November 15 had been $1.35, the futures price (assuming the same 3 cents per bushel basis) would have been $1.38. The loss on the futures market would have been $1.38 — $1.25 = 13 cents, plus the 1 cent per bushel expense, or 14 cents per bushel. Thus, even though the corn would have been sold for $1.35, the net return would still have been only $1.21 per bushel.

Many farmers contract with their elevator instead of hedging directly in the futures market themselves. In this situation, the manager of the elevator would hedge in the futures market to cover his position.

Hedging can be a powerful tool in reducing price risk. More and more farm lenders are recognizing the merits of hedging and are advising their borrowers to use contracts with elevators or futures to protect themselves.

Diversification, Enterprise Selection, and Production Practices. One of the commonest methods long employed to alleviate risk and uncertainty is diversification. By "distributing the eggs among several baskets," the chance of a large loss from a single misfortune or at any one time is reduced. Similarly, by having more than one enterprise in the farm business, the chance of a large loss from a given hazard is reduced. Losses may occur in each enterprise, but chances are against major losses occurring simultaneously in all enterprises, which reduces variability of net income for the whole business. Moreover, since each enterprise is but one part of the total business, a major loss in one enterprise is smaller, relative to the size of the business.

When diversification is given as a means of reducing risk and uncertainty, it is assumed that the diversified business is organized so as to reduce rather than increase risk and uncertainty. It is possible to actually increase risk and uncertainty through diversification by adding risky enterprises to a fairly stable business or by expanding the business materially in the diversification process.[5] For diversification to be most effective, enterprises included in the business should not be subject to the same hazards—or at least not to the same degree. If all crops included are equally affected by drouth at a given time of the year, little will be gained by diversifying. Similarly, if the enterprises added to the business are affected by the same price fluctuations as the enterprises already in the business, little stability of income will be attained by adding the new enterprises. Diversification is effective in combating risk and uncertainty to the extent the enterprises added are affected by different forces, or are basically more stable than those already in the business.

Flexibility. Flexibility has some advantages over diversification as a method contributing to stability and dependability of income.

As time passes and added information is obtained, a flexible business can be adjusted to meet new circumstances, whereas an inflexible business allows little room for change. With an inflexible business, a farmer may anticipate a drop in income, but be unable to do anything about it. Moreover, enterprises that involve great risk and uncertainty usually also hold the possibility of great gain. Reducing risk and uncertainty by diversification simultaneously reduces the pos-

---

5. For further elaboration of these points, see Earl O. Heady, *Economics of Agricultural Production and Resource Use* (Englewood Cliffs, N.J.: Prentice-Hall, 1952), pp. 510–16.

sibility of obtaining a large gain. Flexibility, on the other hand, facilitates adjustments to avoid risk and uncertainty, while still allowing the business to take advantage of larger gains that may be forthcoming.

Flexibility in organization of the farm business can be of three types: time, cost, and product. *Time flexibility* refers to the time involved in producing a product. Beef requires more time to produce than broilers. An orchard represents an inflexible production plan, while considerable flexibility exists with annual crops. A permanent building likewise may be less suited to flexibility than buildings with a shorter life.

Cost flexibility is attained by keeping fixed costs low in relation to total costs. Fixed costs, such as taxes, depreciation, and interest payments, do not vary with volume of production or income. Principal payments on intermediate-term and long-term debts also are fixed outlays that have about the same effect as fixed costs. These fixed costs and outlays can be held down by various methods, for example, custom operators can be used instead of buying expensive machines, and land and livestock can be rented on a share basis and thereby the fixed obligations incurred by cash rental arrangements or by purchase can be avoided. In such ways fixed costs and other obligations can be kept relatively low, enabling the farmer to more readily adjust costs of the business as current conditions justify.

Product flexibility refers to the possibility of adjusting the product produced to meet changing conditions. Grain-livestock producers have the choice of marketing grain or livestock. Ranchers operating on a cow-yearling basis can market either yearlings or calves, depending upon current feed supplies and price conditions. A general-purpose building is constructed to permit a wider range of uses than one designed for a specific product. Products that are storable also add some flexibility to the business since they can be sold or stored, depending upon conditions at the time of harvest.

It is evident that introducing flexibility considerations into the business increases the alternative opportunities open to the farmer and thereby increases the risk-bearing ability. Two cautions should be noted, however: (1) The increase in alternative opportunities means the farmer will have more choices to make and, therefore, will have more opportunities for mistakes; and (2) other things being equal, a highly flexible farm business generally is less efficient than one that is inflexible. Therefore, striving for too much flexibility may actually reduce net income. Some farmers, for example, go heavily into hogs when market prices are high, only to see the market price drop when their hogs are ready to market. Then they may cut back on hogs and have very few to sell when prices go back up. In other words, the successful use of flexibility depends upon accurate market forecasting. Since the level of net income is one factor influencing risk-bearing ability, it becomes clear that there is a limit as to how much flexibility a farmer should strive to achieve.

Ability to reduce operating and living expenses in low income periods contributes to risk-bearing ability by, in effect, reducing the need for it. If operating and living expenses were perfectly flexible there would be no need for risk-bearing ability. If income were low, these expenses could be curtailed as necessary to make ends meet. An extreme degree of flexibility obviously is impractical, but to the extent expenses can be kept flexible, risk-bearing ability is strengthened. Success or failure might well depend upon the ability and willingness of the family members to tighten their belts in poor times. Just a willingness to tighten their belts is not enough; more important is good judgment in knowing which expenses to cut. A farmer with financial problems who buys a new expensive car and a new tractor does not demonstrate an ability to curtail expenses that contribute to risk-bearing ability. In contrast, the farmer who put down an irrigation well and bought fertilizer showed an ability to choose among expenses so as to increase risk-bearing ability.

Producing a Stable and Dependable Income. Stability and reliability of income can be strengthened by measures that alleviate risk and uncertainty. If all risk and uncertainty could be eliminated, the business could be planned and operated to yield a stable income year after year. It is not practical to strive for this goal in agriculture, however, because of the costs involved. In most cases, increasing stability of income reduces profits.

But survival of the business firm is essential to continued production, so failure of the business must be prevented if profits over a period of years are to be maximized. Therefore, it will pay to adopt measures essential to survival even though there may be a certain cost involved.

Producing a stable and dependable income is a matter of following sound farm management practices. Keeping up-to-date on price forecasts will help to time sales of crops and livestock to coincide with periods of favorable market prices. Storage of carry-over feed supplies in good years may alleviate the need to sell breeding livestock in succeeding years because of low feed crop yields. Preventative maintenance of buildings, fences, and farm machinery will cut down on unexpected major repairs. Proper sanitation and the use of preventative medications will avoid major outbreaks of disease in livestock. Proper conservation practices, pest control, and fertilization will offset the effects of adverse weather conditions.

SUMMARY. Risk management is the use of strategies to reduce risk or improve risk-bearing ability. There are five major types of risk and uncertainty in agriculture: production uncertainty, price uncertainty, technological uncertainty, uncertainty caused by actions of other people, and uncertainty caused by sickness, injury, and death.

Farmers use formal and informal insurance strategies to reduce risk and uncertainty and strengthen risk-bearing ability. Informal strategies include holding reserves, hedging, diversifying, introducing flexibility considerations, and following sound production practices to produce a stable and dependable income. The use of formal insurance is covered in the next chapter.

QUESTIONS AND PROBLEMS

1. List the major types of risk and uncertainty in agriculture and give examples of each type for your state or region.
2. Distinguish the terms *formal* and *informal* insurance.
3. Explain how reserves are used to protect against risk and uncertainty. What is the cost of holding reserves?
4. Examine the price quotations of commodity futures in the financial pages of a newspaper. Explain how the manager of a large hog-feeding operation could hedge against an increase in corn prices or a decrease in hog prices.
5. Outline how diversification and flexibility add to risk-bearing ability. What are the costs of these informal insurance strategies?

REFERENCES

Economic Problems in Great Plains Ranching. Proc. of GP-2 Symposium, Bozeman, May 23–24, 1962, Great Plains Council Publ. 22, published by Mont. Agr. Exp. Sta., 1964.

Grossman, P. A., and Headley, J. C. *Yield and Income Variability for Major Crops in Illinois: A Basis for Farm Decisions.* Dept. of Agr. Econ., Agr. Exp. Sta., AERR 73, 1965.

Heifner, Richard G. "Implications of Hedging for the Agricultural Lender." *Agr. Finance Rev.,* vol. 33, ERS, USDA, July 1972, pp. 8–14.

Management Strategies in Great Plains Farming. Proc. of a Workshop held by Great Plains Research Technical Committee GP-2, May 5–7, 1959, Great Plains Council Publ. 19, published by Nebr. Agr. Exp. Sta., 1961.

Manderscheid, Lester V. "Are Futures Markets Useful to Farmers?" *Mich. Farm Econ.,* No. 354, Dept. Agr. Econ., Coop. Ext. Serv., Mich. State Univ., July 1972.

Skold, M. D.; Epp, A. W.; and Hughes, H. G. *Profit Maximizing Plans for Farms in Southeastern Nebraska: By Type and Size of Farm.* Nebr. Agr. Exp. Sta. and Farm Prod. Econ. Div., ERS, USDA, cooperating, Bull. 219, 1965.

Skrabanek, R. L.; Banks, V. J.; and Bowles, G. K. *Farmer Adjustments to Drouth in a Texas County.* Tex. Agr. Exp. Sta. Bull. B-1005, 1964.

CHAPTER 13: RISK MANAGEMENT: FORMAL INSURANCE

FORMAL INSURANCE is a complex subject that deserves a great deal of study. There are many different kinds of insurance and there are many insurance companies to choose from. Thus it is all too easy to end up buying the wrong kinds and the wrong amounts of insurance. Finding a reputable insurance agent can be just as important to financial success as finding a competent attorney or lender. In this chapter, we outline some of the basic principles of insurance and outline the alternatives to provide a basis for choosing insurance.

PRINCIPLES OF INSURANCE. Both formal and informal insurance serve one basic purpose: to provide protection against economic losses arising from adverse events. Automobile insurance, for example, protects the policyholder against losing the asset itself (his car) because of accident, theft, fire, or other calamity. In addition, the liability component of auto insurance protects the policyholder's other assets and his future income against claims for damages or injuries suffered by others. The basic purpose of life insurance is to protect surviving dependents against the loss of income and added expenses that occur when a family member dies.

Insurable Risks. Some risks are more easily insured than others. An event is insurable if the probability of its occurrence can be predicted and the cost of the event to the insured party can be determined. The degree to which these two conditions holds determines in large measure whether the risk can be feasibly covered by formal insurance.

Natural hazards based on the elements vary in their insurability. Those such as fire, lightning, windstorms, and hail have been successfully incorporated into an insurance system because they are not only predictable with reasonable accuracy but they do not cover wide areas. Where the occurrence is isolated, as the usual farm fire, a local insurance company covering a county can handle most of the risks. But where the occurrence is hail or a windstorm that might cut a wide path, a state or nationwide unit is better able to handle the risk than is a county unit.

Crop failures due to drouth that may cover wide areas are difficult to predict, such as a sequence of low crop yields that sometimes occurs in the Great Plains. As a consequence, neither local nor state units are big enough to do the insuring. Only a nationwide agency is big enough to cope with this type of risk.

Personal hazards lend themselves to insurance because they occur with predictable frequency when large numbers are included. It is unlikely that in any one area all individuals will be affected. It is, however, essential that the agency doing the insuring have a large volume of cases so it can be assured of experiencing about the average frequency of loss.

Price fluctuations do not lend themselves to insurance as well as do natural hazards because they are not as predictable and because they are likely to affect wide areas, or even the whole nation at the same time. Prices do not oscillate about a predictable average because they are the result of unpredictable factors such as weather conditions and other natural hazards as well as man's actions—wars, unbalanced budgets, monetary and fiscal policies, tariff regulations, and the like. It is true that "normal" prices are estimated but there are no forces that make prices average out over time equal to this "normal." Hence any agency that attempts to insure against low prices has little actuarial basis on which to operate. For this reason the federal government is the only agency with a large enough resource base to attempt any sizable program of insurance in the price field. So far the government's attempts have included price supports and insurance of certain mortgage loans made through the Farmers Home Administration, both of which have congressional support.

Insurance and Pooling of Risks. Insurance is the combining or pooling of enough small unpredictable risks so that the annual losses for the combined group are a predictable percentage of the total. What is a burdensome risk for the individual becomes in the pool an easily carried, relatively constant, annual loss expense for the insurance agency.

By paying his proportionate share of the losses for the group as a whole, plus his share of the expenses of running the company, the individual is able to avoid the burden of a loss that, if it struck him alone, might put him out of business or set him back for years. The premium paid by the individual can be charged as an expense to take care of the particular risk involved.

Fire insurance illustrates this pooling of risks especially well. The farmer never knows for sure when he leaves for town with his family whether or not a fire may destroy his barn or his home before he returns. For years, or all his life, he may not have a fire, and then again it may strike when he least expects it and result in an extremely heavy loss. In contrast to this extreme fluctuation in annual loss and unpredictability for the individual farmer, there is a predictable annual loss figure per $1,000 of insurance for the farm fire mutuals in the United States. Data published by the United States Department of Agriculture show that over a 60-year period the average loss for mutual fire insurance companies in the United States varied from a low of $1.38 per $1,000 to a high of $2.49. There is relatively little change from year to year in losses experienced.

Insurance, in order to pay, has to cover not only the losses but also the expenses of running the agency, including a profit for the owners of the company. An average figure in recent years would be approximately $2.50 per $1,000 in losses and $1.50 per $1,000 in expenses or a total of $4.00 per $1,000 of insurance. From this it is evident that the expense of the agency itself may be nearly 40 percent of the premium cost, with the actual losses around 60 percent of the premium. Both losses and administrative expenses have been going up in recent years.

In general, the loss component of the premium is found by multiplying the probability of occurrence by the cost of the event. Thus losses of $2.50 per $1,000 coverage would imply that the average probability of fire loss is roughly $2.50 ÷ $1,000 or 0.0025. The premiums for all types of insurance can be analyzed in much the same way. Life insurance, which is treated later in this chapter, is a special case in that the event (death) is certain to occur but the timing of the event is uncertain.

All phases of insurance—fire, crop, liability, and life—rest on the same principle of pooling unpredictable individual risks into a group risk total for which the annual loss can be predicted within narrow limits. Crop insurance presents some special problems because the actuarial base is so indefinite. But fire, liability, life, and associated types of insurance lend themselves readily to the pooling principle. This is not to say that the predictable life or liability rates for large groups never change, because they do, as indicated by rates for automobile insurance. But the changes that do occur can be measured, and appropriate changes can be made in premiums so that insurance cost is kept in line with loss experience and cost of running the insurance company.

The Rationale for Buying Insurance. Since premium costs exceed the cost of pure insurance by the amount of the company's administrative costs, one might conclude that the cost of formal insurance exceeds the benefits. Indeed, many wealthy individuals and government agencies find it more economical to insure themselves against some risks by covering losses with their own funds as they occur. To understand why buying insurance is a rational business decision, one need only look at the alternative. If formal insurance were not available, it would be necessary either to hold enough money or unused credit in reserve to cover any losses that might occur or simply risk being put out of business. As was pointed out in the previous chapter, money and credit held in reserve carry a cost in terms of foregone income from alternative investments.

An example using fire insurance will illustrate this concept. Suppose a farmer owns a barn and contents that can be insured for a premium of $4.00 per $1,000. The alternative to buying a fire insurance policy would be to hold enough reserves of cash, liquid investments, or unused credit to cover any fire losses. As long as the cost of holding reserves exceeds the amount of the premium, it will generally pay to buy insurance. Clearly, fire insurance, based on a premium of $4.00 per $1,000, is a paying proposition for most farmers, because this represents a rate of return of only 0.4 percent. In other words, the cost of holding reserves, which is the difference between the rate of return earned on reserves and the marginal rate of return on investment opportunities, need only exceed 0.4 percent to justify the expenditure for premiums. This same analysis can be applied to all types of insurance, and in some cases it may show that formal insurance does not pay.

In most cases substituting reserves and unused credit for formal insurance is not really a feasible alternative because most farmers use practically all their capital and sometimes most of their borrowing capacity in their business. Reserves can be used for smaller risks such as the $100 deductible for automobile insurance; however, reserves are generally inadequate to cover the $100,000 or $300,000 liability coverage. Deductible clauses in insurance policies are used to avoid the expense of processing very small claims.

KINDS OF INSURANCE. The different kinds of insurance and the factors that determine the amount that should be purchased can be discussed advantageously in five different categories—property, crop, liability, personal (life and health), and social. It should be recognized that several types of insurance can be combined into one policy. Farm owners' policies, for example, usually combine fire, windstorm, theft, and liability insurance into a single policy at a reduced overall premium cost compared to the cost of separate policies.

Property Insurance. Property damage may result from natural hazards such as fire, windstorms, and floods or from human-related actions such as accident, theft, and malicious destruction. In general, property can be insured against most of these hazards at a reasonable premium cost.

Although farm fires frequently result in total building losses because of the absence of fire-fighting equipment, farmers may easily and inexpensively insure their buildings and contents against fire. An invariable role of nearly all mortgage lenders is to require fire and windstorm insurance on the farm buildings located on mortgaged real estate. During recent years, the average cost of fire insurance for the United States has been approximately $4.00 per $1,000. However, there are wide variations between states so that the costs may vary from practically nothing to over $10.00. But a large number of states are in a narrow range, with annual costs in the neighborhood of $4.00 per $1,000 of mutual fire insurance. For a set of buildings and contents valued at $50,000, full coverage fire insurance would cost about $200 a year, a small amount considering the risk and the financial embarrassment to a farm owner if he has a bad fire and no insurance. Farm mortgage lenders usually have the fire insurance policy assigned to them so that they are protected in the event of any fire losses. If a fire should destroy the barn on a mortgaged farm, the lender has the right to insist on using the funds to replace the barn or to reduce the principal of the mortgage.

Windstorm insurance, like fire insurance, is cheap compared to the heavy loss that may be suffered by an individual farmer. In fact, most fire insurance policies include windstorm damage as well. Windstorm damage, including losses from tornadoes, cyclones, and hurricanes, is much commoner in some areas than in others. The Pacific Coast and New England rarely have windstorms, but if such storms do occur, they may be so disastrous as to wipe out the life savings of a farm family.

Windstorm insurance is less costly than fire insurance. An average cost figure that is based on 50 years of experience is $1.35 per $1,000. For a set of buildings valued at $50,000, full coverage would cost only $67.50 a year. Lenders follow the same policy with windstorm insurance as with fire, requiring an assignment so that proceeds from losses may be used in rebuilding or in reducing the mortgage.

In addition to fire and windstorm insurance on buildings, most farmers carry insurance against accidental damage, fire, and theft on their automobiles, trucks, and farm machinery. In the case of motor vehicles, coverage for accidental property losses suffered by the policyholder himself is called collision insurance and the cost of collision insurance should be carefully evaluated. Most policies are sold on a deductible basis, that is, the policyholder is responsible for the first $50, $100, or $250, as the case may be, of any property damage. Substantial savings can often be realized by purchasing collision insurance with the higher deductible amounts. Furthermore, if the market value of the vehicle is low, it probably does not pay to carry collision insurance at all. No general recommendations can be made for collision coverage on motor vehicles because of the wide variation in premium rates. However, it would probably be unwise, for example, to pay $30 per year for $100 deductible collision insurance on an automobile valued at $300, because even in the event of a total loss, the maximum net coverage is only $200. The cost of holding reserves would have to exceed 15 percent ($30 ÷ $200) before collision insurance would pay in this case.

Crop Insurance. There are two main types of crop insurance—*crop-hail* and *all-risk*.[1] Crop-hail insurance is available through commercial insurers and some state insurance departments while all-risk crop insurance is provided through the Federal Crop Insurance Corporation (FCIC), a federal government agency that was established in 1938.

Commercial crop-hail insurance protects against crop loss due to hail and, in some cases, wind or fire, as specified in the policy. Coverage in any amount up to the reasonable value of full yields can be purchased. Premiums are scaled according to the amount of the coverage and the probability of loss in the area.

Payments for claims (indemnities) are based on the percentage of the crop that is destroyed by hail, measured in terms of stand reduction, ears lost, or whatever is appropriate for the particular crop. Thus, if a hailstorm caused a 50 percent reduction in a stand of wheat, for example, and coverage was $30 per acre, the indemnity would be $15 per acre, even though the actual value of the crop might be $50 per acre.

Crop-hail insurance can be purchased any time from before seeding to immediately before the harvest date. Coverage is available in nearly all parts of the country where the risk of hail damage is significant.

All-risk crop insurance from the FCIC covers losses caused by virtually all natural hazards, including drouth, flood, hail, windstorm, frost, insect damage, disease, and other "unavoidable causes." Federal all-risk crop insurance is designed to enable farmers to recover their production expenses rather than compensate them for the full value of the crop. Thus the coverage varies by crops since preharvest production expenses range from around 30 percent of total crop value on wheat to about 60 percent on soybeans, cotton, and tobacco. If a partially damaged crop is harvested, the bushel guarantee is increased to cover harvesting costs.

Federal crop insurance must be purchased on or before a specified

---

1. A more complete discussion of crop insurance is contained in Warren R. Bailey and Lawrence A. Jones, *Economic Considerations in Crop Insurance*, ERS-447, USDA, Aug. 1970.

date prior to the planting date. A yield guarantee is established by the FCIC for each county or district within a county and farmers can select from two or three product price options. Premiums reflect the price option and the probability that yields will fall below the guaranteed level. Premiums are also set high enough to build up reserves, but administrative costs are borne by the government. Premium discounts are available for farmers who report no losses for specified periods. A farmer who reports no losses for 2 consecutive years receives a 5 percent discount. If there are no losses for 3 or 4 consecutive years, the discount is 10 percent and the discount ranges up to 25 percent for no losses in 7 consecutive years.

Indemnities are based on the difference between the yield guarantee and the *average harvested yield* for the insured crop on the *entire* farm. Thus a farmer who loses part of his crop due to flooding, for example, would not receive an indemnity unless the average yield over all acres of that particular crop on his farm fell below the yield guarantee.

The FCIC is expanding its services as rapidly as possible within the limitations imposed by legislation and the availability of funds. In recent years, roughly 10 percent of all United States farms have been using crop insurance for about 25 different crops in about half the rural counties. Total FCIC insurance protection in 1969 was $908 million, compared to $265.9 million in 1960.

Crop insurance, like all types of insurance, is particularly important from a financial standpoint. It enhances borrowing capacity because it can be assigned to a lender as loan collateral. Crop insurance removes a major element of risk in crop farming and should be considered by all farmers located in high-risk growing areas. This is true especially for farmers who are in a low equity position and could not withstand a severe 1-year loss.

Liability Insurance. As was mentioned in the previous chapter, farmers are particularly vulnerable to large liability claims because their assets are highly visible and appear to be indicative of wealth. Thus liability insurance coverage is an essential part of a farm insurance program.

Liability claims arise when a person who suffers physical injury or economic loss can prove that his injuries or losses are caused by someone's negligence. Frequently, liability claims involve not only compensation for actual damages but legal costs as well. Furthermore, there is practically no way of estimating the amount of a liability claim. The claim for a motor vehicle accident, for example, can range all the way from a few dollars to hundreds of thousands of dollars. A fire loss, on the other hand, can be fairly accurately estimated by considering the replacement cost of the building and its contents.

Liability risk takes many forms: the farmer's dog may injure a visitor; a hired man may suffer an accident; or the driver of the farmer's truck may be involved in an accident on the highway. Auto liability insurance would cover this last type. Auto insurance premiums are not very high compared to the peace of mind and security that this coverage provides. In addition to liability for bodily injury or death, liability is also included for damage to the property of others caused by an automobile or truck and the company that has insured the farmer would defend him in court. Several states have adopted no-fault motor vehicle insurance. With no-fault insurance, each driver's own insurance policy pays for damages or injuries which he suffers, regardless of who is at fault in the accident. Under true no-fault insurance, it is not necessary to sue the other driver (or his insurance company) for damages. Some modified no-fault plans do allow lawsuits for damages above specified minimum amounts. Although relatively new, experience thus far indicates that no-fault insurance can result in significant reductions in motor vehicle insurance premiums and faster settlement of claims because long and costly court settlements are largely eliminated.

Other forms of liability are covered in what is termed a comprehensive personal liability policy and an employer's or workmen's compensation policy. The first covers such acts as the dog biting a visitor; the second takes care of an accident to an employee. The workmen's compensation policy has the advantage that it provides medical payments to the injured employee. The laws in some states require employers to carry workmen's compensation insurance. Even if not required, farmers with hired help will do well to make certain that they have protected themselves and their employees against loss of income caused by accidental injuries suffered on the job.

Life Insurance. Life insurance is a widely used form of insurance. Although similar to other insurance in many respects, life insurance has two unique features. First, the insurable event (death) occurs with certainty. Only the *time* of occurrence of the event is uncertain. Second, permanent life insurance policies contain elements of an investment in addition to pure insurance. This means that the *cash surrender value* or *loan value* of the policy builds up over a period of years. This combination of pure insurance along with an investment makes the task of pricing and comparing life insurance policies extremely difficult. If possible, the *insurance* decision should be distinguished from the *investment* decision.

LIFE INSURANCE PREMIUM CALCULATIONS. Life insurance premiums are based on life expectancy data recorded in the form of mortality tables. In its simplest terms, pure life insurance can be interpreted as a savings account. The policyholders make regular "deposits" (premium payments) to the insurance company. These deposits are invested by the company, thus the "savings account" earns interest. As policyholders die, an amount equal to the face value of their policies is "withdrawn" and paid to the beneficiaries as a lump sum or in the form of a regular income.

Like other types of insurance, life insurance premiums must cover the company's administrative expenses. Life insurance is also based on the pooling of risk principle because many policyholders will die before a savings account equal to the face value of the policy is established. Losses on policyholders who die early are recovered from policyholders who live longer than expected. Thus premiums paid by a large enough group of policyholders will, on the average, cover all payments to beneficiaries as well as administrative expenses.

The role of life expectancy data in premium calculation can best be illustrated with a simple example. Suppose that past experience has shown that 30-year-old life insurance policy purchasers have a mean life expectancy of 40 years and that annual premiums can be invested by the insurance company at 4 percent per annum compounded. The annual premium needed to insure all 30-year-old policy buyers for $1,000 is that amount that, when invested at 4 percent compound interest, would accumulate to $1,000 at the end of the 40 years. This would be the level premium to be paid by all 30-year-old policy purchasers for life. The annual premium in this case turns out to be $10.52 per $1,000 face value. The reader should not attempt to compare this estimated premium with actual premiums because many other factors are used to calculate premiums. For one thing, administrative costs have not been considered. Also, there are many different types of insurance policies. The four basic types are discussed below. Furthermore, some 30-year-old policyholders will allow their policies to lapse before death, in which case the company would not have to pay their beneficiaries. Finally, mortality experience and rates of return on investment portfolios vary among individual insurance companies. This latter point suggests that one should make price comparisons when shopping for life insurance.

DETERMINING THE AMOUNT OF LIFE INSURANCE NEEDED. The basic purpose of life insurance is to provide for the financial security of one's dependents when he dies. In this section, we disregard the investment component of life insurance and focus on the pure insurance aspect.

The life insurance coverage decision should begin with the question, "How much money would my surviving dependents need if I were to die now?" The survivors will have immediate financial needs such as funeral expenses, estate settlement costs, taxes, and payment of debts. There will also be continuing financial needs in the form of living expenses. This future financial need must be considered in the life insurance decision.

The total amount of money needed by the survivors consists of immediate expenditures plus the *present value* of projected future needs. An example will illustrate the procedure for establishing financial goals, estimating other sources of income, and arriving at estimated life insurance requirements. The procedure illustrated in this example is basically the same as that used by most life insurance companies. Many companies are using some type of computerized analysis to calculate recommended insurance programs for their clients.

Consider the hypothetical case of a 35-year-old farmer with a 30-year-old wife and two children, ages 3 and 4. He has assumed that if he were to die his three survivors would need $8,000 to cover immediate expenses. He has also projected their future requirements at $6,000 per year until the younger child is 20 years old and $4,500 per year thereafter until his widow is 65. He also wants to leave enough money to permit his wife to purchase an annuity when she reaches age 65.[2] He wants the annuity, together with social security benefits, to provide her with a lifetime income of $4,000 per year from age 65 on. These modest income requirements are based on the assumption that the farm business would be liquidated and the proceeds, after payment of debts and selling costs, would provide enough money to purchase a home.

They have $2,000 in savings, which would partially defray immediate expenses after death. Social security benefits will amount to $3,000 per year until the younger child is 20 years old, and $2,000 per year for the widow from age 65 until her death.[3] Thus the annuity that the widow would purchase at age 65 would have to provide an annual lifetime income of $2,000 and would cost approximately $25,000.

Table 13.1 summarizes the basic procedure for discounting the future income needs of the survivors to estimate the amount of life insurance needed. Columns (1) and (2) show the projected ages of the widow and younger child, who will presumably be financially independent at age 20. Column (3) projects the years from the time of death. Life insurance needs are usually estimated on the assumption that the breadwinner will die in the present year, thus the need for

2. Annuities are contracts sold by life insurance companies that guarantee the purchaser a monthly income for life, beginning at some specified age. Annuities are discussed further in Chapter 16.

3. Social security survivors' benefits would cease when the younger child reaches age 19, unless the child attends college, in which case benefits would continue through age 22.

TABLE 13.1: Summary of Procedure for Estimating Life Insurance Needs

Timing			Survivor's Annual Income—Needs & Sources				Present Value Calculations	
(1)	(2)	(3)	(4)	(5)	(6)		(7)	(8)
Age of widow	Age of younger child	No. years from date of death	Total income needed	Income from sources other than life insurance	Income to be met from life insurance program (4)—(5)		Present value factor (4%)	Present value of column (6) (7)×(6)
30	3	0	$ 8,000	$2,000	$ 6,000		1.0000	$ 6,000
31–47	4–20	1–17	6,000/yr	3,000/yr	3,000/yr		12.1657†	36,497
48–65	...	18–35	4,500/yr	0	4,500/yr		6.4989‡	29,245
65	...	35	25,000	($2,000/yr)*	25,000		0.2534§	6,335
					Estimated Life Insurance Needed			$78,077 or $78,000 (rounded)

* Social security benefits will be $2,000 annually after age 65.
† Present value of $1.00 per annum, 17 years (Appendix Table 4).
‡ Present value of a deferred annuity—$1.00 per annum, years 18 through 35 (see Chapter 3, Footnote 4).
§ Present value of $1.00, 35 years hence (Appendix Table 2).

coverage should be reviewed regularly to make certain that the changing immediate needs and continuing needs of the survivors are taken into account.

Column (4) summarizes the survivor's immediate and future income requirements discussed above. Note that this projection terminates when the widow reaches the age of 65, or 35 years after her husband's death, because it was assumed that she would purchase the life annuity at that time. Column (5) shows the income available from current savings and estimated future social security benefits. The first three entries in column (6) are found by subtracting the entries in column (5) from the corresponding entries in column (4). The last entry in column (6) is the amount needed to buy the annuity.

Procedures for discounting future income streams or future costs associated with investment alternatives were described in Chapter 3. Essentially the same procedure is used in estimating life insurance needs. That portion of the survivor's future income stream that must be provided by life insurance proceeds [column (6) in Table 13.1] is discounted to a present value. This present value figure is the estimated amount of life insurance needed. Column (7) contains the 4 percent present value factors used to discount that portion of the income stream to be met from insurance proceeds. The discount rate used should reflect the rate of return at which the beneficiary could invest the proceeds of the life insurance policies. In this case it was assumed that the widow's investment portfolio would earn 7 percent per annum, but the discount rate was adjusted downwards to 4 percent to compensate for an assumed 3 percent inflation rate.

Column (8) shows the present value of that portion of the survivors' present and future income needs that must be met from the life insurance program. The analysis indicates that this young farmer should carry about $78,000 worth of life insurance. The $78,000 when invested at 4 percent (net return after inflation) would cover the $6,000 needed for immediate expenditures, $3,000 per year until the younger child is 20 and $4,500 per year thereafter until the widow is 65. If all projections materialize there would then be $25,000 available to purchase a life annuity providing a $2,000 annual lifetime income for the widow from age 65 on. All projections are measured in real income. The actual dollar amounts would be higher because of the adjustment for anticipated inflation.

This example illustrates that life insurance is a personal decision and everyone must examine his own situation. The amount of life insurance needed is determined by personal financial goals and the amount of savings and other financial resources, as well as the projected rate of inflation and return on investments. In many cases, a young man with a family will not be able to carry enough life insurance to provide fully for his family's needs so they must balance their outlays for insurance with other living expenditures. In the above example, the future income requirements were modest because the farmer had large enough net worth in his farm business to enable his survivors to purchase a house. In some situations, it might be reasonable to assume that the widow could work (or perhaps remarry), thereby providing a portion of the survivors' income needs and reducing the need for life insurance.

A life insurance program should be regularly reviewed and revised, if necessary. The young farmer's need for insurance differs considerably from that of a middle-aged farmer whose children are grown up. Life insurance needs are normally greatest when the parents and children are young. However, older people should also carry enough insurance to meet the financial needs of their dependent survivors and young men should probably consider purchasing some life insurance while they are still insurable, even before they have family responsibilities, to guarantee that they will be able to buy insurance later on, regardless of health.

SELECTING THE TYPE OF LIFE INSURANCE POLICY. Once the total amount of life insurance needed has been determined, the next step is to select the type of policy or policies. Table 13.2 shows comparative premium rates for the four basic types of life insurance policies.

Term Life Insurance. Strictly speaking, term life is pure life insurance. No savings are involved. It is like fire, auto, liability, or other

TABLE 13.2: Approximate Annual Premium Rates per $1,000 Face Value for Four Types of Life Insurance

Age Taken	Five-Year Term (Renewable and Convertible)	Ordinary Life	Limited-Payment Life (Paid up at Age 65)	Twenty-Year Endowment
15	$ 6.90	$14.05	$15.70	$48.37
20	7.15	15.65	17.70	48.50
25	7.50	17.65	20.20	48.65
30	8.15	20.20	23.60	49.00
40	11.40	27.65	34.65	51.00
50	19.40	40.00	60.90	56.10

SOURCE: Taken from *A Date with Your Future,* published by the Educational Division, Institute for Life Insurance, Health Insurance Institute, New York, 1970.

NOTE: Rates shown are approximate premium payments for life insurance protection for men. Because women live longer, the rates for them would be somewhat less. The premium rates shown here would also be lower per $1,000 of protection if the policies were purchased in units of $5,000 or $10,000.

forms of insurance in that if the event does not happen during the period, there is no payment. If you take out a 10-year or 20-year term policy and do not die in this period, there is no payment at any time during the period or at the end. And similarly, if you had your house insured against fire for 20 years and did not have any fire, you would not expect any payment during the period or at the end.

Term insurance is often used with credit. A farmer buying a farm with a mortgage can take out enough decreasing term insurance to cover this mortgage at a relatively low cost and in this way protect his family against the burden of the mortgage in case he dies. In the same manner, the young farmer can use term insurance to protect his family during the period when his children are growing up and he is accumulating capital to invest in his business.

Term insurance, however, does not provide any savings and coverage is generally not available beyond age 70. For savings and coverage after age 70, an ordinary life, limited-pay life, or an endowment policy must be used. Another disadvantage of term insurance is that premiums increase with age at each renewal date as shown in Table 13.2.

Permanent Insurance: Ordinary Life, Limited-Pay Life, and Endowment Policies. These policies provide what their names signify. *Ordinary life* (also called *straight life* or *whole life*) is a policy on which the insured pays a level premium each year for as long as he lives. Unlike term, though, he is certain that his beneficiary will collect the full amount of the policy when he dies because the policy has no termination other than the death of the insured or cancellation of the policy by the policyholder.

A *limited-pay life,* or similar type policy, provides for a limited number of years in which the insured pays premiums. Variations of this type are those policies that specify "20-pay life" or "paid up at age 65" or at some other age. In all these policies the insured can figure a specific number of years during which he must pay a fixed premium. At the expiration of this period, he has paid-up life insurance for the rest of his life. On his death, the beneficiary receives the face value of the policy. This naturally costs more per pear than ordinary life because the payments cover fewer years.

An *endowment* policy, which includes a larger element of savings than ordinary life and limited-pay life policies, provides for the accumulation of the entire policy sum in a given number of years. At the end of this period, the insured, if he is still living, receives the face amount of the policy.

Since the need for life insurance is generally greatest when the family is young (and often least able to pay premiums), term insurance should be used to cover a major portion of the insurance program for the young farm family. The case of a man who buys a $20,000 ordinary life policy when he really needs coverage of $40,000 is a good example. The rates in Table 13.2 indicate that for the same premium he could have purchased over $40,000 worth of term insurance. For a nominal additional cost, one can purchase *renewable* and *convertible* riders with term insurance policies. The renewable feature guarantees that the policy can be renewed at the end of each term regardless of the policyholder's health. Of course, the premium after renewal will be higher because the policyholder will be older. The convertible feature permits the policyholder to exchange all or part of his term insurance for permanent insurance such as ordinary life any time he chooses to do so. Thus the convertible feature permits a young man to inexpensively cover his family's insurance needs and later convert some of his term insurance to permanent insurance when his financial situation improves.

Most life insurance companies offer some type of family plan that combines permanent and term insurance on the head of the household and other members of the family. These combination plans should be given serious consideration because premiums are often quite reasonable compared to the cost of separate policies. Group life insurance plans available through many employers and farm organizations also offer very favorable rates.

Normally, some permanent insurance should be purchased to provide coverage beyond age 65. The amount of money needed to cover survivors' needs is typically much lower after age 65. Furthermore, most of the survivors' needs can be met from savings and net worth in the business that have accumulated over time. Nevertheless, some insurance may be needed after age 65 to cover the surviving widow's immediate financial needs during the estate settlement period. Life insurance can also provide ready cash to cover estate taxes and other settlement costs. The role of life insurance in retirement and estate planning is covered more fully in Chapters 16 and 17.

Although the rate of return on the savings component of permanent life insurance policies is generally lower than most other savings plans, insurance provides a forced savings plan. The cash surrender value that builds up in a permanent life insurance policy can be withdrawn or used as collateral for a policy loan if needed. Policy loans carry low interest rates compared to other sources of credit.

Health Insurance. The death of the head of a family usually has serious financial consequences; however, illness or injury can also cause a major financial setback. The farm family should carry some form of medical insurance, and disability income coverage may be used to supplement social security benefits.

Hospital-surgical medical insurance plans usually cover most of the costs arising from an illness or injury that requires hospitalization. Routine medical care such as doctors' office calls, checkups, and drugs or medicines are usually not covered. Unfortunately, hospital-surgical medical insurance is fairly expensive compared to other types of insurance. Since group rates are lower, farmers would be well advised to check on the availability of group medical plans from their farm organizations. Many hospital-surgical medical plans are subject to a maximum indemnity, that is, costs in excess of a specified dollar amount or number of days of hospitalization are not covered.

Major medical insurance can be used alone or to supplement a hospital-surgical medical policy. Major medical insurance, like deductible automobile collision insurance, covers all or a specified percentage of costs in excess of the deductible amount ($200, $500, etc.). Thus, while major medical insurance does not cover all medical costs, it will help to eliminate, for a comparatively low cost, ruinous financial losses that could result from serious illness or injury.

Disability income insurance, as the name implies, is designed to replace the breadwinner's income if he should become permanently disabled and unable to earn a living. The question of how much disability income insurance is needed should be approached in basically the same fashion as life insurance. This coverage is fairly expensive, but the cost can be reduced considerably by purchasing a policy with a longer waiting period, that is, a longer period of time between the occurrence of disability and the beginning of the benefits. Typical waiting periods are 30 days, 90 days, and 180 days.

Social Insurance. Some risks cannot be feasibly covered by private insurers. The federal government's involvement in crop insurance, discussed earlier, is an example of this type of risk. Social security and unemployment insurance are two other forms of social insurance that are of primary importance to farmers.

SOCIAL SECURITY. Virtually everyone who earns an income in the United States must channel part of his earnings into social security (or another approved substitute plan). Social security is sometimes misunderstood because many people believe that it provides retirement income only. In addition to retirement benefits, however, social security provides disability income insurance and survivors' benefits. Thus social security not only provides for a retirement income but it also reduces expenditures for life and disability income insurance from private insurers. In the hypothetical case illustrated in Table 13.1, the farmer in question would need about $130,000 worth of life insurance (compared to $78,000) to meet his family's future income needs were it not for estimated social security survivors' benefits. Table 13.3 illustrates the types and amounts of benefits

TABLE 13.3: Examples of Monthly Social Security Benefits

Average yearly earnings after 1950*	$923 or less	$1,800	$3,000	$4,200	$5,400	$6,600	$7,800	$9,000
Retired worker 65 or older / Disabled worker under 65	$ 84.50	$134.30	$174.80	$213.30	$250.60	$288.40	$331.00	$354.50
Wife 65 or older	42.30	67.20	87.40	106.70	125.30	144.20	165.50	177.30
Retired worker at 62	67.60	107.50	139.90	170.70	200.50	230.80	264.80	283.60
Wife at 62, no child	31.80	50.40	65.60	80.10	94.00	108.20	124.20	133.00
Widow at 60	73.30	96.10	125.10	152.60	179.30	206.30	236.70	253.50
Widow or widower at 62	84.50	110.80	144.30	176.00	206.80	238.00	273.10	292.50
Disabled widow at 50	51.30	67.30	87.50	106.80	125.50	144.30	165.60	177.30
Wife under 65 and one child	42.30	67.20	92.50	157.40	217.30	233.90	248.30	265.90
Widowed mother and one child	126.80	201.50	262.20	320.00	376.60	432.60	496.60	531.80
Widowed mother and two children	126.80	201.50	267.30	370.70	467.90	522.30	579.30	620.40
One child of retired or disabled worker	42.30	67.20	87.40	106.70	125.30	144.20	165.50	177.30
One surviving child	84.50	100.80	131.10	160.00	188.00	216.30	248.30	265.90
Maximum family payment	126.80	201.50	267.30	370.70	467.90	522.30	579.30	620.40

SOURCE: Courtesy of Social Security Administration, U.S. Department of Health, Education and Welfare.

* Generally, average earnings are figured over the period from 1951 until the worker reaches retirement age, becomes disabled, or dies. Up to 5 years of low earnings or no earnings can be excluded. The maximum earnings creditable for social security are $3,600 for 1951–1954; $4,200 for 1955–1958; $4,800 for 1959–1965; $6,600 for 1966–1967; $7,800 for 1968–1971; $9,000 for 1972. The maximum creditable for 1973 is $10,800, and beginning in 1974, it will be $12,000. However, average earnings cannot reach these amounts until later. Because of this, the benefits shown in the last column on the right generally will not be payable until later. When a person is entitled to more than one benefit, the amount actually payable is limited to the larger of the benefits.

available from social security. Social security benefits change frequently and a family's benefits will depend upon its annual income and the number of years of credit. The Social Security Administration will provide estimates of retirement and other benefits for individual cases. In recent years medical insurance has been made available through the Social Security Administration in the form of *Medicaid* and *Medicare* plans. There are indications that the federal government will play an even greater role in providing medical insurance protection in the future.

UNEMPLOYMENT INSURANCE. Just as farmers were the last to become eligible for social security benefits, farm workers are the last major group of employees who are not universally covered by unemployment insurance; however, this situation appears to be changing. Farm workers in some states are currently covered by unemployment insurance plans, and federal unemployment insurance legislation covering farm workers is pending. Farmers themselves are not covered by unemployment insurance unless they hold a nonfarm job. Extending unemployment insurance to farm workers will make it easier for farm employers to attract good quality labor who might otherwise choose nonagricultural employment.

SUMMARY. Formal insurance is the pooling of enough small, unpredictable risks so that annual losses for the group are predictable. Thus an insurance company can "play the odds," whereas the individual cannot, because he runs the risk of incurring ruinous financial losses. By purchasing insurance, the individual assumes a small, certain loss (the premium) and eliminates a much larger, uncertain loss.

It would be prohibitively expensive to try to eliminate all risks with insurance. Essential needs should be met first. Essential needs would include enough life insurance to cover the basic financial needs of dependents, certain types of liability insurance, property damage insurance on mortgaged assets, health insurance, and any other losses that would result in financial disaster. Additional insurance should be used to supplement these essential needs, keeping in mind that additional protection always involves added costs. Usually it is more economical to hold enough reserves of cash or unused credit to cover small losses such as routine medical expenses, the first $100 or $250 damages to motor vehicles, or the first 90 or 180 days income lost through disability.

QUESTIONS AND PROBLEMS

1. Explain the principles of insurance. What conditions are needed to set up an insurance company to insure a certain risk?
2. Explain the rationale for buying insurance. Give examples of situations in which it may not pay to buy formal insurance.
3. What are the rates for fire, windstorm, and other property damage insurance on farm buildings in your community? Try to find out if there are major differences in rates among different insurance companies.
4. Explain the differences between commercial crop-hail insurance and federal all-risk crop insurance. Find out what proportion of the farmers in your state use federal crop insurance.
5. Why is liability insurance coverage important? Does your state have no-fault automobile insurance? If so, how do automobile insurance premiums compare with those in effect prior to no-fault coverage? What are the principal arguments against no-fault insurance?
6. How does life insurance differ from other types of insurance? Outline the basic procedure used to estimate life insurance premiums from life expectancy data.
7. Explain the procedure for estimating the life insurance requirements of a young farmer. (If you are married, use the procedure outlined in this chapter to estimate your own life insurance needs.)
8. Discuss the differences among the four types of life insurance policies. Why is term insurance recommended for a young farmer living on a limited budget? Explain why some permanent life insurance should be carried.
9. Contrast the differences in coverage provided by hospital-surgical insurance policies and major medical insurance policies. What are the arguments *for* and *against* making medical insurance available to all citizens through a government health insurance program?
10. Outline the benefits available under social security. (If you are covered by social security, obtain an estimate of your own retirement and survivors' benefits from your Social Security Administration office.)

REFERENCES

Bailey, Warren R., and Jones, Lawrence A. *Economic Considerations in Crop Insurance.* USDA, ERS-447, Aug. 1970.

Botts, Ralph R. *Insurance Facts for Farmers.* USDA Farmers' Bull. 2137, 1963.

Delvo, Herman W., and Anderson, Dale O. *Appraisal of Federal All-Risk Crop Insurance Coverages and Premiums in North Dakota Effective with the 1969 Crop Year.* Dept. Agr. Econ., N.Dak. State Univ., Rept. 65, Mar. 1969.

Delvo, Herman W., and Greer, James D. *Hail Insurance: An Analysis of Policy Forms in Nebraska, 1969.* Dept. Agr. Econ., Univ. of Nebr., Rept. 51, July 1969.

Federal Crop Insurance Corporation. *Annual Reports.*

Garland, S. W. *Insurance for Farmers.* Canada Dept. of Agr. Publ. 1188, 1964.

Jones, Lawrence A. "The Farmowners Insurance Package." *Agr. Finance Rev.*, vol. 28, ERS, USDA, Nov. 1967, pp. 14–22.

Ohio Cooperative Extension Service. *Understanding Life Insurance for the Family.* Bull. 496, June 1968.

Olson, Carl E.; Schaffner, Leroy W.; and Powell, Dennis L. *Effect of All-Risk Crop Insurance on Farm Firm Survival.* Dept. Agr. Econ., N.Dak. State Univ., Rept. 61, Nov. 1968.

CHAPTER 14: CREDIT INSTRUMENTS AND LEGAL ASPECTS OF BORROWING

THE LARGE NUMBER of credit instruments and papers that are a part of loan procedure awe and discourage the farmer when he obtains his first loan. To read and understand all the fine print contained in notes and mortgages seems a formidable task. Reading and understanding the *Uniform Commercial Code,* adopted by practically all the states, is a much more formidable undertaking. When additional affidavits, acknowledgments, releases, waivers, and abstracts have to be obtained or studied, the borrower is truly bewildered. The difficulty lies not only in the large number of documents but also in the unfamiliar legal language included in long paragraphs of small type. The best approach is to take each document by itself and to place most of the emphasis on the main provisions. When this is done, the meaning and the reason for each of the credit instruments are made clear.

THE NOTE. The promissory note is the primary document in most credit transactions. It is the written promise of the borrower to repay the loan. When the lender gives the loan funds to the borrower, he receives in exchange a note signed by the borrower promising to pay the lender a certain stated principal amount with interest on a certain date (see Fig. 14.1).

The dominant position of the note in all credit transactions should be clearly understood. There may be a tendency to overlook the note because it is a small form with much less printed matter than mortgages or extension agreements, but such an oversight may prove costly because the borrower's signature at the bottom of a note is a direct obligation holding him liable for the payment of the loan according to the terms stated on the note. If the property mortgaged by the borrower in connection with the loan fails to cover the amount due at a foreclosure sale, the borrower usually is still liable and the lender may have other nonexempt property of the borrower sold to satisfy the deficiency. Hence, the borrower should *read carefully and thoughtfully* the provisions of the note before he signs it. He should verify the amount, the rate of interest, the penalty provisions if any, and the time and place at which the payment is to be made. Furthermore, he should make a record of these items on an extra note form

OHIO — NOTE (Open-end)
Form PCA 400B (5-70)

Co-Fo. **08-0**   Member No. & Loan Type **31536-8**

John and Mary Doe
Route 1
Anytown

Ohio

(TYPE MAKERS' NAMES AND POST-OFFICE ADDRESSES IN THIS BLOCK)

$ **12,600**

Anytown, Ohio **February 15** 19 **73**

On or before **February 15**, 19 **74**, for value received, I promise to pay to the order of **Marion**

Production Credit Association, 1100 East Center Street, Marion, Ohio _____, negotiable and payable at any office of the payee,

Twelve Thousand Six Hundred _____ **00/100** Dollars, with interest at the

rate of **7 3/4** _____ percent per annum from date of disbursement until paid, or at payee's option and as not prohibited by law, with interest at such other rates as may subsequently be adopted by payee, from date of adoption until note is paid in full.

The payee is hereby authorized to reinstate on this note all sums repaid by the maker on or before the maturity date, provided, however, that the total amount outstanding at any time hereunder shall not exceed the above stated face amount of this note.

In case of failure to perform any of the terms and conditions of this Note or of any Financing Statement and Security Agreement, or any mortgage securing said indebtedness, or in case the holder hereof deems itself insecure, the entire balance of principal and interest shall at the option of the holder be immediately due and payable. Failure to make payments as scheduled on loan applications and other supporting documents shall constitute a breach of performance for which the holder may deem itself insecure. The undersigned hereby authorizes any attorney at law, at any time after the above sum becomes due, to appear for the undersigned in any court in the State of Ohio, and to waive the issuing and service of summons and to confess judgment against any or all of the undersigned in favor of the payee or any holder of this Note for the amount appearing due, and the costs of suit, and thereupon to release all errors and waive all rights of appeal and stay of execution. The makers and endorsers severally consent to any partial release of collateral and extension and waive demand, presentment for payment, protest, notice of protest, notice of non-payment of this Note, and all other defenses to the extent that the Federal Intermediate Credit Bank of Louisville gives or has given value to the payee hereof in reliance upon this Note and do waive all such defenses or rights of offset which they or either of them might have against the payee hereof when this Note is held by said bank, a farm loan registrar, or the successors or assigns of either. The funds evidenced by this Note may be disbursed to any one or more of the undersigned makers and/or endorsers.

This Note is secured by a Financing Statement and Security Agreement (and a Real Estate Mortgage(s) dated **February 15, 1973** _____), and evidences the original indebtedness, any renewal indebtedness and/or any additional advances or disbursements thereunder.

FIG. 14.1—A promissory note. *(Courtesy of the Marion Production Credit Association.)*

so that he will have at hand at all times correct information on the terms of his obligations.

If the lender requires an additional signature to the note—a common condition where the borrower is a young farmer with little capital—the endorser should study the provisions of the note as carefully as if he were the borrower. The importance of the endorsement is evident by the fact that the lender will not make the loan without it. In effect, the endorser himself is borrowing the funds, because he is making himself liable for the payment. Many times, an endorsement, given as a friendly gesture with scarcely a thought, may turn out to be a tragic mistake. A farmer once related that his farm, which had been entirely clear of debt, was mortgaged for all it was worth because an endorsement on a note to a relative caused him to lose almost everything he had.

THE MORTGAGE. The mortgage, which follows the note, is a specific listing of certain property set aside to guarantee the payment of the note. Although mortgages, like notes, may take on a multitude of variations in detail, they are almost identical in their chief provisions (see Fig. 14.2). The provisions not only identify the property to back up the note but they establish a priority of claim among lenders according to the time of filing or recording of the mortgage at the county courthouse. In some places the evidence of debt that accompanies the mortgage is a bond rather than a note, but the general effect is the same.

A mortgage is recorded or filed at the courthouse to give notice to the world in general and all interested lenders in particular that the borrower has given a mortgage or pledge of certain property to a certain lender. Any subsequent lender, therefore, will have to take a second, or junior, mortgage on this same property; and he cannot say he did not know that the property was already mortgaged, because the records or files at the courthouse are kept open for public inspection. Few people among the general public appreciate the significance of these mortgage records and files. It is a large and continuing task, a task that on the whole is handled efficiently.

Real Estate Mortgages. The distinctive features of the real estate mortgage, and of the *deed of trust* that is sometimes used as a mortgage, are the unchanging character of the security, the length of term covered, and the permanence of the mortgage record. Since land does not change position except through erosion, it is relatively easy to describe and to locate through long periods of time. Legal descriptions, especially by rectangular survey, provide a highly efficient

OPEN END MORTGAGE

Know All Men By These Presents:

That _____ John H. Doe and Mary R. Doe _____

_____

_____, the mortgagor, in consideration of the sum of ____ Twenty-Four ____

____ Thousand _____ and $\frac{00}{100}$ ____ Dollars in hand paid by

STATE BANK

of Columbus, Ohio, has MORTGAGED, BARGAINED and SOLD and does hereby GRANT, MORTGAGE, BAR-
GAIN, SELL, and CONVEY unto   STATE BANK   its successors and assigns,
forever, the following real estate situated in ___ Green Township ___ County of ___ Fairfield ___
in the State of Ohio, and described as follows:

S 1/2 of NW 1/4, Section 14, Range 20, Township 14, containing in all 52 acres

more or less.

TO HAVE AND TO HOLD said premises, and all rents, issue and profits therefrom, with the buildings and appurtenances thereunto belonging, including fixtures, and all of the mortgagor's estate, title and interest, either in law or
equity, including right of dower, unto the said grantee and mortgagee, forever. And the mortgagor hereby covenants
with   STATE BANK   that the mortgagor is lawfully seized of the premises aforesaid as a good and indefeasible estate in fee simple and has the right to grant, bargain, sell and convey the same as
herein set forth; and that the premises are FREE AND CLEAR from all encumbrances whatsoever, and that the mortgagor will forever WARRANT AND DEFEND the same with the appurtenances unto the said grantee against the law-
ful claims of all persons whomsoever.

PROVIDED, nevertheless, and these presents are upon these conditions:

That the said mortgagor has executed and delivered to the mortgagee a note of even date herewith for the aforesaid consideration, with interest thereon as provided in the note, conditioned among other things for the payment of
consecutive monthly installments (including interest) of not less than $ __200.64__ each. The final payment of
principal and interest, if not sooner paid, shall be due and payable on ___February 15, 1993___

That upon the reduction of the principal sum due under the debt secured by this mortgage, additional sums of
money may be advanced to the mortgagor, at the option of the mortgagee, to an amount of indebtedness not exceeding the principal amount herein secured, which shall become a part of the principal debt secured by this mortgage
as shall be evidenced by the account records of the mortgagee, and the parties hereto intend that this mortgage shall
secure the unpaid balances of such additional advances as a valid first lien on the real estate herein described. Repayments of said advances shall be in such amounts and upon such terms as may be agreed upon at the time of the
advance. The maximum amount of unpaid loan indebtedness, exclusive of interest, which may be outstanding at any
one time is $ __24,000__ .

That the maturity of all or any part of the debt evidenced by said note and any advances as aforesaid may be
delayed or extended and that any covenants and conditions contained in this mortgage may be waived or modified
without prejudice to the mortgagor's liability as maker of said note, and payment of said note is unconditionally
guaranteed.

That the mortgagor further agrees as follows: To pay all taxes, assessments and other charges that may be assessed against the property herein conveyed or against this mortgage or the debt secured by it promptly as they become due and payable; to keep the buildings on the real estate hereby mortgaged in good and proper repair; to keep
the premises so mortgaged insured against loss by fire, windstorm and other hazards covered by extended coverage
insurance in some reliable fire insurance company acceptable to the mortgagee in an amount not less than the unpaid
balance of said note, with the loss, if any, payable to the mortgagee as its mortgage interest may appear and, when requested by mortgagee, to leave all policies of insurance in the possession of the mortgagee until this mortgage is fully

FIG. *14.2—A real estate mortgage.*

method of designating the exact property concerned, and none other. The importance of land ownership and the relatively high value of land itself has established the practice of making permanent copies of mortgages in the records at county courthouses.

The recording of a mortgage is considered public notice to everyone concerned. Anyone buying a farm may find what mortgages, if any, exist, either by going through the county records or, as is commonly done, by obtaining the information from an abstractor or a title insurance company. Abstracts are used in some parts of the United States and title insurance in others. An *abstract of title* is a brief summary of all recorded transactions or events that have affected the land in question, and of these transactions, mortgages are one of the most important. When an abstract is brought "down to date," it shows the current status of the title, including any outstanding mortgages. Title insurance insures the title to the subject property against defects, except for those shown in the policy. If a recorded mortgage is outstanding against the property, it will be included in the exceptions.

When a mortgaged farm is up for sale, two different methods of purchase may be specified in the deed: the farm may be bought subject to the mortgage; or the purchaser may buy the farm, assuming the mortgage. The difference between "subject to the mortgage" and "assuming the mortgage" is greater than many realize. The term *subject to the mortgage* means that the buyer does not agree to pay the mortgage, although if he fails to pay or meet any of the terms of the mortgage, the lender may foreclose, and the property in due course will be sold at foreclosure sale. The term *assuming the mortgage* means that the buyer, in effect, is endorsing the original mortgage note and hence is liable up to the limit of his property, which may be attached for sale to settle any debts not covered by the real estate mortgaged. This distinction, however, applies only to cases where a farm is bought with a mortgage on it and the mortgage is not paid. If a new mortgage is made at the time of purchase, the purchaser, of course, is liable. Two farmers who bought farms at high prices had experiences that illustrate the difference in the two methods of purchase. Both farmers had 160-acre farms clear of mortgage. They both bought additional quarter-section farms at $300 an acre. Both of the farms purchased had existing mortgage indebtedness averaging $200 an acre. Both farmers paid down $100 an acre in cash, but Farmer A assumed a $200-an-acre existing mortgage while Farmer B bought subject to the $200-an-acre mortgage. During the depression that followed, Farmer A not only lost the farm he bought but also lost his unencumbered farm as well because he had to mortgage it to meet the payments for which he was liable on the second farm. Farmer B, on the other hand, since he had no liability on the $200-an-acre mortgage, allowed the lender to foreclose the mortgage and kept his first farm clear of debt. The original borrowers, in both cases, were still liable even after they had sold the farms to A and B. The person who has signed or endorsed a note is liable for its payment until it is paid or is outlawed by the passage of time after the term has expired.

A real estate mortgage does not mean what it says in one important particular, which may seem a contradictory statement, but a careful reading of a mortgage will bear out the contention. Most mortgages provide for the outright transfer of the property to the lender or mortgagee at the time the mortgage is signed. If the borrower pays the note, however, the property is to be returned to him; that is, fulfillment of the conditions in the mortgage prevents the conveyance from taking effect. In case of default by the borrower, the mortgage specifies that the property is to belong to the lender. But in actual practice this does not occur because the courts have ruled otherwise. Property mortgaged is not transferred to the lender in spite of what the mortgage says, either at the time the mortgage is signed or upon default by the borrower. A lender must take this plea before the court and obtain a judgment, and even then he does not get the actual property mortgaged. The court, in most states, has the sheriff sell the property at a public sale to the highest bidder, the proceeds of the sale being remitted to the lender after costs have been deducted. If the sale brings more than the amount due, the surplus goes to the borrower. If the amount obtained from the sale is not sufficient to meet the judgment and costs, the lender may obtain a *deficiency judgment* against additional property of the borrower.

Interpretation of mortgages varies by states, some states adhering to what is called the title theory and others following a more liberal view, called the lien theory. According to the *title* theory, the borrower actually gives the lender title to the property, but the title reverts to the borrower if he fulfills his obligations. If the borrower defaults, the title, in effect, belongs to the lender even though the lender may have to sell the property or have a sale made by the court in order to obtain a settlement. If the borrower, after defaulting, makes sufficient payment to place the mortgage in good standing, he must obtain a deed from the lender under the title theory to regain his former position.

According to the *lien* theory, the lender with a mortgage obtains only an interest in the property regardless of the wording in the mortgage. If the borrower defaults, the lender has a claim on the property for the amount due, but the lender has no right to the property other than that of obtaining the amount due him. If the borrower, after defaulting, places his mortgage in good standing and if there is no foreclosure action, the borrower's title to the property is the same as before the default.

The contradiction between the wording and meaning of a mortgage may be traced back to the time when the lender did receive title to the mortgaged property as a pledge at the time the loan was made, and the lender became the unquestioned owner of the property if the borrower defaulted. In eighteenth-century England, the mortgagee or lender could take immediate possession of the mortgaged farm if the borrower failed to meet any of the terms in the note or mortgage. Borrowers fought this procedure so vigorously that in time jurisdiction over mortgage defaults was taken over by courts of equity. A lender who sought to collect a defaulted loan could no longer take the mortgaged property directly, he had to appeal to the court, which in turn heard the claims of both sides and, if the lender's pleas were considered valid, sold the property and distributed the proceeds according to priority of lien. But as this change in legal action was taking place there was no corresponding change in the wording of the mortgage; hence, the mortgage of today, handed down by tradition from generation to generation, has lost some of its original meaning.

UNIFORM COMMERCIAL CODE. Laws governing use of mortgages on movable property, called chattel mortgages, have been replaced in practically all the 50 states by provisions of the Uniform Commercial Code. Except for pledges,[1] the emphasis is changed under the code from the form of the agreement to the kind of collateral involved. However, chattel mortgage forms still are usable under the code and, indeed, are used in code jurisdictions. Moreover, they still are utilized in states (and in other countries) where the code has not been adopted.

The Uniform Commercial Code was prepared under the joint supervision of the National Conference of Commissioners on Uniform State Laws and the American Law Institute. It was first adopted by Pennsylvania, where it became effective in 1954.

Two objectives of the drafters of the Uniform Commercial Code were to improve laws relating to commercial transactions and to facilitate uniformity in commercial laws throughout the country. The latter objective was primary, and the bulk of the code remains uniform throughout the states in which it has been adopted. However, in enacting the code a number of states amended some provisions. Therefore, complete uniformity does not exist. Moreover, the authors of the code left some alternatives from which each state could make a

---

1. A pledge is a security interest in chattel property created by manual delivery of the chattel to the creditor under an agreement that the creditor is to retain possession until the debtor has paid in full. A good example is pawning an item of personal property at a pawn shop.

choice, such as the place for filing the "financing statement" under Article 9. The states have selected different alternatives that also add some nonuniformity. Thus the need to check individual state statutes should be recognized.

The Uniform Commercial Code is divided into nine articles that extend over the law of sales, negotiable instruments, documents of title, bank collections, investment securities, bulk sales, letters of credit, and secured transactions. Each article is comprehensive and detailed. Some of the more general provisions of Article 9, which relate to secured transactions, are outlined in this section.

A number of terms new in law are used in the code. Under Article 9, the two parties in a secured transaction are the *debtor* (borrower or buyer) and the *secured party* (lender or secured seller). The secured party obtains a *security interest* (lien) in *collateral* (personal property, given as security) by entering into a *security agreement* (an agreement which creates or provides for a security interest) with the debtor (see Fig. 14.3).

The concept involved in the *security interest* represents a major change in law pertaining to secured transactions. It is a simple, unified concept of a *single* lien. In states that have adopted the code, it replaces the chattel mortgage, reservation of title by a conditional seller, the assignment, and the like. This is true regardless of whether state legislation enacting the Uniform Commercial Code repeals applicable earlier statutes, since a later law supercedes an earlier one where they are inconsistent.[2]

Some concepts involved in *collateral* also represent a new approach in secured transactions. The personal property subject to a security interest may be tangible or intangible. *Tangible* personal property, called *goods,* includes all property that is movable at the time the security interest attaches. Goods are classified into four categories according to the function or purpose they serve: (1) *Consumer goods* include tangible property bought or used for personal, family, or household purposes. (2) *Equipment* consists of personal property that is bought for use *primarily* in business, including farming. (3) *Farm products* include crops, livestock, and supplies *used or produced* in farming operations. They also include *products* of crops or livestock in their unmanufactured states, such as milk, eggs, wool clip, ginned cotton, maple syrup, and honey, if they are in the possession of a debtor engaged in farming operations. If goods are farm products they are neither "equipment" nor "inventory." (4) *Inventory* includes goods held by a person who holds them for sale or leasing, or to be furnished under contract of service. Inventory also includes raw materials, work in progress, or materials used or consumed in a business.

---

2. Charles Bunn et al., *An Introduction to the Uniform Commercial Code* (Charlottesville, Va.: Michie Co., 1964), p. 12.

This Financing Statement and Security Agreement is Presented to the Filing Officer for filing pursuant to the UCC:

1 Debtor(s) (Last Name First) and Address (es)	2 Secured Party and Address	For Filing Officer (Date, Time, Number and Filing Office)
John and Mary Doe Route 1 Anytown, Ohio 43210	PRODUCTION CREDIT ASSOCIATION	2/15/73 1:05 p.m. File No. 19362

This Statement and Agreement covers all of the Debtor(s) interest in the following described property located on the hereinafter described farm land (and additional property and/or farms described on _____ Extension Sheets):

3 CROPS:

4 EQUIPMENT:
As per schedule 1

5 FIXTURES:

6 LIVESTOCK, FARM PRODUCTS AND PERSONAL PROPERTY:
As per schedule 2

7 All property similar to that listed above, which at any time may hereafter be acquired by the Debtor(s) including, but not limited to, all off-spring of livestock, additions and replacements of livestock and poultry, and replacements of and additions to equipment and other personal property above described; and all products of livestock and poultry, and all feed to be used in fattening or maintaining said livestock and poultry.

8 All proceeds of the sale or other disposition of any of the property described or referred to under Items 3 to 7, inclusive above, and of any off-spring, wool, milk and poultry products derived from said property, together with all accounts receivable resulting from such sales.

9 Until this financing statement is terminated, it also applies to debtors interest in crops described above planted or growing on the hereinafter described farms(s) more than 1 year from date hereof and on which crops a separate security agreement is taken.

10 All of the above described crops and property are or will become located on the farm land owned (rented) by _____ located on the _____ Road _____ miles. from _____

This statement and agreement has been executed by parties this 15th day of February 19 73, and IS SUBJECT TO THE TERMS AND PROVISIONS SET FORTH ON THE REVERSE SIDE HEREOF, the same being incorporated herein by reference.

X John Doe
X Mary Doe
Signature(s) of Debtor(s)   (Form PCA 401-I (10-66)

PRODUCTION CREDIT ASSOCIATION
By Robert Miller
Signature of Secured Party - Lender

FIG. 14.3—A financing statement and security agreement. (Courtesy of the Marion Production Credit Association.)

Intangible personal property includes items such as promissory notes, bonds, stock certificates, accounts, and contract rights, which have little or no value in and of themselves but are valuable because of the legal right or rights they represent. It is classified in six groups: (1) *Instruments* include items such as a promissory note, bond, and corporate stock certificates. (2) *Documents of title* are items such as warehouse receipts, dock receipts, and gin tickets. (3) *Chattel paper* means "a writing or writings which evidence both a monetary obligation and a security interest in or a lease of specific goods. . . ." [U.C.C. 9–105 (1) (b).] For example, a farmer buys a tractor "on time," and gives the tractor as the *collateral* for the obligation. The farmer signs a written *security agreement,* which identifies the tractor and acknowledges the debt. Together the *security interest* in the tractor and the *obligation* of the farmer comprise one form of *chattel paper.* (4) An *Account* is any right to payment for goods sold or for services rendered that is not evidenced by an instrument or chattel paper, such as accounts receivable. (5) A *Contract right* is "any right to payment under a contract not yet earned by performance and not evidenced by an 'Instrument' or 'Chattel paper.' " [U.C.C. 9–106.] (6) *General intangibles* are any personal property not included in the above classifications. Rights under insurance policies and passbook accounts are examples.

The classification of goods or collateral involved in a transaction is very important since the classification determines what method is used in the perfection of a security interest against claims of third parties.

A security interest may arise in two ways: in connection with purchase or rental of property, and by obtaining a loan on property already owned. The first, called a *purchase money security interest,* enjoys the greatest protection against the claims of third parties under provisions of the Uniform Commercial Code. Such an interest is created when the seller of collateral retains a security interest to secure all or part of the purchase price. For example, a farmer might buy a tractor "on time," paying $1,000 down and giving the machinery dealer a *purchase money security interest* in the tractor as collateral for the balance of the purchase price. A purchase money security interest is also created when a lender makes a loan to enable the borrower to acquire rights in or use of collateral, providing the loan is in fact made for such purpose. In our tractor example, the farmer might have gone to his banker and told him he wished to borrow the money to buy the tractor. If the bank made the loan and entered into a security agreement with the farmer, the bank would have a *purchase money security interest* in the tractor as collateral for the loan, assuming the loan proceeds were in fact used to purchase the tractor.

To have a *security interest* "attach" to collateral already owned by a farmer (1) there must be a security agreement, (2) value must be given, and (3) the farmer must have "rights" in the property. "Attach" means, loosely, "create." Thus, "a security interest attaches to collateral" means "a security interest is created in collateral." "Value is given" when a loan is made by the lender or "secured party." The farmer has "rights" in crops when they are planted or when they otherwise become growing crops; he has "rights" in the young of livestock when they are conceived. If the security is to cover crops, oil, gas, minerals, or timber to be cut, the land related to the collateral must be described in the security agreement. The security agreement should provide a complete description of the collateral. However, collateral may be referred to by general kind or class if it can be so identified.

To "perfect" a *security interest* that is valid against (immune to attack by) third parties, other than those having a prior perfected security interest or other superior rights, such as tax liens, it is necessary for the lender (secured party), subject to certain exceptions that are discussed shortly, to take possession of the collateral *or* file the proper notice in a public office. Taking possession of collateral is feasible when it is intangible, as in the case of negotiable instruments and investment securities. When tangible security is involved, filing a "financing statement" usually is necessary. The financing statement is not to be confused with a financial statement such as a balance sheet. The financing statement must show the name and mailing address of both the debtor and secured party, and a description of the collateral, together with a description of the associated real property if the collateral is crops or timber. The financing statement must be signed by both the debtor and secured party. No affidavit or witnesses are required. (See Fig. 14.3.)

Policing of collateral by the secured party is not required under the code to validate a security interest. However, as a practical matter, policing is still essential to make certain that the collateral is not being dissipated. A security interest, even though valid, is not very valuable if the collateral is gone.

Filing of the financing statement is in either the county or the state capital, or in both places. The place of filing depends upon which alternative provision of the code was adopted by the state involved.

The financing statement may be filed either before or after the security agreement has been executed. Filing should be done promptly to prevent intervening rights attaching to the collateral. Presentation of the financing statement or a copy of the security agreement to the filing officer, along with the proper fee, and his acceptance of them, constitute filing under the code.

In some instances and under certain circumstances, it is not necessary for the secured party (lender) to file or take possession of the collateral to perfect a valid security interest. This is the case, for example, when there is a "purchase money security interest" in farm equipment having a cash price of less than $2,500. Moreover, in certain cases a security interest is temporarily perfected for a period of 21 days without filing or taking possession by the secured party.

A properly filed financing statement is effective for a period of 5 years from the date of filing. The period can be extended beyond 5 years by filing a continuation statement prior to the expiration date.

When a secured obligation is paid in full and no further commitments to extend credit are contemplated, the secured party must, upon written demand of the debtor, give the debtor a statement terminating the security interest. Failure to provide such a termination statement within 10 days after proper demand is made would subject the secured party to all actual damages suffered by the debtor, plus a penalty of $100 if the failure was in bad faith.

When a secured party desires to assign or transfer his interest in any collateral on which a financing statement has been filed, a statement covering the assignment also may be filed. If an assignment is made concurrently with filing of the financing statement, the assignment may be endorsed on the financing statement before it is filed.

A security interest in crops, growing or to be grown, which is perfected by filing with the proper government official, becomes unperfected when the crops are harvested and removed from the farm. However, if the financing statement covers proceeds, the security interest remains perfected in any income received from sale or other disposition of the crops.

Article 9 permits a lender and a borrower in one transaction and in one financing statement, properly filed, to create a security interest in all the various classes of collateral, including future advances and after-acquired property. The floating lien was invented in pre-code days and used in "factoring" under so-called factor's lien acts of some eastern states. A major contribution of the code was to extend the floating lien beyond the old factoring cases and make it available for use in all states that adopt the code. However, availability of the floating lien may deter extension of open-account credit by suppliers.

The code includes a provision requiring exercise of good faith in all transactions that it covers. Thus a lender with a comprehensive security agreement with a farmer is required to exercise good faith in financing the business. Should he refuse to make further credit extensions, which he may have the right to do under his agreement, there may arise the question of whether he can also prohibit the farmer's seeking funds elsewhere by giving a second security interest in his assets. Under certain circumstances the lender may be held liable for losses suffered by the borrower that resulted from insufficient credit.

PURCHASES ON CONTRACT. Farm chattels are frequently purchased on contract, or what is often called a *conditional sales contract.* In states that have not yet adopted the Uniform Commercial Code, buying chattels on contract means they are bought without the buyer obtaining title to the property. No mortgage is involved because the borrower is not the owner and hence cannot give a mortgage. The borrower gets possession and the lender retains title. The advantage to the lender is that if the terms of the contract are not fulfilled it is possible for the lender to regain possession without the necessity of foreclosure. The advantage to the borrower is that he can purchase equipment and the like with a smaller down payment by this method.

In states that have adopted the Uniform Commercial Code, the situation is much different. Article 2, which deals with the law of sales, is a complete revision and modernization of the Uniform Sales Act that was in force in most of the states. The code covers a much larger area of sales law than the old statute, and provides all sorts of rules and procedures for dealing with problems that arise. The principal change from a financing point of view is that generally the rights of the buyer and the seller are no longer determined by when title to the goods is passed. A sale of goods constitutes passing of title from the seller to the buyer for a price. In other words, in transactions covered by Article 2, title passes to the buyer at the time the goods are delivered, or a contract is entered into for their purchase, regardless of whether payment has been received. Generally, under Article 2 there is no way in which the seller can retain title once the goods are sold or contracted for and, thereby, protect his financial interests as was the case before adoption of the code. However, the seller can obtain the traditional protection of a "conditional sales" contract by entering into a "security agreement" with the buyer, thereby creating a "security interest" in the delivered goods that he can perfect under Article 9 of the code. Article 2 governs the interests of the buyer and seller, while the interests of the debtor and creditor are governed by Article 9.

Land purchase contracts are often used as a method of buying land (see Fig. 14.4). In fact, many farmers would not be able to purchase otherwise because they do not have the down payment required for purchase with a deed. Land contracts may provide for the transfer of a deed when the buyer has paid from 30 to 50 percent of the purchase price, or when the full purchase price has been paid. Some insurance companies who prefer not to sell on contract sell with a

CONTRACT FOR SALE OF REAL ESTATE

LAND CONTRACT

THIS AGREEMENT, Made and entered into at __Cole__ , __Wayne__ county,
Ohio, this __20th__ day of __March__ __1973__ by and between __James R. Brown__
party of the FIRST PART and John H. Doe, _____

_____

_____

party of the SECOND PART.

WITNESSETH, That said first party has this day agreed to sell and convey
to the second party, their heirs and assigns forever, and the second party has
agreed to purchase from the first party the following described real estate,
situated in the Township of _____Green_____ , County of _____Wayne_____
State of Ohio, bounded and described as follows:

SW 1/4 of Sec. 3, Township 83, Range 24, West, containing in all 160 acres more
or less.

Said premises being known as the previously described real estate.

Said second party hereby agrees to pay to the first party for the real estate
and personal property aforesaid the sum of $__Sixty-Four Thousand__ ————————
———————————————————— ($__64,000__).

The rate of annual interest on this contract of purchase shall be __7 1/2__
percent and the length of loan __20__ years, payable as follows:

Six thousand four hundred dollars ($6,400) on the execution of this agreement and
the remaining sum of $57,600 in semi-annual principal payments of $1,440 plus
interest on the unpaid balance commencing on September 20, 1973 . . .

Second party agrees to pay all taxes and assessments of every kind that
may become due or payable on said premises on or after the date of these presents,
i.e., beginning with the __August, 1974__ collection.

Second party agrees to keep all building structures located on said premises insured against loss by fire and windstorm for not less than $__45,000__
during the continuance of this contract, and said policy shall

FIG. 14.4—A real estate contract.

down payment of 25 percent and give the deed at the time of the sale. Sellers on contract, however, frequently sell with down payments of not more than 10 percent at the time the buyer takes possession.

Farmers who buy land on contract should read their contracts carefully to understand fully their position in case of default. Failure to pay any amount due on the date specified may cause the entire amount to become due and payable and may give the seller the right to repossess the property, with all previous payments of the buyer considered as rent payments and liquidated damages. Although the buyer may have only one more payment to make before being eligible to receive a deed, failure to make a required payment on the date due may forfeit all the previous payments and place the buyer in the same position as a tenant whose lease has expired. Instead of instituting foreclosure of a mortgage, the seller has only to serve legal notice on the buyer of his default on the contract and take possession after the period of time provided by law has elapsed. If the buyer takes the case to court, he will have to contest the provisions in the contract that he voluntarily signed when he purchased the farm.

Since the buyer on contract is often in a poor bargaining position, it is important for him to compare the price he is paying, including not only the quoted price but the financing charges as well, with the price he would have to pay if he were buying the same goods or land for cash, or if he were buying with enough down payment to obtain title and give a mortgage for the difference. On the other hand, the lender or seller will want to make sure that the buyer is not making as small a down payment as possible, with the intention of using the land or goods as long as possible before they are repossessed.

OTHER CREDIT INSTRUMENTS. A large number of written instruments may be encountered in farm credit that have not been discussed up to this point. Of these the most important are abstracts, title insurance, waivers, nondisturbance agreements, extensions, assignments, and releases.

An *abstract of financing statements* is a record of any security interests in property owned by the borrower. A *real estate abstract* contains a brief account of all deeds, mortgages, foreclosures, and other pertinent facts that affect the title to the land. Before a buyer completes a farm purchase he should insist on an up-to-date abstract and should have the abstract examined by a competent attorney to make sure that the seller has good title. In some areas *title insurance* is used in place of the real estate abstract. It is issued by a licensed title insurance company upon payment of a premium, and insures the buyer or mortgagee against defects in the title other than those that may have been specifically excluded.

Efforts have been made at different times to introduce a system of titles based on registration and certificates. This system, called the *Torrens system* after Sir Robert Torrens who started it in Australia, provides for public registration of the property by the owner if he can establish clear and undisputed ownership. Registration entitles the owner to a certificate that carries with it complete evidence of ownership. When the property is sold the new owner has the old certificate canceled and a new one issued in his name.

A *waiver* is a relinquishment of a claim. A landlord may waive his lien on a tenant's crop in favor of a lender who wants to make the tenant a loan. In some areas lenders will not extend short-term credit to tenants without a waiver of the landlord's lien. The landlord's lien is the right that the landlord has to the crops produced on his land in settlement of any amounts that the tenant may owe the landlord. In some states the landlord lien extends to all property owned by the tenant, but the trend in state legislation is definitely toward a limitation of the lien to the crop raised by the tenant.

A *nondisturbance agreement,* as the term implies, is a promise by one lender to a second lender that he will not start any action against the borrower during a stated period of time. A short-term lender may be unwilling to lend to a borrower with a heavy mortgage debt unless the mortgage holder will sign a nondisturbance agreement to cover the period of the short-term loan.

An *extension agreement* is a written statement setting forth the terms on which a lender agrees to postpone a payment due him.

An *assignment* is a transfer of notes, mortgages, and other property from one party to another. A common *assignment* is the transfer of a mortgage from a mortgage company that makes the original loan to an insurance company that buys the note and mortgage. The mortgage company in this instance is the assignor, and the insurance company is the assignee.

A *release* or *satisfaction* is a cancellation of a claim, usually of a real estate or security interest. A release when recorded gives notice to all concerned that the mortgage to which it refers no longer exists as a claim against the property specified. A *partial release,* commonly used when a highway strip, portion of a farm, or some livestock are sold, cancels the mortgage claim against that part of the property that is sold.

FORECLOSURE OF MORTGAGES. The foreclosure of a farm mortgage may be divided conveniently into four steps: default on the mortgage by the borrower; court proceedings; foreclosure sale of the land by the sheriff; and redemption period.

Default on the mortgage occurs when one of the numerous terms of a mortgage is not met. If a mortgage provides for fixed payments on principal in addition to interest, and if the principal payment is not made when required or within the period of grace allowed, the mortgage is in default, and the lender has the right to start foreclosure proceedings even though the interest is paid and all other terms have been met. These other terms include payment of all taxes and assessments when due, and payment when due of premiums on fire and tornado insurance on buildings. Actually, few lenders start foreclosure proceedings on a minor default in payment, although they have this right if the term is specified in the mortgage. Foreclosure is commonly recognized as a last resort after every other means of settlement has been tried. There is good reason to support this policy since lenders are not primarily operators of farmland. Moreover, the present operator as an owner is usually willing and able to pay the lending agency as much as or more than he would as a tenant. Finally, farms acquired by lending corporations must be rented on a short-term basis, since they are for sale. Because tenants with short-term leases are not interested in maintaining buildings and improvements, lenders find it to their advantage to work out loan extensions or deferments to help the present owner retain title to the farm.

Court proceedings vary by states but usually consist of three parts: (1) the institution of foreclosure by the lender, (2) the hearing of the case, and (3) the rendering of the decision by the court. Since most foreclosure cases are clear-cut defaults about which there is no argument, the judge almost invariably renders a judgment against the borrower for the amount due plus accumulated interest and costs. In the depression period beginning in 1931, however, a successful defense by borrowers against foreclosure was made in the form of a plea for a moratorium.

The *foreclosure sale* is a public auction conducted by the sheriff. In depressed periods most sales are perfunctory affairs, with the only bid being that of the lender who has brought suit. A common practice followed by lenders is to bid an amount slightly less than the amount due and then ask the court that they be appointed as receiver during the redemption period to collect the rents and apply them on the deficiency.

The *redemption period* is an interval following the foreclosure sale in which junior creditors and the previous owner may purchase the farm by paying the amount of the foreclosure sale plus interest and other costs after the sale. The period allowed varies by states from no time at all to more than 2 years.

In states that have adopted the Uniform Commercial Code, the procedure for foreclosure on secured nonreal-estate loans is set forth in Part 5 of Article 9. When a debtor is in default under a security agreement, the secured party, with certain exceptions, has the rights and remedies provided in the security agreement. In general, these may include repossession, sale, acceptance of the collateral in satisfaction of the debt, or any other available judicial procedure. Except in the case of certain consumer goods, a secured party who takes possession of collateral after default may, providing proper notices are given as specified in U.C.C. 9–505, keep the collateral in satisfaction of the indebtedness if a written objection is not received within certain time limits. However, if the debtor makes a timely written objection, the secured party must sell, lease, or otherwise dispose of the collateral (U.C.C. 9–504). Disposition of the collateral may be by private or public proceedings, as a unit or in parcels, at any time and place, and on any terms, but "every aspect of the disposition, including the method, manner, time, place, and terms, must be *commercially reasonable. . . .*" (U.C.C. 9–504.) The secured party may purchase the collateral if it is disposed of at a public sale, and also under certain other circumstances. The debtor (or any other secured party) may redeem the collateral any time before its disposition, providing he has not agreed otherwise in writing after default. To redeem, the debtor must make all payments due, including reasonable expenses incurred by the secured party in retaking, holding, and disposing of the collateral (U.C.C. 9–506). The secured party must account to the debtor for any surplus after disposition of collateral (U.C.C. 9–504). Unless otherwise agreed or provided in the security agreement, the debtor is liable for any deficiency. The secured party is obligated to comply with the code in taking action on a default; otherwise, the debtor or any other person with proper rights may recover damages or loss caused by the failure to comply with the code provisions.

BUSINESS FAILURE. Most legal instruments used in credit transactions serve to protect the lender in the event the borrower should default. It should be recognized that foreclosure is used only as a last resort. Most reputable lenders attempt to work out alternative solutions with the borrower by extending loans for longer periods or by deferring principal and possibly interest payments to give the borrower a chance to resolve his financial difficulties.

Nevertheless, some businesses do fail despite the efforts of owners and creditors. Failure is usually due to a combination of factors, including crop failure, disease, poor management, personal problems, illness, and the like. If the assets of the business are more than sufficient to cover outstanding debts, creditors usually try to persuade the borrower to voluntarily liquidate the business before his net worth becomes further impaired. If the total amount of debts outstanding exceeds the value of the assets, bankruptcy is often the only alternative. Bankruptcy proceedings can be initiated voluntarily by the borrower or they can be brought about by his creditors.

Legal bankruptcy occurs when a person (or a corporation) is unable to pay his debts and he must allow a legal distribution of his assets among his creditors.[3] All bankruptcy cases are handled in the federal courts. Upon declaration of bankruptcy, a court-appointed *referee* meets with the creditors to establish the amounts of their claims. A *receiver* (or *trustee*) is appointed to oversee the liquidation of assets and to distribute the proceeds among the creditors.

Once the bankruptcy proceedings have been completed, the creditors involved have no further legal claim against the borrower, even though some of them may have been repaid only a fraction of the debts owed. Thus bankruptcy in a sense offers a form of legal protection for the insolvent borrower. In fact, many people have gone back into business following bankruptcy despite the obvious difficulties of reestablishing a credit rating. Bankruptcy, like foreclosure, should be considered only as a last resort, to be used when other solutions have failed. A record of bankruptcy puts a permanent blemish on one's credit rating, making it difficult, perhaps even impossible, to ever borrow money on reasonable terms again.

FAIR CREDIT REPORTING ACT. Credit is vitally important to the nation's economy and accurate credit ratings are an essential part of this system. Historically, lenders checked credit worthiness on a more or less informal basis by checking courthouse records and by contacting other lenders with whom prospective loan applicants had done business. In recent years a national network of credit reporting agencies has evolved to the point where a preliminary evaluation of a prospective borrower's credit rating can be obtained by simply calling a local credit bureau.

Courthouse records are still carefully checked before loans are closed and other creditors may also be contacted, but credit reporting agencies have greatly improved credit service. Now, loan applications can be given at least tentative approval within a matter of hours, where formerly it may have taken several days to check a person's credit rating.

Some people have been unjustly denied credit, as well as employment or insurance, because their credit files contained inaccurate or erroneous information. Passage of the Fair Credit Reporting Act in 1971 has eliminated many of the problems of inaccurate credit reports.

The Fair Credit Reporting Act (not to be confused with Truth

---

3. Many large corporations continue as going concerns following bankruptcy when they are reorganized under the provisions of the Bankruptcy Act. Most bankruptcy cases involving small businesses require liquidation.

in Lending) essentially provides that anyone who is refused credit (or employment or insurance) has a right to know why. If the refusal was due to an unfavorable credit report, the lender must reveal the source of this information. This act also has disclosure requirements that enable individuals to learn the contents of their files. This disclosure requirement means that an individual can dispute any obsolete or erroneous information and have such information deleted from his file, if justified. The Fair Credit Reporting Act also specifies that information contained in their files may be revealed only to lenders, employers, insurance companies, and others who have a legitimate need for such information.

QUESTIONS AND PROBLEMS

1. Why are so many credit instruments needed in farm credit transactions?
2. What are the main characteristics of a note that should be remembered? Of a mortgage?
3. Has the Uniform Commercial Code been adopted in your state? How does the code affect the legal aspects involved in use of credit?
4. What is the difference between buying a farm *subject to the mortgage* and *assuming the mortgage?* Between buying a farm *on contract* and *with a mortgage?*
5. Explain how a real estate foreclosure is conducted.
6. What is an abstract? Title insurance? Compare the two.
7. What is a waiver? When would it be used?
8. Why might there be a need for a nondisturbance agreement? For an extension agreement?
9. Explain how an assignment is used.
10. What is meant by a "release" or "satisfaction" of a claim? Can a borrower obtain a release of a "security interest"? If so, explain how this is accomplished.
11. Explain how bankruptcy proceedings are conducted.
12. Discuss how the Fair Credit Reporting Act protects borrowers and improves credit service.

REFERENCES

American Jurisprudence, 2nd ed., vol. 15. Lawyers Cooperative Publ. Co., Rochester, N.Y., 1964, pp. 729–91.
"A *Permanent* Frazier-Lemke Law?" *Farm Policy Forum,* vol. 3, no. 8, Iowa State Univ. Press, Aug. 1950.
Bunn, Charles, et al. *An Introduction to the Uniform Commercial Code.* Michie, Charlottesville, Va., 1964.
Cameron, Arnold G. *The Torrens System: Its Simplicity, Serviceability, and Success.* Houghton Mifflin, New York, 1915.

Hawkland, William D. *A Transactional Guide to the Uniform Commercial Code,* vols. 1 and 2. Joint Committee on Continuing Legal Education of the Am. Law Inst. and the Am. Bar Assoc., 101, N. 33rd St., Philadelphia, Pa. 19104.

Krauz, N. G. P. *Installment Land Contracts for Farmland.* Univ. of Ill., Agr. Ext. Serv. Circ. 823, June 1967.

Levi, Donald R. *Agricultural Law.* Lucas Bros., Columbia, Mo., 1971.

Luce, Kenneth K. *The Uniform Commercial Code.* Wis. Bar Bull., Apr. 1963, pp. 27–33.

Montague, William L. *Uniform Commercial Code's Article 9—When Filing Is Not Required to Perfect a Security Interest.* Ky. Law Jour., vol. 52, no. 2, pp. 422–28.

Nelson, A. G., and Davis, Ray J. *The Uniform Commercial Code As Related to Arizona Agriculture.* Ariz. Agr. Exp. Sta. Rept. 243, Nov. 1967.

Schrampfer, William H. *Law in Its Application to Business,* revised ed. Holt, Rinehart, and Winston, New York, 1961.

Spivack, Oscar. *The Uniform Commercial Code.* Tenn. Law Rev., vol. 31, no. 1, pp. 20–33.

CHAPTER 15: LENDER'S ANALYSIS AND SERVICING OF A LOAN

THE PRECEDING CHAPTERS have outlined principles and practices relating to agricultural credit. While most of the discussion applies to both borrowers and lenders, the point of emphasis has been somewhat more from the viewpoint of the borrower. Moreover, those who have not had firsthand experience in borrowing money tend to view the matter with a certain degree of awe, and possibly skepticism. A broader knowledge of loan and service policies of lenders and of their obligations and responsibilities will aid the borrower in formulating plans for use of credit. Such information will enable the borrower to understand better the viewpoint of the lender and why he must do certain things, thereby contributing to a greater degree of mutual understanding essential for most effective teamwork. The objective of this chapter is to help provide this type of information regarding specialized lenders.

LENDER'S BUSINESS IS "SELLING" LOANS. A lender's business is "selling" credit and loan services in a competitive market, and this fact has an important bearing on his loan and service policies. He must offer a competitive product to stay in business. A lender's major source of income is usually interest on loans. It follows that, other things being equal, the larger the volume of loans a lender has outstanding, the larger his income. Therefore, he competes in the market for loans in a similar manner that other businesses compete for business. His methods may assume a little different emphasis. Lacking a tangible product to display—things such as a shiny new car and a new dress design that attract public attention because they are new and different—he tends to emphasize building goodwill through superior service, supporting worthwhile community projects, building business and social relationships with other businesses, and cultivating the friendship and support of various agricultural organizations and leaders by supporting their programs. But he also competes on the basis of price and product, the same as any other business. The lender's price tags are in terms of interest rates, loan-closing fees, and the like. His products are comprised of various types and sizes of loans and loan services. He competes by offering improved service, by developing new types and terms of loans that better meet the needs of agriculture, by increasing the size of loans, and sometimes by cutting interest rates and loan fees.

Competition among lenders encourages them to review continually their loan policies and practices with a view to making improvements that will increase their business. It encourages lenders to "keep on their toes." In general, competition helps insure against credit abuses. Most areas of the United States have enough lenders to provide a fairly competitive loan market, particularly in prosperous times. (Somewhat in contrast with other business, competition among lenders tends to diminish during recessions and depressions.) The government-sponsored cooperative Farm Credit banks and associations, and direct government loans through the Farmers Home Administration and other government agencies, add competition and provide credit service in areas and for farmers with limited opportunity for loans from commercial lenders.

LENDERS GENERALLY LEND OTHER PEOPLE'S MONEY.

Most lenders do not own the money they lend. Lenders may loan some of their own capital (part of the capital and surplus of the institution) but the bulk of their loan funds are either owned by other people or represent contractual obligations for insurance coverage and the like. It is not our purpose here to study the source of loan funds—that subject will be covered in the chapters dealing with various lenders in Part III of this book. But it is important here to understand and recognize the basic ownership of loan funds since it has an important influence upon loan and service policy of lenders.

Since lenders lend money belonging to someone else, they, in effect, serve as managers or trustees of the money. In their role as manager they are obligated to obtain the maximum return consistent with good business practices. In their role as trustee, lenders are obligated to take proper safeguards in investing the funds to insure against loss.

To help protect the financial interests of the public, numerous federal and state laws have been enacted to govern the activities of lenders. As will be brought out in subsequent chapters, these laws outline the legal framework within which lending institutions operate. They define the type, size, and quality of individual loans, as well as the aggregate amount of loans that may be made. Real estate loans, for example, are generally limited by law to about 85 percent of the appraised value of the security. The size of individual loans is further limited either in absolute terms or relative to the capital structure of the lending institution. In addition to limits on size of individual loans, lenders are limited by law in the aggregate amount of loans they may extend. For example, commercial banks must maintain specified reserves and the banks and associations of the Farm Credit System cannot exceed specified ratios of loans to capital. Moreover, the law provides for periodic examinations by federal or state examiners to determine whether operation of the institution is in accordance with the law under which it is operated. One part of this review is examination of the loans of the institution to help assure that they meet standards for sound investments. Loans that do not meet these standards must be made good. The lender may be able to do this by working with the borrower either to obtain more collateral or a partial payment that will strengthen the security position of the loan. If the loan cannot be made good by such a procedure, the lending institution is obligated to "write the loan off." Loans that are charged off are carried as undeclared assets on the books of the institution. They are eliminated from the balance sheet, or from assets pledged as security for loans.

To the extent of their resources, lenders must stand the losses realized on loans they make. Depositors, policyholders, or bondholders realize a loss only when the lending institution becomes insolvent. Using other people's money to make loans possibly totaling several times the capital and surplus of the lending institution subjects the lender to great risk if the loans are not properly made. The risk assumed by the lender multiplies, as illustrated by the *Principle of Increasing Risk* discussed in Chapter 4. If unforeseen conditions develop that adversely affect a substantial portion of the outstanding loans, it is easy to see how rapidly the lender's capital and surplus could disappear. A small percentage of loan breakdowns is a natural expectation. Farmers suffer losses from drouths, excessive rainfall, and other natural hazards, and they, or members of their families, suffer from sickness, injury, or death. Family quarrels, poor management, or mistakes in appraisal sometimes make it necessary to foreclose a mortgage. Every farm loan institution should be prepared for a small percentage of loan breakdowns for such reasons. But they must guard against any large-scale breakdown of loans. The life of the lending institution depends upon avoiding such a catastrophe.

PROCEDURE FOLLOWED IN MAKING LOANS. The procedure lenders follow in making loans varies somewhat in detail, but the general principles are the same. Lenders develop their own detailed forms and approaches and, as would be expected, these vary somewhat. The procedure followed also varies from borrower to borrower. With a new applicant, the lender must gather more information and make a more detailed study of the business than with a borrower who has been doing business with the lender for a period of time, and of course the procedures must be adjusted to fit the type of loan being considered. But through all this variation run some common practices, and the purpose of this section is to outline these in general terms. The information needed by the lender is discussed first, and then the general procedures followed in making loans are considered.

To give a complete picture of loan procedures it is assumed, unless otherwise indicated, that the application of a new borrower is being considered. Some shortcuts are often possible with established borrowers. It is also assumed that the loan being considered involves a large amount of money. Lenders generally dispose of very small loans rather promptly by either deciding to make them as quickly as possible or, on the basis of a brief review of the facts involved, decline to extend the credit. This statement should not be interpreted to mean lenders generally frown on small loans. The average lender is not inclined to say "No" very readily. But he must consider the economical use of time, as must any businessman, and, therefore, small loans usually are handled with dispatch.

Information Needed—the Credit File. The lender needs certain information relative to the applicant, his family, and his business for use in analyzing a loan application. For this purpose he sets up a credit file or loan folder for each borrower. The credit file generally includes the following basic records:

1. Loan application
2. Comment sheet (often not used for real estate loans)
3. Balance sheet
4. Income statement
5. Inspection report if a nonreal-estate loan, or an appraisal report if a real estate loan
6. Miscellaneous records such as resolutions, legal papers, and insurance policies where required

A more complete credit file will also include other information—depending upon the type of loan—such as inventory forms, schedule of advances and repayment agreement, mortgage abstracts or abstracts of liens, aerial photographs, photographs of buildings, and soil maps. Frequently, correspondence pertaining to the loan is also kept in the credit file. The objective in developing the credit file is to have a place to assemble information pertinent to a loan for convenient reference. It should contain all information that may have a bearing on success or failure of the loan.

FINANCIAL RECORD—AGRICULTURE

SECTION I—LOAN APPLICATION

APPLICANT(S) .... Name Leopold Whistlemeier Date Jan. 8, 1965 Telephone 030-9999

Address R#7 Westford

Age 51 Married: yes ☑ no ☐ Wife's Name Patricia

No. of Dependents 2 Ages: Boys 17 14 Girls

Farming Experience: Total 30 yrs. Present Farm 10 yrs.

LOAN REQUEST .... Amount $5,200 Maturity 11/30/65

Purpose Annual operating Capital

Collateral Offered Livestock and growing Crops

Repayment Plan From Sept., Oct., and Nov. sales of hogs, Cattle, and Corn.

Comments

FARM OPERATED .... Location Green Valley Township

Total Acres 436 (Owned) Tillable 290 Other 146 (Rented)

Landlord: Name None

Address

Lease Expires 19 Annual Cash Rent $

Major Product(s) Sold Hogs

Contracts for Sale of Products None (To whom and terms of contract)

FINANCIAL FACTORS ...... Checking Account: Amount $600. Bank Green Valley State Bank

Savings Account: Amount $ -0- Bank

Contingent Liabilities $ None

Explain

Pending Judgments or Lawsuits

Explain None

REFERENCES .... Credit Green Valley State Bank, 101 W. Main St., Westford (Name) (Address)

Westford Mortgage Co., 220 W. Main St., Westford

Farmers Friend Feed Co., Brice St., Westford

Business (trade) Green Valley Tractor and Implement Co., Brice St., Westford (Name) (Address)

Central Hardware Co., Long St., Westford

Personal Mr. Josiah Friendly R#7 Westford (Name) (Address)

Mr. A. M. Upp 10 W. Main St., Westford

REMARKS .... Mr. Whistlemeier wishes to transfer his banking business to us.

I (we) the undersigned certify that the foregoing statement and representations constitute to the best of my (our) knowledge true and correct statements.

Date signed Jan. 8, 1965 Signature /s/ Leopold Whistlemeier

FIG. *15.1a—Financial Record—Loan Application. (Courtesy of the American Bankers Association.)*

LOAN APPLICATION. The loan application is the initial document involved in a loan transaction. It usually shows the date, name, address, and telephone number of the applicant, as well as the amount of credit requested, the purpose for which the funds are to be used, the proposed plan of repayment, and the security, if any, the applicant offers. For convenience, the balance sheet and the income statements sometimes are made a part of the application. A sample

SECTION II—FINANCIAL STATEMENT

Financial Statement of:

Name *Leopold and Patricia Whistlemeir*

Address *R # 7 Westford*

TO: *Westford State Bank*

Major Enterprise(s) *Hogs*

Statement Date *Jan. 1* 19*65*.

ASSETS				LIABILITIES			
CURRENT				**CURRENT**			
Cash on Hand			$ -0-	Notes Payable to Our Bank	(Sched. I)	$	-0-
Cash on Deposit (Bank *Sun Valley Nat. Bank*)			600	Notes Payable to Relatives	(Sched. I).		-0-
Notes Receivable	(Sched. A)		-0-	Notes Payable to Others	(Sched. I)		1,400
Accounts Receivable	(Sched. A)		-0-	Accounts Payable	(Sched. I)		800
Livestock Held for Sale	(Sched. B)		3845				
Crops Held for Sale and Feed	(Sched. C)		9,980	Portion of Intermediate-Term Debt Due Within 12 Months	(Sched. J)		-0-
Cash Investment in Growing Crops	(Sched. C)		-0-				
Securities (Marketable)	(Sched. D)		-0-	Portion of Long-Term Debt Due Within 12 Months	(Sched. K)		2,400
Cash Surrender Value of Life Insurance	(Sched. E)		1,800	Rent, Taxes, and Interest Due and Unpaid			-0-
Other (Specify)			-0-	Loans Against Cash Surrender Value of Life Insurance			-0-
	TOTAL CURRENT		$ 16,225	Other Debt Due Within 12 Months			-0-
					TOTAL CURRENT	$	4,200
INTERMEDIATE				**INTERMEDIATE-TERM**			
Autos and Trucks (Net)	(Sched. F)		$ 888	Notes Payable to Our Bank	(Sched. J)	$	-0-
Machinery and Equipment (Net)	(Sched. F)		14,417	Notes Payable to Others	(Sched. J)		-0-
Breeding and Dairy Livestock	(Sched. B)		12,512				
Securities (Not readily marketable)	(Sched. D)		-0-	Maturities of over 1 but under 10 years for other than seasonal needs—less portion applied to current liabilities.			
Other (Specify)			-0-				
	TOTAL INTERMEDIATE		$ 27,817		TOTAL INTERMEDIATE-TERM	$	-0-
				LONG-TERM			
FIXED				Mortgages on Farm Real Estate (Less portion applied to current liabilities)	(Sched. K)	$	73,600
Farmland	(Sched. G)		$ 103,500				
Farm Improvements (Net)	(Sched. G)		8,000				
Nonfarm Real Estate	(Sched. H)		-0-	Mortgages on Other Real Estate (Less portion applied to current liabilities)	(Sched. K)		-0-
Household Furnishings			-0-				-0-
Other (Specify)			-0-	Other (Specify)			-0-
	TOTAL FIXED		$ 111,500		TOTAL LONG-TERM	$	73,600
					TOTAL LIABILITIES	$	77,800
					NET WORTH*	$	77,742
	TOTAL ASSETS		$ 156,542		TOTAL LIABILITIES & NET WORTH	$	156,542

*Net worth resulting from upward reevaluation of fixed assets ($ 18,500)

GENERAL INFORMATION

1. Insurance
   a. Real and Personal Property *Complete coverage for mach., livestock, bldgs., and household*
   b. Liability *$ 50,000 Rural Mutual Insurance Co.*
   c. Workmen's Compensation *One hired man equivalent*
   d. Other *Hail*

2. Taxes
   a. Personal Property *est. $315.*
   b. Real Estate *est. $1,265.*
   c. Income *est. $800.*
   d. Other

For the purpose of procuring and maintaining credit from time to time in any form whatsoever with the above-named bank, the undersigned submit(s) the above Financial Statement as being a true, complete, and accurate statement of my (our) financial condition on the above date, and agree(s) that if any change occurs that materially reduces the means or ability of the undersigned to pay all claims or demands against me (us), the undersigned will immediately notify the bank in writing; and unless the bank is so notified, it may continue to rely upon the statement herein as a true, complete, and accurate statement of the financial condition of the undersigned.

Signed /s/ *Leopold Whistlemeir* Date *Jan. 8* 19*65*.

/s/ *Patricia Whistlemeir*

Certified by:

FIG. *15.1b—Financial Record—Financial Statement. (Courtesy of the American Bankers Association.)*

application form, complete with financial statement, supporting schedules, and profit and loss statement, is reproduced in Figures 15.1a to 15.1e.

COMMENT SHEET. The comment sheet provides a record of miscellaneous information to supplement other forms. Since the farm household and farm business are integrally related, personal information about the borrower and his family often is recorded on

SECTION III—SUPPORTING SCHEDULES

A. RECEIVABLES

	Type	From Whom	Amount Original	Amount Present	Date Due	Collateral
Notes		None	$	$		
....		TOTAL	$	$		
Accounts		None				
		TOTAL	$	$		

B. LIVESTOCK

	No.	Description	Value Per Unit	Total Value
	150	Market Hogs @ 90 lbs.	$ 13	$ 1,950
Held for Sale	80	Market Hogs @ 25 lbs.	7	560
	13	Beef Cattle	95	1,235
	5	Dairy Calves	20	100
			Total	$ 3,845
....	44	Sows	$	$ 2,052
Held for Breeding (Including Dairy)	2	Boars		85
	36	Beef Cows & Heifers		6,275
	3	Bulls		600
	19	Dairy Cows & Heifers		3,500
			Total	$ 12,512

C. CROPS

	Units	Description	Value Per Unit	Total Value
	7,000 bu	Corn	$ 1.10	$ 7,700
Held for Sale or Feed	300 bu	Oats	.60	180
	140 ton	Hay	15.00	2,100
			Total	$ 9,980
	Acres			Investment to Date
....	94	Hay & Pasture		$ —0—
Growing	31	Seeding to Legumes & Grass		—0—
			Total	$

D. SECURITIES

	Description	Present Total Value	Pledged	Amount Owed
	None	$		$
Marketable				
	Total	$		$
....	None			
Nonmarketable				
	Total	$		$

E. LIFE INSURANCE (OWNED)

Face Value	Company	Insured	Present Cash Surrender Value	Annual Premium	Pledged	Amount Owed
$ 10,000	Utopian Insurance Co.	Leopold	$ 1,800	$ 264	no	$ —0—
$	Total		$	$		$

FIG. *15.1c—Financial Record—Supporting Schedules. (Courtesy of the American Bankers Association.)*

the comment sheet. Information on the family's needs, wants, and desires helps the lender understand goals of the family and provides background knowledge useful in analyzing a loan application. The number and ages of children at home not only help indicate family living costs but also the amount of family labor available, which in turn influences the amount of labor to be hired. Health of the family members, their spending habits, and their interest in the farm all

Section III—Supporting Schedules (continued)

F. MACHINERY AND EQUIPMENT (MAJOR ITEMS)

	Article	Year Purchased	Cost	Accumulated Depreciation	Present Value
Auto and Truck	*Auto (sedan)*	1961	$ 2,216	$ 1,328	$ 888
	Total		$	$	$
All Other	*No. 1 Tractor*	1964	$ 5,700	$	$ 5,090
	No. 2 Tractor	1961	4,800		2,000
	Corn Picker	1961			1,600
	All other mach. & equipment				5,727
	Total		$	$	$ 14,417

G. FARMLAND AND IMPROVEMENTS

	Date Purchased	Description	Purchase Cost	Present Value	Title
Land	3/16/55	*190 A. Tillable plus 146 A. Nontillable*	$ 48,000	$ 66,500	*Leonard & Patricia*
	9/1/63	*100 A. Tillable*	45,000	45,000	" "
	Total		$ 93,000	$ 111,500	

	Date Purchased	Description	Cost of Improvements	Accumulated Depreciation	Present Value
Improvements (Farm Structures)	3/16/55	*Residence ($6,000 Value)*	$	$	$
		40' x 60' barn ($1,000 Value)			
		And other buildings ($1,000 Value)			
		included above			
	Total		$	$	$

H. NONFARM REAL ESTATE

	Date Purchased	Description	Purchase Cost	Present Value	Title
	None		$	$	
	Total		$	$	

I. NOTES AND ACCOUNTS PAYABLE

	Date Originated	Original Amount	Balance Due	Holder	Terms Collateral	Terms Repayment
Notes	9/1/63	$ 9,000	$ 1,000	*Green Valley State Bank*	*Livestock Equip*	3/15/65
	Total	$	$			

	Amount Due	To Whom	Repayment Arrangements
Accounts	$ 800	*Farmers Friend Feed Co.*	*Sale of hogs in Spring*
	$	Total	

J. INTERMEDIATE-TERM LIABILITIES

	Date Originated	Original Amount	Balance Due	Holder	Purpose
		$ None	$		
	Total	$	$		

K. LONG-TERM LIABILITIES

	Date Originated	Original Amount	Balance Due	Holder	Repayment Arrangements
Farm	3/16/55	$ 39,000	$	*Hartford Mortgage Co.*	*$2400 principal in Oct.*
	9/1/63	36,000			*plus interest at 5 3/4%*
	Total	$ 75,000	$ 76,000	*Mortgages combined in 1964*	
Other					
	Total	$	$		

FIG. *15.1d—Financial Record—Supporting Schedules (continued). (Courtesy of the American Bankers Association.)*

have an important bearing upon success of the business, and the lender seeks to obtain as much of this type of information as possible.

If the applicant is a new borrower, the lender is interested in learning of his experience and ability as a farmer, his credit history, and related information. These things are recorded on the comment sheet if other forms do not provide for the information. Information

SECTION IV—PROFIT AND LOSS STATEMENT

Statement of: *Leopold Whistlemier Farm*
Address: *R#1 Hereford*
Prepared for: *Hereford State Bank*

Period Covered:
Jan. 1 19 *64* through *Dec. 31* 19 *64*

RECEIPTS

Gross from Sale of Livestock and Livestock Products (describe):

	Units	
Cattle	(35)	$ 2,545
Hogs	(443)	13,378
Milk	(45,000 lbs.)	1,552
Eggs	(630 doz.)	138
	Subtotal Livestock	$ 17,613

Gross from Sale of Crops (describe):

Corn	(2,104 bu.)	$ 2,378
Soybeans	(124 bu.)	319
Gov't. Payment	( )	2,171
	( )	
	Subtotal Crops	$ 4,868

Other from Farming (describe):

Misc.		$ 580
	Subtotal Other	$ 580

Gross Receipts From Farming .... $ 23,061

OPERATING EXPENSES

Feeder Livestock Purchased	$ —0—
Feed Purchased	3,302
Hired Labor	3,553
Fertilizer and Lime	1,245
Pesticides	136
Seeds and Plants Purchased	612
Machine Hire	722
Machinery Maintenance and Repairs	1,471
Fuel and Oil	1,052
Livestock Expenses (breeding, veterinary, medicine)	746
Maintenance and Repairs (other than machinery)	781
Rent and Leases	—0—
Utilities (farm share)	177
Taxes and Insurance (farm share)	1,577
Farm Interest	2,008
Other Cash Expenses (specify):	
Auto	215
Hail Insurance	140
Misc	421

Total Cash Operating Expenses .... $ 18,158

Net Cash Income From Operation .... $ 4,903

Adjustments for Change in Inventory:

	Feed	Market Livestock	Supplies
Beginning Inventory	$ 7,140	$ 4,778	$
Ending Inventory	10,130	4,866	
Net Change (±)	$ +2,990	$ + 88	$

(Plus if increased, minus if decreased) .... (±)$ + 3,078

Net Operating Profit .... $ 7,981

Adjustments for Capital Items:

	Machinery and Equipment	Breeding Livestock	Improvements
Beginning Inventory	$ 8,862	$ 11,427	$ 9,072
Plus: Purchases	4,802	67	363
Less: Ending Inventory	10,933	11,577	8,080
Sales	—0—	2,990	
Net Change (±)	$ −2,731	$ +3,073	$ −1,355

.... (±)$ − 1,013

Profit (Loss) From Operation .... $ 6,968

Information Only

Depreciation taken this year:

Machinery and Equipment	$ 2,731
Breeding Livestock	—0—
Improvements	1,355
Total	$ 4,086
Annual Nonfarm Income:	$ —0—

I (we) hereby certify that the above is a complete and accurate statement of my (our) profit and loss record during the period shown to the best of my (our) knowledge and belief.

Signature(s) /s/ *Leopold Whistlemier*

Date *Jan 8* 19 *65*

FIG. *15.1e—Financial Record—Profit and Loss Statement. (Courtesy of the American Bankers Association.)*

on the credit rating of the applicant obtained from other businesses may be recorded on the comment sheet. A comment sheet also provides a convenient place to make a record of visits to the farm after the loan is closed.

BALANCE SHEET AND INCOME STATEMENT. If the loan applied for appears reasonable and appears to be for a sound purpose, the balance sheet and income statement are prepared. The loan officer and the applicant may complete the two financial statements together or the applicant may be given the forms and asked to prepare them at his convenience.

It often happens that the financial statements need to be confirmed or supplemental information needs to be obtained. In such instances the lender may advise the applicant that he would like to visit his farm. The lender summarizes the results of his visit to the farm in an inspection report. This report is used especially if an unsecured loan or a loan secured by movable property is made. If a real estate mortgage is taken to secure a loan, a real estate appraisal report is obtained. With a nonreal-estate loan, the lender studies the business from the viewpoint of its management and operation, while with real estate loans, greater emphasis is placed upon the appraisal report.

Where data are available, many lenders develop comparison statements and a loan history sheet for the borrower. Past records in the credit file of established borrowers provide a good source of such information. The comparison statements show the trend of balance sheet and income statement items over a period of years to facilitate trend analysis as illustrated in Chapters 7 and 8 and in Figure 15.2. The loan history sheet provides a record of credit used and repaid over a period of time.

INSPECTION REPORT. The purpose of the inspection report is to provide firsthand information on the farm family and business that will be used in analyzing the loan and preparing the financing statement. Prepared by the loan analyst himself or by his representative, the inspection report generally gives a detailed list of all property owned by the applicant to give a complete picture of what he has to work with. Any property that is not to be taken as collateral is properly identified on the record form. Each item of property is described in reasonable detail to facilitate identification at a later date if necessary and to provide information for the financing statement. Description of items listed in the financing statement must be reasonably explicit since, when filed, it constitutes a public notice of items covered. A conservative market value is given for each item of property for use

COMPARATIVE ANALYSIS SHEET—AGRICULTURE

Name *Leopold H. Austemeier*   Address *R.#7 Siegfried*

Statement date	1/1/61	1/1/62	1/1/63	1/1/64	1/1/65	
ASSETS						
1. Cash	600	0	20	1,600	600	
2. Receivables						
3. Inventory held for sale and feed	12,466	16,245	15,384	12,242	13,825	
4. Marketable securities and CSVLI	1,450	1,450	1,450	1,700	1,800	
5. Cash investment in growing crops						
6. Other						
7. **Total Current Assets**	14,515	17,695	16,824	15,542	16,225	
8. Autos and trucks (net)	120	886	666	444	888	
9. Machinery and equipment (net)	8,100	10,614	12,119	12,866	14,417	
10. Breeding and dairy livestock	12,380	10,205	10,775	12,365	12,512	
11. Securities (not readily marketable)						
12. Other						
13. **Total Intermediate Assets**	20,600	21,705	23,560	25,675	27,817	
14. Farm land	66,500	66,500	66,500	111,500	103,500	
15. Farm improvements (net)					8,000	
16. Other				0		
17. **Total Fixed Assets**	66,500	66,500	66,500	111,500	111,500	
18. **Total Assets**	101,615	105,900	106,884	152,717	156,542	
LIABILITIES AND NET WORTH						
19. Notes payable	2,500	4,000	1,000	9,000	1,000	
20. Accounts payable	100	210	150	2,070	800	
21. Portion of intermediate- and long-term debt due within next 12 months					2,400	
22. Rent, taxes, and interest due				tax 200		
23. CSVLI loan						
24. Other debts due within 12 months						
25. **Total Current Liabilities**	2,600	4,210	1,150	11,270	4,200	
26. **Total Intermediate-Term Liabilities**						
27. Mortgage on farm real estate	36,000	34,000	33,000	32,000	73,600	
28. Mortgage on nonfarm real estate				36,000		
29. **Total Long-Term Liabilities**	36,000	34,000	33,000	68,000	73,600	
30. **Total Liabilities**	38,600	38,210	34,150	79,270	77,800	
31. **Net Worth**	63,015	67,690	72,734	73,447	77,742	
PROFIT AND LOSS STATEMENT						
32. Gross receipts from farming	22,806	21,364	25,773	23,061		
33. Total cash operating expenses	17,949	17,004	17,491	18,158		
34. Net change in inventory	+1,562	+412	-2,450	+3,078		
35. Net change in capital items	+1,833	-442	-1,875	-1,013		
36. **Profit (loss) from operation**	8,252	4,405	3,927	6,968		
37. Other income						
FINANCIAL TESTS—RATIOS						
38. Current (line 7 ÷ line 25)	5.58	4.20	14.63	1.38	3.86	
39. Debt to Worth (line 30 ÷ line 31)	.61	.56	.47	1.08	1.00	
40. Gross Receipts to Total Assets (line 32 ÷ line 18)	.22	.20	.24	.15		
41. Profit to Total Assets (line 36 ÷ line 18)	.081	.042	.037	.046		
42. Annual Debt Servicing to Gross Receipts				.36		
AMOUNT PER $100 OF GROSS RECEIPTS						
43. a. Cash operating expenses	79	80	68	79		
44. b. Profit	36	21	15	30		
MANAGEMENT FACTORS						
Crop Yields						
45. (Kind) *Corn* (Unit) *bu/a.*	93	90	73	85		
46. *Soybeans bu/a.*		-	43	28		
47. *Oats bu/a.*	40	30.	67	35		
48.						
Livestock Production Rates						
49. (Kind) *Pigs* (Unit) *per litter*	5.6	4.8	6.7	6.1		
50. *Hogs fed cost per 100# gain*	$10.17	$10.37	$10.55	$10.20		
51. *Beef cattle fed cost per wt.# gain*	$12.61	$15.06	$9.54	$14.82		
52.						
53. Value of Crops per Tillable Acre						
54. Livestock Returns per Dollar Feed Fed *Hogs*	$1.62	$1.52	$1.17	$1.34		
55. Man Work Days per Farm						
56. Man Work Days per Man						
57. Power and Machinery Cost per Tillable Acre	$25.73	$36.21	$31.63	$22.12		
58. Value of Farm Production per Tillable Acre	$118.25	$108.05	$102.27	$87.90		
59. Cost of Farm Production per Tillable Acre						
60. Other						
61.						
62.						

FIG. *15.2—Comparative Analysis Sheet. (Courtesy of the American Bankers Association.)*

in analyzing the loan. Income and expenses for the coming year also are estimated for use of the loan analyst. The inspector adds remarks at the end of his report to explain any unusual items about the family and business, and to provide additional pertinent information not covered otherwise in the report.

APPRAISAL REPORT. The main purpose of appraising a farm for a real estate loan is to obtain a dependable estimate of the value of the land and buildings. An indication of the debt-carrying capacity of the farm and its operator also may be gotten from the appraisal. In addition, the appraisal will alert the lender to any risks or other special features connected with the farm.

Preparation of an appraisal report for a real estate loan generally is a somewhat more specialized job than preparing an inspection report on personal property. As the terms indicate, the one is an inspection and the other is an appraisal. Farm and ranch appraisal comprises a major field of specialization in and of itself. It constitutes one of the major agricultural professions, and many agricultural colleges and universities have a course of study devoted exclusively to the subject.[1]

Analysis of Loans. The analysis a lender makes of a loan consists primarily of determining how much credit should be extended, together with the repayment plan, and the collateral to be required. In discussing these points it is assumed the borrower has applied for a maximum loan. Where less than a maximum loan is involved it may be possible to shorten the analysis. It is also assumed that the lender has the ability and desire to work with the borrower in analyzing use of credit.

HOW MUCH CREDIT? The information assembled in the credit file, together with the material covered in earlier chapters, indicates the type of analysis followed in extension of credit. Needs, wants, and desires of the family provide one indication of how much credit should be extended. Along with this information the lender considers the current financial position of the applicant and the trend of his financial progress. Other things being equal, a strong and improving financial position generally is considered a favorable factor while a weak and declining financial position is considered a danger signal. Looking to the future, the banker analyzes the farm business as a basis for judging how much it will pay the farmer to borrow: With what amount of credit will returns *added* by the use of the *added* funds just cover the *added* costs? He also analyzes the amount of credit that should be extended from the viewpoint of repayment capacity and risk-bearing ability. *Returns, repayment capacity,* and *risk-bearing ability* are sometimes referred to as the "three R's" of credit.

REPAYMENT PLAN. Many lenders strive to schedule loan payments to come due when income for loan repayment is available, as was outlined in Chapter 11. With this objective in mind, the ma-

---

1. For a comprehensive treatment of the subject, the reader is referred to the text, *Farm Appraisal and Valuation,* 5th ed., by William G. Murray, Iowa State Univ. Press, Ames, 1969.

jority of real estate loans made by commercial lenders are written on a long-term, amortized repayment basis, and some short-term and intermediate-term loans are made on the budget basis. However, this is far from a universal rule. Many of the real estate loans made by individuals provide for a lump sum payment at the expiration of the term. Some lenders make short-term loans payable upon demand, while some have notes come due several times during the year, primarily to bring the borrower in to see the lender periodically to discuss progress.

The majority of short-term and intermediate-term loans are written on a 3-, 6-, 9-, or 12-month basis. When some of these loans are made, it is recognized a balance will still be outstanding at the end of the term and will be renewed. This procedure has been successfully used by some lenders for years, with some borrowers being provided with intermediate-term credit on an annual renewable basis for 10 to 20 years. In this connection it should be recognized that annual renewals work well as long as all goes well. In fact, the lender can logically loan more on an annual renewable basis than on an intermediate-term loan basis. But the difficulty arises when the going gets tough either for the borrower or for the lender. Then the borrower may find himself confronted with meeting a substantial intermediate-term debt at the end of a 12-month period. To help alleviate this possibility and, in some cases, to provide a basis for more credit, lenders have started making some loans on an intermediate-term basis, for example, credit for bulk milk tanks, machinery, and breeding stock. Usually such loans are written on an amortized basis for a term of 1 to 7 years, depending upon the item financed and some related factors.

SECURITY REQUIREMENTS. The next step in analysis of a loan involves consideration of security requirements. While collateral security is almost universally required for real estate loans, little unanimity of opinion exists among lenders concerning collateral for nonreal-estate loans. Some lenders make a large percentage of their nonreal-estate loans on an unsecured basis; others make few such loans that are not protected by specific collateral. There are also wide differences geographically that seem to be a matter of custom.

Credit Rating of Applicant. The most important consideration in determining whether collateral is necessary for a loan is the credit rating of the applicant. It is determined by the credit character of an individual. Credit character comprises those qualities of a borrower that make him want or intend to pay when a loan is due—qualities of honesty and integrity, denoting determination to fulfill his obligations irrespective of contingencies that may arise. To live up to the promise above their signatures, some borrowers are willing to sacrifice much more than others, making great sacrifices and denying themselves and their families the prime essentials of life. On the other extreme, there are those having little regard for moral obligations, who would escape payment through a legal loophole if they could find one.

A borrower's previous record in meeting obligations is much more impressive to a lender than any amount of promises. A farmer cannot live in a community even for a few years without indicating to the businessmen of the community and to other neighboring farmers the amount of respect that he has for his financial obligations. Credit ratings from credit reporting agencies, which have developed to a high degree in cities on the basis of monthly bill payments, exist also in most rural areas.

One farmer with a good financial statement and earning record applied for a loan a few years ago to buy livestock and to pay operating expenses. After the local bank refused to make the loan, the farmer applied to a federally sponsored agency in a town in an adjoining county. The agency's examination and analysis of the financial statement and income record indicated that the applicant was entitled to a loan. But a routine request for references revealed that this farmer had declared bankruptcy twice and had refused to cooperate with another federally sponsored agency that sought to work out a method of payments that would eventually put the real estate mortgage in good standing. The local bank claimed it had lost over $1,200 on a $1,600 note, and the mortgage agency had been forced to take a loss through foreclosure. The farmer was a money-maker, however, and had staged a quick comeback. When he was confronted with his personal record, he admitted that a lender had good reason to hesitate before making him a loan but he protested that he would never again attempt to cheat his creditors. The record itself was the decisive factor, however, and this farmer did not get the loan.

Physical Security. Lenders generally consider it desirable to require security if one or more of the following situations prevail:

1. The borrower has a "split line" of credit; that is, where credit is obtained from two or more lenders. Established legal procedures in all states permit seizure of certain kinds of unencumbered property for satisfaction of overdue debts. Under such circumstances the lender usually protects his interests by requiring security that, in turn, may help the borrower repay the loan by assuring continuity of the farm operation during the life of the loan.
2. The borrower has had no opportunity to build a credit rating in the community. The lender usually requires security when the

borrower has not established the fact that he will perform according to his promise.

3. The lender does not have full information about the character and personal ability of the farmer and his farm. The lender usually tries to secure full information, but where this is impracticable he makes the loan if it appears justified and the security is adequate.

4. The borrower's loan is "full," that is, the borrower has the maximum amount of credit that it is safe for him to use. The lending institution that does a good job by its borrowers endeavors to provide them with all the credit they can profitably and safely use.

The usual form of pledging property as security is for the borrower to give the lender a security agreement or a real estate mortgage on specific property he owns. Other forms include depositing with the lender collateral consisting of negotiable stocks, bonds, notes, and other similar property rights of value to be forfeited if the loan is not paid.

The security agreement usually covers not only the property purchased with the loan proceeds but also additional property. If the borrower obtains a loan to buy six dairy cows, it is natural that the six dairy cows should be given as a pledge for the loan payment. The same may be said for loans to purchase all kinds of livestock, tractors, equipment, and other farm property. But the lender usually wishes to include property other than that bought with the loan funds unless the borrower has invested a substantial sum of his own. In making a loan to buy six dairy cows, for example, the lender may ask for a total of twelve dairy cows as security; in advancing funds to buy a carload of feeder cattle, he may ask for a security agreement covering not only the cattle purchased but also hay, grain, and other feed equal in value to the value of the cattle purchased; or in making a $30,000 loan for operating expenses he may ask for security valued at $50,000. Sellers of equipment have similar requirements in the form of cash down payments.

Lenders often make the mistake of specifying the amount of security required by using a fixed ratio or percentage. They may require, for example, that the security shall have a value equal to twice the amount of the loan. Any fixed proportion will later be recognized as too liberal for a poorly managed business and too conservative for a superior farm manager. A more reasonable plan is for lenders to adjust their security requirements according to the borrower's ability and other factors affecting the risk of the loan.

Endorsement. When inadequate physical security is available, the borrower may meet the lender's requirements by securing an endorsement. Endorsement means obtaining an additional signature on the front or back of the note. The person who adds his signature becomes liable for payment of the note if the borrower fails to do so, the same as though he had borrowed the money himself. Too many farmers have taken the obligation of an endorser altogether too lightly in the past. Before endorsing a note, the endorser should study the loan as outlined above and be convinced that the borrower can repay the loan. No borrower should ask a friend or relative to endorse his note unless this friend or relative is fully aware of the obligations he is assuming in endorsing the note.

Closing the Loan. When a lender has decided to make the loan, the actual closing process is relatively simple. The procedure varies in some degree from state to state due to statutory requirements and custom. The procedure also is slightly different for chattel than for real estate loans. But the main steps are as follows:

1. Verify the borrower's title to the property offered as security by a search of the public records. This step is necessary, of course, only when the loan is to be secured by a mortgage or security agreement.
2. Preparation and execution of the note (or bond) and mortgage or security agreement if the loan is secured by such an instrument. In some states a deed of trust is used rather than a mortgage for real estate loans. All loans need to be accompanied by a signed note as evidence of the fact that an obligation exists between the borrower and lender. The usual policy of most banks is to have the husband and wife jointly sign the note and mortgage or security agreement.
3. Recording of the mortgage or security agreement or deed of trust if one was prepared.
4. Examination of insurance policies covering property pledged as collateral for the loan to determine that coverage is reliable and adequate, and that the loss-payable clause is made in favor of the lender.

As soon as the required legal instruments have been signed and other requirements of the closing process completed, the proceeds of the loan are made available to the borrower.

SERVICING LOANS. The progressive lender has two broad objectives in servicing loans: (1) to fulfill his responsibility in safeguarding funds entrusted to the lending institution, and (2) to help the borrower make effective use of the credit, thereby adding to goodwill and business potential of the lender in the community. Safeguarding the funds involves checking the borrower's compliance with the purposes for which the credit was extended. A part of the loan procedure involves an agreement between the lender and borrower concerning the use to be made of loan proceeds and the general operating program for the farm business and household. The lender is responsible for checking on the borrower's compliance with this agreement and on his general progress. Some modification of mutually agreed upon plans often is advisable as conditions develop, and good business practices require that the lender keep abreast of the borrower's affairs.

The second objective of creating goodwill by assisting the borrower in making effective use of credit is related to the objective of safeguarding loan funds. Services that help the borrower and create goodwill usually also strengthen the loan. Notwithstanding conscientious efforts of both the lender and the borrower to forecast accurately all cash requirements, frequently because of some modification of plans, unusual weather, or other unforeseen conditions, the need arises for additional advances. Handling these in an intelligent and businesslike manner is an important phase of loan servicing that can both strengthen the loan and build goodwill.

The type of loan service needed varies somewhat with the type of loan. Real estate loans usually are on the books for a fairly long period of time and involve somewhat different servicing than chattel loans. Installment notices on real estate loans are mailed to the borrower, and under normal circumstances most payments are made as scheduled. Loans that become delinquent or require other servicing, such as partial releases for road right-of-ways, are investigated either directly by the lender or by his correspondent (representative) to determine the proper procedure. Insurance on improvements and other property must be kept in force and since unpaid taxes create a prior lien, tax records must be checked periodically to be sure taxes are current. Such things are involved in the minimum service for real estate loans. Progressive lenders give additional service, as outlined above, with a view to developing goodwill and additional business.

Service on nonreal-estate loans is somewhat broader than on real estate loans. Since nonreal-estate loans involve movable property that generally is much more subject to depreciation and can be disposed of more readily, the lender is obligated to keep a closer check on the property. Most borrowers are honest, but some become careless, and others do not fully realize that the security is not being kept up. Still others sometimes inadvertently dispose of security without keeping the lender informed. Attention also must be given to taxes and insurance on personal property the same as on real estate. When loans are secured by cash crops, the lender maintains a careful check on progress and needs of the crop, and at harvest time makes proper arrangements for liquidating the loan.

The type of service rendered by progressive lenders on farm loans was summarized in a letter to the authors:

> After the loan is approved the modern and progressive banker then usually considers that particular farmer and the loan made to him as his personal obligation and responsibility and he watches this line of credit to see if the agreed upon repayments are being complied with, and visits the farm often enough to keep in touch with the farm operations and the progress being made by the farmer. This type of work is what we consider servicing farm loans. In our bank, for instance, we try to keep one jump ahead of everything that takes place on the farms of our farm customers. It is our plan to anticipate things that happen to our borrowers. We try to know, for instance, if there is an adequate amount of roughage stored on the farms of each of our customers to feed his animals out properly during our seven-month stabling season. We visit the farms often enough to check on the care and attention given to the livestock. We are continually making observations as between farms to determine the quality of the over-all farm operations. We try to see our customers often enough to establish a certain feeling of confidence between the loaning officers and the borrowers. In this manner our customers will discuss with us their future plans and present problems so that we can give the benefit of our advice and experience.
>
> In the case of an established customer, we would do exactly the same thing, but perhaps visit the farms of those making satisfactory progress less frequently and devote a little more time to those owing us large sums and involved in one kind of a problem or another for various reasons.

A well-trained and experienced lender can contribute a great deal to a borrower's success, particularly if he will take time to visit the farm and discuss problems and opportunities with the farmer. A farmer will do well to select a lender who can and will render this service.

QUESTIONS AND PROBLEMS

1. Explain why lenders are obligated to take proper safeguards when making loans.
2. Describe the principal documents and records kept in a lender's credit file.
3. Discuss the principal factors used by lenders in analyzing loan applications.
4. What is involved in *closing* and *servicing* loans?
5. Visit agricultural lenders in your area and compare their policies and procedures followed in analyzing and servicing farm loans.

REFERENCE

American Bankers Association. *Agricultural Finance.* Am. Inst. Banking, Section of Am. Bankers Assoc., New York, 1969.

CHAPTER 16: FARM RETIREMENT AND INVESTMENTS

MOST FARM BUSINESSES are operated as sole proprietorships, partnerships, or small corporations, and the principal operator or operators of an independent or closely held business must eventually withdraw from active participation because of advancing age or extenuating circumstances such as ill health. Failure to carefully plan for retirement and the ultimate transfer of the estate at death can result in serious problems such as lack of financial security, personal and family dissatisfaction, disruption of the farm business, and needless capital losses. This chapter and the following one outline the importance of retirement and estate planning and cover some of the basic procedures that can be used to facilitate a smooth transfer of the farm business.

LIFE CYCLE OF A FARM BUSINESS. Farm businesses operated as sole proprietorships, and to a somewhat lesser degree, those operated as partnerships and small corporations typically follow a firm growth cycle that is closely related to the age of the owner or owners.[1]

In the *establishment stage,* general plans regarding the type and size of the farming operation are made and the necessary financing is obtained for the beginning resource base. The second phase is the *expansion stage* in which emphasis is placed on increasing the total size of the business to raise net income to some desired level. Farmers in the expansion stage often rely heavily on borrowed or leased capital to acquire resources. Following the expansion stage, many farm businesses go through the *consolidation stage* in which efforts are made to maintain and stabilize the income stream. Repayment of borrowed capital often takes precedence over the acquisition of more assets in the consolidation stage, that is, the emphasis is on *protecting* the current assets and income positions rather than increasing them.

In the *disinvestment* or *withdrawal stage,* the owner, either voluntarily through planned retirement or involuntarily through illness or death, withdraws his labor, management, and capital from the farm

---

1. For a more detailed discussion of the farm firm growth cycle, see J. R. Brake and M. E. Wirth, *The Michigan Farm Credit Panel: A History of Capital Accumulation,* Res. Rept. 25, Agr. Exp. Sta., Mich. State Univ., East Lansing, 1964.

business. Getting out of active farming can be just as difficult as getting started, perhaps more so, because the training and experience gained from years of active farming are of little help in dealing with the complex personal, financial, and legal problems that accompany the retirement and estate transfer phases.

GOALS OF RETIREMENT AND ESTATE PLANNING

Financial Security during Retirement. One of the primary considerations of the disinvestment stage is ensuring that there will be sufficient income for the retiring farmer and his wife for the rest of their lives. Retirement income expectations should be realistic and in line with past income and the amount of wealth accumulated prior to retirement. Procedures for estimating sources and amounts of retirement income are covered later in this chapter.

Continuity of the Farm Business. Many retiring farmers are understandably anxious to transfer their farm business to a younger operator as a "going concern." The opportunity to transfer the business to a family member or other competent young farmer often provides an ideal method for gradually retiring from active farming. Properly handled, this arrangement can result in a reliable source of retirement income and a place to live for the retiring member as well as a source of financial help and management assistance for the beginner. Furthermore, the value of farm capital can be preserved since some selling expenses are avoided.

Equitable Treatment of Heirs. Most successful farmers accumulate sizable amounts of wealth throughout their farming careers; hence, they should be concerned as to how this wealth will be distributed after their death. *Equitable* treatment of heirs does not necessarily mean *equal* treatment. Although distribution of one's property is a highly personal decision, it would be reasonable to consider the individual needs of all survivors. The financial needs of the surviving spouse should be given due priority and a child suffering from a physical handicap or other misfortune may deserve special consideration. The son who has made a personal and financial sacrifice to stay home and farm may also deserve a higher proportion of the estate than other members of the family. Equitable treatment of heirs can avoid a great deal of family dissatisfaction and financial insecurity.

Minimizing Capital Losses. The wealth accumulated throughout a farming career can be severely depleted in the retirement and estate transfer process if the withdrawal from active farming is not properly planned. Taxes and commissions for professional services often consume a substantial portion of the retiring farmer's wealth or a deceased farmer's estate. Capital gains taxes, income taxes, realtors' and auctioneers' commissions, brokerage fees, federal and state inheritance taxes, and legal fees are some of the expenses to be considered in planning the retirement and estate transfer programs. Many of these expenses can often be reduced or completely eliminated through careful planning without sacrificing other important goals.

ANALYZING RETIREMENT ALTERNATIVES. The retirement and estate transfer phases of the life cycle cannot be approached independently.[2] Estate transfer decisions affect retirement and vice versa. Nevertheless the retirement phase precedes the estate transfer stage chronologically. Thus the remainder of this chapter deals with retirement income and investment considerations. The next chapter deals with estate transfer.

Farmers and their families should make definite plans for retirement before a serious illness or other extenuating circumstances force them to do so. Most retiring farmers face two alternatives: (1) liquidate the entire farm business and reinvest the proceeds in nonfarm securities, or (2) sell only the farm chattels and rent the farmland. While many people continue to farm beyond age 65, most farmers or their surviving spouses must eventually select one of these two alternatives. Continuing to operate the farm business beyond the age of 65 may reduce social security benefits, hence, there is a financial incentive to withdraw from active farming.

Of course personal goals are important. Bringing a family member into the business, ill health, or a desire for a more leisurely way of life may suggest liquidation. A desire to remain on the farm or in the farm home could be sufficient reason for selecting the rental alternative.

In a financial analysis of retirement alternatives, life expectancy, capital losses, and the risks and returns associated with each alternative must be considered. In general, average life expectancy is a poor basis for budgeting annual retirement income. For example, a 65-year-old man has a mean life expectancy of about 13 years. However, the life expectancy data in Table 16.1 show that he has a 20 percent chance of living 20 more years. Hence, retirement income should be budgeted so that the retiree has a low probability of outliving his income. A 65-year-old couple might adjust their rate of spending so

---

2. See W. F. Lee and J. R. Brake, *Conversion of Farm Assets for Retirement Purposes,* Res. Rept. 129, Agr. Exp. Sta., Mich. State Univ., East Lansing, 1971.

TABLE 16.1:   Life Expectancy Probability Table

Remaining Lifetime (years)	Present Ages							
	55		60		65		70	
	Male	Female	Male	Female	Male	Female	Male	Female
5	0.92	0.96	0.87	0.93	0.82	0.90	0.75	0.84
10	0.80	0.90	0.71	0.84	0.61	0.75	0.48	0.62
15	0.65	0.81	0.53	0.70	0.39	0.55	0.24	0.36
20	0.49	0.67	0.34	0.52	0.20	0.32	0.09	0.14
25	0.31	0.50	0.17	0.30	0.07	0.13	0.02	0.03
30	0.16	0.29	0.06	0.12	0.01	0.03	*	*
35	0.06	0.11	0.01	0.02	*	*	*	*
40	0.01	0.02	*	*	*	*	*	*
Mean Life Expectancy (years)	19.5	23.8	16.0	19.7	13.0	15.9	10.3	12.4

SOURCE: Calculated from U.S. Bureau of Census, U.S. Life Tables, 1959–61.
* Less than 0.01.

that their assets will last them for a period of 25 to 30 years. The probability that either of them would outlive this time period would be less than 13 percent.

Evaluating Investment Risks and Returns. The retiring farmer must balance risks and returns when selecting investments. Investment risks include the possibilities of (1) a decline in asset earning power, (2) market risk, an example of which is a decline in the price per share of common stock, (3) increasing interest rates that would lower the value of a fixed income security, such as a bond, and (4) a decline in the real value of an asset because of increases in general price levels. This last risk is "purchasing power risk"—the decreasing real value of a fixed dollar asset, such as a bond, during periods of rising prices. In short, a bond redeemed during inflation will not buy as much as the original investment would at the time of bond purchase.

In evaluating assets, it is also important to separate *income returns* (profits, rents, or interest) from *price returns* or *capital gains* (an increase in value of an asset over time). Capital gains add to the investor's stock of wealth, but they cannot be spent until the asset is sold.

During a period of economic prosperity, the investor should devote a large proportion of his portfolio to *equity* assets such as farm real estate, common stocks, or mutual funds. If a period of economic depression seems likely, the investor should reduce his holdings of equities and switch to longer-term *fixed income* securities such as bonds or mortgages. Of course one never knows what type of economic era he is entering, so some diversification seems wise. Historically, the most stable total returns (including both income and price returns) have been associated with farm real estate. However, the income returns on nonfarm equities such as common stocks and mutual funds have on the average been higher in certain periods than for farm real estate.

Liquidity is very important to the elderly investor. Farm real estate, installment land contracts, and farm mortgages are popular investment alternatives among retiring farmers, but these investments tend to lack liquidity. Farm real estate cannot always be sold readily to meet large medical or other expenses. Land contracts and mortgages, though similar to bonds in some respects, do not have the liquidity of bonds because they are sold in limited local markets, usually at a substantial discount. Nonfarm securities, such as common stocks, mutual fund shares, and bonds, can generally be liquidated quickly and in comparatively small units with minimum expense.

Mutual funds have advantages and disadvantages for the small investor. They provide needed diversification and professional management, but they have two important drawbacks. First, many funds are sold by salesmen, whose commission charges or "load fees" may run as high as 7 to 9 percent of the amount invested. These commissions can be avoided by purchasing "no load" mutual funds that are purchased directly, thus avoiding the sales commission. Second, care and evaluation are needed before selecting a mutual fund. Some mutual funds have shown consistently poor historical performance. Hence, the investor must carefully evaluate mutual funds and select a fund whose investment goals are similar to his own.

Investments should also be easy to manage. Investments requiring extensive analysis prior to purchase or close supervision thereafter are generally not good for retirement age farmers. Farm real estate is usually easily manageable for them, since they are familiar with its investment characteristics. Their general lack of experience in managing nonfarm securities poses a serious difficulty for most retiring farmers. Perhaps this is why most of them express a negative attitude toward stocks, bonds, and mutual funds as investments.

Those who wish to invest in nonfarm securities may find it difficult to obtain reliable and unbiased investment advice. The investor must evaluate many sources of information to make a sound investment decision. The novice investor should begin by reading a good textbook on investment analysis and keep informed by reading regularly one or two periodicals that cover market developments. He may also wish to consult one or more advisory services. Often, recent issues of advisory service letters are available at brokerage offices.

The investor's broker is probably the most important single source of information and advice. Ordinarily the broker can supply the investor with detailed current and historical information on stocks and bonds under consideration. A good broker should be aware of his client's personal investment goals and be willing to help achieve those goals regardless of the size of the investor's account. Investment advice and counseling can also be obtained on a formal or informal basis from most commercial banks. Farmers who have over $100,000 to invest in stocks and bonds may wish to turn their portfolios over to a Chartered Financial Analyst who would manage their investments for a relatively small percentage charge per year.

The investor must evaluate sources of information and be aware of potential biases. For example, a bank representative may recommend investing in his bank's saving accounts even though equity securities are in the investor's best interest. A broker may recommend unnecessary changes in the investor's account to increase his commission income. Mutual fund salesmen typically recommend only the shares issued by the fund they represent. Finding qualified investment counsel is probably one of the more difficult aspects of investing in stocks, bonds, and mutual funds.

Estimating Capital Losses. The retiring farmer who contemplates selling his farm real estate and reinvesting the proceeds in nonfarm securities should consider the possible capital losses involved. When farm assets are liquidated, capital gains taxes, realtors' and auctioneers' commissions, brokerage fees, and the purchase or rental of a nonfarm retirement dwelling generally reduce considerably the amount of funds that can be reinvested.

Complete liquidation of the farm business will cost 10 to 40 percent of the original value of assets owned prior to liquidation, depending on exact capital gains taxes, commissions, and the type of retirement home purchased. Purchase of a dwelling is not, strictly speaking, a capital loss, but it does reduce the amount of capital available for purchasing income-producing assets.

Budgeting Investment Income. Annual retirement income can be budgeted from the amount of assets, the expected rate of return on assets, and the amount of social security benefits or other pension income. An important aspect to consider, however, is rate of inflation in the general price level. Obviously, increasing prices reduce the purchasing power of a fixed annual income.

Suppose, for example, the retiring farmer purchases $10,000 worth of bonds that yield 7 percent, for an annual income of $700. If the rate of inflation is 3 percent per year, the real rate of return of this investment would be only 4 percent and he would have to reinvest 3/7 of his income each year so that annual returns and the real value of the bond would keep pace with inflation; otherwise, the real value of the security and its income would gradually decline over time. Reference to Appendix Table 2 will show that a 3 percent annual rate of inflation reduces the purchasing power of a dollar to 50 cents in about 23 years. A 5 percent annual rate of inflation reduces the purchasing power of a dollar to 50 cents in only 14 years.

Another question that has to be considered is whether to use only the income from the invested capital or to use the capital itself. Appendix Table 3 shows the annual income that can be expected from each dollar invested, assuming the principal is liquidated over a specified number of years. For example, consider a $10,000 savings account that pays 5 percent per year interest. If the principal itself is not used, the income per year will be $500. However, if the investor needed more than $500 per year, he could gradually use some of the $10,000 principal as well. If he chose to use up all the principal over a 20-year period, multiplying the entry in the 5 percent column of Appendix Table 3, for $n = 20$, by $10,000 shows that he could withdraw $802 per year. If that were still not enough, he could withdraw $1,295 per year, but the principal would be used up at the end of 10 years.

AN ILLUSTRATION OF RETIREMENT INCOME BUDGET-
ING. The retirement income budgeting procedure can be illustrated for a case that might be typical of the situation confronting a retiring farmer. Suppose a retiring farmer and his wife own $100,000 worth of productive assets consisting of a $70,000 farm, $20,000 worth of livestock and farm machinery, and $10,000 in cash, savings accounts, and other liquid assets. By inquiring at the local office of the Social Security Administration they find that their social security retirement benefits will be $2,650 per year. Based on past experience, these social security benefits can be expected to increase to keep pace with inflation.

It was assumed for this example that farm real estate prices will increase by 3 percent per annum and that net rental income from farm real estate would be $3\frac{1}{2}$ percent. Bonds were assumed to yield 8 percent per annum and savings accounts 5 percent. Nonfarm equities were assumed to have a 5 percent per annum price increase and a 4 percent per annum income return. A 3 percent per annum rate of inflation was assumed.

Table 16.2 shows the estimated amount of investment income that the typical retiring farmer could expect to receive with the farm rental alternative. It is assumed that if they rent their farm out they can continue to live in the farm home. This arrangement is usually

TABLE 16.2:   Estimated Annual Investment–Annual Income under the Farm Rental Alternative

Type of Asset	Amount Invested	Price Returns*	Income Returns	Total Returns
Farm Real Estate	$ 70,000	$2,100	$2,450	$4,550
Bonds	30,000	0	2,400	2,400
Savings	5,000	0	250	250
Total	$100,000	$2,100	$4,550	$6,650
Reinvestment needed to compensate for inflation				−3,000
Real annual income without asset liquidation				$3,650
Real annual income with asset liquidation in 25 years				$4,370

* Also referred to as capital gains.

possible because tenants are interested mainly in renting the cropland, not the buildings.

If he rented out his farm and invested his liquid funds in bonds and savings accounts as shown, he would receive a total annual investment income of $6,650. This income would be equivalent to a 6.65 percent overall rate of return on the $100,000 worth of assets; however, the assumed 3 percent rate of inflation would reduce the *real* rate of return to only 3.65 percent. This 3.65 percent net real rate of return indicates that his annual investment income would always be equivalent to $3,650 if he reinvested enough each year to compensate for inflationary losses. The $2,100 price returns from the farm real estate would be automatically reinvested because of the expected 3 percent annual increase in land prices. In addition he would have to reinvest $900 of the $4,550 in income returns each year to fully compensate for the 3 percent rate of inflation.

The amount of real annual retirement income could be increased to a maximum of $4,370 by gradually liquidating the bonds and savings accounts over the 25-year planning period. The $2,100 return on the bonds and savings accounts is equivalent to a 7 percent rate of return before inflation, or 4 percent after taking the 3 percent rate of inflation into account. Appendix Table 3 indicates that if $30,000 worth of bonds and savings yielding 4 percent per annum were gradually liquidated over a period of 25 years, they would provide a real annual income of $1,920 ($30,000 × 0.0640, from Appendix Table 3). This income from the liquid assets, together with the $2,450 in rental income, would amount to $4,370 annually in terms of real annual income.

The expected amount of annual real income under the farm business liquidation alternative can be budgeted in a similar manner.

TABLE 16.3: Estimated Annual Investment–Annual Income under the Farm Business Liquidation Alternative

Type of Asset	Amount Invested	Price Returns*	Income Returns	Total Returns
Nonfarm Equities	$40,000	$2,000	$1,600	$3,600
Bonds	30,000	0	2,400	2,400
Savings	5,000	0	250	250
Total	$75,000	$2,000	$4,250	$6,250
Reinvestment needed to compensate for inflation				−2,250
Real annual income without asset liquidation				$4,000
Real annual income with asset liquidation in 25 years				$5,505

* Also referred to as capital gains.

If the farm were sold, capital losses and the purchase of a modest dwelling would reduce the value of assets available for reinvestment to around $75,000. The estimated investment income from one possible $75,000 investment portfolio is shown in Table 16.3. The nonfarm equities, together with the bonds and savings, yield a total annual income of $6,250, which is equivalent to an 8⅓ percent overall rate of return on the $75,000 portfolio. With the 3 percent annual inflation, the real rate of return would be only 5⅓ percent or $4,000.

Under the business liquidation alternative, all assets would be in a highly liquid form, so the entire $75,000 portfolio could be gradually liquidated. Interpolation between the 5 and 6 percent columns in Appendix Table 3 indicates that a $75,000 portfolio yielding a 5⅓ percent real rate of return would provide a real annual income of about $5,505 for 25 years.

The amounts of real annual retirement income under the two alternatives, excluding social security benefits, are summarized in Table 16.4. It is obvious that even with $100,000 worth of productive assets and social security benefits of $2,650 per year, the typical retired farmer must live within a fairly tight budget regardless of which retirement alternative he selects. The need to set aside and reinvest

TABLE 16.4: Budgeted Amounts of Real Annual Investment Income from Two Retirement Alternatives

Alternative*	Without Asset Liquidation	With Asset Liquidation in 25 years
Farm Rental	$3,650	$4,370†
Sale of Farm Business	$4,000	$5,505

* Does not include estimated social security benefits.
† Asset liquidation is limited to nonreal-estate assets since farmland cannot be readily liquidated in small units.

enough of the investment income each year to protect against inflationary losses reduces the amount of retirement income substantially.

The need to budget carefully retirement income is even more critical for retiring farmers who have smaller amounts of assets. A retiring farmer who has only $50,000 to invest should expect to receive only about half as much investment income as the farmer with $100,000 worth of productive assets. The problem of portfolio liquidity is also more critical for the low net worth situation. The desirability of holding assets in a highly liquid form so that they can be sold gradually throughout the retirement years suggests that the sale of the entire farm business may be the better retirement alternative for the low net worth case. However, the low net worth retiree cannot assume large amounts of risk. Thus he should probably invest in savings accounts, high quality bonds, and nonfarm equities.

Most farmers with larger amounts of productive assets will be able to achieve a satisfactory retirement income under either alternative. Even so, the high net worth retiree would be advised to guard against unnecessary expenditures. An expensive retirement dwelling or failure to protect assets against inflationary losses could have serious consequences even for the retiring farmer who has $200,000 to invest.

OTHER SOURCES OF RETIREMENT INCOME. Social security benefits and investment income are probably the two major sources of retirement income for most retiring farmers. However, if retirement planning is started early enough in life, additional sources of income can be generated.

One possibility is to establish a pension plan under the Self-Employed Individuals Tax Retirement Act, sometimes referred to as "HR-10" or the "Keogh Plan." The Self-Employed Retirement Act permits farmers and other self-employed individuals to establish a retirement pension plan and make annual contributions in amounts based on their annual income. Federal income taxes on these contributions are deferred until after retirement when the money is withdrawn. Some highly profitable farming operations are subject to very high tax brackets; hence, the possibility of deferring income until after retirement, when one is likely to be in a lower tax bracket, may be a real advantage.

Annuities can also be used to provide retirement income. Annuities are contracts sold by life insurance companies that guarantee the purchaser a monthly or annual lifetime income, beginning at some specified age. For example, a 65-year-old male would pay approximately $10,000 for a variable annuity that would provide an income of about $900 per year for the rest of his life, or "10 years certain."

He could also purchase the annuity by making regular payments over several years prior to age 65. The term *variable* means that the income would fluctuate slightly with the rate of return on investments held by the issuing company. The *10 years certain* clause means that if, for example, the purchaser of the annuity should live for only 5 years after payments begin, his survivors would receive the payments through the tenth year.

Permanent life insurance, such as limited-pay life and endowment policies, can also be used to accumulate a retirement income fund. Premiums on these types of policies normally cease at, or prior to, retirement age and the policyholder can withdraw the cash value either as a lump sum or as a regular monthly income.

The main disadvantage of a self-employed retirement plan, annuities, life insurance, or any savings plan for that matter, is that funds must be diverted from investments in farm assets, family living, and other, possibly higher-yielding, alternative uses. Farmers and their families should definitely consider their financial needs and resources for retirement long before reaching retirement age. However, they should also avoid becoming heavily committed to forced retirement savings plans to the extent that current consumption and farm investments are unduly restricted.

SUMMARY. Small, independent or closely held businesses typically follow a life cycle which is closely related to the life cycle of its owner or owners. Thus farmers should carefully plan for their retirement and the transfer of their estates. The principal goals of retirement and estate planning are (1) financial security during retirement, (2) continuity of the farm business, (3) equitable treatment of heirs, and (4) minimizing capital losses.

The retirement phase involves the conversion of farm capital into sources of retirement income. Income from investments, together with the social security base, are the two major sources of retirement income for most farm families. Factors to be considered in budgeting investment income are life expectancy, investment risks and returns, and capital losses.

QUESTIONS AND PROBLEMS
1. Describe the four phases of the typical life cycle of a farm business.
2. Discuss the four main goals of retirement and estate planning.
3. Why are "mean life expectancy" figures a poor basis for estimating the number of years over which retirement income will be needed.

4. Explain the terms: business risk, market risk, interest rate risk, and purchasing power risk. To which types of investment risk are the following investments most susceptible: bonds, common stocks, farm real estate, installment land contracts, real estate mortgages, mutual funds, saving accounts?
5. Explain why *liquidity* and *ease of management* are desirable attributes of an investment. Discuss the investments listed in problem (4) in terms of liquidity and ease of management for retiring farmers.
6. Discuss the problems of obtaining reliable investment advice and counseling. Which sources would you recommend for a retired farmer?
7. Outline the procedure for estimating the amount of retirement income for a farmer. Point out the effects of life expectancy, capital losses, and inflation.

REFERENCES

Cohen, Jerome B.; Zinbarg, Edward D.; and Zeikel, Arthur. *Investment Analysis and Portfolio Management,* revised ed. Richard D. Irwin, Inc., Homewood, Ill., 1973.

Lee, W. F. "Retirement Planning for Farmers." *Econ. Information for Ohio Agr.,* No. 511, Dept. Agr. Econ. and Rural Sociol., Ohio Coop. Ext. Serv., Sept. 1970.

Lee, W. F., and Brake, J R. *Conversion of Farm Assets for Retirement Purposes.* Dept. Agr. Econ., Mich. State Univ., Res. Rept. 129, Jan. 1971.

Sauer, H. M.; Bauder, W. W.; and Biggar, J. E. *Retirement Plans, Concepts and Attitudes of Farm Operators in Three Eastern South Dakota Counties.* Dept. Rural Sociol., S.Dak State Univ., Bull. 515, June 1964.

Smith, Robert S. *Farmers and Retirement.* Dept. Agr. Econ., Cornell Univ., Coop. Ext. Serv., Bull. 5, Jan. 1971.

CHAPTER 17: ESTATE PLANNING AND FARM OWNERSHIP TRANSFER

AN ESTATE transfer plan is an arrangement for the orderly transfer of one's possessions to his heirs before and after death. The large amount of capital involved in commercial farming today means that many farmers accumulate sizable estates; however, estate planning is also important for small estates. Anyone who owns property, whether young or old, should give serious thought as to how his estate will be transferred.

Estate planning is a personal matter and the specific plan should be tailored to personal and family goals. As was mentioned in the previous chapter, the primary goals may include (1) financial security during retirement, (2) continuity of the farm business, (3) equitable treatment of heirs, and (4) minimizing estate taxes, legal fees, and other transfer costs.

Estate planning usually involves many complicated legal and financial matters and the legal aspects vary from one state to another. Thus legal advice from a qualified attorney usually is essential, and depending upon the circumstances, the professional services of people such as an accountant, trust officer, insurance agent, or an investment counselor may also be needed.

PROPERTY INCLUDED IN AN ESTATE. An *estate* consists of all real property as well as tangible and intangible personal property that one owns or has an ownership interest in. Real property includes all land and buildings or other permanent improvements. Tangible personal property includes items such as automobiles, farm equipment, livestock, inventories, cash, and personal items such as jewelry and antiques. Intangible personal property includes securities such as stocks, bonds, bank accounts, notes, mortgages, life insurance policies, and annuities. One of the first steps in designing a transfer plan is to make a complete inventory of *all* assets and liabilities so that an attorney and others can properly analyze the situation.

ESTATE SETTLEMENT. The affairs of the deceased are handled by the state through the probate courts. The basic purposes of probate proceedings are (1) to satisfy creditor's claims, (2) to pay any state and federal estate taxes due, and (3) to distribute the remaining assets of the estate among heirs in line with the wishes of the deceased or in accordance with state law.

The probate court appoints an administrator or executor for the estate. The assets of the estate are inventoried and appraised. Public notice of the death is placed in newspapers to alert creditors and give them a time period in which claims may be filed. If necessary, assets may be sold to satisfy creditors' claims and taxes. Eligible heirs are determined and located and the property is distributed among them at the final estate closing.

Some property need not go through probate, such as life insurance proceeds payable to named beneficiaries and property held in joint tenancy with right of survivorship. However, such property is included, totally or in part, in the estate for purposes of calculating state and federal taxes due.

METHODS OF TRANSFERRING AN ESTATE. There are several methods of arranging for the orderly transfer of an estate. These methods can be discussed advantageously under the following headings: wills, life insurance and annuities, coownership and life estates, transfer by sale or gift, trusts, and incorporation.

Wills. A will forms the basis of most estate transfer plans. The purpose of a will is to specify how property is to be distributed upon the death of the owner. In addition, the maker of the will can name a qualified executor who will administer the estate, as well as a guardian or a trustee who will look after the interests of minor children or other survivors who might have difficulty in handling financial matters.

Virtually every property owner, regardless of his age or the size of his estate, should have a will prepared with the help of a qualified attorney. Studies have shown that fewer than half of all farmers have made a will—a serious situation when one considers the consequences of dying *intestate,* that is, without having made a valid will. In the absence of a will naming an executor, an administrator is appointed by the court and the estate is distributed according to the intestate law of succession. Intestate laws of succession vary from state to state, but generally, they specify, for example, that the widow receives from one-third to one-half of the estate and the remainder is divided *equally* among the surviving children of the deceased or their heirs. Without a will, several undesirable situations may occur. The share of the estate passing to the surviving spouse may be inadequate, particularly if minor children are involved. The farm property may become divided into inefficient units. The estate may remain unsettled or undergo a long and costly settlement. In most states, minor children are placed under the care of a court-appointed guardian if both parents die simultaneously without having made wills in which they have named a guardian of their choice.

Clearly, there are many advantages of having a will. However, there may be some drawbacks. A badly outdated or improperly prepared will can sometimes be worse than no will at all. Wills should be reviewed regularly and amended if necessary to account for changing family circumstances and goals. A birth, death, or divorce are examples of events that would call for a thorough review of the will. A will does not guarantee that discord among heirs will be eliminated. Occasionally wills are contested, causing long and costly estate settlements.

A will, by itself, generally, is not a desirable method of transferring a farm business. The person who hopes to inherit the business may not know the precise terms of the will, and even if he does, he will still be uncertain as to when he will finally gain full control of the business. Also, since it is the *last* will and testament that is probated, there is always a possibility that a family quarrel may result in a change in the will that would disinherit the successor. The resulting uncertainty may make it impossible for him to properly finance the farm business or operate it efficiently. Hence, a will in conjunction with one or more of the other estate transfer plans discussed below usually is more suitable.

Life Insurance and Annuities. Most farmers overlook the role that life insurance can play both in creating an estate and facilitating the orderly transfer of the estate. The payment of life insurance proceeds to named beneficiaries will not be delayed until the estate has been settled; thus life insurance provides immediate cash to cover family living expenses, taxes, debts, and settlement costs that arise during the settlement period. The availability of ready cash may enable the survivors to continue operating the farm business by preventing the forced sale of assets to meet settlement costs and taxes. Life insurance may also be used in a father-son partnership where the son insures the father's life as a means of providing money to purchase the business assets after the father's death. In this situation, however, the premiums are likely to be high because of the father's age and they may hinder the son's ability to accumulate capital in the business before the father's death.

Annuities may also be used to facilitate the transfer of a farm business. *Commercial annuities,* which were discussed in the previous chapter, are sold by life insurance companies. A son, for example, could purchase an annuity for the parents equal to the purchase price of the farm. In return, the insurance company would pay the parents an annual lifetime income. Care should be taken to be sure that the premiums will not unduly hinder the son's capital accumulation and that the income for the parents will be adequate. With a *private annuity,* the business might be sold to the son who in turn would agree to pay the parents monthly or yearly income for the rest of their lives. Private annuity arrangements should be carefully thought out because there are many possibilities for family friction. The annual income for the parents may be inadequate and equitable treatment of other heirs may be difficult. A disadvantage of both life insurance and annuities is that they offer no protection against inflation. With a 3 percent rate of inflation, for example, the purchasing power of an annuity paying $300 a month would be only $225 per month in 10 years.

Coownership and Life Estates. Coownership refers to the situation where two or more persons own property together. Although state laws vary with respect to coownership, there are two basic forms: *tenancy in common* and *joint tenancy with right of survivorship.* If the coowners hold the property as tenants in common, each owner holds an undivided interest in the property, and this undivided interest would, in the event of an owner's death, become part of his estate, and would be ultimately transferred to his heirs. Generally, the tenancy in common form of coownership should be used only if qualified legal advice has been sought and only if the owners have utmost confidence in each other. If the coowners are joint tenants with right of survivorship, the deceased owner's share automatically passes to the surviving owner or owners rather than to his heirs.[1] Joint tenancy with right of survivorship prevents the transfer from being delayed while the estate is being settled.

Joint tenancy with right of survivorship is used by many farmers to facilitate the transfer of property to their heirs; however, it should not be considered a substitute for a will. If a husband and wife who own property as joint tenants with right of survivorship should die simultaneously without wills, their jointly owned property would be transferred according to the intestate laws of succession. Intestate laws of succession would also take effect upon the death of the surviving spouse in the absence of a properly drawn will.

Some farm families transfer farm property by means of a *life estate.* A life estate, usually created by deed or will, provides that the holder of such an estate (the life tenant) can use the property during his lifetime, and upon his death the property passes to another person, known as the *remainderman* (or *remaindermen*). Some farmers transfer their property to their children and retain a life estate for themselves. A farmer may deed or will the farm to his wife for her lifetime

---

1. *Tenancy by entireties,* another form of coownership that contains the right of survivorship feature, can be held only by husband and wife.

with the provision that after her death it shall go to his children. Other types of arrangements are also possible.

While life estates have advantages as a means of providing support for parents and transferring the farm, they also have a number of disadvantages. The life tenant may not improve the farm and may even exploit the land and buildings in an effort to secure maximum income during his lifetime. He may be held responsible by the remainderman for destruction of permanent improvements, trees, and the like, but the life tenant cannot be forced to keep up the farm. Even if such provisions were made in the law, it is very doubtful that a family member who is to inherit the property would bring legal action against aged parents. Moreover, the parents may not want to neglect the farm, but conditions may have changed so that more income is needed than was contemplated. Since economic and social changes both inside and outside the family cannot be foreseen, the life estate may work a hardship on both the parents and the son. Moreover, the son has no specific commitment as to when he will become the owner and be able to put his plans for the farm and a home into effect. Another disadvantage of the life estate is that the remainderman's cost basis for tax purposes is the same as the former owner's cost. Should the remainderman want to sell the farm, he would be faced with higher taxes on capital gains than would be the case if he had inherited the property directly. The cost basis of inherited property is generally its market value at the time the transfer takes place.

Transfer by Sale or Gift. If transfer of the business to a son or other successor is an important goal, selling or giving property to the incoming operator prior to death is probably the most businesslike way of making the transfer. Typically, a partnership, corporation, or other family agreement is used to enable the successor to gradually increase his financial interest in the business. This method gives the successor some control and enables him to acquire a financial interest in the business early in life. Assuming the sale price reflects the fair market value of the property, equitable treatment of other heirs is possible.

In many cases, the retiring farmer provides financing for the successor. Very often, the real estate is sold on a land contract or mortgage. The land contract sale has two possible advantages for the seller: (1) if the down payment is less than 30 percent of the purchase price, capital gains taxes may be significantly reduced and (2) the regular payments of principal and interest provide a regular source of income. However, retiring farmers may want to avoid having a major portion of their assets in land contracts or mortgages because they lack liquidity. If the father should need a large amount of money, the son might be forced to refinance the loan with another lender or the father might have to sell the contract or mortgage, perhaps at a substantial discount.

Gifts to heirs prior to death can be used to reduce estate taxes on large estates. Property given away prior to death is exempt from federal estate taxation as long as the gift program was not started in contemplation of death. Generally, the gift program must have been in effect for more than 3 years prior to death to meet this requirement.

Large gifts are subject to federal gift taxes; however, gift tax exemptions are liberal, and even if gifts exceed the exemptions the gift tax rates are lower than corresponding estate tax rates. Thus, with large estates, gifts can achieve two objectives of estate planning: (1) transfer of the business to a successor, and (2) reduction of estate taxes and other settlement costs.

Single lifetime gifts of up to $30,000 ($60,000 for a married couple) are exempt from federal estate taxes, as are gifts of up to $3,000 per year ($6,000 for a married couple) to *each* beneficiary. That portion of gifts in excess of these exemptions are subject to the federal gift tax. Many farmers use gifts in conjunction with a land contract sale to the son. The farm property is sold to the son but all or part of the payments due on the land contract are treated as gifts. If the business is operated as a partnership or corporation, gifts of shares in the partnership or stock in the corporation can be made in the same manner.

A carefully thought-out sale and gift program is generally recommended as a method of transferring a farm business to a successor. However, the method used should be consistent with the goals and needs of the donor. Also, care should be taken to insure that all heirs are treated equitably. Gifts or sale of the business under unusually favorable terms to one heir might constitute inequitable treatment of other heirs, although, as was pointed out in the previous chapter, the disposition of one's property among his heirs is a personal decision.

Trusts. Another tool for estate planning is a trust. Trusts are especially useful when the estate is large and minimizing taxes is an important goal. A trust is a legal arrangement whereby a property right is held by one party, the *trustee,* for the benefit of others, the *beneficiaries.* The trustee manages, controls, and has title to the property, but all income (less the trustee's management fee) goes to the beneficiaries. Final ownership is eventually assigned to designated beneficiaries. Any kind of property can be placed in a trust, but usually only income-producing property or property that can be invested by the trustee is placed in trust.

Trusts are of two types: *living* and *testamentary.* Living trusts are subdivided further into *revocable* and *irrevocable* trusts. With a revocable trust, the trust creator reserves the power to terminate the trust at any time; thus the revocable trust may reduce income taxes but it will generally not reduce estate taxes significantly. The irrevocable trust is binding on the trust creator for the term of the trust in that it cannot be revoked, altered, or amended; thus the irrevocable trust can reduce both estate taxes and income taxes. A living trust can be set up in any manner the creator desires, with even the possibility of naming himself both trustee and beneficiary. The testamentary trust is created in a will by making the trust the beneficiary of the estate rather than a specific individual or individuals.

Much careful planning must be done to anticipate all changes that may occur when creating either an irrevocable living trust or a testamentary trust. One situation in which the farmer might want to consider a trust is when he wants to be relieved of the burden of management or when he believes that his survivors cannot assume management responsibilities. When setting up a trust, the creator is obtaining the management services of the trustee, whether it is a person or an institution such as the trust department of a bank. Perhaps some farmers do not consider using trusts because of skepticism of the management capabilities of the trustee, and sometimes this skepticism is well founded. Many institutional trustees lack experience in managing specialized businesses such as farms. Thus the trustee should be carefully selected if the farm business is to be placed in a trust.

Many of the larger rural banks employ qualified farm managers in their trust departments. If there is no farm manager, the trust can be written to specify that the farming operation will be placed under the supervision of a qualified farm manager. In many cases a trust is more satisfactory if the farm assets are sold and converted to liquid assets such as stocks and bonds because it is often easier to find trustees who are experienced in the management of nonfarm investments.

Incorporation. Corporations were discussed in Chapter 6 as a method of acquiring equity capital to farm. But perhaps the most important advantage of incorporating a farm business is that it can help to facilitate the transfer of a business to heirs either before or after death. When a corporation is formed, the owners of the business own shares of stock instead of real property and tangible personal property. The fact that the owners' claims in the business are represented by undivided, homogeneous interests has important implications for farm transfer. If one owner should die, his shares of stock become part of his estate. Since the physical assets of the business are not directly involved in the estate settlement, the business need not be reorganized, as in the case of the proprietorship or partnership forms of business organization. In addition, transfer of the business prior to death is easier, since any sale or gift transactions involve shares of stock instead of physical property.

When carefully planned, incorporation of a farm business will help to achieve a smooth transfer as well as a possible reduction in estate taxes and settlement costs. However, incorporation alone cannot be regarded as a substitute for other estate transfer methods. A will is still needed and, furthermore, if there are insufficient liquid assets in the estate to meet settlement costs and taxes, some of the assets may still have to be sold even though the business is incorporated. Thus it generally is desirable to carry sufficient life insurance to cover anticipated estate settlement costs. As was pointed out in Chapter 6, there are several disadvantages of incorporation. The corporation is a more complex organization and is subject to organizational fees, more rigorous record-keeping requirements, and some state and federal taxes that do not apply to proprietorships and partnerships.

ESTATE SETTLEMENT COSTS AND TAXES. Many people fail to realize just how much shrinkage takes place in an estate as a result of settlement costs and taxes. The total shrinkage, expressed as a percentage of the gross value of the estate, may range from about 10 percent on small estates to 40 percent or more on estates over $200,000.

Estate settlement costs consist of four basic items: (1) executor's or administrator's fee, (2) federal estate taxes, (3) state and local inheritance or estate taxes, and (4) legal fees. In addition, there may be additional expenses for an accountant, appraiser, and other professional services if the estate is unusually large or complicated.

Federal estate taxes usually comprise the largest single expense in settling larger estates. Table 17.1 shows the current schedule of federal estate tax rates applicable to taxable estates up to $2.5 million. The *taxable estate* is calculated by taking the *gross estate* (which is essentially the value of all property in which the deceased had a full or partial interest) and subtracting all *deductions* and *exemptions*. *Deductions* for federal estate taxes include the following: (1) debts, funeral expenses, costs of administering the estate and losses from fire, storm, and other casualty or theft during the settlement of the estate; (2) the amount of money or property left to charitable, religious, and educational organizations; and (3) the marital deduction for the amount of money or property passing without reservation to a surviving spouse. The marital deduction cannot be more than 50 percent of the adjusted gross estate (gross estate less the deductions listed in item 1 above), even though more than one-half actually goes to the spouse. The marital deduction permits a person to leave roughly half of his estate to his spouse free of tax. In addition to these three types

TABLE 17.1:   Computation of Federal Estate Tax

Taxable Estate Equaling (1)	Taxable Estate Not Exceeding (2)	Tax on Amount in Column 1 (3)	Rate of Tax in Excess over Amount in Column 1 (4)
(dol)	*(dol)*	*(dol)*	*(%)*
	5,000		3
5,000	10,000	150	7
10,000	20,000	500	11
20,000	30,000	1,600	14
30,000	40,000	3,000	18
40,000	50,000	4,800	22
50,000	60,000	7,000	25
60,000	100,000	9,500	28
100,000	250,000	20,700	30
250,000	500,000	65,700	32
500,000	750,000	145,700	35
750,000	1,000,000	233,200	37
1,000,000	1,250,000	325,700	39
1,250,000	1,500,000	423,200	42
1,500,000	2,000,000	528,200	45
2,000,000	2,500,000	753,200	49

SOURCE: Internal Revenue Service.

of deductions, an *exemption* of $60,000 is allowed to all estates. This means that the first $60,000, after all deductions are subtracted, is exempt from tax. Thus, if a person had an adjusted gross estate of $120,000 and left at least half of it outright to his wife, there would be no federal estate tax because the marital deduction would reduce the taxable estate to $60,000 and the $60,000 estate exemption would offset that amount.

There are full or partial *credits* against the federal estate tax for state inheritance or estate taxes paid. Property in the estate that was inherited from someone else and on which federal estate taxes were levied within the preceding 10 years is also subject to a partial credit. A credit is also allowed for gift taxes paid on gifts that were included in the estate because they were judged to have been made in contemplation of death.

Other settlement costs vary widely among states and among counties within states. Thus it is not possible to accurately estimate estate settlement costs for all states. Farmers would be well advised to contact a qualified attorney or their Cooperative Extension Service for information on these matters.

ILLUSTRATION OF ESTATE PLANNING. The potential for reducing federal estate taxes through estate planning can be illustrated using a hypothetical example. Consider the case of a successful farmer who has accumulated total assets of $400,000. The estimated value of his adjusted gross estate, that is, the amount remaining after deductions for administrative expenses, payment of debts, funeral expenses, and charitable bequests, is $300,000. He wants to leave his wife $150,000 to cover her living expenses after his death. He has three children. One son hopes to take over the farm business while another son and a daughter are employed in nonfarm occupations. It is assumed (as is often the case) that the husband predeceases the wife.

Table 17.2 illustrates the amount of federal estate taxes that would be paid on this farmer's estate and subsequently on that part of his wife's estate that she inherits from him. No attempt was made to calculate state inheritance or estate taxes, and other settlement costs are only approximated. It should also be noted that there are many methods of transferring an estate other than those illustrated.

Plan 1 is really no plan at all. According to state law, one-third of his estate would go to his wife and the remaining two-thirds would be divided equally among the three children, which may or may not be in accord with his wishes.[2] Failure to make a will does not necessarily result in the highest total amount of federal estate taxes on the two estates, as this illustration shows; however, the surviving spouse would receive far less than the $150,000 that he feels she would need for living expenses following his death.

Under Plan 2 he wills everything to his wife and (it is assumed that) she subsequently wills her entire estate to the children. Notice that the tax on the husband's estate is lower than under Plan 1 because the full marital deduction is used; however, there is no marital deduction for the wife's estate. Consequently, the amount of tax on her estate would be quite high.

Under Plan 3 he wills half of his estate to his wife, thereby taking full advantage of the marital deduction and providing her with nearly $150,000 for living expenses. The other half of the estate could be willed directly to the children, or it could be placed in a trust naming the children as the ultimate beneficiaries of the property. If desired, he could direct that all or part of the income from the trust be paid to his wife during her lifetime. In any case, Plan 3 reduces the amount of property in the wife's estate, thereby resulting in a significant reduction in federal estate taxes and other settlement costs on her estate compared to Plan 2.

Under Plan 4 he establishes a gift program several years before his death and reduces the value of the adjusted gross estate to $200,000. He wills $150,000 to his wife; however, since the adjusted gross estate is only $200,000, only $100,000 would qualify for the

---

2. As was pointed out previously, intestate laws of succession vary among states.

TABLE 17.2: Estimated Federal Estate Taxes under Four Possible Estate Transfer Plans

	Plan 1 (No will)	Plan 2 (Will leaving all to wife)	Plan 3 (Will leaving half to wife)	Plan 4 (Gift program & will leaving three-quarters to wife)
HUSBAND'S ESTATE:				
Adjusted gross estate	$300,000	$300,000	$300,000	$200,000
Less: Marital deduction	100,000	150,000	150,000	100,000
Estate exemption	60,000	60,000	60,000	60,000
Taxable estate	140,000	90,000	90,000	40,000
Federal estate tax*	31,500	17,500	17,500	4,800
Net estate	268,500	282,500	282,500	195,200
WIFE'S ESTATE:				
Gross estate†	$ 89,500	$282,500	$141,250	$146,400
Less: Administrative expense‡	6,700	21,200	10,550	11,000
Adjusted gross estate	82,800	261,300	130,700	135,400
Less: Estate exemption	60,000	60,000	60,000	60,000
Taxable estate	22,800	201,300	70,700	75,400
Federal estate tax*	2,000	48,420	12,250	13,530
TOTAL TAX ON TWO ESTATES	$ 33,500	$ 65,820	$ 29,650	$ 18,330
NET AMOUNT PASSING TO CHILDREN§	$259,800	$212,880	$259,700	$270,670

* Adjusted for federal estate tax credit, where applicable.
† Share of husband's net estate under plan designated.
‡ Estimated as 7.5% of gross estate. Administration expenses vary widely.
§ Husband's adjusted gross estate less all taxes and administrative expenses paid on the two parents' estates.

marital deduction. Even so, the transfer of $100,000 prior to his death results in a substantial reduction in estate taxes on both estates compared to Plans 1, 2, and 3.

This illustration points out the importance of taking full advantage of the marital deduction feature of the federal estate tax. Since the marital deduction is not available on the surviving spouse's estate, estate taxes on the second estate will normally be quite high. Property can be kept out of the second estate by willing it directly to the children or transferring it to them through a trust. Estate taxes on *both* estates can be reduced significantly by making transfers prior to death through a gift program. In the case illustrated, a gift program would enable the son who plans to take over the farm to acquire a financial interest in the business early in life.

SUMMARY. Estate planning can be used to achieve important personal and financial goals such as financial security during retirement, transfer of the farm business to a successor, equitable treatment of heirs, and reduction of estate settlement costs. Careful consideration of these goals is a logical first step in designing an estate transfer program.

The will should form the basis of nearly all estate transfer programs. The will can be supplemented with other estate transfer aids such as life insurance and annuities, coownership of property, life estates, sales and/or gifts prior to death, trusts, and incorporation. It should be emphasized that estate planning is not a "do it yourself" project. The assistance of a qualified attorney is needed to insure that all legal requirements have been met. In addition, an accountant, insurance adviser, and a trust officer may also be needed to formulate the estate transfer plan.

QUESTIONS AND PROBLEMS

1. Explain why anyone who owns property, regardless of the size of his estate, should have an estate transfer plan.
2. Discuss the purposes of probate proceedings.
3. Discuss the purposes of a will and indicate some of the possible consequences of not having a valid will. Find out how property is transferred in your state under the intestate law of succession.
4. How can life insurance and annuities be used in an estate transfer plan?
5. Explain the differences between the *tenancy in common* and *joint tenancy* forms of coownership.
6. What are the advantages and disadvantages of transferring property through a life estate?
7. Explain why a sale and gift program is a businesslike method of transferring farm property to a successor.

8. Describe the three basic types of trusts and discuss the role of trusts in estate planning.
9. How does incorporation facilitate the transfer of property?
10. List the major deductions, exemptions, and credits under the federal estate tax law. Illustrate the importance of the marital deduction in reducing federal estate taxes.

REFERENCES

Graham, John R. *Basic Principles of Estate Planning: An Introduction.* Agr. Ext. Serv., Univ. of Ark., July 1970.

Harl, Neil E. *Farm Estate and Business Planning.* Agri Business Publications, Glenview, Ill., 1973.

Hepp, Ralph E., and Kelsey, Myron P. *A Study Outline for Estate Planning and Farm Transfer.* Agr. Econ. Misc. Series 1966-11, Dept. Agr. Econ., Coop. Ext. Serv., Mich. State Univ., 1966

Hill, Elton B., and Harris, Marshall. *Family Farm Transfer and Some Tax Considerations.* NCR Publ. 127, Mich. State Univ., Agr. Exp. Sta. Spec. Bull. 436, 1961.

Johnson, Jerome E., and White, James P. *Family Estate Planning.* N.Dak. State Univ., Agr. Exp. Sta. Bull. 463, revised 1969.

Krause, Kenneth R. *Family Estate Planning.* N.Dak. State Univ., Agr. Exp. Sta. Circ. 177, revised May 1967.

Levi, Donald R. *Agricultural Law.* Lucas Bros., Columbia, Mo., 1971.

Maynard, Cecil D.; Jeffrey, D. B.; and Laughlin, Glenn. *Estate Planning.* Okla. State Univ., Ext. Circ. E-726, Oct. 1968.

Moore, John E. *Property Planning Transfer Considerations.* Dept. Agr. Econ. and Rural Sociol., Ohio Coop. Ext. Serv., Ohio State Univ., 1971.

Pinna, W. P.; Wells, R. C.; and Harwood, D. J. *Estate Planning for North Carolina Farmer Families.* Dept. Agr. Econ., N.C. State Univ., EIR-15, 1970.

University of California. *Estate Planning for Farmers.* Calif. Agr. Exp. Sta. Circ. 461, revised May 1968.

PART 3: FINANCIAL MARKETS AND AGRICULTURAL LENDING AGENCIES

CHAPTER 18: FINANCIAL MARKETS

THE FINANCIAL MARKET (also referred to as the capital, credit, funds, or money market) in its broadest sense includes all transactions in financial instruments, such as currency, bank deposits, charge accounts, loans, mortgages, bonds, and shares of corporate stock. Farmers and farm lenders are participants in this market. When a farmer buys supplies or equipment on credit, when he borrows or repays a loan, or when he buys a stock or a bond, he is participating in the financial market. Similarly, when a farm lender obtains funds in the money market and lends them to farmers, he is directly involved in this market.

The financial market is a heterogeneous market consisting largely of institutions and individuals at various locations throughout the country connected by telephone, telegraph, and mail facilities. At the same time, the market is a vast complex mechanism that has evolved to serve the vast and complex financial needs of businessmen (including farmers) and other individuals, as well as corporations and government.

As an aid in understanding the scope of these markets, *an outside assignment* is proposed at this point. Study a financial newspaper, particularly the pages that report transactions and quotations for the different types of financial instruments. Outline the different markets and instruments for which quotations are listed. Note the quotations for Federal Land Bank bonds, Federal Intermediate Credit Bank debentures, and Bank for Cooperatives debentures. These banks, discussed in some detail in a subsequent chapter, make loans to farmers and farmer cooperatives with the money obtained in the financial market. Estimate the number of items listed in each market or group. Students usually are impressed by these figures. But keep in mind that the quotations carried by financial papers reflect only a part of the transactions in the financial market.

As already indicated, the financial market is, in effect, comprised of many financial markets. There are different markets for different types of financial instruments such as stocks, bonds, commercial paper (unsecured short-term promissory notes generally issued by large well-known firms), negotiable bank certificates of deposit, and various types of government agency and government securities. The distinction between markets for debt issues, such as bonds, and for equity issues, such as stocks, should be noted. For some purposes a distinction is made between money markets comprised of short-term instruments with a maturity of 1 year or less and capital markets that handle instruments with a maturity of more than 1 year. It should also be recognized that there are different markets for different economic units (individuals, households, businesses, and governments) and for different geographic areas—the national financial market and the local financial markets. Financial transactions may involve individuals, nonfinancial businesses, financial institutions, and governments, or various combinations of these.

A general picture of the function and operation of the financial markets is presented in this chapter. One exception is made in omitting financial transactions between individuals such as a farm mortgage loan made by an individual to a farmer. In the discussion that follows, the essential elements of the financial process are discussed first, followed by consideration of financial intermediaries such as commercial banks. The latter part of the chapter is devoted to national and local financial markets.

FUNCTIONS OF FINANCIAL MARKETS.
Financial markets have two basic functions: to facilitate transfer of capital from suppliers to users and to ration capital among users. Keep in mind that farmers are included among the users and, therefore, compete in financial markets for available funds. The return of capital from users to suppliers also is a function of the financial markets, but it comprises an auxiliary service function and is not dealt with specifically in this chapter.

Transfer of Capital.
The transfer of capital from suppliers to users is essential to the functioning and growth of a market economy.

Without this function, every economic unit would be, of necessity, financially self-sufficient. Expenditures of each unit would be limited to its own funds; moreover, there would be no outlet for unused savings.

Two basic economic functions are involved in the transfer of capital from suppliers to users. One consists of acquisition of funds that, in turn, are "packaged" and loaned. The funds may be acquired directly, as by an individual depositing funds in a bank, or they may be acquired by selling a new issue of a financial instrument, such as a

Federal Land Bank bond, in which case an intermediary such as the Federal Land Bank is involved. These transfers are often referred to as primary financial market activities.

The second basic economic function consists of transfer of outstanding financial instruments among financial units, such as those reflected by quotations in financial papers. These transfers usually involve services of an agent such as a broker or dealer in securities. Transactions of this type, generally referred to as secondary capital market activities, are essential to give the financial market liquidity. Without a secondary market, the original purchaser of a financial instrument would have to hold it to maturity. Under such circumstances, financial instruments would need to have very short maturities, or all portfolios would become frozen. Either alternative would seriously limit the usefulness of financial instruments and functioning of the financial markets. Moreover, short maturities for financial instruments related to fixed investments would reduce the inclination to borrow and might at times endanger the stability of the financial market. Lack of negotiability in financial instruments would sharply reduce purchases by potential buyers and thus reduce the volume of new issues and raise interest rates.

Rationing Capital. A basic function of financial markets—as of any market—is to allocate scarce resources among competing ends. In other words, through operation of financial markets, the limited supply of funds that is available is allocated to farmers and other economic units in the economy that have need for funds. If the markets function well, the funds will be allocated to uses yielding the highest returns. As indicated in Chapter 2, the allocation will be optimized when the marginal productivity of capital is equal for all uses.

The market mechanism for rationing capital among users is theoretically demand versus supply. In conventional simplified form, the demand function or curve for capital indicates the amount that buyers or users are willing to take at various interest or yield rates and repayment terms at a given time. The supply function or curve provides comparable information regarding the amount suppliers are willing to provide. The intersection of the two curves indicates the amount of capital that is transferred and the associated interest or yield rates and terms.

There are, as indicated above, many financial markets and many types and denominations of financial instruments. The demand and supply functions or curves for the various financial instruments in various markets are closely interrelated, but this does not mean that they are one and the same. Financial instruments vary greatly in terms of yield, liquidity, and risk. Preferences of suppliers and users vary with respect to these same criteria. Hence, the market mechanism offers alternatives to suppliers and users of funds that, in turn, provide some flexibility in the rationing process. For example, within limits, a corporation has the option of debt financing through a bank loan or a bond issue, or of equity financing through a common or preferred stock issue. The choice will depend upon terms and conditions prevailing at the time.

Demand and supply in financial markets tend to arise from activities of particular sectors of the economy—consumers, businesses, and governments—and, therefore, tend to be focused first in a particular financial market. Enlarged borrowing by a sector tends to be reflected in the particular financial market most closely related to its financial needs. For example, a greater demand by farmers and other businessmen for credit may first be reflected in a rise in commercial bank interest rates. Because of the interrelationships of financial instruments and of markets, such a development is soon felt to some degree throughout the whole financial market structure. The rise in interest rates serves as both a stimulant to greater savings and as a rationing device in use of funds first, and most importantly, in the market directly involved and then to some degree in the financial market as a whole.

Availability of capital in financial markets depends upon the flow of funds into those markets directly and also on the ability of financial institutions to obtain funds in one market and make them available in another. This important function of the financial market is elaborated upon in the following section dealing with financial intermediaries.

ROLE OF FINANCIAL INTERMEDIARIES. Financial intermediaries are firms whose assets are comprised primarily of claims on others and whose liabilities consist primarily of obligations to others. For example, assets of commercial banks consist primarily of loans and of investments in government securities, both of which are claims on others, and their liabilities consist primarily of deposits that are obligations to the depositors. By way of contrast, assets of nonfinancial business firms, such as farms, consist largely of physical property such as real estate, machinery, and equipment, while their liabilities consist of notes, mortgages, etc. Along with commercial banks, the major types of financial intermediaries are insurance companies, stock and bond exchanges, mutual funds, thrift institutions such as savings and loan associations and credit unions, investment bankers or underwriters, and federally sponsored and owned credit

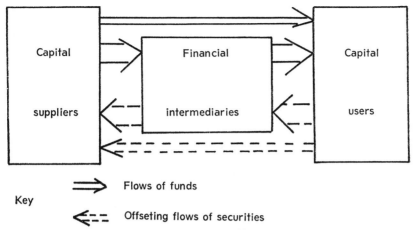

Key

⟹ Flows of funds

⟸--- Offseting flows of securities

FIG. *18.1—Flow of capital from suppliers to users.*

institutions.[1] In addition to the suppliers and users of funds, the financial intermediaries are the principal participants in financial markets. In this role they perform the functions of these markets as outlined above.

Intermediaries are Middlemen. The position of financial intermediaries in the financial markets is illustrated by Figure 18.1. They occupy an intermediate or middleman position between suppliers and users of capital. In other words, they supply the linkage between the suppliers and the users, as, for example, a rural commercial bank between depositors and farm borrowers, or a Federal Land Bank between investors in a distant city and farm borrowers. Note that there is a flow of funds from suppliers to intermediaries and on to users and an offsetting flow of securities (notes, mortgages, bonds, etc.) from users to suppliers. Providing this linkage is an extremely important function. In some cases an intermediary will perform the function alone, but often two or more intermediaries are involved. A brief review of the operations and flow of funds in the major types of financial intermediaries will further clarify their role.

Commercial Banks. Commercial banks obtain the major part of their funds from suppliers as demand deposits and savings and time deposits. Large commercial banks augment their deposits by

---

1. The Federal Reserve System is also a major financial intermediary. However, since it functions primarily as a monetary authority, as discussed in Chapter 19, which directly regulates the operations of member commercial banks and indirectly affects all financial intermediaries, it is not included here.

issuing negotiable, large-denomination certificates of deposit (CDs)—receipts for funds deposited in a bank for a specific period at a given interest rate—and bankers acceptances—short-term prime negotiable paper. Since deposits show wide seasonal or other temporary variations, banks use a major part of their funds for short-term and intermediate-term loans and investments, although they do put some funds in long-term investments. At the longer-term end of their loan portfolios are real estate mortgage loans that are made for a number of years. Installment loans and some other loans to business and individuals are for an intermediate term of from 1 to about 3 years. Their short-term loans, the major part of their loans to business (including farmers), consumers, and others, are for comparatively short periods, generally ranging from a few days to a few months with few if any exceeding 1 year. Bank investments in securities are largely in Treasury securities and state and local government bonds. They hold relatively few corporate bonds or corporate shares. Treasury securities are important in commercial bank portfolios due to their liquidity.

Insurance Organizations. Insurance organizations, including life insurance companies, fire, marine, and casualty insurance companies, and private and public pension funds, obtain funds from households, businesses, and governments either on the basis of contracts (insurance policies) or by contributions to pension funds. Life insurance companies are unique in the financial markets because of the relative regularity of the funds they receive from the household sector on the basis of long-term voluntary contracts. Similarly, private and public pension funds receive a regular flow of funds because of compulsory contributions by or for employees. The various types of insurance organizations differ considerably in the use of their funds due either to government regulation or tradition. Life insurance companies invest a major part of their funds in long-term farm and other mortgages and in corporate bonds. They invest a relatively small proportion in corporate shares and government securities. Other insurance companies invest largely in corporate and government securities. Private pension funds invest primarily in corporate securities, particularly in common and preferred stock. State and local government pension funds also invest primarily in corporate securities, but their emphasis is on bonds. They also put some funds into mortgages and government securities. Federal retirement funds are invested in Treasury securities, as provided by law. These investment policies have made life insurance companies and pension funds the decisive factor in the market for corporate bonds. Life insurance companies are also very important in the apartment and commercial building mortgage markets. Pension funds are very important in the market for corporate shares.

Thrift Institutions. Thrift institutions—the two main groups being mutual savings banks concentrated in New England and New York and savings and loan associations operating throughout the nation and the third group being the very numerous but mostly small credit unions—obtain their funds as savings deposits from households. Savings and loan associations invest a major part of their funds in home mortgages and are the most important single supplier of funds in this market. Savings banks also invest heavily in home mortgages, but put a substantial proportion of their funds in other mortgages and some in corporate securities. Credit unions use their funds mainly for personal loans to members.

Finance Companies. Finance companies obtain funds primarily by sale of bonds and short-term paper sold in the open market and from commercial bank loans. They use their funds primarily for short-term and intermediate-term installment loans to individuals. They also extend some short-term and intermediate-term loans to business for inventories and credit to customers, but except for farm equipment financing, finance companies are relatively unimportant sources of farm credit.

Government-Sponsored and Owned Institutions. Government-sponsored and originally government-owned credit institutions, including the Federal Land Banks, Federal Intermediate Credit Banks, Banks for Cooperatives, Federal Home Loan Banks, and Federal National Mortgage Association obtain funds primarily by sale of their own debt securities. These are not explicitly guaranteed by the government, but most investors feel there is a strong moral obligation in this regard. The first three bank systems, as indicated above, provide credit for agriculture. The Federal Home Loan Bank system makes loans to savings and loan associations on the basis of mortgages pledged as security. The Federal National Mortgage Association ("Fannie Mae") buys and sells home mortgages—provides a secondary market for mortgages—as a means of adding liquidity in the market and increasing the attractiveness of mortgages as an investment for financial institutions, thereby increasing the supply of mortgage funds available to home buyers.

Government-owned finance institutions, including the Farmers Home Administration, the Commodity Credit Corporation, and the Federal Housing Administration, operate with federal funds. The Farmers Home Administration, which also uses funds obtained in the financial markets, provides direct loans, and insures loans of other lenders to agriculture and others in rural areas. This agency is discussed in detail in a later chapter. The Commodity Credit Corporation provides commodity price support loans to farmers. The Federal Housing Administration and the Veterans Administration insure or guarantee mortgages made by private financial institutions and thereby substantially increase the flow of capital into home mortgages.

Investment Bankers. Investment bankers, or underwriters, including other firms that perform investment banking functions, such as member firms of national security exchanges, are the chief intermediaries between firms selling new issues of stocks and bonds and the suppliers of capital. They typically underwrite new issues of securities, that is, purchase the issue outright, either alone or as a member of an underwriting group or syndicate, and subsequently sell the securities to investors. Hence, they are referred to at times as underwriters.

Investment bankers, or groups of bankers, also do some "standby" underwriting of new security issues, which involves an agreement with the issuer to buy and subsequently sell any part of a new issue of securities that the issuer is unable to sell to investors. With the more speculative issues, investment bankers ordinarily do not function as underwriters but may serve as agents for the issuing corporation in selling, either alone or as a member of a group, as much of the new issue as possible. This arrangement may also be used with nonspeculative issues that are expected to sell well when it is not essential that the entire issue be sold.

Investment bankers perform a number of additional intermediary functions. For example, they participate in distribution or transfer of large blocks of outstanding securities, including transfer of part or all of the ownership of closely held businesses. They perform the function of security substitution, selling their own securities backed by a broadly diversified portfolio, and using the funds derived to invest in various types of securities and firms less well suited to the investing public. Investment bankers also function in private placements of new security issues as, for example, the negotiated sale of a new issue of securities to a life insurance company or pension fund.

Investment Companies. Investment companies, now predominantly mutual funds, raise capital by selling their own shares, primarily to individual investors, and invest most of their capital in corporate shares. As a result of their size and their relatively rapid portfolio turnover, they have become an important factor in the stock market, along with private pension funds and other institutional investors.

Securities Markets. The securities markets, although not directly involved in the movement of capital from suppliers to users, perform an important facilitating function by providing a secondary market for securities. Liquidity is an important factor to potential investors, and marketability is an important element in liquidity. By providing the facilities for marketing securities, the network of stock exchanges, securities dealers, and brokers facilitates the initial distribution of securities.

In addition to the investing public, the securities market consists of the organized stock exchanges and their member firms, the over-the-counter markets, and the appurtenant brokers and dealers. The securities markets are organized auction markets where buyers and sellers, through their brokers, effect transactions in securities. Securities admitted to listing on the exchanges are traded in the stock markets, and unlisted securities for which a market is maintained are traded in the over-the-counter markets.

Summary. As indicated by the above discussion, financial intermediaries perform a number of important functions, individually or in combination with others, in the transfer of capital from suppliers to users. The initial function of assembling funds from suppliers involves not only accepting deposits but developing and providing various means of attracting capital such as different types of accounts. A somewhat similar role is played with securities. While securities of many nonfinancial firms are acceptable to the investing public and are traded regularly on the exchanges, many are not suitable, due to factors such as risk, lack of knowledge regarding the issuing firm, and size and term of the instrument. Therefore, financial intermediaries offer their own securities, including their own shares, to the investing public in units and on terms that are most acceptable to facilitate obtaining or assembling funds from suppliers.

Perhaps the most important function in the intermediation process is the transformation of funds or the modification of the risk and liquidity aspects. Funds received by financial intermediaries vary greatly in amount and in the term for which they are deposited or invested. Intermediaries, therefore, must modify the heterogeneous supply of funds, so they are suitable for the users. Small amounts must be aggregated into large units with appropriate time dimensions, and in some cases perhaps large blocks of funds, such as those obtained by commercial bank sale of large-denomination certificates of deposit, must be broken down to meet the needs of smaller users. Intermediaries incur risk in the transformation of funds not only by issuing their own securities, which generally are more liquid and less risky than the instruments they themselves hold, but through modification of time and cost elements of various types of funds acquired.

A third function of financial intermediaries is transferring funds from one location to another. Capital available in a community seldom equals the amount used and, therefore, intermediaries move capital around the country as needed. If funds are scarce and expensive in one center, local intermediaries may augment the supply by bringing in funds from centers where funds are more abundant and less costly. For example, Federal Land Banks sell bonds in the national financial market to serve local farm mortgage needs. Intermediaries may also shift some of the local demand to centers where the supply of funds is more adequate. For example, many rural commercial banks maintain correspondent relationships with larger commercial banks in urban centers through which the urban bank participates with the local bank in larger farm loans.

A fourth function of financial intermediaries is rationing the supply of funds available to the various users as outlined above in the discussion of financial markets.

NATIONAL AND LOCAL FINANCIAL MARKETS. In the early part of the chapter, reference was made to the various financial markets, one classification of which was the national market and the local markets. Some detail on these markets will add to an understanding of the financial processes.

National Financial Market. The national financial market is centered in New York City, where all the major financial intermediaries in the nation or their representatives are located within a fairly small area or district. The large dealers in government securities, underwriters, and dealers in other types of equity and debt securities are located there. The banks of the farm credit system maintain a fiscal agent in the district. Most of the nation's large commercial banks are headquartered in the district, as are representatives of large banks located elsewhere. The head offices of a number of large insurance companies and industrial corporations also are located in the area. Firms located elsewhere are linked to the market through security dealers, banks, or other financial institutions, and by a network of communication media. Many of the participants in the national financial market are both suppliers and users of funds.

Instruments traded in the national market generally are of high quality, broadly acceptable to a wide range of investors, and readily marketable. Treasury securities (United States government securities), state and local government securities, corporate bonds, and corporate shares are the major issues traded. Other issues, such as federal funds (commercial bank deposits in a Federal Reserve Bank), United States government agency issues, commercial paper, certificates of deposit, bankers acceptances, and insured mortgages are traded in the market, but the volume is smaller. When the volume is small, the market tends to be thin, and price fluctuations may be relatively large.

Many issues traded in the national financial market are traded in the over-the-counter market. Treasury and state and local government securities are traded in this market, as are also some corporate bonds. The over-the-counter market also trades in corporate shares, mainly those of medium-sized and small, less-seasoned corporations as well as those of most banks and insurance companies. The organized stock exchanges handle shares primarily of large-sized and medium-sized nonfinancial corporations.

Treasury securities play a unique role in the financial market. Treasury bills are widely used as the balancing item in portfolios of many financial institutions and businesses, including some farm businesses. When temporarily unneeded funds accumulate, bills are purchased and subsequently sold as needs for cash develop. Treasury securities constitute the primary issue purchased and sold by the Open Market Account of the Federal Reserve System, discussed in the following chapter, as the primary means of expanding or contracting the monetary base of the nation.

The national financial market provides large suppliers and users of capital an effective and efficient means of placing and obtaining funds. The market, through a complex yet flexible network of international, national, regional, and local intermediaries, provides facilities for continuous and close linkage between suppliers and users of capital.

Local Financial Markets. Local financial markets are comprised of local suppliers and users of capital and the local financial intermediaries that serve them, such as commercial banks, savings and loan associations, insurance companies, merchants and dealers, finance companies, local affiliates of federally sponsored and owned credit agencies, and local stock and bond brokers. As was evident from the above discussion of intermediaries, they differ greatly in the type of service provided and the geographic area served, and the lending institutions vary in the type and terms of loans extended. The local intermediaries also vary in their access to the national financial market, some having more or less direct connections, while others are limited primarily to the local market.

The effectiveness or degree of perfection of local financial markets in the overall financial framework of the nation depends in large measure on their connection or linkage with the national market. It would be possible, of course, for local markets to achieve optimum intermediation between locally originated funds and the local demand for capital. This balance could be achieved if rates paid for savings (interest plus other inducements to save) and rates charged for capital (interest, fees, and other costs associated with loans) were such as to just equate the local supply and demand for capital. However, under such circumstances, rates probably would vary considerably from one local market to another. Adequate and effective linkage with the national financial market is essential to achieving relative uniformity in rates among local financial markets.

Even with theoretically perfect linkage among financial markets, rates probably would vary somewhat among them. If the local demand for capital exceeds the local supply so funds must be attracted from outside the community, local rates would exceed those that such funds would earn in the national financial market by a margin equivalent to the costs of attracting the capital to the local market. On the other hand, if the community generated a surplus of funds, rates in the local market would be lower than rates in the national market, the difference being equal to costs of placing the funds in that market. Costs in both cases would include those involved in transferring the funds, as well as other intermediary costs pertaining to size of transaction, maturities, risk, and management.

As the financial markets throughout the nation and means of intermediation have improved over the years, linkage among markets and with the national financial market has improved. These developments, along with federally sponsored and owned finance institutions, have contributed substantially to elimination of wide differences in rates that existed in the 1920s and earlier in various parts of the country. However, there are indications that rates still are out of line (either high or low) in many local financial markets and that these markets are quite insensitive to changes in rates in the national market. Custom, inertia, and lack of knowledge probably are the major factors. Moreover, the policy of federally sponsored and owned financial institutions of charging uniform rates throughout a district (that is, district served by a Federal Land Bank) has overcorrected the situation in some areas by not allowing sufficient flexibility in rates to compensate for differences in risk and other loan costs, thereby contributing to an imbalance among areas.

Imperfections among financial markets regarding interest rates (including other inducements to save and fees and other costs associated with loans) affect the level of economic activity and resource utilization and development in the market areas. With theoretically perfect linkage, comparable uses of funds (loans) would carry comparable rates in all financial markets adjusted for costs of attracting funds to the community if it were a capital-deficient area or the costs of moving funds out of a capital-surplus area. Since there appear to be imperfections in the financial markets, it follows that there probably are imbalances in economic activity. In those areas where rates are relatively low, the level of business activity, employment, and resource utilization and development is relatively high. On the other hand, those areas where rates are relatively high are at a disadvantage in these respects.

Market imperfections are noticeable in many rural areas. Most, if not all, areas are served by commercial banks and, theoretically, the entire country is served by local affiliates of the Farm Credit System (Production Credit Associations [PCAs] and Federal Land Bank Associations [FLBAs]). However, many PCA territories are large and some offices are operated only on a part-time basis. In these areas the commercial bank, in practice, becomes the main source of farm production credit other than merchant and dealer credit. If the commercial bank is not aggressive, linkage with the national financial market may be very weak. When this is the situation, local interest rates generally are relatively insensitive to economic forces elsewhere in the country.

Imperfection within local financial markets affects the balance or mix of economic activity within the area. Where imperfections exist, some sectors of the economy obtain more than their share of the available capital, with the result that production expands, and returns per unit of resources are relatively low. On the other hand, the sectors that obtain less than their share of available capital are forced to limit production, with the result that they realize relatively high returns per unit of resources employed. Hence, imperfections in a financial market not only cause an imbalance in production but lower the overall productivity of the available capital since the marginal productivity of capital is not equal in all sectors.

Imperfections within markets arise from a number of causes. Federally sponsored and owned finance institutions, as well as some other lending institutions, make loans to only certain sectors of the economy, and in some cases it appears this causes some distortion in the allocation of capital. Federal farm programs, crop insurance, deposit insurance, and the like, may also distort the flows of capital. Legal limitations on the level of interest rates that may be paid on savings or charged on loans also affect capital flows within a financial market.

QUESTIONS AND PROBLEMS
1. Explain what is meant by a financial market. What connection does it have with agricultural credit?
2. List and explain the functions of a financial market. How do they affect a farmer?
3. Distinguish between primary and secondary financial market activities. Use farm examples. Why is a secondary market essential in operation of the financial system?
4. What is a financial intermediary?
5. Discuss the role of financial intermediaries in financial markets.
6. List the major types of financial intermediaries and discuss the flow of funds in each. Identify those that make loans to farmers and indicate the source of their loan funds.
7. Discuss the national financial market. What is its function?

8. What are the characteristics of financial instruments traded in the national financial market? Give examples from agricultural credit.
9. Discuss the characteristics of local financial markets.
10. Outline the types of imperfections that exist in local financial markets and explain the reason for each.
11. Study the financial and business statistics in the *Federal Reserve Bulletin,* or a comparable source, and determine the volume of various financial instruments outstanding.
12. Make a list of the financial intermediaries in your community. Study their sources and uses of funds and the functions they perform.

REFERENCES

Baughman, Ernest T. "The Economic Role of Financial Intermediaries: Challenges of a Changing Agriculture." *A New Look at Agricultural Finance Research,* Agr. Finance Program Rept. 1, Dept. Agr. Econ., Univ. of Ill., 1970.

Board of Governors, Federal Reserve System. *Federal Reserve Bulletin* (monthly).

——. *The Federal Reserve System.* Washington, D.C., 1963.

Dougall, H. F. *Capital Markets and Institutions,* 2nd ed. Prentice-Hall, 1970.

Gerstenberg, C. W. *Financial Organization and Management of Business,* 4th ed. Prentice-Hall, 1960.

Goldsmith, R. W. *Financial Intermediaries in the American Economy since 1900.* Princeton Univ. Press for Natl. Bureau of Econ. Research, 1958.

Meek, Paul. *Open Market Operations.* Fed. Res. Bank of New York, 1969.

Polakoff, M. F., et al. *Financial Institutions and Markets.* Houghton Mifflin, 1970.

CHAPTER 19: **MONETARY AND FISCAL POLICY**

THE FINANCIAL MARKETS discussed in the preceding chapter operate within the monetary and fiscal policies of the nation. These policies, along with federal and state laws, provide the framework within which the financial markets operate. All participants are affected in one way or another. The objective in this chapter is to examine these policies relative to operation of the financial markets. Fiscal policy is treated briefly, following which the major part of the chapter is devoted to monetary policy.

FISCAL POLICY. Fiscal policy means government policy regarding expenditures and taxation. By these means government can significantly affect the level and pattern of economic activity and development. With stable or sustaining monetary and tax policies, an increase in government spending theoretically raises the level of business activity, income, and savings. The flow of funds from suppliers to users increases, as well as the level of business of financial intermediaries. On the other hand, when government spending is cut, the process is reversed.

Changes in tax policy theoretically have similar effects. With stable or supporting monetary and spending policies, a reduction in taxes normally raises the level of disposable income, business activity, and savings—and vice versa. These changes also are reflected in the flow of funds from suppliers to users and in the level of business of financial intermediaries.

The type of fiscal measure employed affects the pattern of economic activity and development. For example, a larger appropriation for the Farmers Home Administration (FHA), discussed in a later chapter, would enable it to make and guarantee more farm loans. The farmers receiving the loans could then expand their production. They would purchase more inputs from local merchants and dealers and sell a larger volume of products to marketing firms. Thus, as illustrated by this example, a change in government spending for farm loans affects the farm sector directly, and indirectly affects those sectors that serve the farm sector. Similarly, a change in government spending for rural development affects those sectors directly and indirectly involved in or influenced by rural development. Changes in tax policies bearing on specific sectors of the economy have similar effects.

The federal government, in particular, has instituted many programs and policies affecting financial aspects of the economy. Among these are the Farm Credit System, Farmers Home Administration, and agencies that support farm commodity prices. These institutions and agencies generally are considered instruments of monetary policy, but they also involve fiscal policy to the extent that government expenditures are incurred for loans, loan insurance, operating expenses, and interest or other subsidies. The distinction between fiscal and monetary policy is not always clear and sharp—and need not be since the two are often used together to accomplish an objective. However, the two also may conflict and have offsetting effects.

MONETARY POLICY. Monetary policy is concerned with the volume of money and credit in the economy and under what terms they are available. By regulating the supply of funds and terms on which they are available, the government can significantly influence the level of economic activity. The pattern of economic activity also can be modified by measures that affect the supply of funds for selected sectors of the economy.

The Federal Reserve System constitutes the primary monetary regulatory authority in the nation. The organization, function, and operations of the system are outlined first, following which the effect of government-sponsored and government-owned institutions on monetary policy is briefly considered.

Federal Reserve System. The Federal Reserve System is comprised of the Board of Governors and the 12 Federal Reserve Banks. The Board of Governors is a governmental agency in Washington, D.C., consisting of seven men appointed for 14-year terms by the president of the United States, with the advice and consent of the Senate. The board is responsible for supervising the Federal Reserve System and has a major hand in formulating national monetary and credit policies. The 12 Federal Reserve Banks (with a total of 24 branches) are corporations chartered by the Congress of the United States. The 50 states are divided into 12 districts, each with its own Reserve Bank. The capital stock of each Federal Reserve Bank is owned by member banks in the district. However, the Federal Reserve Banks are operated, not for profit of stockholders, but in the public service.[1] Each of the 12 banks has its own board of directors.

---

1. The return to member banks is limited by law to a 6 percent annual dividend on stock owned. Income above amounts needed to cover dividends, expenses, and any additions to surplus necessary to maintain a capital:surplus ratio of 2:1 is paid to the Treasury. (Source: *The Federal Reserve System, Purposes and Functions*, Board of Governors of the Fed. Res. System, Washington, D.C., 1963, pp. 196–97.

The Federal Reserve System, through power entrusted to it by the Congress of the United States, exerts very significant influence on commercial banks and on the supply of credit. Practically all the larger banks in the country are members of the Federal Reserve System. Member banks have over 80 percent of the commercial banking assets. The system exerts direct influence on policies of these banks, primarily through actions that affect bank reserves. Some of these actions also influence credit policies of nonmember banks. Moreover, member bank policies, in turn, affect nonmember banks since member banks typically perform many of the same functions for nonmember correspondents that the Federal Reserve Banks perform for members. Reflecting the impact of monetary policy on the credit supply of the economy in general, Federal Reserve policy also affects other lenders, such as merchants, dealers, Federal Intermediate Credit Banks, Federal Land Banks, and insurance companies. The nature of this influence will be indicated later in the chapter.

FUNCTIONS OF THE FEDERAL RESERVE SYSTEM. The basic function of the Federal Reserve System is to use its broad powers "to foster growth at high levels of employment, with a stable dollar in the domestic economy and overall balance in our international payments."[2] This means that the Federal Reserve System has a responsibility to the nation's economy as a whole, and not to any one segment alone. It means that the system should develop and maintain a national monetary policy supported by financial machinery as needed to provide an economic climate in which private enterprise will develop, grow, and prosper. To facilitate achieving this objective, authorities should take action to help counteract both inflationary and deflationary movements.

In carrying out this basic function, the Federal Reserve System relies primarily on its power to regulate the supply of credit. The job is to allow an adequate flow of credit "to foster growth at high levels of employment" without going too far so that inflation develops. The following paragraphs from a publication of the Board of Governors of the system are pertinent.

> In a dynamic and growing economy, enough credit and money is that amount which will help to maintain high and steadily rising levels of production, employment, incomes, and consumption, and to foster a stable value for the dollar. When credit, including bank credit, becomes excessively hard to get and costs too much, factories and stores may curtail operations and lay off employees. Smaller payrolls mean hardship for workers, who curtail their purchases; merchants feel the decline in trade and reduce their orders for goods. Manufacturers in turn find it necessary to lay off more workers. A serious depression, unemployment, and distress may follow.

2. Ibid., p. 2.

When credit is excessively abundant and cheap, the reverse of these developments—an inflationary boom—may develop. An increase in the volume and flow of money resulting from an increase in the supply and availability of credit, coupled with a lowering of its cost, cannot in itself add to the country's output. If consumers have or can borrow so much money that they try to buy more goods than can be produced by plants running at capacity, this spending only bids up prices and makes the same amount of goods cost more. If merchants and others try to increase their stocks so as to profit by the rise in prices, they bid up prices further. Manufacturers may try to expand their plants in order to produce more. If so, they bid up interest rates, wages, and the prices of materials. In the end they raise their own costs.[3]

Since such a large part of the Federal Reserve System's primary function depends upon regulating the supply of credit, commercial banks of the nation play an important role in the undertaking. This is because commercial banks are the financial institutions through which credit can be created, so it is through them that the credit supply of the nation is controlled.

MEANS OF INFLUENCING CREDIT EXPANSION. There are a number of means that the Federal Reserve System can use to control credit expansion, but the three most important are:

1. Adjusting reserve requirements of commercial banks
2. Open market operations
3. Changing the Federal Reserve discount rate

These methods constitute *active* means of control since the system takes initiative in bringing about desired changes through their use. All three are effective through their influence on bank reserves.

Adjusting Reserve Requirements. The Board of Governors of the Federal Reserve System has authority to change reserve requirements of member banks within limits set by law. The reserve maximum and minimum requirements, given as a percentage of deposits, are shown in Table 19.1.

Authority to change reserve requirements gives the Federal Reserve System a powerful tool to use in controlling bank credit since the amount of reserves a bank has, compared with the required reserves, governs its potential loan volume. As long as a bank has excess reserves it may make additional loans—assuming there is a demand for more credit. However, if the bank has a reserve deficiency it must make up the deficiency by borrowing, selling securities, allowing repayments to exceed loan extensions, acquiring additional deposits

---

3. Ibid., p. 11.

TABLE 19.1: Maximum and Minimum Reserve Requirements of Federal Reserve System Member Banks

| | Demand Deposits | | Time Deposits |
| | Country banks | Reserve city banks | All banks |
Reserve Requirement			
	(%)	(%)	(%)
Minimum	7	10	3
Maximum	14	22	10

SOURCE: *Fed. Res. Bull.,* Board of Governors, Fed. Res. System, Washington, D.C., Sept. 1972, p. A10.

without offsetting loan increases, or by a combination of these means. Thus, if the Federal Reserve System wants to encourage an increase in the amount of credit, it can do so by lowering the reserve requirements (within the range provided by law), thereby giving banks more excess reserves for loans. On the other hand, if the Federal Reserve System wants to restrict the supply of credit, it can achieve this end by increasing the reserve requirements.

An example will help clarify the effect of a change in reserve requirements. Since the creation of deposits is accomplished by the banking system as a whole, all commercial banks are considered as a unit in the example and it is assumed that their combined assets and liabilities are as shown in Table 19.2.

Starting with Situation I shown in Table 19.2, the reserve requirement is assumed to be 12 percent, giving a dollar reserve requirement of $72 billion, the same as reserves assumed to be available. In other words, with conditions assumed in Situation I, the banking system has no excess reserves. Under such circumstances the

TABLE 19.2: Assets and Liabilities of All Commercial Banks in the United States (Hypothetical data with all dollar amounts in billions)

Assets		Liabilities	
Loans	$428	Deposits (demand)	$600
Bonds	200	Borrowings	50
Reserves	72	Capital and surplus	50
Total	$700	Total	$700

Memo:	Situation I	Situation II	Situation III
Reserve requirement	12%	10%	14%
Actual reserves	$ 72	$ 72	$ 72
Required reserves	$ 72	$ 60	$ 84
Excess reserves	$ 0	$ 12	$ 0
Reserve deficiency	$ 0	$ 0	$ 12

commercial banking system is not in a position to expand loans or investments.

Now assume that the Federal Reserve System believes additional funds are needed to meet credit needs of the country and that it, therefore, lowers the reserve requirement to 10 percent as shown in Situation II. This action lowers the amount of required reserves to $60 billion, leaving $12 billion of excess reserves. The banks are then free to expand their loans and investments until all their excess reserves are used up. With the assumed 10 percent reserve requirement, loans and investments can be increased by $120 billion. To keep the illustration simple, assume the entire $120 billion deposit expansion takes place through making new loans and that all the proceeds of the loans are kept on deposit. Loans shown in Table 19.2 would then total $548 billion and deposits $720 billion. It is evident that lowering the legal reserve requirement releases a given amount of reserves that can lead to an increase of several times that amount in loans.

Comparison of Situations I and III in Table 19.2 illustrates the effect of an increase in reserve requirements. In Situation I the reserve requirement is 12 percent and the dollar amount of reserves available is just equal the required reserves. Increasing the reserve requirement to 14 percent of deposits raises the amount of reserves required to $84 billion, which causes a reserve deficiency of $12 billion. The banking system could remove this deficiency by one method or a combination of methods: reducing the volume of loans (probably as payments are received), selling bonds, or borrowing from the Federal Reserve. Assume the system decides to reduce the volume of loans and thus absorb deposits. With the reserve requirement at 14 percent, the $72 billion of available reserves will support approximately $514 billion of deposits. In other words, deposits have to be reduced by about $86 billion to remove the $12 billion reserve deficiency. Thus, with a 14 percent reserve requirement, the ratio is about 7:1. Again the powerful impact of action by the Federal Reserve System is evident, this time in the direction of contraction rather than expansion. By adjusting reserve requirements, the system can exert great influence over credit conditions. Reserve requirements, along with open market operations and discount rate changes, lie at the heart of monetary control.

Open Market Operations. The term *open market operations* refers to buying and selling securities—mostly short-term government issues— by the Federal Reserve System in the national financial market. Open market transactions are conducted under the direction of the Federal Open Market Committee, comprised of members of the Federal Reserve Board and presidents of five of the Federal Reserve Banks.

The primary influence of open market operations on credit extension is exercised through their effect on reserves of commercial banks. When analyses made by the Federal Reserve System indicate that increased availability of credit would help achieve desired expansion of economic activity, the Open Market Committee buys securities. Purchases of government securities by the Open Market Committee increase bank reserves and enable the banking system to increase loans and investments, thereby creating more deposits. For example, assume the Open Market Committee buys securities from a bank, insurance company, broker, or individual and gives in payment a check drawn on a Federal Reserve Bank. The seller of the securities deposits the check in his account at a member bank, and the bank in turn receives a credit to its reserve balance at its Reserve Bank when the check is collected. Reserve funds created by this transaction are *newly created* by the Federal Reserve System. While the receiving bank's reserve balance is increased in exactly the same way that a draft drawn on another commercial bank would add to its reserves, the difference is that the check drawn on a Reserve Bank does not produce an offsetting reduction in the reserve balance of another commercial bank. Thus the net result is an increase in reserves of the commercial banking system and an equal addition to Federal Reserve System holdings of government securities.

When analysis of the Federal Reserve System indicates inflationary pressures are developing and that the rate of growth in the supply of money should be restricted, the Open Market Committee sells securities, which reverses the above procedure. Sale of government securities by the Federal Reserve System reduces member bank reserves and thereby curtails credit extension.

The way in which open market operations affect commercial bank lending might be further clarified by referring again to Table 19.2. Assume that excess reserves are nil as in Situation I. Having no excess reserves, the banking system is unable to create additional deposits through loans. Now suppose the Open Market Committee concludes credit should be eased and directs that $1.0 billion of government securities be purchased in the open market. The effect of this action on reserves of "All Commercial Banks" considered in Table 19.2 is shown by comparing Situations I and IV in Table 19.2 Continued.

Federal Reserve purchase of $1.0 billion of securities increases the dollar reserves of commercial banks by $1.0 billion (to $73 billion), thereby creating a billion of excess reserves. If all the excess reserves are used for credit expansion, a *maximum* of about $8.3 billion of new loans could be made with reserve requirements at 12 percent.

Comparison of Situations I and V illustrates the effect of a sale

TABLE 19.2 Continued (Dollar amounts in billions)

	Situation I (From Table 19.2)	Situation IV	Situation V
Reserve requirement	12%	12%	12%
Actual reserves	$ 72	$ 73	$ 71
Required reserves	$ 72	$ 72	$ 72
Excess reserves	$ 0	$ 1	$ 0
Reserve deficiency	$ 0	$ 0	$ 1

of $1.0 billion of securities in the open market by the Federal Reserve System. Reserves of commercial banks are reduced by $1.0 billion, causing a reserve deficiency of $1.0 billion. If this deficiency is removed by reducing loans, the total volume of loans outstanding in Table 19.2 would be reduced by about $8.3 billion, with the assumed 12 percent reserve requirement.

Changing reserve requirements of commercial banks and open market operations by the Federal Reserve System are merely two different methods of accomplishing the same objective: changing the amount of excess reserves held by commercial banks and thereby influencing their loan and investment policies. In practice the two methods are used to supplement each other. Generally, reserve requirements are not changed often and only when fairly substantial changes are needed in reserves. On the other hand, open market operations are used to adjust reserves for daily and seasonal variations in requirements.

Changing the Discount Rate. With approval of the Board of Governors of the Federal Reserve System, the Federal Reserve Banks can adjust the discount rate (the rate of interest charged member banks on loans from the Reserve Bank) as a means of influencing extension of credit to the public. Member banks may borrow from Reserve Banks to a modest degree under usual conditions (and to a considerably greater degree in extreme circumstances) on the basis of government securities and other assets that are eligible and acceptable. Nonmember banks, other financial institutions, and nonfinancial businesses (including individuals) also may borrow from and discount paper with the Federal Reserve Banks to meet emergency conditions broader than the institution itself, that is, emergency conditions in the community or nation. When banks are borrowing, an increase in the discount rate increases their costs and thereby tends to discourage borrowing. But, more important, it serves as a warning that credit extension needs watching, and banks know that if such warnings are not heeded, the more positive and forceful tools of adjusting reserve requirements and open market operations may follow. Thus a major influence of adjusting the discount rate is psychological, and as such it is a potent influence not only on commercial banks but on business generally.

Adjustments in the discount rate may serve also as a signal of easier credit conditions. A reduction of the rate lowers the cost of commercial bank borrowing and, in turn, encourages commercial banks to make business loans. It also provides a psychological effect in that business may feel more inclined to undertake expansion plans if credit promises to be adequate and lower in cost.

While changes in the discount rate are directly effective on member banks, the effect is passed on indirectly to nonmember banks through correspondent relationships, and to the economy in general through the effect on the general interest rate structure.

Two or more monetary control measures may be used jointly at times to effect a policy change. For example, open market operations may be used to smooth credit market adjustments caused by a change in the discount rate. The controls may also be used to encourage bankers to follow advice of the system. For example, in a recent inflationary period, commercial bankers were advised to limit their loans to business and were told that the discount window was open to those conforming to the policy. Such indirect use of controls is effective in operation of monetary policy.

INDIRECT EFFECT ON OTHER LENDERS. In the initial discussion of the Federal Reserve System, it was indicated that monetary control measures applied to commercial banks have broad indirect influence on other lenders. A couple of examples will help clarify the nature of this influence. Commercial banks usually purchase a substantial proportion of the debentures sold by the Federal Intermediate Credit Banks (FICBs) in the national financial market. As outlined in a later chapter, the proceeds of these sales are used to fund loans made by Production Credit Associations (PCAs) to farmers. Hence, when the Federal Reserve System reduces the amount of excess reserves held by commercial banks, the commercial banks may restrict their purchases of FICB debentures and demand a higher rate of return on those they do purchase. These effects are, in turn, passed on to the PCAs and to the farmers. The situation is similar with merchants and dealers, who obtain a substantial amount of funds for loans to farmers from commercial banks. When the Federal Reserve System restricts commercial bank reserves, the banks will likely raise their interest rates and restrict their loans to merchants and dealers. In turn, these effects will likely be passed on to their farmer customers.

Other Institutions. The federally sponsored and owned financial institutions are instruments of monetary policy along with the Federal Reserve System. The Federal Reserve System can have an effect on various sectors by open market operations that, say, raise long-term interest rates relative to short-term rates. It can even provide financing for individual businesses when necessary to prevent the spread of emergency conditions. However, most of its activities are at the overall level, affecting the economy as a whole. Moreover, its primary function is monetary control.

In contrast, the primary function of the federally sponsored and owned financial institutions is to increase the supply of credit or improve the loan terms for specific sectors of the economy. For example, the Farm Credit System and the Farmers Home Administration, discussed in later chapters, were organized by the federal government to provide more adequate financing for agriculture. Funds loaned by the banks and associations of the Farm Credit System are obtained by the sale of bonds and debentures in the national financial market. Therefore, the effect of their operations from the viewpoint of monetary policy is to shift funds to agriculture from other sectors of the economy. Most of the loans made by the Farmers Home Administration (FHA) have a somewhat similar effect since they are funded from the financial markets. However, the federal government provides some funds for FHA loans, interest subsidies, and operating expenses. When government funds are loaned or spent, the total supply of funds in the economy is increased, assuming other fiscal and monetary policies are stable. Hence, operations of government financial institutions such as the FHA have both fiscal and monetary effects.

QUESTIONS AND PROBLEMS
1. What is meant by fiscal policy? Monetary policy?
2. What are the relationships of fiscal and monetary policies to the financial markets?
3. What is the primary instrument of monetary policy?
4. What is the Federal Reserve System? Obtain a copy of the Federal Reserve Bulletin and outline the boundaries of the 12 districts.
5. Outline the objectives of the Federal Reserve System.
6. Give the three primary methods used by the Federal Reserve System to influence credit extension.
7. Explain how a change in reserve requirements can affect the loan volume of commercial banks.
8. Explain how open market operations affect commercial bank loan volume.
9. Explain how adjusting the discount rate affects extension of credit by commercial banks.

10. Compare changing reserve requirements, open market operations, and changing the discount rate in their effects on commercial bank loans.
11. What is the current policy of the Federal Reserve System with regard to commercial bank loans?
12. How does the Federal Reserve System affect the farmer and the financial institutions that serve him?
13. How are the federally sponsored and owned financial institutions involved in fiscal and monetary policies?

REFERENCES

Annual Reports of the Federal Reserve System. Board of Governors, Washington, D.C.

Davis, Carlisle R. *Credit Administration.* Am. Inst. of Banking, Am. Bankers Assoc., Chap. 16.

The Federal Reserve System, Purposes and Functions. Board of Governors, Fed. Res. System, Washington, D.C., 1963.

How Our Reserve Banking System Operates. Monetary Study No. 2, revised ed. Economic Policy Commission, Am. Bankers Assoc.

Lenhart, Harry, Jr. "Uniquely Independent Fed Wields Power over Economy." *National Jour.*, vol. 2, no. 44, Oct. 31, 1970, pp. 2375–92.

Modern Money Mechanics. Fed. Res. Bank of Chicago, revised 1970.

Money: Master or Servant? 5th ed. Fed. Res. Bank of New York, 1970.

Roosa, Robert V. *Federal Reserve Operations in the Money and Government Securities Markets,* Fed. Res. Bank of New York.

CHAPTER 20: FINANCIAL INTERMEDIARIES SERVING AGRICULTURE

As THE NATION has grown and developed, some financial intermediaries, such as commercial banks, have continued to serve all sectors of the economy. However, other intermediaries have developed that serve only certain sectors. The purpose of this chapter is to provide information on agricultural credit related to the overall credit picture and on lenders that make agricultural loans, including their current relative importance and trends in their market shares. The limited activity of some farms in the equity markets is considered in the latter part of the chapter.

AGRICULTURAL CREDIT IN PERSPECTIVE. Demand for credit comes from governments and a wide variety of private sources, including agriculture. Data on public and private debt at the beginning of 1972, and comparative figures for three earlier years, are given in Table 20.1. Note the strong growth trends in each debt category. Note, also, the three major groups—governments, corporations, and individuals and unincorporated enterprises—and the relative importance of each. Credit used by agriculture is included in the latter group and comprises about 3 percent of the total debt. It is clear, therefore, that agricultural producers do not have their own individual supply of credit but must compete with all other segments of the economy for borrowed funds, and the competition is very impressive.

Financial intermediaries serving agriculture are a part of the national and local financial markets as outlined in Chapter 18. They function within these markets. They mobilize available funds from the multitude of individual sources throughout the country and channel or distribute them to those who want to use the credit. Those with surplus funds naturally look for the highest returns consistent with the risk and uncertainty involved. Those wanting to borrow similarly look for the lowest cost. When the supply of funds is fully adequate to meet demands, as was the case for a period following World War II, lenders compete for loans, and interest rates and related costs drop. On the other hand, when credit is tight (the supply is inadequate to meet all demands) lenders raise their interest rates and loan requirements, which serves as a means of rationing

TABLE 20.1: Public and Private Net Debt Outstanding in the United States, January 1 of Selected Years (Billions of dollars)

Item	1950	1960	1970	1972
Total Public and Private Debt	448	846	1,723	1,996
Total public debt	237	299	452	534
Federal government	218	240	289	326
State and local governments	18	56	132	168
Federal financial agencies*	1	4	31	40
Total private debt	212	547	1,271	1,463
Corporations	118	283	715	827
Long-term	56	130	307	380
Short-term	62	153	408	447
Individuals and unincorporated enterprises	94	264	556	636
Farm	12	23	56	64
Mortgage	6	12	29	31
Nonmortgage	6	11	27	33
Nonfarm	82	241	501	572
Mortgage	51	161	305	352
Nonmortgage†	31	80	196	220
Memo: Total Farm Debt as Percent of Total Public and Private	2.7%	2.8%	3.2%	3.2%

SOURCE: *Survey of Current Business,* U.S. Dept. of Commerce. Data for state and local governments are for June 30 of the preceding year. Figures may not add up to totals, due to rounding.

* Debt of federally sponsored agencies in which there is no longer any federal proprietary interest. Includes obligations of Federal Land Banks beginning 1950, debt of Federal Home Loan Banks beginning 1955, and debt of the Federal National Mortgage Association, Federal Intermediate Credit Banks, and Banks for Cooperatives beginning in 1968.

† Comprises debt incurred for commercial (nonfarm), financial, and consumer purposes, including debt owed by farmers for financial and consumer purposes. Financial debt is debt owed banks and brokers for purchasing and carrying securities and debt owed life insurance companies by policyholders.

available loan funds. Thus the financing institutions provide the means whereby changes in supply and in demand for funds are reflected in the ease or tightness of credit and in the general interest rate structure. Availability of and interest rates on agricultural credit are closely affected by this overall situation since the institutions financing agriculture are a part of the financial markets.

INTERMEDIARIES MAKING FARM LOANS. Lenders extending credit to agriculture fall naturally into groups, depending upon the type of institution involved. Five different types of lenders discussed in subsequent chapters are as follows:

1. Commercial banks
2. Insurance companies

3. Merchants, dealers, and others
4. The Farm Credit System
5. The Farmers Home Administration

Data on agricultural loans customarily are divided into two classes: real estate and nonreal-estate loans. Lenders making real estate loans are referred to as long-term credit agencies and those making nonreal-estate loans as short-term and intermediate-term credit agencies. Some lenders, of course, make both types of loans. The volume of outstanding loans held and those made by the various types of lenders is one indication of their relative importance in the agricultural credit picture.

Farm Real Estate Mortgage Loans. During the year 1971, the volume of farm real estate mortgage loans *made* in the 48 contiguous states of the United States totaled $6,779 million. Data for Alaska, Hawaii, and Puerto Rico were not available. The breakdown by type of lender is given in Table 20.2.

The three major institutional lenders—commercial banks, insurance companies, and Federal Land Banks (FLBs)—make the major

TABLE 20.2:   Farm Mortgage Loans *Made* in the United States by Type of Lender during the Year 1971.

			Volume	
			---	---
		Average		% of
Lender	Number	Size	Amount	total
	(thou)	*(thou)*	*(mil)*	
Commercial Banks and Trust Companies*	79.4	$19.1	$1,516	22.4
Insurance Companies*	5.1	79.6	403	6.0
Federal Land Banks†	40.8	38.6	1,576	23.2
Farmers Home Administration‡	19.4	19.3	375	5.5
Production Credit Associations*§	33.2	33.9	1,126	16.6
Savings and Loan Associations*	14.3	20.3	290	4.3
Individuals*	43.9	28.3	1,242	18.3
Miscellaneous*‖	9.6	26.2	251	3.7
All Lenders	245.7	$27.6	$6,779	100.0

SOURCE: *Farm Real Estate Mortgages Recorded,* Farm Credit Admin., June 1972. Data for 48 contiguous states only. Estimates for Alaska, Hawaii, and Puerto Rico are not available.

* Estimates made by Federal Land Banks from farm mortgages recorded in sample counties.

† Actual numbers and amounts of loans made, including outstanding balances of borrowers obtaining funds.

‡ Data provided by the Farmers Home Administration. The average size is based on number and amount of initial advances only.

§ Mortgages secured by farm real estate primarily as additional security for operating and capital purpose loans.

‖ Includes mortgages of investment companies, state and local government agencies, and any cases where the mortgage cannot be specifically identified.

portion of real estate loans, accounting for 51 percent of the number and 52 percent of the volume of such loans in 1971. The large number of commercial bank farm real estate loans is due in part to real estate mortgages taken as additional security for short-term and intermediate-term loans. The large volume of real estate loans made by commercial banks is partly accounted for by those that they subsequently transfer or sell to insurance companies. In addition to loans obtained through commercial banks, insurance companies as a group make a substantial volume of loans to farmers both directly and through middlemen.

Individuals also comprise an important source of farm real estate credit. This group represents a wide range—the farmer-owner who sells his farm on contract or who takes a mortgage as part of the sale price of the farm, a relative of the farm buyer who lends a portion of the funds to buy the farm and is given a first or second mortgage as security, the professional man in the small town who lends his savings to the farmer on farm mortgage security, and finally, the private investor in some distant city who buys a farm mortgage as an investment from a bank or loan agency.

In many tabulations, loans by individuals and miscellaneous lenders are grouped together. The miscellaneous lender group, which also encompasses widely divergent types of lenders, includes real estate loans made by investment companies, credit unions, endowment funds of schools, fraternal societies, cemeteries, hospitals, and the like. Such institutions are interested in obtaining a good return on a long-term investment without having to bother with frequent reinvestment of their funds. Farm mortgage companies, loan agents, and investment companies occasionally make farm mortgage loans from their own funds, but in the main these agencies act as mortgage middlemen between farm borrowers on the one hand and individual investors, insurance companies, banks, and other farm mortgage holders on the other. The miscellaneous group also includes loans made by state and local government agencies.

Production Credit Associations (PCAs), included in the miscellaneous group in many tabulations, appear out of place in a farm mortgage loan tabulation since, as is pointed out in Chapter 24, they are chartered to make short-term and intermediate-term loans. Farm mortgages recorded by PCAs are taken primarily as additional security for operating and intermediate-term capital loans. Also, it should be recognized that while real estate loans usually are long term, they do not necessarily have to be.

Note the relative size of loans made by the various types of lenders shown in Table 20.2. The average size of insurance company loans is twice to four times the average size of loans made by other lender

TABLE 20.3: Farm Mortgage Loans *Held* in the United States, by Type of Lender, January 1, 1972

Lender	Unpaid Balance Outstanding	% of Total
	(mil)	
All Operating Banks	$ 4,214	13.4
Life Insurance Companies	5,562	17.8
Federal Land Banks	7,862	25.1
Farmers Home Administration	310	1.0
Individuals and Others	13,386	42.7
All Lenders	$31,334	100.0

SOURCE: *Farm Mortgage Debt*, ERS, USDA. Data for the 48 contiguous states. Complete data for Alaska and Hawaii are not available.

groups. Reasons for this variation in size of loans will become evident as the various types of lending institutions are discussed in subsequent chapters.

The volume of farm real estate mortgage loans *outstanding* (unpaid balance) January 1, 1972, totaled $31,334 million (see Table 20.3). In this tabulation, "Individuals and Others" include the latter four groups given in Table 20.2; that is, individuals, miscellaneous, PCAs, and savings and loan associations. These lenders as a group hold the largest proportion of the outstanding real estate loans. As of January 1, 1972, they held 43 percent of the total. Federal Land Banks are the second most important source of long-term credit, holding $7,862 million, or 25 percent of the total on January 1, 1972. Life insurance companies ranked next with 18 percent, and commercial banks fourth with 13 percent. The smaller percentage of loans *held* than *made* by commercial banks results partly from the relatively shorter term of commercial bank real estate loans and partly from transfer of loans to insurance companies, as indicated above. The Farmers Home Administration (FHA), which makes government loans, held a relatively small proportion of the real estate loans.

Data on farm mortgage loans given in Tables 20.2 and 20.3 show the relative importance of the various types of farm mortgage lenders as of a recent date, but consideration should also be given to the long-term picture. The relative importance of the various groups has changed in the past and probably will change in the future as economic conditions and alternative investment opportunities change. Thus the long-run picture becomes even more important than the short-run situation in appraising the relative importance of various types of lenders in providing mortgage credit for agriculture.

The farm mortgage debt held by major lenders as of January 1 from 1910 to 1972 is portrayed in Figure 20.1. Note the predominance of loans made by individuals and others in recent years and during

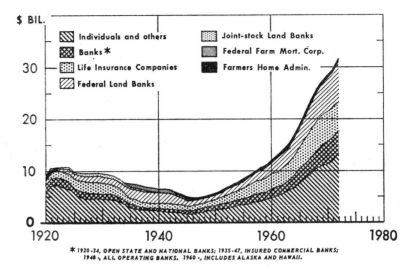

FIG. 20.1—*Farm mortgage debt held by major lenders groups, United States, January 1, 1910–72. (Courtesy of ERS, USDA.)*

the early 1920s. But note also their shrinking importance starting in the late 1920s and extending into the 1940s—the time when farm foreclosures reached their peak and many farmers were in desperate need of credit. Individuals generally are an unsatisfactory source of long-term credit since just at the time when the farmer most needs the finances, the individual also needs them. Moreover, individuals who hold long-term mortgages may be seriously hurt when low farm income prevents the farmer from meeting his payments of interest and principal. Retired people and others depending on such payments for a livelihood sometimes suffer hardships.

The trends of farm mortgage loans held by insurance companies and commercial banks follow somewhat the same pattern as that of individuals. Historically, these groups have expanded their loans during favorable or prosperous years and contracted their financial service during depressions. During recent years the availability of loan funds has significantly affected their volume of loans. The reason for this pattern of lending is perfectly logical, as will be shown in chapters dealing with these lenders. But the point is brought out here, in connection with the historical review of farm mortgage loans, to show that these lenders are not always as important, relatively, as they are at the present time.

During unfavorable or depression years, loans by the government or government-sponsored agencies expand. Note the great expansion of FLB loans in the 1930s. (Today some people disagree with calling the FLBs government-sponsored institutions since they are entirely farmer owned, but there is little question that they were government sponsored, and operated by virtue of government financial support during the 1930s.) The federal government created the Federal Farm Mortgage Corporation in 1933 as an affiliate of the FLBs to help provide urgently needed financing for agriculture during the Great Depression of the 1930s. The corporation was abolished in 1961. Most of its loans had been repaid by that time and the balance were sold to the FLBs. The FHA, originally called the Resettlement Administration, was also created during the Great Depression to assist in financing agriculture. It was created too late to share, to any great degree, in the mammoth real estate financing undertaking of the government in the 1930s, but there is little question but that it would shoulder a major part of the government load in any future depression.

Nonreal-estate Farm Loans. Nonreal-estate loans of farmers outstanding January 1, 1972, totaled about $35.6 billion as shown in Table 20.4. Of this total, $1.4 billion was accounted for by price-support loans made or guaranteed by the Commodity Credit Corporation, which will be discussed later in this chapter. Excluding these loans from the total, as often is done in referring to the nonreal-estate

TABLE 20.4:   Nonreal-Estate Loans Outstanding in the United States, by Type of Lender, January 1, 1972

Lender	Volume Outstanding	% of Total	
		Including CCC	Excluding CCC
	(bil)		
All Operating Banks	$12.5	35.1	37.5
Production Credit Associations	6.1	17.1	18.3
Other Financing Institutions—Loans and Discounts from Federal Intermediate Credit Banks	.2	.7	.7
Farmers Home Administration	.8	2.2	2.3
Nonreporting Creditors*	13.7	38.5	41.2
Total, Excluding CCC Loans	33.3	93.6	100.0
Commodity Credit Corporation	2.3	6.4	
Total, Including CCC Loans	35.6	100.0	

SOURCE: *1972 Balance Sheet of the Farming Sector,* Farm Prod. Econ. Div., ERS, USDA. Some of the loans have real estate as security but all have short and intermediate terms. Data include 48 contiguous states.
   * Includes loans and credits extended by dealers, merchants, finance companies, individuals, and others.

farm debt, leaves a balance of $33.3 billion. This figure probably is less accurate than that for the farm mortgage debt because a considerable amount of short-term debt is not recorded or filed at the courthouse. Accurate data, however, are available for the institutional lenders.

A large proportion of the short-term and intermediate-term credit used in agriculture is extended by miscellaneous lenders. This group, which held 41 percent of this type of debt outstanding January 1, 1972, is comprised of two types of lenders: (1) business concerns which provide credit to farmers as a supplementary service either in selling equipment and materials or in buying the farmer's produce, and (2) individuals and miscellaneous lending institutions. Commercial companies or businesses selling goods to farmers are an important source of farm credit. Implement companies and feed stores often extend credit in connection with sales. Dealers who contract to buy the farmer's produce or are interested in handling the produce as a middleman may advance funds during the growing season or production period and deduct the principal and interest when the crop or commodity is delivered. Individuals making nonreal-estate loans to farmers include relatives, landlords, and other individuals in the local community. Nonrelated private investors at a distance from the farm are not able to provide this type of credit satisfactorily because of distance, short duration of this type of loan, and the nature of the security. Rural credit unions, building and loan associations, and similar lenders are important sources of credit in some communities where such facilities have been developed to serve agriculture.

Loans by commercial banks outstanding January 1, 1972, amounted to $12,487 million, or 38 percent of the total, which indicates their predominant role in nonreal-estate financing of agriculture. Production Credit Associations accounted for 18 percent and the FHA for 2 percent of the nonreal-estate loans outstanding January 1, 1972. Loans of these lenders are discussed in some detail in later chapters.

A historical picture of nonreal-estate farm loans held by banks, Production Credit Associations, and the Farmers Home Administration is given in Figure 20.2. Throughout much of recorded history commercial banks have played an important role in financing short-term and intermediate-term needs of agriculture. However, during periods of depression, and when farm income has been depressed for other reasons, their importance has declined. Figure 20.2 shows the great contraction in commercial bank loans during and following the Great Depression. The demand for credit generally increases during such periods but commercial lenders often are unable to meet demands due to reduced farm income and lower security values. Lending ability of commercial banks also is influenced by the shrinkage of deposits that occurs during such periods. Thus they often are

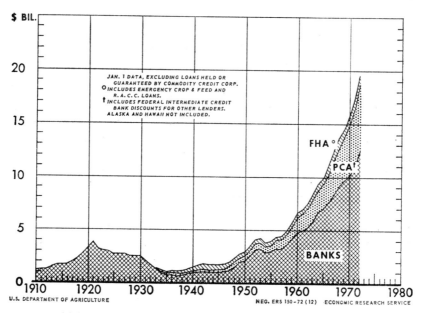

FIG. *20.2—Nonreal-estate loans to farmers held by banks and federally sponsored agencies, United States, 1910–72. (Courtesy of ERS, USDA.)*

unable to supply the credit needs of many farmers, especially tenants and smaller farmers who have little equity in real estate. To fill the gap, government-sponsored and government credit agencies were created during the Great Depression. The PCAs were sponsored by the government to provide a means, as will be explained in a later chapter, whereby farmers could provide their own credit. The FHA also was created to help alleviate the situation by making direct government loans to farmers. As is shown by Figure 20.2, these two types of agencies were important sources of credit during and following the Great Depression. It was not until the late 1940s that commercial banks again took major leadership. Production Credit Associations also expanded their loan volume along with commercial banks, while credit extended by the FHA decreased since, in accordance with the law under which it operates, it makes loans only to farmers who cannot obtain credit upon reasonable terms from other lenders.

Commercial lenders probably will continue to restrict their agricultural loans during periods of low farm income as they have done in the past, leaving the load for the government to carry. A severe widespread depression such as that which prevailed during the 1930s fortunately has not occurred in recent years. However, small areas have suffered severe financial distress. Experience indicates commercial lenders are unwilling or unable to supply needed credit to many farmers, especially tenants with smaller units and full or part owners whose equities in real estate are low. Production Credit Associations, which the government sponsored in the 1930s to enable farmers to provide for their own credit needs, contract their service along with commercial banks. The FHA alone is left to relieve distress by expanding direct government loans to agriculture.

COMMODITY CREDIT CORPORATION LOANS. Reference was made above to $2.3 billion of nonreal-estate loans made by the Commodity Credit Corporation (CCC) in connection with its farm commodity price support operations. These are not ordinary loans; they usually are made "without recourse," which means in most cases the borrower need not pay the balance if the commodity upon which a CCC loan is made does not sell for enough to pay the loan. The corporation absorbs losses while the farmer benefits from any gains associated with price increases during the term of the loan. With such a policy, losses are practically inevitable.

Since these are not ordinary loans, they are not discussed in later chapters, as are the regular types of loans.

The CCC, organized in 1933, is an agency of the United States Department of Agriculture. It is managed by a board of directors appointed by the president and confirmed by the Senate, subject to the general supervision and direction of the secretary of agriculture, who is, ex officio, a director and chairman of the board.

ACQUIRING FARM EQUITY CAPITAL IN THE FINANCIAL MARKETS. Innovative arrangements are being used increasingly to acquire equity capital in the financial markets for use in farming. These were discussed in terms of finance principles involved in Chapter 6. The objective here is to briefly outline how some of the arrangements are utilized. Limited partnerships, sale of purebred beef cattle herds, and common stock offerings are discussed. The material presented is based primarily upon studies by William H. Scofield and Errol Bragg, Economic Research Service, USDA.[1]

Sale of Limited Partnerships. A limited partnership has appeal for some nonfarm investors since the financial liability of each partner is limited to his original investment; the partnership does not require, and in fact prohibits, direct involvement of the limited part-

---

1. William H. Scofield, "Nonfarm Equity Capital in Agriculture," *Agr. Finance Rev.,* ERS, USDA, July 1972; and William H. Scofield and Errol Bragg, *Agribusiness Notes,* FPED Working Paper, ERS, USDA, Aug. 1972.

ners in management; and it provides a direct conduit for income tax deferral and pass-through of profits and losses. Scofield found that of 42 registration statements pertaining to agricultural ventures filed with the Securities and Exchange Commission (SEC) during 1970–71, more than one-half were offerings of limited partnership interests. Of the 24 partnership offerings, 14 were to raise capital for cattle feeding, and 8 were to establish citrus groves, nut orchards, and vineyards.[2]

Sale of limited partnerships to raise equity capital for financing commercial feeding of cattle has become significant in recent years.

> The 14 registrations examined could have raised nearly $150 million in equity capital from about 35,000 investors if the total amounts registered were sold in minimum units. Actual sales of such national offerings were undoubtedly somewhat less than these amounts, but it is known also that many private placements have been made that did not require SEC registration. Also, feeding companies can seek equity capital within a State by meeting the registration requirements of that State, without SEC clearance.[3]

The increase in sales of limited partnerships has stemmed from the recent rapid growth of cattle feeding firms, as well as their prospects for further growth. Operation and growth of these firms are dependent upon acquiring large amounts of equity capital. A 30,000-head lot requires about $8 million for cattle and feed for a typical 6-month feeding period. Such a firm will require some $2 million of equity capital, assuming it is able to borrow $3 for each dollar of equity.

Organizational aspects of creating and selling limited partnerships are not particularly complicated. An existing firm, such as an incorporated feedlot, forms a subsidiary corporation to act as general partner. Following registration with the appropriate state agency, the general partner files a registration statement with the SEC if an interstate offering is planned. When SEC clearance is obtained, the general partner proceeds with the sale of the limited partnerships, either directly or through security dealers.

Sale of Livestock Breeding Herds. Of the 42 registration statements pertaining to agricultural ventures filed with the SEC during 1970–71, Scofield found 13 offerings of beef breeding herds, mostly purebred, or so-called exotic or European breeds.[4] With this arrangement, firms that have owned or leased lands and other facili-

---

2. Scofield, p. 37.
3. Ibid., p. 38.
4. Ibid., p. 37.

ties needed to care for cattle sell beef breeding herds through public offerings. A herd usually consisted of 5 or 10 cows, with breeding arrangements and a contract providing for annual payments to cover maintenance of the herd. Such investments have appeal for persons in high tax brackets, due to the tax advantages offered.

Sale of Corporate Stock. Historically, a few incorporated farms have been sufficiently large and profitable to attract investors in the public financial markets. Some have produced agricultural products alone, while others have also operated farm-related businesses. Scofield found that firms making most of the recent public common stock offerings were involved in both production of agricultural products and in one or more related activities, such as farm supply or processing and marketing.[5]

QUESTIONS AND PROBLEMS

1. Using summary groupings, explain who borrows money in the United States.
2. What proportion of the total credit being used is attributable to farmers? Is the proportion increasing or decreasing?
3. If your home farm community had to rely on local savings for credit, do you estimate it would have sufficient or insufficient credit? Would the period of loans be acceptable to both borrowers and lenders? Discuss.
4. Discuss the function of financial intermediaries serving agriculture.
5. List five different types of lenders who make loans to farmers. Discuss the relative importance of each type from the viewpoint of the amount of real estate and nonreal-estate loans made to farmers. From the *Agricultural Finance Review,* determine the proportion of loans made by each type of lender to farmers in your state.
6. Why do individuals account for such a large proportion of all farm mortgage holdings? Why do they figure less prominently in short-term loans?
7. Why do commercial banks have a small proportion of long-term farm loans and a large proportion of short-term farm loans?
8. What is the function of the Commodity Credit Corporation? What type of loan does it make? Could similar loans be made successfully by a commercial lender without the government insurance feature?
9. Discuss the methods used to obtain equity capital for use in farming from the financial markets. Do these hold promise for growth? What is their significance for farmers?

---

5. Ibid., p. 40.

REFERENCES

Agricultural Finance Review. USDA (issued annually).
Agricultural Statistics. USDA (issued annually).
Balance Sheet of Agriculture. USDA (issued annually).
Farm Mortgage Debt. USDA (issued annually).
Survey of Current Business. U.S. Dept. of Commerce (issued monthly).

CHAPTER 21: COMMERCIAL BANKS AND FARM LOANS

THE COUNTRY BANK ranks high among farm credit lenders in both number of institutions and volume of credit extended. A large majority of the 13,900 commercial banks in the United States are located in towns with less than 10,000 population. In a limited sense, these rural banks are farm credit service stations, leading all agencies in volume of nonreal-estate farm loans and ranking high in real estate loans made. From the farmer's point of view, commercial banks have several advantageous features. First, they give prompt credit service with a minimum of red tape; second, they are readily accessible; and third, they alone provide a full range of financial services, including checking accounts, savings accounts, trust counseling, estate planning, investment counseling, farm management services, charge cards, and safety deposit boxes.

NATURE OF COMMERCIAL BANKS. Commercial banks are corporations chartered under federal or state law. Banks that are chartered under federal law are called national banks and obtain their charter from the Comptroller of the Currency, a bureau of the Treasury Department of the federal government. State banks are chartered by state chartering authority, usually known as the superintendent of banking, commissioner of banking, bank commissioner, or banking board.

As corporations, commercial banks are legal and economic entities the same as other incorporated businesses. They are capable of doing business, owning property, making contracts, and the like, as defined by their charters. Since corporations are recognized as separate entities from the people who own, manage, and work for them, they can continue indefinitely without interruption.

Commercial banks are owned by stockholders of the corporation. Stock of many smaller banks is held by individual families, or by a few individuals, while that of larger banks usually is bought and sold on over-the-counter markets and is owned by a wide variety of investors. Thus commercial banks are organized as private profit-making businesses and operate within a framework of competition, the same as other commercial enterprises, although they are regulated in somewhat greater detail than most businesses.

Commercial banks are controlled by a board of directors, elected by the stockholders on the basis of one share, one vote. The National Bank Act provides that each national bank shall have not less than 5 or more than 25 directors, each elected for a term of 1 year. Provisions for election of directors of state banks vary widely among states. A major requisite of a director is that he be a man in whom the public has confidence since, particularly in small communities, the public judges a bank to a considerable degree by its directors. Major lines of business from which the bank draws its customers generally are represented on the board by directors who are well and favorably known in their field. By this means, expert opinion on general prospects and developments in the various fields of business and industry is provided the board. Moreover, such a selection of directors facilitates mutual understanding with various segments of the public.

Federal and state supervisory agencies have been given broad powers over the banking system to insure that banks comply with the extensive body of regulatory law under which they operate. This fact has an important bearing on bank operations and loan and investment policy that is sometimes overlooked by the public. State chartered banks are subject to supervision and examination by banking departments or agencies in the respective states. The Comptroller of the Currency has the primary responsibility for supervision and examination of national banks. The Board of Governors of the Federal Reserve System and the Federal Reserve Banks have broad powers of examination and supervision over member banks. Since the comptroller is specifically charged with responsibility by law for supervision and examination of national banks, the board and reserve banks rely primarily on the comptroller for examination of national banks and direct their main efforts to examination and supervision of state member banks. The Federal Deposit Insurance Corporation, which provides deposit insurance, examines insured state banks that are not members of the Federal Reserve System.

From the foregoing discussion it is evident that commercial banks are similar in many ways to other incorporated businesses. They are privately owned and operated on a commercial basis and, like other lending institutions, are examined and supervised by public agencies. However, commercial banks are *distinct from all other lenders in their ability, as a group, to create money* in the form of bank deposits by making loans and investments. The way in which this distinctive function is accomplished will be discussed shortly, but first, we consider the reserves that commercial banks are required to maintain, since these are an essential part of the money-creating process.

COMMERCIAL BANKING SYSTEM CREATES LOAN FUNDS.

In contrast to all other lenders, who can lend only their own capital or money entrusted to them by others, commercial banks create most of the funds that they lend. In making loans, commercial banks create deposits, each loan normally giving rise to a deposit placed to the credit of the borrower. When checks are drawn against the deposit and placed or deposited in other banks, the newly created funds are dispersed throughout the banking system. Thus each loan that is made adds an equivalent amount to the deposit total of the banking system. When a loan is repaid, the reverse situation occurs, with the deposit total of the banking system being reduced by the amount of the loan payment.

An individual bank cannot make an unlimited expansion in its loans and investments, of course. The limit is roughly determined by the bank's excess reserves. A borrower obtains a loan for the purpose of using the funds, and therefore the bank that makes the loan must be prepared to supply cash or settle through the clearing house for checks deposited in other banks. A bank that expands its loans and investments beyond the amount of its excess reserves runs the risk of a reserve deficiency.

An illustration of how the multiple expansion of deposits works will help clarify the process by which funds are created. Assume reserves required equal 20 percent of deposits and that there is a demand for all the funds that can be created with such a required reserve ratio. Also assume that Bank A has no excess reserves and that it receives a deposit of $1,000 in currency that had previously been withdrawn from circulation and kept in a safe-deposit box. Receipt of this deposit of "new money" gives Bank A $1,000 of reserves, of which 20 percent, or $200, are required as reserves for the $1,000 deposit. The remaining $800 are excess reserves, and Bank A can increase its loans and other investments by that amount. Bank A makes a loan of $800 and creates a deposit of $800. To keep the illustration simple, assume the borrower checks out the entire amount to pay a bill and the $800 is deposited in Bank B. The result is that reserves of Bank B are increased $800, of which $160 are required as backing for the added $800 of deposits, leaving $640 of excess reserves for loans or other investments. Bank B makes a loan of $640 and creates a deposit of $640. The $640 plus the $800 makes a total of $1,440 created by Banks A and B. If the $640 is checked out and deposited in Bank C, Bank C would have $512 of excess reserves for loans after deducting its 20 percent required reserve, raising the total amount of funds created to $1,952. The amounts of excess reserves available as each successive loan is checked out and deposited in another bank, together with related figures, are shown in Table 21.1.

Assuming deposits newly created through the making of loans are withdrawn and redeposited in other banks, as illustrated in Table 21.1, the process can continue until the whole of the initial $1,000 deposit has been absorbed by the 20 percent reserve requirement. Maximum potential deposits total $5,000 or five times the

TABLE 21.1:   Illustration of the Potential Multiplying Power of Fractional Reserves, Assuming 20 Percent Required Reserves

Bank	Amount Deposited	Reserves Gained	Excess Reserves	Amount Loaned	Cumulative Deposits Created
(1)	(2)	(3)	(4)	(5)	(6)
A	$1,000	$1,000	$ 800	$ 800	$ 800
B	800	800	640	640	1,440
C	640	640	512	512	1,952
D	512	512	410	410	2,362
E	410	410	328	328	2,690
F	328	328	262	262	2,952
G	262	262	210	210	3,162
H	210	210	168	168	3,330
I	168	168	134	134	3,464
J	134	134	107	107	3,571
Total, ten banks shown	$4,464	...	...	$3,571	...
Total, other banks	$ 536	$ 536	$ 429	$ 429	$4,000
Total, all banks	$5,000	...	...	$4,000	...

original deposit, and the maximum potential amount loaned totals $4,000.

This example illustrates how commercial banks as a group are able to create deposits. It also illustrates the fact that when *maximum* deposit expansion is accomplished, the initial deposit becomes entirely tied up within the banking system as required reserves. All the credit extended has been created. It should be noted, however, that for this expansion process to take place, the initial deposit must represent truly *new* reserves and not merely a deposit transfer between businesses or individuals. Moreover, the expansion illustrated is the *maximum* that can take place with the assumed 20 percent reserve requirement. In actual practice the multiple normally is not as constant nor as large as used in the example, due to differences in reserve requirements, cash needed for day-to-day transactions, and policies of various banks.

It may be well to note that a multiple contraction of deposits can occur as well as a multiple expansion. Assuming there are no excess reserves, withdrawal of funds from the banking system generally causes a multiple contraction of deposits in much the same way that addition of new funds permits a multiple expansion.

SIGNIFICANCE OF THE MONEY-CREATING POWER. The ability of the commercial banking system to create loan funds has great economic significance. By regulating the volume of reserves available to banks, the Federal Reserve System imparts an elasticity to the nation's credit system essential for economic progress and stability. Without such flexibility, farmers and other businessmen would have to maintain more permanent operating capital to meet fluctuating and uncertain financial requirements. Large sums might be held idle for extended periods, while at other times available funds would prove insufficient to meet seasonal needs or other peak requirements.

The money-creating power of the commercial banking system affects the credit supply available to agriculture both directly and indirectly. It influences commercial bank loans to farmers as well as bank financing of merchants, dealers, processors, and the like, through which farmers obtain considerable credit. At the same time it influences investment policies of commercial banks and, thereby, the flow of credit to farmers through other lending institutions.

ARRANGEMENTS TO INCREASE LENDING CAPACITY. Lending capacity of commercial banks is limited by two primary factors: (1) reserves, as outlined above, and (2) bank capital. Reserves limit the *aggregate volume* of loans and investments a bank can carry, whereas bank capital limits the *size* of *individual* loans. Section 5200 of the National Bank Act limits the size of loan that a national bank may grant to any one customer to a given percentage of the bank's unimpaired capital and surplus. Feeder-cattle loans are limited to 25 percent, and farm real estate and other agricultural loans to 10 percent of the bank's capital and surplus. Some state laws are more restrictive while others are more liberal than the National Bank Act regulations.

Limitations on the size of loans often are important to smaller country banks in a community of larger farms, since loan requirements of such farms often exceed the lending limit of the bank. The rapid and continuing growth in size of farms has accentuated the problem, since the capital structure of many country banks has not grown as fast, relatively, as the size of farms. Moreover, with the trend being toward larger farm units, it appears that the problem of farm loan size relative to bank capital loan limitations may become increasingly acute.

Commercial banks have developed a number of ways or methods that facilitate increasing their lending capacity and handling larger lines of credit. One of the most important of these is development of branch banking systems.

Branch Banking. As a means of expanding their business and of providing more adequate and convenient service to the public, banks frequently establish branch offices known as *branch banks*. State laws vary widely in this regard; whereas some states permit branch banking without restriction or with certain limitations, some others prohibit branches entirely. The National Bank Act, under which national banks are chartered, permits establishment of branches according to state law where the bank is located. Branches, like new banks, may not be established without approval of the appropriate supervising authority.

Other things being equal, branch banking facilitates handling a larger total volume of loans by shifting funds from one area to another as the need arises. Consider, for example, two banks in a community with approximately the same volume of deposits, one an independent bank and the other a branch bank office. The independent bank is limited in its loan volume (excluding loans carried on a correspondent basis, etc., to be discussed later) by its own reserves. On the other hand, the branch bank office has the benefit of all reserves in the banking institution of which it is a part. It is evident, therefore, that the branch office may have a very large volume of reserves at its disposal. Of course, all branches must be served from the "pot of reserves" and, therefore, when money is tight (reserves are scarce) the branch bank office will be restricted in the volume of loans it can carry, the same as the independent bank. In fact, a branch banking operation could draw funds from a local community to serve head office loan customers. When a branch bank has a number of offices serving a fairly large area, all communities served by the institution seldom have simultaneous peak demands for loans, even in periods of prosperity. This helps make funds available for individual branches according to their needs.

Branch banking also facilitates making larger individual loans since branch banking institutions generally have more capital and surplus than independent country banks serving agriculture. In the example used in the preceding paragraph, the independent bank is limited in the size of individual loans it can make by its own capital and surplus. In contrast, the size of individual loans the branch bank office can make depends upon the capital and surplus of the entire banking institution of which it is a part. Thus it is probable that the branch bank office could make larger individual loans than the unit bank.

Correspondent Bank Relationships. Business arrangements by which commercial banks in the United States coordinate their efforts in rendering bank services are referred to as *correspondent bank relationships*. Through correspondent relationships, two or more banks can team up to provide funds for loans and to handle large loans. In addition, correspondent bank relationships facilitate many other operations and services essential in banking and needed in rural areas, including bank management assistance for country banks, transfer of funds, check clearance, bond and stock portfolio counseling, and servicing of rural accounts held by city banks.

Banks of any size can have correspondent relationships with other banks. In practice, however, a smaller bank usually becomes a correspondent of a larger bank or banks.

REASONS FOR CORRESPONDENT BANK RELATIONSHIPS. Correspondent bank relationships constitute a method of economizing on bank reserves, or of making fuller use of reserves, similar to branch banking. Loan requirements in some agricultural areas may double during peak lending seasons and reserves of local banks often are inadequate to meet such demands. Excess reserves of city banks can be made available through correspondent relationships, and used to supplement those of the country bank. Thus, as branch banking provides a means of using excess reserves for loans anywhere in the area served by the branch bank, correspondent bank relationships similarly facilitate making use of excess reserves for loans in any part of the area served by the correspondent banks. Of course, with both branch banking and correspondent banking, this benefit to the smaller bank is dependent upon reserves being available. If a city correspondent bank has no excess reserves, it can be of little help to the country bank.

Country banks use correspondent relationships to help provide loans larger than they are permitted to make on the basis of their own capital and surplus. Through correspondent relationships even the smallest commercial bank theoretically can take care of any credit requirement of good quality in the community except possibly for long-term real estate loans.

Correspondent relationships also provide a method of spreading risks associated with credit extension. Whereas the lending authority of a country bank may permit carrying a certain line of credit, the risk involved may be such that the bank would rather provide only part of the funds. Similarly, some loans may be "bankable," but involve enough risk so that the local bank is reluctant to carry too many in its loan portfolio. By participating with one another on such loans, commercial banks are able to meet more of the credit needs of agriculture without individually incurring excessive risk.

Bank Holding Companies. A bank holding company is a corporation that holds a controlling interest in the stock of one or more banks or related businesses. The degree of control over the banks varies. In some cases the individual banks operate virtually as independent banks, while in other cases the controlled banks operate almost as branches of the same bank. Holding companies may expand the type of their service, as well as their geographic coverage. They may enter and have entered into bank-related activities. They have acquired mortgage companies and other financial concerns in distant places, which serves to lessen the significance of state lines in the banking sector.

Multibank holding companies have grown rapidly since the passage of the 1970 amendments to the Bank Holding Company Act that placed one-bank holding companies under the same regulatory standards as the multibank companies. Hence, except in states where statewide branching is permitted or where multibank holding companies are prohibited, many one-bank holding companies have become multibank holding companies by establishing new banks or acquiring existing banks.

Studies by the Federal Reserve System[1] indicate that holding companies exercise the greatest control in areas relating to bank investments and correspondent relationships of the subsidiary banks. Banks acquired by holding companies tend to switch out of treasury securities and into state and local government securities and loans. These portfolio changes suggest holding companies result in acquired banks making more credit available in their local financial markets. Some other studies[2] support the view of informed persons who feel that holding companies, as well as branch banking systems, result in draining away of rural savings for urban or other remote investments. Theoretically, with proper linkage among financial markets, funds will be allocated so as to equalize demand and supply, as was pointed out in Chapter 18. If rural and agricultural demands are less able to compete on a market basis, the funds will flow elsewhere. Conversely, if the local demand is stronger than elsewhere, funds will be drawn to the area.

Other services that holding companies may provide could strengthen the position of local financial markets. For example, a holding company may create a subsidiary to insure loans. Such a service could materially increase the use of funds in local financial markets.

Chain Banking. Chain banking refers to arrangements where one or more individuals control, or have the potential to control, several banks through stock ownership. Some authors broaden this definition to include control or potential control via common directors

---

1. Robert J. Lawrence, "Operating Policies of Bank Holding Companies—Part I," *Fed. Res. Bull.*, Apr. 1971, pp. 283–84; and Samuel H. Talley, "The Effect of Holding Company Aquisitions on Bank Performance," *Fed. Res. Bull.*, Feb. 1972, p. 105.

2. Richard L. Gady, "Performance of Rural Banks and Changes in Bank Structure in Ohio," *Econ. Rev.*, Fed. Res. Bank of Cleveland, Nov.–Dec. 1971.

or officers of two or more banks. Not much is known about these types of arrangements, probably because there is no formal organization of the banks involved, and only limited data have been assembled on the informal ties. However, data that are available indicate a significant proportion of the unit banks is included in chain systems.[3]

It would appear that bank chains could operate in much the same way as multibank holding companies. Some differences may arise, however, from the number and size of banks involved. The typical bank chain is small in terms of number of banks affiliated. A large majority of the chain systems have only 2 to 4 banks, but some have 20 or more. However, the typical chain bank is slightly larger in terms of assets than the typical member bank. Chain affiliated banks generally are located in the same area.

Chain banking apparently exists on a larger scale in the states that have unit banking than in those that have branch banking. Chain banking may not have developed as an alternative to branch banking, but it appears that states having prohibitions against branching may only be inviting some other form of multiple-office banking to emerge.

Borrowing from Other Banks. Another method used by commercial banks to increase their loan funds is to borrow from other banks.

An unusual or unexpected withdrawal of deposits, or demand of loans, for example, may deplete a bank's reserves. Under such circumstances a bank may find it necessary to borrow. Such situations have stimulated development of the market for federal funds where a larger bank temporarily short of reserves can borrow funds to meet its requirements. Various limitations prevent small banks from participating directly in the federal funds market, although some do so indirectly through correspondent relationships. A bank that is a member of the Federal Reserve System generally may borrow from its Federal Reserve Bank, while a nonmember bank borrows from its correspondent bank. Note that such borrowings provide loan funds by augmenting the borrowing bank's reserves.

Banks legally have discounting privileges with Federal Intermediate Credit Banks (discussed in a later chapter) either directly or through an affiliated agricultural credit corporation. However, the privileges carry several restrictions. Moreover, the discounting is on a recourse basis that precludes a bank from discounting loans that exceed its legal lending limit. This avenue of increasing lending capacity has never been very important, although there was some increase during the 1960s.

---

3. Information in this section is based primarily on Jerome C. Darnell, "Chain Banking," *Natl. Banking Rev.*, Mar. 1966, pp. 307–31.

Bank-PCA Participation. The Farm Credit Act of 1971 allows Production Credit Associations (discussed in a later chapter) to participate in loans made by commercial banks. This provision could be beneficial to rural banks short on loanable funds and, also, in handling large loan requests that exceed bank lending limits.

Arrangements with Life Insurance Companies. In the recent past some commercial banks had arrangements with life insurance companies whereby farm mortgage real estate loans made by the bank were subsequently taken over without recourse by an insurance company. The mechanics of these arrangements have changed somewhat in recent years. Banks now function primarily as "finders," with the insurance company, rather than the bank, disbursing the mortgage funds. These arrangements are important since they allow rural banks to provide financing for local real estate credit needs, including overline requests, without committing their funds to long-term maturities normally associated with such loans.

FARM LOAN POLICY. Bank policy is necessary since a number of different individuals are involved or affected by the way the bank is operated. Depositors are concerned with safety of their funds; stockholders with a safe, profitable investment; and borrowers with the bank's loan policy. Interests of these three groups must be molded into a single policy.

The framework of a bank's policy is established by legislation under which it is chartered and by regulations issued by supervisory agencies. Within this framework general policy outlines are formulated by the bank's board of directors. Officers and supervisory personnel, in turn, fill in the details as necessary to facilitate operations. The bank's loan committee has considerable to do with formulating loan policies.

Since banks are independent corporations organized by people, their policies naturally vary greatly. Two banks may look alike to the public, but in reality they may be very different institutions. This is an important fact to keep in mind in selecting a lender. One bank may have a progressive farm policy and be interested in making loans, while another bank may invest the bulk of its assets in nonfarm loans and securities. Some banks maintain a flexible policy designed to meet the needs of the community, while others make few changes.

From the viewpoint of credit extension, two of the more important policy considerations pertain to:

1. The distribution of the bank's earning assets
2. The policy followed in making and servicing loans

TABLE 21.2:   Loans, Investments, and Deposits of All Commercial Banks in the United States for Given Dates

June 28, 29, or 30	Total Loans and Investments	Loans Amount	% of total	Investments Amount	% of total	Total Deposits	Loan Deposit Ratio	Investment Deposit Ratio
	(bil)	*(bil)*		*(bil)*		*(bil)*		
1920	$ 36.3	$ 28.1	77.4	$ 8.2	22.6	$ ...*	...*	...*
1930	48.9	34.5	70.6	14.4	29.4	55.0	62.8	26.1
1940	41.1	17.4	42.3	23.7	57.7	60.3	28.9	39.3
1950	121.8	44.8	36.8	77.0	63.2	143.8	31.1	53.5
1960	188.9	114.8	60.8	74.1	39.2	209.0	54.9	35.4
1970	423.2	296.1	70.0	127.1	30.0	432.4	68.5	29.4
1972†	535.6	365.4	68.2	170.2	31.8	538.6	67.8	31.6

SOURCE: Data for 1972, 1970, 1960, and 1950 are from the *Fed. Res. Bull.* Loan and investment data for earlier years are from *Banking and Monetary Statistics*, Board of Governors, Fed. Res. System, 1943, p. 19. Deposits for 1940 are from the Ann. Rept. of the Fed. Dep. Ins. Corp. for the year ended Dec. 21, 1940, p. 140. Deposits for 1930 are from the *Fed. Res. Bull.* for that year (p. 650) and are for all banks, exclusive of interbank deposits.
* . . . = not available.
† Preliminary.

Policy with regard to the bank's earning assets determines the amount of funds put into loans, and loan policy indicates the way or the terms upon which those funds are made available to borrowers.

Effect of Earning-Asset Distribution on Loans. Assets of banks often are grouped on the balance sheet as cash, loans, investments, and other assets. Of these, loans and investments generally are the largest items. These two groups comprise the major earning assets of banks and the allocation of funds between them indicates the relative importance of the bank's loan program. Table 21.2 portrays the dollar volume of loans and investments of all commercial banks in the United States over a period of several decades. Note the relative decrease in importance of loans from the 1920s to the 1940s, and the reversal of this trend in the 1950s. Traditional theory of commercial banking, evidenced to a degree in the original Federal Reserve Act, held that the banking system should adjust its earning assets to the needs of the business world. The commercial banking system was considered merely an adjunct to the productive process. However, during the decades between the two World Wars, and particularly during and following World War II, revolutionary changes occurred in commercial banking. Among other things, investments of commercial banks in securities (primarily United States government obligations) grew much faster than loan volume.

Investments in securities provide commercial banks flexibility to adjust to changing conditions. They provide secondary reserves for deposits to supplement required reserves, enabling a bank to readily adjust to a run-off in deposits if such should occur. They can also be liquidated to provide funds for loans should a favorable opportunity arise. The latter often occurs in prosperous times when interest rates are relatively high and security prices relatively low. Thus such flexibility may carry a fairly high price tag if securities have to be sold below cost. When this is the case, a bank's management may decide to place funds from new deposits or maturing securities in loans but be unwilling to sell securities at a loss to accommodate additional credit demands.

The amount of flexibility provided by securities naturally varies with the amount and type of securities owned by commercial banks. When securities comprise a relatively unimportant item in the balance sheet, the flexibility provided is limited, and vice versa. It is evident, therefore, that the flexibility of the commercial banking system declined during the 1950s and 1960s. The relative importance of investments in securities declined considerably during these decades, while the relative amount of loans increased (see Table 21.2). Concomitantly, the loan:deposit ratio increased to a record level. Many banks probably were operating at or above their preferred loan:deposit ratios, somewhat as manufacturing concerns operate above their preferred capacity:utilization ratios in periods of strong demand. Consequently, a high level of loans to deposits generally becomes a constraining factor in bank lending.

A high loan:deposit ratio does not necessarily mean, however, that banks in general are overextended. The changing composition of commercial bank liabilities in the 1960s contributed to the acceptability of higher loan:deposit ratios. Time and savings deposits, as well as bank capital accounts, grew far more rapidly than demand liabilities. Savings deposits generally have good stability, as do also many time deposits. However, marketable certificates of deposit may be unstable should available rates on other money market instruments become relatively more attractive.

The upward trend in the loan:deposit ratio during the 1950s and 1960s was accompanied by a decline in the investment:deposit ratio to a near record low. Many banks probably were operating below their preferred investment:deposit ratios. Under such circumstances a further reduction in holdings of securities relative to deposits is resisted. This appears to have been the case in the early 1960s since the investment:deposit ratio increased from 1970 to 1972. Thus, when the investment:deposit ratio is low, the volume of loans made by commercial banks is governed primarily by the amount of excess reserves generated by current operations.

Banks vary greatly in their loan-investment policies. Country banks tend to have a smaller proportion of their earning assets in

TABLE 21.3: Variation in the Loan-Deposit Ratio of Member Banks in the Seventh Federal Reserve District with Total Deposits under $100 Million, June 28, 1972, by State

Loan-Deposit Ratio	Illinois	Indiana	Iowa	Michigan	Wisconsin	Seventh District
(%)			(% of banks)			
75 and above	3	4	8	24	20	10
70–74	5	5	12	25	20	12
65–69	10	21	12	21	14	14
60–64	14	22	23	15	13	17
55–59	15	8	17	8	12	13
50–54	18	19	10	3	9	13
45–49	11	7	8	2	6	8
40–44	9	4	3	1	4	5
Under 40	16	10	7	1	2	9

SOURCE: *Banking Briefs,* Research Dept., Fed. Res. Bank of Chicago, Oct. 10, 1972.

loans than larger city banks. In mid-1972, for example, loans accounted for 63.7 percent of total loans and investments of country member banks (of the Federal Reserve System). In comparison, reserve city member banks averaged 77.8 percent in loans in New York and 75.2 percent in loans in Chicago. Other reserve city member banks averaged 72.6 percent in loans.[4]

A further indication of differences in bank policy regarding loans is provided by differences in the loan:deposit ratio among banks. The range for medium-large and small member banks in the Seventh Federal Reserve District as of mid-1972 is shown in Table 21.3. Note the wide spread in the ratios from under 40 to 75 and above. Moreover, the relatively large proportion of banks with a ratio under 40 in some of the states indicates some of the banks may have had ratios in the 30s and 20s or lower.

Banks with a low loan:deposit ratio probably do not have an aggressive loan program. Loans that such banks make often are conservative. Banks with an average or higher loan:deposit ratio often do a better job in credit extension. However, a bank should not have an excessive loan:deposit ratio. A bank that is "loaned up" may have to reduce its loan volume in case something happens in the community to cause a reduction in deposits. Also, a bank that is loaned up may be unable to provide additional credit needed to meet seasonal loan requirements.

The credit service of a bank to farmers in the community is indicated not only by its distribution of earning assets between loans and investments but also by its policy regarding farm versus nonfarm

---

4. *Fed. Res. Bull.,* Board of Governors of the Fed. Res. System, Washington, D.C., Sept. 1972.

loans. A bank may have a satisfactory loan:deposit ratio and still make few farm loans. Progressive banks generally are interested in the entire community and, in periods when credit is tight, allocate a portion of their funds to each type of loan in accordance with need. However, banks vary greatly in this regard and a farmer would do well to inquire regarding the bank's policy. Published bank statements generally do not show a farm and nonfarm breakdown of loans.

Farm Loan Characteristics. Two primary considerations of commercial banks in making farm loans are (1) service to borrowers, and (2) risk involved in making loans. Banks make loans to all types of farmers, but some farmers merit more credit than others. Bankers must be able to evaluate the applicant's request and either approve a loan as requested (or with modifications) or decline it and indicate the reasons for doing so. Success of the banker in handling this task determines to a large degree how successful the bank is in serving the farm community and the stockholders.

Bankers usually have a knowledge of their customers that is distinctly helpful in handling farm loans. The banker is in an excellent position to know the credit standing of the farmer who has been carrying a checking account and doing business with him for several years. If the farmer pays his bills promptly, has no long-standing debts, is accumulating property, and is a man of high moral standards, the local banker generally knows it. If the reverse situation exists, the banker usually is likewise aware of it. This information is only a part of that desired for a long-term loan, but it is a major requirement in making short-term advances. If an individual customer with a good record asks for a 2-month loan to pay taxes because his livestock are not ready to market, the banker is able to act promptly on such a request. On the other hand, the customer who is heavily in debt and fails to measure up on other counts is likely to be refused. Short-term credit agencies not having the local knowledge that bankers possess are forced to safeguard themselves against losses by more restrictions. They must obtain security interests, waivers from landlords, nondisturbance agreements from other lenders, and make inspections, some of which would not be necessary if they were in a position to know the local conditions as well as the local banker.

The local bank has the added advantage of being close to the farmer. Other short-term credit agencies may be located only at county seat towns or in larger cities, and consequently many farmers have to make a special trip to see them. Where there is a bank in the local trading area, the farmer can drop in when he is in town for other purposes. The bank is the logical place for the farmer to apply for short-term and intermediate-term credit, particularly when he is using a checking account and other bank services. Since the bank has to have a certain amount of income to operate, farmers may actually lower the cost of other services by borrowing from the bank. Moreover, the service the bank may be giving him and the knowledge his banker has about his financial standing make it easy for the farmer to give the additional information needed in the balance sheet, income statement, and cash flow budget required for a loan.

The general policies of commercial banks in making farm loans are indicated by various characteristics of loans they make. Four primary characteristics are discussed briefly in the following paragraphs.

Types of Loans. The most important type of farm loans made by commercial banks is production loans to provide funds for current farm operations—for items such as seed, fertilizer, tractor fuel, repairs, labor, feed, and feeder livestock. Loans for intermediate-term purposes, such as machinery and equipment, milk cows, and breeding livestock, rank second in importance. Real estate loans rank third.

According to material presented in Chapter 20, short-term and intermediate-term loans account for about three-fourths of the total volume of commercial bank credit outstanding January 1, and real estate loans account for the balance. This comparison probably understates the relative importance of commercial bank production loans since many of them are made and repaid within the year and, therefore, are not reflected in January 1 data.

Loans for intermediate-term purposes comprise an important part of nonreal-estate loans made by commercial banks. Loans made for such purposes comprised 42 percent of the number and 38 percent of the amount of total nonreal-estate loans held by commercial banks June 30, 1966.[5] Intermediate-term loans gradually increase in relative importance over time, due to the increasing relative importance of machinery and some other working assets.

Maturity of Loans. Maturity of farm loans made by commercial banks naturally varies considerably with the type or purpose of the loan. Current operating loans generally are payable when the cash flow they generate is received, which customarily is in less than 1 year. The phrase "payable on demand" is sometimes used in extending credit to established customers when the period of time the funds will be needed is uncertain. However, its use is of questionable merit since it sometimes reflects lack of planning in use of credit. Moreover, while bankers generally do not expect to "demand" payment of such

---

5. Emanuel Melichar, "Bank Financing of Agriculture," *Fed. Res. Bull.,* June 1967. Derived from Table 18.

loans, such a provision in a note should not be lightly dismissed. Conditions beyond the control of the banker may force him to exercise legal prerogatives.

Loans made for intermediate-term purposes generally have maturities exceeding 1 year. Three-year or 4-year terms are quite common and terms of up to 7 years are not uncommon. However, some intermediate-term loans still are written for 1 year or less. When these loans are made, it often is mutually understood that the note will be extended at maturity, but the caution mentioned in the preceding paragraph should be noted in such cases.

Interest Rates. Interest rates charged by commercial banks vary from time to time, depending upon demand for credit, general economic conditions, policy of the Federal Reserve System, and rates charged by other lenders. Since the general level of interest rates has moved up to relatively high levels in recent years, state usury law limitations have also affected commercial bank interest rates in some states. The situation appears inequitable since commercial banks and other private lenders such as insurance companies are restricted in the rates they may charge by state usury laws, while the government-sponsored and government-owned lending agencies such as the Production Credit Associations and Federal Land Banks are exempt from these laws because of their federal charters. As a result, the latter's rates rose to levels much higher than those permitted by some state usury laws. This flexibility permitted them to obtain funds to lend while the supply of commercial bank farm loan funds in the states affected was restricted.

A number of factors are considered by commercial banks in determining the interest rate to charge on a loan. With today's computers, progressive commercial banks can collect and store total information on a customer, that is, his time and demand balances, trust business, total loan picture, and the like. These are all considered in setting the interest rate. Rates charged by a bank typically have a range of about 2.0 percentage points, such as from 6.0 to 8.0 percent or from 7.0 to 9.0 percent. The modal rate customarily is a little below the midpoint of the range.

In the past, the type of loan had an influence on the interest rate, with rates on real estate loans being lowest and those on operating loans the highest. However, with the rise in the general level of interest rates, these differences have largely disappeared. In fact, in some cases the situation has been reversed, with the highest rates being charged on real estate loans.

Security for Loans. A primary consideration of commercial banks, as well as of all lenders, is the risk involved in making a loan. Lenders make only loans they feel are sure to be repaid. However, the certainty of repayment varies. Some loans are practically riskless, some involve a small amount of risk, and some are moderately risky. Moreover, unforeseen developments often arise that lower the quality of loans after they have been made.

Policy relative to requiring security naturally varies among banks. Farmers who are regular customers and have a good credit rating may not be required to give security. Many banks loan considerable sums entirely on a character basis. On the other hand, when a banker considers some risk exists, collateral is required, primarily to insure that the borrower's farm operation continues intact so as to generate a cash flow from which the loan can be repaid. Of course, *all* loans need a signed note to provide evidence that an obligation exists.

BANK AGRICULTURAL SPECIALISTS. With the increasing use of capital in agriculture and the growing complexity of the farming business, many commercial banks have employed men trained in agriculture to work on this part of their business. These banks recognize that it is important to have a man in the bank who understands commercial farming and is able to talk with farmers. Some of these men have advanced into the officer ranks, thereby further strengthening commercial bank service to agriculture.

As part of their work on agricultural loans, the bank agricultural specialists work with customers on their farms, analyzing their credit needs and providing information and counsel on the use of capital in their businesses. Many farmers can profitably use more credit. Moreover, many farmers could improve on use of available capital. For example, some farmers have adequate cash to pay all current operating expenses. However, this cash is kept on hand, often in a checking account earning no interest. Bank agricultural specialists can assist these farmers in managing their cash flow by pointing out the alternatives: (1) place the cash in a savings account or buy short-term securities until the money is needed, or (2) invest in savings accounts or longer-term securities and borrow short-term operating funds. Such service can be of material assistance to farmers and of great value to the bank in modifying its service and adapting loans to meet the needs of farmers.

QUESTIONS AND PROBLEMS
1. Explain the nature of a commercial bank. By what authority does a bank operate?
2. Who owns commercial banks? Discuss the significance of ownership in operation of a bank.
3. Discuss the role of directors in affairs of a bank.
4. Explain how bank reserve requirements limit the amount of loans a bank may make.

5. How does the source of commercial bank loan funds differ from those of other lenders?
6. Explain how the commercial banking system creates deposits. Can one bank alone create deposits?
7. Compare branch banking and correspondent bank relationships as a means of providing loan services.
8. Compare chain or group banking with branch and correspondent banking from the viewpoint of financing agriculture.
9. Discuss commercial bank arrangements with insurance companies and Production Credit Associations as means of broadening bank loan service to agriculture.
10. What is meant by bank policy? Why is it needed?
11. What or who determines a bank's policy?
12. Outline the things considered by commercial banks in developing a farm loan policy.
13. Discuss the types of loans made by commercial banks and to whom these are made.
14. Discuss the term of loans made by commercial banks. What term do loans for intermediate-term purposes carry?
15. How are commercial bank loans secured?
16. Interest rates charged vary by size of loan. Why? Are these differences justifiable?

REFERENCES

Agricultural Banking Developments, 1971. Am. Bankers Assoc., Washington, D.C.
The Bank Agricultural Officer. Am. Bankers Assoc., Washington, D.C.
Darnell, Jerome C. "Chain Banking." *National Banking Review,* March 1966, pp. 307–31.
The Federal Reserve System, Purposes and Functions. Board of Governors, Fed. Res. System, Washington, D.C.
How Our Reserve Banking System Operates. Monetary Study No. 2, revised ed. Economic Policy Commission, Am. Bankers Assoc.
Mayo, Robert P. "The Challenges for Small Banks." *Business Conditions,* Fed. Res. Bank of Chicago, Mar. 1971.
Meier, Harvey A. "Agricultural Lending: A Reflection of Attitudes, Practices and Activities of Ohio Commercial Bankers." *The Ohio Banker,* vol. 65, no. 8, Oct. 1972, p. 12.
Melichar, Emanuel. "Bank Financing of Agriculture." *Fed. Res. Bull.,* June 1967, pp. 927–53.
———. "The Farm Business Sector in the National Flow of Funds Accounts." *1970 Proc. of the Business and Economic Statistics Section,* Am. Statistical Assoc., Washington, D.C.
———. "Seasonal Discount Assistance to Rural Banks: Evaluation of a Federal Reserve Proposal." *Agr. Finance Review,* USDA, July 1969.
Our Financial System at Work. Monetary Study No. 1, revised ed. Economic Policy Commission, Am. Bankers Assoc.
"Rural Bank Needs for External Funds." *Business Conditions.* Fed. Res. Bank of Chicago, May 1972.

CHAPTER 22: INSURANCE COMPANY FARM LOANS

LIFE INSURANCE COMPANIES are an important source of long-term mortgage credit for farmers, being the second largest institutional lender in the farm mortgage field.[1] Of the $31,334 million of farm mortgage loans outstanding January 1, 1972, insurance companies held $5,562 million, or 18 percent (see Table 20.3, Chapter 20). However, their share of the farm mortgage business has declined in recent years. Throughout the 1950s and up until 1968, insurance companies ranked first among lending institutions in volume of farm mortgage loans. Their volume continued to increase in 1969 but at a slower rate than the total. Following that time it gradually declined. The major reasons for this trend are discussed later in the chapter.

Life insurance companies are among the largest financial institutions in the nation, their group assets totaling about $230 billion. Moreover, their growth has been very rapid. Except for the Great Depression of the 1930s, their assets have nearly doubled each decade. With such a rate of growth it appears likely that life insurance companies could continue to be important in the farm mortgage field. However, their activity in this area will depend upon company management, alternative uses for investment funds, and other factors.

OWNERSHIP AND CONTROL OF INSURANCE COMPANIES.

Life insurance companies are of two types: stock companies and mutual companies. *Stock companies* are owned by the stockholders who provide the capital required by the company. Policy premiums for such companies are calculated to cover as closely as possible the anticipated actual cost of the insurance protection which is sold. Stockholders carry the risk of loss that might be sustained, and also receive any profit that is realized the same as in any stock corporation.

Mutual insurance companies are cooperative associations of per-

---

1. Life insurance companies make practically all the farm mortgage loans that are made by insurance companies. Property and casualty insurance generally represent short-term contracts that do not require that long-run policy reserves be accumulated. For this reason reserves of such companies generally are put in short-term investments.

sons established to provide insurance on their own lives. Policy-holders are "members," corresponding to stockholders in the stock company. Thus mutual insurance companies are owned by the policyholders. Insurance written by mutual companies is generally participating insurance, which means that policyholders participate in earnings of the company. Since there is no stock ownership, as in the stock company, to absorb unusual losses, premiums collected are set high enough to cover almost any eventuality, and then the excess of premiums over costs is returned to policyholders as dividends.

Insurance companies are corporations organized under state law and are controlled by the board of directors of the corporation. Directors of stock companies are elected by the stockholders, usually on the basis of one vote for each share of stock owned. Directors of mutual companies are elected by member policyholders.

The board of directors, in turn, elects officers and employs a staff to carry on affairs of the company in accordance with the company's charter and general policy established by the board.

Insurance companies are supervised by the state insurance department, which is headed by an official generally referred to as Commissioner of Insurance, Superintendent of Insurance, or Director of Insurance. This official has general control, supervision, and direction over all affairs of insurance companies operating in the state. Each company is required to submit an annual report giving certain specified information to the state department of insurance. These reports enable the commissioner to keep currently informed on operations of companies. Moreover, the commissioner may at any time deemed advisable examine a company or inquire otherwise into its affairs. Most states require that all insurance companies be examined periodically. Expert examiners having special training and knowledge not possessed by regular examiners of the insurance department may be employed where necessary to facilitate a thorough examination. The costs of all examinations are charged to the company examined.

Ownership and control of insurance companies have an important bearing upon their function as farm mortgage lenders. To grow and prosper they must operate on the basis of sound business principles, which involves fair treatment of both policyholders and borrowers. Lending policies must be such that needs of borrowers are met without incurring excessive risk that subsequently might lead to serious financial problems or foreclosure, and loans generally are distributed so as to contribute most to public goodwill. It should be kept in mind that the primary responsibility of an insurance company is to its policyholders. A stock company is organized for the purpose of selling insurance to make a profit. Mutual insurance companies are organized to provide insurance protection for policyholders. Responsibility to borrowers is of secondary importance since loans serve only as a means of profitably utilizing reserves associated with insuring of policyholders.

LOAN FUNDS. Life insurance companies issue, for the most part, long-term policies on which reserve funds are slowly accumulated as the insured grows older and the policy matures. When an insured dies, the beneficiary may request that proceeds of the policy be paid in installments rather than in a lump sum. Thus life insurance companies accumulate large sums of money in connection with their insurance program and hold such money for long periods of time. These funds are invested and, in turn, produce income that adds additional assets for investments.

Policyholders have first claim on a life insurance company's available funds. Most life insurance contracts allow policy owners to borrow the cash value of the policy. During periods of high interest rates, the specified rate in the insurance contract is often considerably below the market level, which results in an increased demand for policy loans. These loans have substantially reduced the flow of funds available for other investments during some periods.

After the prior claim of policyholders has been met, insurance company policy regarding allocation of funds to various types of investments is established, subject to provisions of law, by the board of directors, with advice of officers of the company. Three principal considerations usually are involved: (1) security of principal, (2) adequacy of yield, and (3) diversification of investments.

Security of principal is important since the primary object of a life insurance company is to pay claims. Insurance obligations generally are fixed in terms of a given number of dollars, and a company's ability to meet its fixed claims is of paramount importance. For this reason insurance companies generally give more importance to security than to either of the other two considerations in selecting investments.

While security is important, *adequacy of yield* must also be considered to facilitate reducing the cost of insurance to policyholders. Competition is keen in the insurance field, and the rate earned on investments plays an important role in determining the company's competitive position. Thus an insurance company may sacrifice some security on a part of its investments to increase the average yield.

The practice of *diversification of investments* is followed to reduce risks and to develop goodwill. It is considered sound policy to spread investments among different businesses or classes of investments as well as to spread them geographically. Such a policy reduces

TABLE 22.1:   Distribution of Assets of Life Insurance Companies in the United States

Item	1950	1960	1965	1972
Total Assets, Jan. 1 (bil dol)	59.6	113.6	149.5	221.6
Percent Invested in:				
Government securities	29.8	10.0	8.2	5.0
Securities of business and industry	39.0	43.9	42.5	44.9
Mortgages:				
Farm	1.9	2.5	2.9	2.5
Nonfarm	19.7	32.0	34.0	31.6
Policy loans	3.7	4.1	4.8	7.7
Miscellaneous	5.9	7.5	7.6	8.3
Total	100.0	100.0	100.0	100.0

SOURCE: *Life Insurance Fact Book*, Inst. of Life Ins., New York, N.Y.; also *Spectator Life Insurance Year Book*, a Chilton publication. Data for 1965 and 1972 are from the *Fed. Res. Bull.*, Sept. 1972, pp. A39 and A52. Figures in the table represent total assets, both in and out of the United States, of companies incorporated in the United States.

the probability of loss and makes funds available for home financing, farm purchases and improvements, business developments, and the like, as a means of creating goodwill for the company.

Mortgage loans as a class generally satisfy well the investment requirements of life insurance companies (see Table 22.1). They provide a relatively high degree of security, particularly since almost all loans are now amortized. Periodic loan payments, therefore, gradually strengthen the security position of the investment. However, in gearing their investment policies to an inflationary economy, life insurance companies have reduced their emphasis on mortgages and other long-term "fixed-income" investments, while equity-type and short-term investments have increased. The proportion of life insurance company assets in corporate shares increased from 5.3 percent in 1965 to 9.3 percent in 1972.

Farm mortgage loans generally do not seem to be as acceptable to life insurance companies as nonfarm mortgages. During the past decade or so only 2.5 to 3.0 percent of their assets have been invested in farm mortgages (see Table 22.1). These are average percentage figures that include hundreds of companies that do not make farm loans. Note also that the share of life insurance company assets invested in farm mortgages declined relatively more from 1965 to 1972 than the proportion put in nonfarm mortgages. A number of factors are involved. Making farm mortgage loans is a relatively specialized business. Earning capacity of the farm must be considered along with value and permanency of the security, and a specialized staff is needed to make and handle such loans. Moreover, interest income tends to be lower on farm than on city loans, and more expense is involved in obtaining an adequate appraisal of farm property and in travel and time due to the greater distances.

The situation is aggravated by the legal advantages enjoyed by the Federal Land Banks, the primary competitors of life insurance companies. Being instrumentalities of the federal government, interest rates on Federal Land Bank loans are not restricted by state usury laws as are rates charged by insurance companies. When interest rates were at record levels in recent years, usury laws in many important agricultural states prevented insurance companies from lending at market rates.

> In 20 states where the interest that private lenders can charge is limited by usury laws, the FCS [Farm Credit System]—unencumbered by such restrictions—has emerged as the major institutional source of farm credit. The situation is so severe in some areas, including such major agricultural states as Minnesota, Kentucky, and North Carolina, that some insurance companies have either closed their loan offices or pared their staffs to one or two men.
>
> The national figures don't show the tremendous gains in FCS loans in states whose usury levels are below the going rate for money. There, the system this year [1970] accounts for as much as 75% of the agricultural loans made by institutional lenders.[2]

To maintain perspective, it should be recognized that the general level of farm interest rates has been lower than state usury law ceilings throughout the past half century except for the period referred to above. Of course they may play a part in the future if interest rates again rise above usury levels.

The income of Federal Land Banks is not subject to taxation, and the bonds they sell and the income therefrom are exempt from state, municipal, and local taxation. Pertinent parts of the Farm Credit Act of 1971 are quoted in Chapter 24. The Federal Land Banks claim these tax exemptions are appropriate concessions for serving the sound credit needs of otherwise uneconomical lending areas and setting aside a portion of their earnings as reserves. As provided in the 1971 Farm Credit Act:

> Each Federal Land Bank shall . . . carry to reserve account a sum of not less than 50 percentum of its net earnings for the year until said reserve account shall be equal . . . to the outstanding capital stock . . . of the bank. Thereafter a sum equal to 10 percentum of the year's net earnings shall be added to the reserve account until the account shall be equal to 150 percentum of the outstanding capital stock . . . of the bank.

---

2. Jon A. Prestbo, "The Ever-Growing Farm Credit System," *Wall Street Jour.*, Nov. 3, 1970.

Insurance company farm lenders feel these tax exemptions give the Federal Land Banks a definite competitive advantage in farm lending. A major insurance company farm lender stated in private correspondence that "insurance companies could lend their money at from one-fourth of 1% to three-fourths of 1% less gross rate and achieve the same net as they now receive if they enjoyed the same tax status as that of the land banks." In other words, with the same contract rates, the net received by insurance companies would be 0.25 to 0.75 percentage point lower than that realized by the Federal Land Banks. This differential, insurance company men point out, is a double-edged sword. It not only puts them at a disadvantage in competing for farm mortgage loans but also puts them at a disadvantage within their own companies in competition for investment funds. Note the following statement, from private correspondence, by an insurance company farm loan representative:

> The farm loan department of any company has to compete with the other investment departments within its company for funds. The investment department is charged with the responsibility of earning as much money as possible and will funnel the funds in the proper direction to accomplish this. If the agricultural loan department cannot earn as much as other departments, over the long run, it will be forced out of business.

As indicated by this quotation and by the above material, funds of life insurance companies available for farm loans depend primarily upon company policy. It is true, as some contend, that farm loan funds are influenced by reserves available for investment. Insurance companies cannot create loan funds. During periods of severe financial strain, growth of reserves may be slow and policy loans and policy surrender demands may be high. Under such circumstances, it may be necessary to curtail loans and other investments. It should be noted that under such difficult conditions other lenders also are forced to curtail their loans.

Forward commitments on urban mortgage loans may restrict insurance company funds available for farm loans during tight money periods. The head of the mortgage loan department of a major life insurance company explained their experience in a letter to the authors, adding that he felt "confident it was rather typical."

> Farm loans, as I'm sure you know, are generally committed and closed in a rather short period of time. Large commercial and apartment house loans in urban centers are in most part committed against plans and specifications, with interim construction financing by a third party and the permanent financing funded from one to three years later.
> We, therefore, entered the tight money period, initiated by a slowdown in cash flow, with a very large backlog of forward commitments—

this together with a large increase in demand for policy loans literally "soaked up" funds otherwise available for immediate investment.

Company officials customarily make an allotment of funds to the various types of investments early in the year, based upon an estimate of the amount of assets that will be available. As a result, farm loans may be restricted at times. For example, a farm loan department may be allocated $25,000,000 for loans during the year. If demand for loans is strong, this amount may all be loaned out by September or October, in which case the company would be out of the farm loan field for the balance of the year. In practice, however, a company farm loan department generally does not run itself entirely out of funds. If demand is strong, the company is a little more choosy in the loans it makes, and by this means conserves some funds for good loans throughout the year. Company officials may, if conditions warrant, make some additional funds available in the interest of maintaining a reputation of being a dependable source of credit.

LOAN POLICY. Insurance companies provide a strong competitive source of credit in areas where they concentrate their lending activity. They usually give farm mortgage credit to farmers in these areas on favorable terms and at rates as low as they would to comparable borrowers in business or other lines of activity. The farmer who has a good farm mortgage to offer for a long-term loan is in a position to benefit from the competition among insurance companies, and between insurance companies and other lenders eager to make this type of farm mortgage loan.

Life insurance companies generally make only first-mortgage loans on farm and ranch property. In some states they are prohibited by law from making short-term loans. Furthermore, they generally have little interest in short-term loans because of the character of their reserves and the extensive supervision required by such loans.

Insurance companies that are active in the farm mortgage field choose the territory in which they lend. Smaller companies with limited farm loan funds concentrate their lending activity in selected areas to facilitate economy of operations and to obtain maximum returns. Larger companies also choose their areas of operations with a view to obtaining the greatest return possible with the smallest amount of expense and risk consistent with other company objectives. Having no obligation to serve all farmers, they select those areas where a fair degree of safety is combined with a large volume of business at a rate as high as possible under these conditions. Preference is given to areas where larger commercial farms predominate in number, where soils are fairly uniform, where precipitation or irrigation water is dependable, and where investment return is consistent with risk.

Insurance companies choose the loans they make in areas where they operate. Over the years they have loaned on typical types of farms somewhat larger than the average. Their loans run for a long period of time, during which ownership or operation of the farm may change and the probability of getting a good operator on a typical type farm is greater than on a specialty operation. Similarly, typical type farms generally provide relatively more security than specialty operations. These considerations continue to be fundamental in insurance company loan policy. However, with the continued advance of technology and the economy, some types of farms that formerly were atypical have become commoner, and management has become much more important. Such changes combined with the higher opportunity cost of loan funds, inflationary trends, and increased competition for farm loans have caused some modification in traditional farm loan policy. Loans are now made on feedlots, elevators, citrus groves, and the like. Some insurance companies use part of their farm loan funds for joint ventures or other arrangements that provide for participation in ownership and income. They also make loans that involve agribusiness features such as a processing or marketing facility combined with a farm. Management is stressed, and many loans include a clause to protect the company against changes that would reduce the level of management. The following clause was taken from a mortgage recorded in Iowa:

> Mortgagor agrees to reduce principal of said note to $15,000 before conveying said premises and further agrees that this mortgage shall become due and payable forthwith at the option of the mortgagee, if the mortgagor shall convey said premises, or if the title thereto shall become vested in any person or persons in any manner whatsoever before the principal amount of said note is reduced to said amount.

Such a clause fairly well protects the company since it gives them the right to call for payment of the mortgage should the farm be sold.

Insurance companies make quite a number of loans on part-time farms adjoining residential areas of cities and larger towns. They generally do not loan on large estates with costly pretentious buildings that have a limited sales value, but rather on moderately valued farms with useful buildings that have appeal to many within a practical price range. Their interest centers on property located on good roads and within easy commuting distance to business and retail shopping centers, schools, churches, and the like.

SIZE OF LOANS. There are no limits on the size of insurance company loans except for a self-imposed minimum and a maximum based upon the appraised value of the security. The minimum generally is set in the range of $5,000 to $10,000, depending upon individual company policy, with a view to avoiding the relatively high expense and possible risk associated with such loans. One insurance company official explained it this way in a personal letter to the authors:

> There are two very good reasons why insurance companies have a minimum size of loan they are willing to make. One is that most loans below $10,000 are on small, marginal, inefficient units. Regardless of the interest rate charged or the safety of the investment from a sale of the security standpoint, because of the limited volume of business and the limited income produced by the security, there is a substantial amount of servicing required with such small loans. The other reason is that the cost for handling each dollar invested on a small loan is pretty high and, therefore, the larger loans are somewhat more desirable. The first reason, however, is the most pressing.

Insurance companies are permitted by law to make mortgage loans up to 75 percent of the appraised value, as established by the company's appraisers or loan representatives. Most loans are limited to about 65 percent of the appraised value. In terms of dollars, their loans are relatively large. As was indicated in Chapter 20, life insurance company loans made in 1971 averaged $79,600, compared with $38,600 for Federal Land Banks and $19,100 for commercial banks. It should be recognized, however, that the higher insurance company average is due in part to some very large loans that they make.

TERM OF LOANS AND REPAYMENT PLANS. Insurance company loans generally range in terms from 5 to 25 years, with most of them being written currently for a 20-year term. Where the security is adequate, the term may be extended to 25 years or more, depending on company policy. Similarly, where the security is subject to an unusual hazard, such as soil erosion or an uncertain supply of irrigation water, a shorter term may be used to give the company latitude to periodically review each individual loan and thereby reduce the risk involved.

While the majority of insurance company loans are written for about 20 years, they often are amortized at a somewhat slower rate. On good farms with no unusual hazards, principal payments may be set as low as 2 or 3 percent of the face amount of the loan, depending upon company policy. With a low loan:value ratio, no principal payments may be required during the life of the loan. In such cases the balance is due as a balloon payment at maturity. Interest is in addition to the principal payments and gradually decreases as the loan is repaid.

Some insurance companies have developed noteworthy modifications in the amortization schedule. The policy of one company provides that if the loan does not exceed 50 percent of the appraised value, annual principal payments may be as follows:

1. First 5 years—3 percent of the face amount of the loan
2. Second 5 years—2 percent of the face amount of the loan
3. After 10 years—no principal payments

When a larger proportion of the appraised value is loaned, amortization payments the first 5 years are increased to 5 percent.

A "double diminishing" repayment plan used for some time by another major insurance company accomplishes about the same objective. With this plan, principal payments are set at a fixed percentage of the *unpaid* balance of the loan rather than of the original face amount of the loan. Thus both the principal and interest payments diminish as the loan is repaid. And after the loan is reduced to 50 percent of the original amount, no further principal payments are required until the loan matures.

Both of these plans have desirable features. They enable an insurance company to amortize a loan at a relatively rapid rate until it is reduced to an unquestionably safe amount, and then to retain the loan as an investment. They also may be of help to the farmer by encouraging him to reduce his loan to a safe amount through larger payments in the earlier years. Moreover, the option of discontinuing principal payments when the loan is partially repaid has the advantage of letting the farmer choose whether he should continue to accumulate savings through principal payments on the farm or whether he would gain more satisfaction by using his funds in other ways.

Insurance companies generally restrict prepayments (payments ahead of schedule) during any one year to 20 percent of the original amount of the loan. Some companies permit a larger payment if the funds are derived from farm income. Most companies also permit a larger prepayment upon payment of a premium equal to, say, 2 percent of the amount of the payment. The restriction on prepayments arises because of the large costs involved in placing a loan on the books. Life insurance companies generally do not charge loan-closing fees except to cover direct cash outlays for legal services, recording the mortgage, and the like, and, therefore, major costs of putting the loan on the books must be covered by interest income. Thus insurance companies feel it is necessary to be assured that loans will stay in their portfolio a reasonable length of time or that they will be reimbursed for loan acquisition costs in the event of premature payment in full.

Some companies allow additional prepayment privileges up to, say, 20 percent of the principal amount of the loan to build a reserve payment fund to meet future loan payments if needed. Such payments ordinarily are not subject to withdrawal. Interest generally is allowed on such funds at the rate paid on the loan.

LOAN PROCEDURE. The home office of most insurance companies is located in centers of population some distance from major farming areas. Under such circumstances insurance companies make farm loans through their own branch offices or salaried field representatives reporting directly to the home office, or through correspondents who negotiate and close the loans and assign them to the insurance company. Some companies have their own branch offices or field representatives in part of the country and use correspondents in other parts. Most companies that have their own field organization use middlemen such as banks, realtors, insurance agents, and attorneys who originate loan applications. These middlemen also are often called brokers or correspondents.

Branch Offices and Field Representatives. Insurance companies generally locate their branch (or district) offices and field representatives in the centers of good agricultural areas where there are prospects for a relatively large volume of high quality loans. Companies that operate pretty much throughout the entire country generally use branch or district offices to facilitate operations and management, whereas companies that operate in only certain parts of the country use field representatives without district offices.

Each branch or district office is supervised by a manager who is responsible to the farm loan department of the home office of the company. The branch manager employs a staff, often in consultation with the home office, to carry on functions of the office. The staff includes fieldmen well trained in farm and business management and in appraisal to develop farm loan business for the company. Field representatives of companies that do not maintain branch offices perform about the same function as these fieldmen.

While procedures vary considerably among insurance companies, activities of branch offices and field representatives can be classified into three general groups: (1) loan procurement, (2) loan investigation and closing, and (3) loan servicing. The first two of these groups are discussed here and the third pertaining to servicing loans in the territory is covered later in the chapter.

Regarding *loan procurement,* branch office personnel and field representatives develop some business on their own, but with most companies the majority comes from contacts with parties who have financial dealings with farmers and farm owners and are in position to know when long-term real estate financing is needed. A large percentage of loans results from farm real estate sales and, therefore, a primary contact is with real estate brokers. Other contacts include loan offices, banks located usually in small and medium-sized towns, attorneys, tax accountants, and the like. With most companies these contacts direct business to the attention of the company, and for this service a commission is paid on loans that are closed. The loans are negotiated by the company's branch office fieldman or field representative, depending upon the type of field organization.

The second phase of the field operation pertaining to *investigation and closing of the loan* includes a thorough investigation of the applicant as to such things as managerial capability, financial progress and responsibility, credit reputation, age, health, and family financial requirements. It includes an appraisal of the property to determine its normal productivity and related factors, and whether net income produced under normal circumstances will be sufficient to support the operator and his family and leave an adequate surplus to cover interest and principal payments. It includes the "loan closing," a term that covers all the activities attending the actual making of the loan. Notes and mortgages have to be signed and acknowledged, previous mortgages paid and released, and the new mortgages recorded. Any slip in the loan-closing negotiations may be costly, as illustrated by the local agent who allowed a day to intervene between the release of the old mortgage and the recording of the new. During that intervening day, a bank that had an unrecorded second mortgage put that mortgage on record at the courthouse, thus making it a first mortgage ahead of the agent's mortgage.

A company with a branch office field organization that closes its loans through attorneys or title insurance companies generally proceeds as follows:

1. The branch office sends the *Advice of Loan Approval* to the borrower, and a copy to a local attorney or title company in the community where the farm is situated. Blank mortgage forms are also sent to the attorney or title company.
2. The local attorney or title company examines the title and, if everything is in order, prepares the mortgage and authorizes the branch office to disburse the loan proceeds (funds). If any imperfection is found in the title, it is called to the attention of the branch office.
3. The branch office escrows the loan proceeds with the local attorney or title company who pays out the funds when any defects in the title have been removed and any other conditions stipulated by the company have been complied with.

Companies that have a field representative type of farm loan organization follow a somewhat similar procedure. The field representative sends the loan application, appraisal report, and financial statements, along with his recommendations to the home office of the company where they are considered by the farm loan department. When the application is approved, loan papers generally are sent out to a local attorney who represents the company in the actual closing of the loan.

Agreements with Commercial Banks. Some insurance companies have developed arrangements with commercial banks whereby the bank does more than merely direct the attention of the company to a loan prospect. Some of these arrangements are informal. On the other hand, some are formal business contracts. These arrangements have an advantage for the commercial bank, and at the same time provide the insurance company with a source of long-term investments. The borrower may also benefit by having a source of long-term credit available from his local bank, particularly if the bank is providing his short-term and intermediate-term credit. The bank and farmer can then work out an overall financial plan for the farm.

Farm Mortgage Correspondents. Other than commercial banks, which have already been discussed, farm mortgage correspondents of insurance companies generally are mortgage bankers or individuals associated with mortgage companies, real estate offices, and the like. They are not always easy to recognize because they combine their loan business with other business endeavors. A mortgage company, for example, may make many different types of loans, with farm loans representing only a small segment of the business. A real estate agent may arrange to be a correspondent for an insurance company to provide a source of long-term financing as a means of facilitating farm sales. Lawyers, insurance agents, tax accountants, and abstractors sometimes act as loan correspondents as an accommodation for their customers and to expand their business.

The term *correspondent* has come to have a rather broad meaning in connection with the making of farm mortgage loans by insurance companies. Originally it referred to some local mortgage company that originated loans for an insurance company and continued to service them on a fee basis throughout their life. Some insurance companies use this type of correspondent today in place of a field organization. Companies with a field organization use middlemen or loan brokers who procure loan applications but do not negotiate the loan, and these are now also commonly called correspondents.

Insurance companies uniformly reserve the right to accept or reject loans. In other words, the insurance company decides whether or not it will make or buy a loan. For loans that it makes or buys, the insurance company carries all the risk. Correspondents do not carry any risk on loans they originate except for expenses associated with extra services they might render on problem loans.

A correspondent may act as an agent for more than one insurance company, particularly if he has different types of loans. Some insurance companies specialize in the type and quality of loan they will make, and to properly service his clients, the correspondent may represent more than one company.

LOAN SERVICING. With profit being their motive for operation, insurance companies give careful attention to loan service as a means of building goodwill for the company generally and to help build their loan volume. Competition between profit-motivated companies encourages superior service in many instances. They recognize that well-satisfied customers are their best advertisement for new loans, as well as for their insurance business generally.

Servicing of loans involves a number of things that may be grouped into three general categories: (1) checking to see that the loan continues in good standing, (2) working with problem loans that may develop, and (3) performing general services such as processing partial releases. Note the following statement, taken from a letter to the authors from a major company with a branch office field organization.

> Our loan servicing includes the following:
> a. We check annually on all of our loans to see that the real estate taxes are paid since they are a prior lien. In some offices we check with the county tax collector and in other offices we engage a special tax searching service who makes the tax search for us.
> b. When a loan becomes delinquent, we follow up by correspondence and personal contact to see that it is paid. Our philosophy is that if a borrower can pay without unreasonable sacrifice, he must pay. If he can't pay, we analyze his situation to see if he can work it out or if we must foreclose as a last alternative.
> c. We process partial releases and modifications as requested. The principle involved in partial releases is that the remaining security must adequately secure the loan regardless of the value of the land being released.

The following statement is taken from the originating and servicing agreement of a major insurance company with its farm mortgage correspondents:

> In servicing such loans, Correspondent undertakes to perform, under the Company's direction, all acts and duties which a reasonably prudent

mortgage lender would perform with respect to its own mortgages. Without limiting the generality of the foregoing: . . .

Correspondent will keep adequate records respecting the mortgages, which records shall be the property of the Company and shall be open to inspection and audit by the Company, and Correspondent will furnish reports on request regarding the status of mortgages. Once a year, Correspondent will furnish proof acceptable to the Company of the payment of all taxes, assessments or other public charges affecting the mortgaged premises. Correspondent will at all times use due diligence to keep buildings and other improvements on the mortgaged premises adequately insured as required by the mortgage, and to prevent liens superior to the mortgages from attaching to the mortgaged premises. It will promptly notify the Company of any facts coming to its attention which might have an adverse bearing on the Company's investment. It will make inspections of the mortgaged premises at reasonable intervals as requested from time to time by the Company and, in any event, at least once a year, filing reports with the Company on forms approved by the Company. It will, in the event of casualty, assist in collecting insurance moneys and, if requested by the Company, in having the properties restored and will cooperate with the Company in any legal proceedings affecting the loans or the mortgaged premises. It will not accept sums in reduction of principal in excess of the amounts permitted by the loan terms.

To protect its investment an insurance company must make certain that real estate taxes, assessments, or other public charges are paid, since they become a prior lien against the property ahead of the mortgage. Attention must be given to keeping insurance on buildings in force and to seeing that they and the farm generally are kept in repair, otherwise the company's security could deteriorate and the loan might become impaired. In addition to impairment of the security, such defaults often serve as a warning of possible loan weakness from other causes. For example, a temporary tax delinquency increases the borrower's operating costs and may be an indication of a careless attitude toward his obligations. Similarly, a lapse of an insurance policy may indicate carelessness and may prove to be a disaster financially to the borrower, should fire or natural forces destroy the improvement.

Servicing delinquent loans generally is not much of a problem during periods of economic prosperity. The relatively few borrowers who become involved financially often find a better situation in nonfarm employment, with the result that their farms generally are taken over by financially stronger operators in the community. However, during less prosperous times delinquency can become quite a problem.

The procedure involved in dealing with delinquent loans varies somewhat from company to company, but in general the pattern is as follows: when payment is not received in response to the initial notice, a second reminder notice is sent; if no response to the reminder notice is received, the case is turned over to a member of the company's service group who analyzes the case and decides whether collection should be attempted by further correspondence or whether it should be turned over to the branch office or company correspondent.

Insurance companies generally are as lenient as possible with worthy borrowers during periods of difficulty. Loans are made with the understanding that they will be repaid, of course, and the prospective borrower should fully realize that an insurance company's first responsibility is to its policyholders. However, insurance companies also realize that because of the dynamic character of the farm business, income fluctuates widely. To help offset the effect of income fluctuations, some companies have set up reserve payment plans, as referred to above, through which borrowers can build reserves to help meet payments in low income periods. And insurance companies generally realize that some deviation may be necessary in their regular and planned collection policy. Interest payments generally are insisted upon, if at all possible, to keep the loan from building up to an unwarranted amount. But principal payments often are extended or deferred, or the loan is rewritten, when it is felt that such action is justified, and when the borrower has a reasonable prospect of working out of his difficulty. Insurance companies generally have no desire to force a farmer out of business. Foreclosure action is taken only as a last resort when careless management and misuse of funds lead the company to believe a loan extension would merely postpone the day of reckoning.

In regard to partial releases, subordination agreements, and the like, insurance companies make an effort to cooperate with and accommodate the borrower in such matters. Whenever the release involves a loss of a substantial portion of the security, the field office or correspondent usually is asked to study the situation and to obtain a new appraisal as a basis for determining the amount that should be paid on the loan. In making this determination, the company considers not only the value of the remaining security but also what the earning capacity of the unit will be after the release is effected.

QUESTIONS AND PROBLEMS
1. What type of loans do insurance companies make?
2. How important are insurance companies as farm lenders in your state? In the nation? Is their volume of loans increasing or decreasing? Are they increasing or decreasing in importance relative to other lenders?
3. Who owns and controls insurance companies? What significance does this have from the viewpoint of the farmer wanting to obtain a loan?
4. What is the primary source of insurance company loan funds? Evaluate this source of funds from the viewpoint of dependabil-

ity of loan service. Compare this source of funds with the primary source of commercial bank loan funds.

5. What factors do insurance companies consider in determining how much of their assets to put into farm loans?
6. Outline the loan policy generally followed by insurance companies. Do they give much consideration to the operator?
7. Explain the repayment plans used by insurance companies. Appraise their repayment policy.
8. Appraise the advisability of discontinuing principal payments when the loan is, say, one-half repaid.
9. Is it possible to have too much competition in the farm mortgage loan business? What may be the consequences?
10. Does the loan and service procedure followed by a lender make any difference to the borrower? Discuss.
11. Is there an insurance company loan office or representative in your locality? How would you go about making contact with an insurance company about a loan?
12. Why do insurance companies have branch or district offices? Field representatives? Correspondents? Compare these and discuss their functions.
13. Discuss and appraise the procedures used by insurance companies in making loans; in servicing loans.

REFERENCES

Federal Reserve Bulletin. Board of Governors, Washington, D.C.

Fletcher, George A. "Joint Ventures in Agricultural Finance." *Jour. Am. Soc. Farm Managers and Rural Appraisers,* Apr. 1971, pp. 33–38.

Krause, K. R.; Atkinson, J. H.; and Snyder, J. C. *Specialized Illinois and Indiana Farm Mutual Insurance Companies in a Changing Competitive Environment.* Purdue Univ., Agr. Exp. Sta. Res. Bull. 771, Dec. 1963.

Life Insurance Fact Book. Inst. of Life Ins.

Penson, John B., Jr., and Warren, Forest G. *Life Insurance Company Farm-Mortgage Loans: A Statistical Study of Loans Outstanding, September 30, 1966,* USDA, ERS-439, Washington, D.C., June 1970.

Sharpe, Dennis B. *Agricultural Letter.* Fed. Res. Bank of Chicago, Sept. 29, 1972.

Warden, Denzil C. "Joint Ventures in Agricultural Finance." *Jour. Am. Soc. Farm Managers and Rural Appraisers,* Apr. 1971, pp. 39–43.

Warren, Forest G., and Mitchem, Nan P. *Farm Mortgage Lending.* ERS, USDA (issued twice yearly).

CHAPTER 23: MERCHANTS, DEALERS, AND OTHER LENDERS

MERCHANTS, dealers, processors, individuals, and other types of noninstitutional lenders are an important source of credit for farmers. They have extended a substantial proportion of the credit used by farmers over the years and probably will continue to do so. Technological developments in agriculture cause the volume of credit obtained from these sources to increase over time. As purchased inputs become increasingly important in the operation of the farm business, the amount of noninstitutional credit increases.

The objective of this chapter is to portray a general picture of agricultural financing by major types of noninstitutional lenders. Real estate financing is considered first, following which nonreal-estate credit is discussed. A major part of the chapter is devoted to merchant and dealer credit.

In considering financing by noninstitutional lenders, it should be recognized that there probably is greater variability in their policies and procedures than in those of institutional lenders. Objectives of noninstitutional lenders in extending credit vary widely, and as a result, their policies and procedures also vary widely.

REAL ESTATE CREDIT. As indicated in Chapter 20, noninstitutional lenders held 43 percent of the real estate debt outstanding January 1, 1972.[1] This proportion has been high consistently over the years. These lenders as a group extend more real estate credit to agriculture than any one of the institutional lenders.

Practically all the noninstitutional lender real estate debt is held by individuals, mostly by those who have sold their farms using a mortgage, deed of trust (an arrangement whereby a limited power of sale over property is placed in one or more trustees by deed, to secure payment of money and performance of other conditions),[2] or a pur-

---

1. The 43 percent includes a relatively small amount of farm real estate debt held by institutional lenders, such as Production Credit Associations and savings and loan associations, but the major part is held by individuals, merchants, dealers, and other types of noninstitutional lenders.

2. Fred L. Mann, *A Comparative Study of Laws Relating to Low-Equity Transfers of Farm Real Estate in the North Central Region*, North Central Regional Publ. 136, Univ. of Missouri Res. Bull. 782, p. 14.

chase contract—also called a sales contract, installment land contract, contract for deed, etc. In the year ended March 1, 1972, sellers financed 38 percent of the credit-financed farmland transfers, 31 percent using a purchase contract and 7 percent using a mortgage. In periods when credit available from institutional lenders is tight, seller financing may increase. In 1970, for example, 53 percent of the credit-financed farmland transfers were financed by sellers, 46 percent by purchase contracts, and 7 percent by mortgages. In that year sellers provided 61 percent of the total volume of credit extended for real estate purchases.[3]

The use of purchase contracts was discussed in Chapter 14. As was brought out there, since the down payment with a purchase contract usually is lower than with a mortgage, a farmer with limited equity can use a purchase contract as a means of acquiring a farm or of adding to his farm. This is one feature that accounts for their popularity. Another is the tax advantage to the seller. Most farms sold these days bring more than their cost. In such cases, a capital gain is realized, and with present tax laws, if more than 30 percent of the sale price is received in the year of sale, the total capital gain is taxable income in that year. On the other hand, if the down payment is less than 30 percent, capital gains realized on the sale may be spread out over a period of years.

According to conventional economic theory, low-equity financing will bring more buyers into the market and, in turn, increase the price of land. The theory appears to be reflected in practice where unusual circumstances are not involved. A survey by the Economic Research Service indicated that the "sales prices per acre tend to be higher when financed by land contract, as much as 10 to 20 percent in many instances."[4] Examples of unusual factors that may neutralize the effect of increased buyers are close kinship or friendship between buyers and sellers and income tax considerations.[5]

The interest rate with a purchase contract theoretically would be higher than with a mortgage since the down payment with the former usually is lower than with the latter. It appears the theory holds in practice where special circumstances are not involved.[6] However, it also appears that special circumstances are involved in most instances. In addition to kinship, a major factor is the tax advantage in converting ordinary income (interest) into capital gains (sale price). In other

3. *Farm Real Estate Market Developments*, ERS, USDA, July 1972, p. 23.
4. John F. Gale, "Installment Land Contracts in Financing Farm Real Estate Transfers," *Agr. Finance Rev.*, Aug. 1964, p. 43.
5. For a fuller discussion of such factors see Marshall Harris and N. William Hines, *Installment Land Contracts in Iowa*, Agr. Law Center Monograph 5, Univ. of Iowa, Jan. 1965, pp. 24–25.
6. Ibid., pp. 25–26.

words, it usually is to the seller's advantage taxwise to hold down the interest rate and to compensate by raising the sale price.

Being one means of borrowing, the principles applying in use of capital apply in use of purchase contracts. Particular attention should be given to terms of the contract, as outlined in Chapter 14, and also to repayment capacity and ability to carry the risk involved since use of purchase contracts generally requires more of both.

NONREAL-ESTATE CREDIT. Noninstitutional lenders, as indicated in Chapter 20, held 41 percent of the nonreal-estate debt January 1, 1972. The share held by these lenders always has been high, although the proportion declined about one percentage point over the past decade.

A sample survey taken in 1966 as a supplement to the 1964 *Census of Agriculture* provides information on the relative importance of three types of noninstitutional lenders: merchants and dealers, individuals (landlords, relatives, friends, estates, etc.), and miscellaneous (unpaid bills for hospital, medical, and veterinary service; utility bills; taxes or insurance premiums past due; and debts for other purposes). The proportion of commercial farm operators with nonreal-estate debt borrowing from each source was as follows: merchants and dealers, 62 percent; individuals, 11 percent; and the miscellaneous group, 31 percent. For comparison, the proportion borrowing from commercial banks was 40 percent.[7]

It is evident that merchants and dealers are the major noninstitutional suppliers of nonreal-estate credit. Merchants and dealers stand out not only among the noninstitutional lenders but also in comparison with the institutional suppliers of nonreal-estate credit. Commercial banks, generally considered the major source of nonreal-estate credit, serve only about two-thirds as many farmers as merchants and dealers.

Merchants and dealers are also important in terms of *volume* of credit extended, ranking second only to commercial banks. They accounted for 21 percent of the combined operator and landlord nonreal-estate farm debt reported in the sample survey compared with 39 percent for commercial and savings banks. The proportion held by individuals was 7 percent, and the miscellaneous group held only 3 percent.[8] While these figures are not directly comparable with those given above, a comparison of the two indicates that the average amount of credit extended per borrower by merchants and dealers and

---

7. Derived from *Farm Debt*, 1964 U.S. Census of Agriculture, vol. 3, part 4, p. 35 and p. 184. Since many farmers borrow from more than one source, the percentages who borrow from the various sources add to more than 100.

8. Ibid., p. 422.

the other noninstitutional lender groups is substantially less than the average loan extended by commercial banks.

Merchants and dealers are the most widely used sources of non-real-estate credit in all regions of the country. They stand out particularly in the South not only in the proportion of borrowers financed but in the fact that they provide credit to nearly three times as many farmers as commercial banks.

Why Do Merchants and Dealers Extend Credit? Sales promotion usually is the primary reason why merchants and dealers extend credit to farmers. It facilitates sales of gasoline, feed, fertilizer, supplies, etc., particularly when these items are delivered and the farmer is not at hand to make payment. It also helps in selling items where large amounts are involved. Machinery dealers often extend credit to help close a sale; livestock commission companies make loans to farmers for purchasing livestock.

Credit is also used as a magnet by marketing firms. Dealers who contract to buy fruits and vegetables from farmers sometimes make advances for operating expenses; cotton gins provide financing for cotton farmers as a means of increasing their ginning business; farm cooperatives provide credit in some cases to their members for whom they process and sell products or purchase supplies.

What has been said and the fact that merchants and dealers extend credit to a large proportion of farmers should not be interpreted as meaning they like the role. While some manufacturers and dealers extend credit in part because of the profit they realize on the lending itself, the large majority would prefer not to extend credit. The following from private correspondence is pertinent:

1. I belong to the National Credit Organization of both the Feed and Agricultural Chemical Groups, and two things stand out very clearly.
   a. Nearly all dealers and/or manufacturers are doing as much as possible to have farmers finance through normal lending institutions in order to make more money available for purposes other than accounts receivable.
   b. Most manufacturers and/or wholesalers have curtailed, reduced or even eliminated dealer financing again for the same reasons as above. They are leaving it up to the dealer to obtain his own financing through normal lending institutions.
2. The advent of Regulation Z under the Truth-in-Lending Legislation which classifies farmers as consumers has caused some dealers to eliminate cash discount and to curtail their financing as much as possible due to the complications imposed by Regulation Z.

Types of Merchant-Dealer Credit Arrangements. Credit extended by merchants, dealers, processors, some manufacturers, and other types of middlemen takes many forms. The form may vary considerably from one type of dealer to another. For example, feed dealers generally offer different credit arrangements from machinery dealers. Moreover, a given merchant may have a different form of credit arrangement with one customer than with another. When vertical integration is involved, funds provided by the middleman may be more in the nature of an investment of equity capital in the farm venture than of a loan to the farmer.

The various arrangements under which credit is extended by merchants and dealers may be generally classified into three groups: open account credit, extended open account credit, and credit extended under formal contract. In addition to these, vertical integration and financial leases, discussed in Chapter 6, constitute means whereby a farmer can obtain use of capital.

Open account credit is extended by many retailers, including some manufacturers who sell direct to farmers, when frequent sales are made for relatively small amounts. Customers usually are billed once each month. This procedure is more convenient than cash payment for each purchase, particularly when supplies are delivered to the farm and the farmer is not at hand to pay for them.

Some feed, fertilizer, machinery, and similar manufacturers also provide open account financing for farmers through their local distributor. Manufacturers sometimes are involved with the larger accounts, which they may carry in entirety or in conjunction with a local distributor.

Practically all equipment dealers extend credit on an open account basis. Unless special arrangements are made, these accounts are due by the 10th or the 15th of the month following the month of purchase. In recent years some dealers have offered as an alternate various bank credit cards to enable their customers to stretch payments over a longer period of time if they wish.

Open account credit carried more than 30 days is customarily referred to as extended open account credit. Oil dealers customarily extend credit to farmers for 90 days, and in some cases for longer periods. Some dealers in seed, fertilizer, and other supplies provide extended open account credit to farmers, with payment to be made at harvest time when crops are sold. Similarly, some feed dealers provide extended open account credit with payment to be made when livestock are sold. Some manufacturers also provide extended open account credit either alone or on a participation basis with local dealers.

Formal written contracts, such as promissory notes and conditional sales contracts, are used by some merchants and dealers, and by some manufacturers, to secure credit transactions with farm customers. Formal contracts usually are negotiated at the time of sale. However, they may stem from "past-due" extended open account credit lines that are converted to a formal contract basis. Almost all the financing provided by dealers on a contract basis is, in turn, assigned to the manufacturer or to a lending institution. In a very few instances, dealers have set up their own finance companies to handle their financing.

Cost of Merchant-Dealer Credit. Farmers using merchant and dealer credit may find it extremely costly, moderately priced, or relatively cheap, depending on the policy of the lender and the type of credit arrangement. Dealers usually impose a finance charge after a period of time on both *open account credit* and *extended term financing*. The free period varies. However, in most cases farmers get 30 days free, and with some items the free period may even extend to 6 months. The finance charge usually runs from 1 to 1½ percent per month, depending upon the state usury law.

Credit extended under formal contracts usually carries an interest charge. The rate fluctuates with the availability of money and the general level of interest rates.

Interest charged by merchants and dealers is commonly higher than that charged by financial institutions extending credit for the same purpose. Since the federal Truth in Lending Act was passed, the annual percentage rate of interest must be disclosed, which should make farmers aware of the actual charge imposed. Why, then, do farmers pay the higher rates? Undoubtedly there are a number of reasons. Some may not have taken time to compare the alternative costs. Other farmers use it because they cannot obtain credit elsewhere, or think they cannot, at lower rates. However, some farmers use merchant-dealer credit in spite of its high cost because of the convenience, the relatively liberal terms provided, etc. From the farmer's standpoint, the relevant consideration is the total cost—the sale price plus the cost of credit measured in terms of money, inconvenience, and time required—with one arrangement compared with another.

A number of factors contribute to the comparatively high cost of merchant-dealer credit. Expenses per dollar of credit granted tend to be high compared with those of financial institutions serving farmers. Many small advances to customers by merchants without an efficient method of handling accounts adds to costs of extending and collecting credit. In some cases additional time is required on the part of sales personnel to explain the credit policy to customers. Collection costs and bad debt losses tend to be heavier than for financing institutions since merchants often are less thorough in credit analysis, items sold on credit such as feed and fuel cannot be repossessed when they have been used, and the security is often inadequate or nonexistent. Moreover, if the merchant must borrow the money that he, in turn, lends to his customers, his cost for loan funds may well be higher than the corresponding cost of money for financial institutions.

Source of Merchant-Dealer Loan Funds. Merchants and dealers who extend credit to farmers usually must be financed themselves.

Major sources of this financing are local commercial banks, larger city banks, banks for cooperatives, and manufacturers. If the merchant or dealer is a cooperative institution with farmers owning shares, the financing is likely to come from a bank for cooperatives or a commercial bank. Other merchants and dealers are quite likely to be financed by local commercial banks. However, if the merchant or dealer is a large operator and uses an extensive line of credit, he may go directly to a large city bank for his financing. Manufacturers may provide dealer financing for a wide variety of items such as machinery and equipment, machine repair and overhaul, fertilizer, and feed. In such cases the manufacturer may obtain financing either by retaining earnings, by sale of commercial paper and debentures in the national financial market, or by borrowing from large commercial banks.

Financing arrangements between dealers and feed manufacturers vary considerably. With some arrangements the dealer is fully liable for defaulted contracts, while with others he carries no financial responsibility. With some financing plans the dealer pays part of the finance charges, while with other arrangements the farmer carries the full load. Finance charges may be in the form of a nominal interest charge or, more commonly, in the form of a flat fee per ton in addition to the cash price.

Financing arrangements between dealers and machine manufacturers also vary, but to a somewhat lesser extent than in the feed industry. The general provisions of a contract used by a major machinery manufacturer are outlined to indicate what is involved.

A dealer who obtains financing from a manufacturer enters into a contract with the manufacturer that spells out the terms and conditions under which the credit is obtained. Credit normally is extended on the basis of customers' notes or contracts, which must meet the requirements of the manufacturer. Notes and contracts include finance charges, computed as prescribed by the manufacturer. All payments on the note or contract are made by the note or contract maker directly to the manufacturer. The dealer is liable for the payments if the customer defaults. To insure the funds are available to meet this obligation, a "dealer's reserve account" is set up by the manufacturer. Reserves in this account are built and maintained from the finance charges on notes and contracts accepted by the manufacturer. The reserve account is separate and distinct from the dealer's regular account or statement that reflects indebtedness of the dealer to the manufacturer.

If any note or contract accepted by the manufacturer is not paid in full, the loss is charged to the dealer's reserve account, together with related expenses incurred by the manufacturer. However, under certain conditions the manufacturer may stand part of the loss.

Merchants and dealers also have used various financing arrangements with lending institutions to provide customer credit without having to carry it on their own books. For example, machinery dealers and commercial banks have worked out plans whereby the bank purchases the farmer's note from the dealer. The commonest arrangements are (1) the full-endorsement plan, (2) the limited-recourse plan, (3) the repurchase plan, (4) the nonrecourse plan, and (5) the mutual reserve plan.[9]

The *full-endorsement plan* provides that the dealer is fully liable to the bank for all defaulted obligations. The responsibility of making collections generally is transferred to the bank, but the dealer continues as the primary creditor. This plan is not looked upon with favor by representatives of dealers and farm equipment manufacturers. Their view is that the dealer should be relieved largely from the credit aspects of the business. Moreover, their belief is that banks may tend to lean too heavily upon the recourse crutch and give too little attention to quality of the credit. A full-recourse arrangement can easily lull the lender into a false sense of security that, in turn, can lead to bad credit practices on the part of both the dealer and the lending institution.

The *limited-recourse plan* limits the liablity of the dealer as to time or amount on individual or aggregate sales contracts bought by the bank. Thus with this plan the bank assumes some direct liability on loans and, in return, the plan provides for building specified reserves to cover losses incurred. Generally, to encourage making sound sales, the dealer is relieved of full liability only after a specified number of payments have been made on the sales contract.

The *repurchase plan* provides that the dealer repurchase farm equipment repossessed by the bank for the unpaid balance of the contract. Various types of arrangements can be made under this plan. The bank can assume responsibility for any legal action that becomes necessary. Reserves similar to those with the limited-recourse plan can be built to cover losses. This plan, as well as the limited-recourse plan, puts the dealer on a participation basis with the bank, which tends to facilitate fuller cooperation.

The *nonrecourse plan* provides for the bank to buy the equipment sales contract and become the primary creditor. The bank has no recourse to the dealer if the purchaser of the equipment defaults on payments. Naturally banks are quite selective in contracts that

---

9. *Farm Equipment Financing by Banks,* American Bankers Assoc., New York.

they buy on a nonrecourse basis and, therefore, such arrangements are not very popular.

With the *mutual reserve plan* the dealer sells his paper to the bank without recourse, but a sufficiently large reserve is created to protect the bank against losses. When and if the dealer's paper pays out in full, he receives the entire amount in the reserve. The major difference between this plan and the repurchase plan is that the dealer is not obligated to repurchase repossessed equipment with the mutual reserve plan.

Through arrangements with sales finance companies and other organizations, such as General Motors Acceptance Corporation, C.I.T. (Commercial Investment Trust), and Financial Corporation, merchants and dealers make a substantial amount of credit available to their customers without having to provide it themselves. Such companies finance credit transactions by purchasing customer notes or accounts from the merchant or dealer. Another device used by merchants, dealers, and manufacturers is to establish subsidiary credit corporations. In such cases the initial capital is ordinarily furnished by the parent firm, and loan funds are obtained by selling commercial paper and debentures in the national financial market and discounting customer notes with, or borrowing from, commercial banks. Where the financing agency is organized by a farmer cooperative, it may obtain loan funds by borrowing from a Bank for Cooperatives.

QUESTIONS AND PROBLEMS

1. Discuss the importance of various types of noninstitutional lenders as sources of credit for farmers.
2. What types of loans do noninstitutional lenders make to farmers?
3. Who provides most of the real estate credit extended by noninstitutional lenders? Is this a dependable source of credit?
4. Why do land contracts offered by farm owners selling their land often provide for a lower interest rate than is charged on farm mortgage loans?
5. Why do merchants and dealers offer credit?
6. Does merchant credit cost the farmer more than other credit? If so, why does he use it?
7. Are merchants justified in the rates they charge for credit? What are the main items of cost?
8. Where do merchants and dealers obtain the funds they loan to farmers?
9. Are merchants and dealers a dependable source of credit? Discuss.
10. Appraise merchant credit as a source of financing. Does it contribute to optimum balance in the use of capital in the farm business?

REFERENCES

Benson, Richard A. "Trade Credit in the Fertilizer Industry: Theory and Practice." *Agr. Finance Review,* July 1969, pp. 21–33.

Clark, Chaplin D., and Berry, Russell L. *Buying Farmland on Installment Contracts.* S.Dak. Agr. Exp. Sta. Circ. 164, 1964.

Emde, Kenneth, and Raup, Philip M. *The Minnesota Rural Real Estate Market in 1971.* Inst. of Agr. Econ., Univ. of Minn., Study Rept. 572-2, 1972.

Farm Real Estate Market Developments. Published annually by ERS, USDA.

Gale, John F. "Installment Land Contracts in Financing Farm Real Estate Transfers." *Agr. Finance Review,* ERS, USDA, Aug. 1964, pp. 37–44.

Hamlin, Edmund T. *Manufacturer Financing of Farm Machinery and Equipment Sales and Rentals to Farmers, 1963–1970,* Farm Prod. Econ. Div., Working Paper, ERS, USDA, May 1972.

Harris, Marshall, and Hines, N. William. *Installment Land Contracts in Iowa.* Univ. of Iowa Agr. Law Center, Monograph 5, 1965.

Reinsel, Robert D. "Effect of Seller Financing on Land Prices." *Agr. Finance Review,* ERS, USDA, July 1972, pp. 32–35.

Structure of Six Farm Input Industries. Farm Prod. Econ. Div., ERS, USDA, 1968.

Taylor, Fred R., and Bredahl, Maury E. *Merchant-Dealer Credit in North Dakota: Merchant-Dealer Problems and Practices.* N.Dak. Agr. Exp. Sta., Agr. Econ. Rept. 63, 1969.

Taylor, Fred R., and Huber, Hilmer. *Merchant-Dealer Credit in North Dakota: Farmer Use and Importance.* N.Dak. Agr. Exp. Sta., Agr. Econ. Rept. 62, 1969.

CHAPTER 24: **FARM CREDIT SYSTEM**

THE FARM CREDIT SYSTEM is composed of the Farm Credit Administration, 12 Farm Credit Districts, and the cooperative banks and associations that were organized and put into operation by the United States government as a means of helping farmers to help themselves. No other segment of the economy has been thus favored. The organization of the Farm Credit System is portrayed in Figure 24.1. The Farm Credit Administration and Farm Credit Districts are considered first, following which the Federal Land Bank System, the Production Credit System, and the Banks for Cooperatives are discussed in that order.

FARM CREDIT ADMINISTRATION. The Farm Credit Administration (FCA), an independent agency in the executive branch of the United States government, consists of the Federal Farm Credit Board, the governor, and his staff. It is a supervisory organization—it makes no loans. Loans are made by the banks and associations of the Farm Credit System, which are supervised by the FCA. However, certain loans in each of the three bank groups are submitted to the FCA for approval. This is a rather unusual function for a regulatory agency as it generally is not done by supervisory agencies such as the Federal Reserve Board and Federal Deposit Insurance Corporation. Some auditing and examination of the banks and associations are also carried on as part of supervision performed by the FCA.

The Federal Farm Credit Board is comprised of 13 members. Twelve members of the board, 1 from each of the Farm Credit Districts, are appointed (on a staggered basis—2 each year) for 6-year terms by the president of the United States, with the advice and consent of the Senate, after giving consideration to nominations made by borrowers of the district banks and associations. The 3 groups of borrowers (the Federal Land Banks, the Production Credit Associations, and the cooperatives borrowing from the district Banks for Cooperatives) each nominate 12 men, making a total of 36. To date, the selection has been made from these men, on a nonpartisan basis, to provide approximately equal representation for each of the 3 borrowing groups. The thirteenth member of the board is appointed by the secretary of agriculture as his representative.

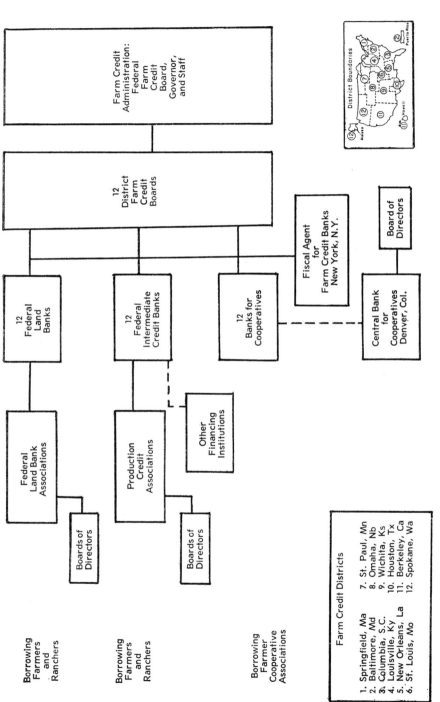

FIG. 24.1—*Organization of the Farm Credit System.*

Farm Credit Administration: Federal Farm Credit Board, Governor, and Staff

12 District Farm Credit Boards

District Boundaries

12 Federal Land Banks

12 Federal Intermediate Credit Banks

12 Banks for Cooperatives

Fiscal Agent for Farm Credit Banks New York, N.Y.

Central Bank for Cooperatives Denver, Col.

Board of Directors

Federal Land Bank Associations

Production Credit Associations

Other Financing Institutions

Boards of Directors

Boards of Directors

Borrowing Farmers and Ranchers

Borrowing Farmers and Ranchers

Borrowing Farmer Cooperative Associations

Farm Credit Districts

1. Springfield, Ma
2. Baltimore, Md
3. Columbia, S.C.
4. Louisville, Ky
5. New Orleans, La
6. St. Louis, Mo
7. St. Paul, Mn
8. Omaha, Nb
9. Wichita, Ks
10. Houston, Tx
11. Berkeley, Ca
12. Spokane, Wa

The Federal Farm Credit Board appoints a governor to administer affairs of the FCA. The governor and his staff are housed in what is termed the Washington Office, located in Washington, D.C.

In addition to supervision of the banks and associations of the system, the governor has funds at his disposal that may be used to purchase stock in one or several of the Federal Land Banks, Federal Intermediate Credit Banks, Production Credit Associations, and Banks for Cooperatives as a temporary investment to meet emergency credit needs of borrowers. The banks and associations in which such investments are made are subject to pertinent provisions of the Government Corporation Control Act during the time such stock is outstanding. Because government control would be thereby increased, it appears unlikely that this source of capital will be used unless widespread emergency conditions exist, since the Farm Credit Act of 1971 provides alternative means whereby such needs can be provided for within the system.

FARM CREDIT DISTRICTS. The 12 Farm Credit Districts of the Farm Credit System encompass the entire United States and Puerto Rico. They are designated by number and name of the headquarters city (see Fig. 24.1). Each district includes a District Farm Credit Board, a Federal Land Bank (FLB) and its affiliated Federal Land Bank Associations (FLBAs), a Federal Intermediate Credit Bank (FICB) and its affiliated Production Credit Associations (PCAs), and a Bank for Cooperatives.

The District Farm Credit Board is made up of 7 members. Six of the directors are elected, 2 by borrowers from the FLB, 2 by borrowers from the PCAs, and 2 by borrowers from the Bank for Cooperatives. The 7th director is appointed by the governor of the FCA with the advice and consent of the federal board. The District Farm Credit Board is the board of directors of each of the 3 banks in the district.

The 3 banks in each district are housed in the district offices located in the headquarters city.

FEDERAL LAND BANK SYSTEM. The Federal Land Bank System comprises that part of the Farm Credit System through which farmers and other eligible applicants obtain long-term mortgage loans. The 12 FLBs and their affiliated FLBAs are the system's intermediaries.

Federal Land Banks. Each FLB is a corporation chartered as a permanent institution under the Federal Farm Loan Act of 1916 and continued under the Farm Credit Act of 1971. The act specifies that they "shall continue as federally chartered instrumentalities of the United States."

Policies of the FLBs are determined by the respective District Farm Credit Boards. The board is authorized, subject to provisions of the law under which the bank is chartered and supervision of the FCA, to exercise all such powers as are necessary to carry on business of the bank. The board employs a staff to manage and operate the bank.

The FLB in each district has certain responsibilities for supervising the FLBAs in the district. The banks, by mutual agreement with the associations, have delegated to the associations many functions involved in making and servicing loans to association members. The banks have a responsibility to make certain the delegated authority is properly exercised. In addition, the FCA has authorized the FLBs to perform a number of its powers and duties in supervision of the associations.

Federal Land Bank Associations. Each FLBA is a corporation, organized by borrowers from the district FLB, which operates in a specified area under a federal charter.

As is the case with all corporations, each FLBA is controlled by a board of directors. The board, elected by members of the association who own voting stock, employs a manager who serves as the executive officer of the association.

The volume of loans made by the FLB in an area depends in large degree on the association serving the area. The association is the unit of the system that originates the business and maintains first-hand contact with the public.

Ownership. The FLBs, organized and originally owned by the federal government, are owned by the FLBAs, and the FLBAs are owned by the borrowers. Each borrower purchases capital stock or participation certificates in the FLBA equal to 5 percent of the face amount of the loan. Farmers acquire voting stock while the other classes of borrowers, discussed subsequently, receive nonvoting stock or participation certificates, so they have no voice in affairs of the association. The FLBA in turn purchases a like amount of capital stock or certificates in the FLB in the district. Bank and association stock and certificates are retired when the loan is paid in full.

In addition to capital from the sale of stock and certificates, the banks and associations have accumulated substantial amounts of surplus and reserves over the years. Part of these are earnings on the initial government capital that were left in the system when the government capital was retired.

Loan Funds. The primary source of FLB loan funds is from the sale of consolidated federal farm loan bonds in the national financial markets through the fiscal agent for the banks located in New

York City. These bonds are the joint obligation of the 12 banks. The maturities, rates of interest, and terms and conditions of each issue are subject to approval by the governor of the FCA. The governor informs the treasury of all public financing plans and actions by the banks of the Farm Credit System.

The size of each bond issue sold is determined by the 12 banks individually estimating how much money they will need to refund maturing bonds and to provide for new loans until the next issue of bonds is sold.

Each FLB generally obtains some funds between bond issues by borrowing from other land banks, from other banks in the Farm Credit System, or from commercial banks. The FLBs may also borrow from other financial institutions, such as insurance companies, federal agencies, or Federal Reserve Banks, under certain conditions with FCA approval.

With the approval of the governor and concurrence of the boards of directors of all the banks, the banks of the Farm Credit System may join together in issuance of system-wide notes, bonds, debentures, and other obligations. This provision of the Farm Credit Act of 1971 has not been used to date.

Bonds sold by the FLBs may not exceed 20 times the capital and surplus of all the banks. Notes and mortgages of land bank borrowers are the primary collateral for the bonds.

Loans and Loan Service. Federal Land Banks make first-mortgage loans to (1) farmers, including partnerships and corporations engaged primarily in farming, (2) persons and businesses furnishing farm-related services (custom-type on-farm services performed for farmers), and (3) owners of rural homes. Loans may not exceed 85 percent of the appraised value of the security. Certain types of loans require prior approval by the FCA. The conditions for prior approval are set by regulations.

The appraised value, with some exceptions, is the market value of the property. It is defined as the amount a property will bring providing there is a reasonable time to find a purchaser, and both the seller and the prospective buyer are fully informed, with neither being under abnormal pressure. The exceptions pertain to property near urban centers, timber land, land in orchards and the like, land dependent upon leases or permits, land subject to serious problems such as a depleting water supply, and lands involving minerals. Appraisals in each district are made in accordance with standards established by the land bank and approved by the FCA.

Loans to farmers are made for any purpose and for a term of 5 to 40 years. Most loans are amortized over a period of 5 to 35 years.

Federal Land Banks may own and lease, or lease with option to purchase, facilities needed by farmers in their operations.

Loans to persons or businesses furnishing farm-related services may be made for land and improvements, equipment, and initial working capital. Rural housing loans are restricted to single-family, moderate-priced dwellings and their appurtenances in rural areas, including towns and villages with a population of 2,500 or less. Rural housing loans are amortized over periods not exceeding 30 years. Farm loans and farm-related service loans have precedence over rural housing loans if circumstances arise that curtail loan funds for the system.

Federal Land Bank loans run directly from the bank to the borrower. They are made through the FLBA, which is the local contact point through which borrowers obtain loans. The association receives applications for loans, elects loan applicants to association membership, and performs functions in closing loans. It can be delegated authority in making loans commensurate with its demonstrated ability to extend and to administer credit soundly in accordance with established policy.

The making or closing of land bank loans largely follows conventional lines except that the procedure is split between the bank and the association. Either designated local attorneys or land bank attorneys consider the abstract of title to the property and determine whether the applicant has proper title to the farm. In parts of the country where title insurance is used in place of abstracts, the bank's legal staff examines any exceptions specified in the preliminary report of the title insurance company to determine adequacy of the title. A *remittance statement* is prepared setting forth requirements to be met before the loan proceeds are released and specifying the way in which the money is to be paid out. If part of the funds are to be used for buildings or other improvements, that part of the funds may be held in trust until all the costs are known. The association completes the final loan-closing steps. This involves carrying out the requirements specified in the remittance statement, having the applicants sign the note and mortgage, and recording the mortgage in the county recorder's office.

Servicing of land bank loans is carried out by the bank and the association. Checking on payment of real estate taxes and keeping insurance on buildings in force is done by the association. Services involving partial releases and the like can be handled by the bank but usually are delegated to the association. Delinquency problems are usually handled by the association, with the bank being directly involved only in the more difficult cases.

As shown in Chapter 20, the FLBs and their affiliated associations have been major farm mortgage lenders for several decades. They have grown considerably both in volume of loans and in relative importance in the farm mortgage field, particularly in recent years. The proportion of the farm mortgage debt held by the FLBs increased from 15 percent January 1, 1955, to 25 percent January 1, 1972. Practically all of this increase was at the expense of life insurance companies, the primary competitors of the land banks.

Interest Rates and Dividends. The policy in setting interest rates is to provide credit at the lowest reasonable cost consistent with sound business, taking into account the cost of money, necessary reserves and expenses, capital requirements, and services provided to borrowers. Interest rates are determined by the bank board, subject to approval of the FCA. The following types of interest rate programs may be employed: (1) fixed rates, the rate specified in the note being the maximum rate chargeable during the period of the loan; (2) variable rates, permitting rates charged on outstanding loan balances to be changed during the period of the loan to conform with the policy set forth above; (3) fixed interest spread, where the interest rate charged on outstanding loan balances is the cost of money to the bank plus a percentage as necessary to conform with the stated policy; and (4) differential rates, whereby different rates are established for different classes of loans based on type, purpose, amount, or quality of loan, or any combination of these factors.

Formerly land banks used only the fixed-rate plan, so interest on a rapidly diminishing number of outstanding FLB loans is still calculated on this basis. However, all the FLBs now use the variable rate plan in making loans.

Since the Farm Credit Act specifies that the FLBs are federally chartered instrumentalities of the government, they are not considered subject to state usury laws limiting the rate of interest that may be charged. This exemption is a distinct advantage when, during periods of unusually high interest rates, regular commercial lenders may be restricted by state usury laws.

Dividends may be paid by the land banks when earnings exceed the cost of money, operating expenses, and reserve and capital requirements. The dividends are paid on stock and participation certificates owned by borrowers. The rates may be varied for different classes and issues of these instruments, depending on the comparative contribution of the holders to the earnings of the bank.

Taxation. Federal Land Banks and FLBAs are not subject to taxation, except for taxes on real estate that they own. As specified in the Farm Credit Act of 1971, they ". . . shall be exempt from Federal, State, municipal, and local taxation, except taxes on real estate held. . . . The . . . notes, bonds, debentures and other obligations issued by the banks and associations . . . and the income therefrom shall be exempt from all Federal, State, municipal, and local taxation, other than Federal income tax liability of the holder thereof. . . ."

As indicated in Chapter 22, the FLBs feel these tax exemptions are justified since part of the FLBAs include some uneconomical lending areas, and since the land banks are required by law to set aside a substantial proportion of their earnings as reserves until they equal 150 percent of the outstanding capital stock of the bank. A different point of view is presented by life insurance company farm lenders, historically the primary competitors of the land banks. The insurance companies feel the tax exemptions give the land banks an interest rate advantage of about one-half percentage point. In other words, with the same contract rates, the net after-tax rate of return to insurance companies would be about one-half percentage point lower than the rate realized by the land banks.

PRODUCTION CREDIT SYSTEM. The Production Credit System comprises that part of the Farm Credit System through which farmers and other eligible applicants obtain short-term and intermediate-term loans. The 12 FICBs and the PCAs are the system's intermediaries.

Federal Intermediate Credit Banks. Federal Intermediate Credit Banks are "federally chartered instrumentalities of the United States," continued under the Farm Credit Act of 1971 as permanent institutions similar to the land banks. They are primarily "wholesalers" of credit, and as such, discount loans for and make loans to the PCAs, which are their primary local outlets for loan funds. The FICBs also discount agricultural loans for other financing institutions as outlined below.

Policies of the credit banks are determined by the respective District Farm Credit Boards. The board is authorized by law, subject to supervision of the FCA, to exercise all such powers as are necessary in conducting the business of the bank. A staff employed by the board manages and operates the bank.

The FICBs have certain responsibilities in supervision of the PCAs in their respective districts. They have the responsibility for developing credit policies, procedures, and standards, and for making certain that these are carried out by the associations. The credit banks also perform delegated supervisory functions for the FCA.

Production Credit Associations. Each PCA is a "federally chartered instrumentality of the United States," the same as the credit banks. Members of the PCA with voting stock elect a board of directors from among its members, each member having one vote. This board establishes policies of the association and employs a staff to conduct its affairs.

Most PCAs serve fairly large areas, including several counties and one or more trade centers. Some associations cover a whole state. Generally, territories do not overlap, although in some instances associations financing specialized or large operations duplicate other association territories. As one means of making their services more readily accessible, many associations have established field or branch offices. Most of these are operated on a full-time basis, but some may be serviced only 1 or 2 days each week. In some cases the field and branch offices are housed with the FLBA, in which case the FLBA manager may serve as the PCA field representative.

Other Financing Institutions. The FICBs may make loans to and discount agricultural paper for commercial banks and other financing institutions (not members of the Farm Credit System) that meet specified requirements. These lenders are commonly referred to as "other financing institutions," or OFIs. The OFIs are one feature that distinguishes the Production Credit System from the Land Bank System because there are no comparable provisions which permit the FLBs to buy or discount farm loans made by other lenders.

Commercial banks and other institutions applying for discount privileges must (1) prove a continuing need for such discounts in order to maintain a volume of agricultural loans at least equal to the past 3-year average, (2) prove that the need for discounting is not the result of denial of loan funds by customary sources, (3) establish that they have a capital structure and actual or potential loan volume to permit a reasonably efficient lending operation, and (4) establish that they are capable of extending and administering on a sound basis the volume of lending anticipated. In addition, commercial banks or agricultural credit corporations affiliated with a commercial bank must (1) have an agricultural loan volume equal to at least 25 percent of total loans or if less than 25 percent, prove that it is making a special effort to serve the credit needs of its rural area; (2) have a loan:deposit ratio of at least 60 percent at the seasonal peak; and (3) establish that participation with PCAs (outlined subsequently) is either unavailable or would not be of assistance. Further provisions apply to agricultural credit corporations, which are not affiliated with a commercial bank.

These provisions appear to be major hurdles. Only a small number of OFIs discount with the FICBs. As shown in Chapter 20, the volume of OFI loans discounted with FICBs January 1, 1972, comprised only 0.7 percent of the nonreal-estate debt outstanding. Moreover, this proportion has declined somewhat over the past two decades.

Ownership. The FICBs, organized and owned for many years by the
federal government, are now owned by the PCAs through purchases of stock and participation certificates issued by the bank.
Each PCA is owned by current and former borrowers who hold stock
or participation certificates issued by the association. With proper
stockholder approval, a PCA may also raise capital by selling preferred
stock to investors.

Each PCA borrower is required to own stock or participation
certificates in the association equal to 5 percent of the loan and may
be required to own as much as 10 percent. In contrast to FLB loans
where equity issues are retired when the loan is paid, PCA stock and
certificates are not retired upon payment of the loan since doing
so might weaken the capital structure of the system at times, considering the short term and intermediate term of loans made. Farmers and
producers or harvesters of aquatic products, who are current borrowers, hold voting stock, which entitles each borrower to one vote in
affairs of the association. Other borrowers and noncurrent borrowers
hold nonvoting stock or participation certificates, so they have no
voice in affairs of the association.

In addition to capital raised by the sale of stock and participation certificates, FICBs and PCAs have accumulated substantial
amounts of surplus and reserves. Part of these funds are earnings
from the use of government capital, which were left in the banks and
associations when the government capital was retired.

Loan Funds. Federal Intermediate Credit Banks obtain the major
part of their loan funds from the sale of debentures in the national financial market. These debenture bonds are similar to
bonds sold by FLBs in that they are fully collateralized. However,
there are some differences in other respects. One difference is in term
of years; FLB bonds tend to have longer terms, although some bonds
are issued with terms of 1 year or less. Most FICB debentures have a
term of 9 months, however, they have been issued with maturities up
to 3½ years and may be for longer periods. Federal Land Bank bonds
usually have an interest rate coupon and may be offered at par, at a
discount, or at a premium, depending on the market. When FICB
debentures have a maturity of no more than 9 months, they merely
carry a stated rate of interest, are sold at par, and at maturity the
principal is paid with accrued interest. The present policy is for the
FICBs to issue debentures so that about 75 percent will have a 9-
month maturity and about 25 percent will have intermediate maturity.

The FICB debentures are the joint obligation of the 12 banks,
and issues are subject to approval by the governor, who reports the
financing plans to the treasury. Procedures in planning sales of
debentures are similar to those outlined above for FLB bonds. Pro-

visions for FICBs to borrow from each other, other banks of the system, and from other financial institutions are the same as for FLBs. Debentures issued, plus long-term notes and other similar obligations, may not exceed 20 times the capital and surplus of the banks.

Production Credit Associations obtain the major part of their loan funds by discounting borrowers' notes with or borrowing from the FICB in the district.

PCA Loans. Loans obtained through the Production Credit System are made by the PCA. The PCA then uses the borrowers' notes and mortgages as collateral to obtain funds from the FICB of the district. Production Credit Associations with adequate capital of their own may make loans with such funds that are pledged to the FICB as additional collateral.

This arrangement in making loans constitutes a major difference compared with the Land Bank System. Whereas FLB loans run directly from the bank to the borrower, Production Credit System loans generally are made outright by the PCA, which carries all the primary risk. The 1971 Farm Credit Act provides, however, that FICBs may enter into participation agreements with PCAs, and PCAs may enter into participation agreements with each other in making and servicing loans. In all districts, the PCAs have adopted either participation or mutual loss-sharing loan plans. These provisions facilitate handling large loans and spreading risk.

Production Credit Associations may make loans to (1) farmers, including certain partnerships, corporations, and other legal entities engaged primarily in farming; (2) producers or harvesters of aquatic products; (3) persons and businesses furnishing farm-related services (custom-type services performed on-farm for farmers); and (4) owners of rural homes. It will be recognized that these are the same groups financed by the FLBs except for the addition of producers and harvesters of aquatic products.

Production Credit Associations may make loans to farmers and to producers or harvesters of aquatic products for any purpose. Operating loans usually are made with maturities coinciding with the normal marketing season for the enterprise being financed. Intermediate-term loans are amortized over the useful life of items financed not exceeding a period of 7 years. However, *special* intermediate-term loans, made only to *farmers* under certain circumstances, may provide for a balloon payment at the end of the 7-year term, realizing that forebearance or extension may be necessary at that time. These loans are intended primarily to finance items with a useful life exceeding 7 years.

Production Credit Associations may make loans to farm-related businesses for working capital, equipment, and operating needs related to the custom-type services performed on-farm for farmers.

Terms and repayment provisions for operating and regular intermediate-term loans are similar to those outlined in the preceding paragraph.

Loans made by PCAs to eligible rural residents may be for buying or building a single-family, moderate-priced dwelling, including a mobile home, but are largely for modernization and repair, due to the statutory limitation on the term of the loan to 7 years. The limitations on FLB lending in this category also apply to the PCAs.

Both secured and unsecured loans are made by PCAs. Normally, primary security taken consists of first liens on personal property and crops. While it is not intended that PCAs ordinarily make first-mortgage real estate loans to farmers, real estate or other security may be taken when deemed necessary and in accordance with district policy.

Recovery value is the basis used by PCAs in determining the worth of personal property and crops taken as security. Appraised value, as defined in the discussion of FLB loans, is used when real estate is the primary security. Recovery value is defined as the amount that the lender should be able to realize from the sale of the property on reasonable terms after deducting maintenance and selling costs and any prior liens and encumbrances.

As shown in Chapter 20, the PCAs have grown both in volume of loans and in relative importance in the nonreal-estate loan field. The proportion of nonreal-estate loans held by PCAs increased from 12 percent on January 1, 1960, to 18 percent January 1, 1972. During this same period the percent of nonreal-estate loans held by commercial banks, the major competitors of PCAs, declined from 42 percent to 38 percent.

PCA-Commercial Bank Participation. The Farm Credit Act of 1971 provides that PCAs may, with proper approval, participate in loans with local commercial banks and other lenders. Participation agreements with commercial banks must include certain provisions to assure that the banks do not substantially shift their lending away from agriculture. Other lenders must provide evidence of financial responsibility and capability to service and control loans as prerequisites for PCA participation.

The objective in providing for PCA participation is to enable commercial banks and other lenders who are unable to meet the entire credit needs of some of their customers to provide for these needs locally.

Interest Rates, Fees, and Dividends. The policy in setting PCA interest rates is the same as for FLB loans. Production Credit Associations also may choose among the four interest rate programs outlined above. Many associations use the "fixed-interest spread" program, adding the costs of operating the association and requirements for reserves to the cost of money from the FICB.

Interest rates vary somewhat among PCAs primarily because of differences in operating expenses that, in turn, depend to a large degree upon the size and the volume of loans made.

Some PCAs also charge moderate loan service fees, the amount of which depends upon local conditions and the size of the loan made. These fees are charged to help meet the expenses incurred by the association in making loans, such as visits to farms and searching lien records.

Interest and discount rates charged the PCAs and OFIs by the FICBs depend to a large degree upon the rates the banks have to pay on debentures sold. Rates vary a little among FICBs, due largely to differences in operating costs that must be added to the cost of money.

The FICBs and PCAs may, with proper approval, pay dividends on their capital stock and participation certificates when earnings exceed the cost of money, operating expenses, and reserve and capital requirements. The rate of dividends may vary among different classes and issues of stock and participation certificates, depending on the relative contributions of the holders to earnings.

Taxation. The FICBs are exempt from taxation except for taxes on real estate, the same as the FLBs. The Farm Credit Act of 1971 provides that they ". . . shall be exempt from Federal, State, municipal, and local taxation except taxes on real estate held. . . . The . . . notes, bonds, debentures, and other obligations issued by the banks . . . and the income therefrom shall be exempt from all Federal, State, municipal, and local taxation, other than Federal income tax liability of the holder thereof. . . ."

Real and tangible personal property owned by a PCA is subject to taxation. Each PCA is also subject to income taxes on the same basis as any other corporation.

BANKS FOR COOPERATIVES. The 13 Banks for Cooperatives—12 district banks and the Central Bank located in Denver, Colorado—comprise that part of the Farm Credit System through which farmers can obtain credit for their cooperatives. The Banks for Cooperatives are "federally chartered instrumentalities of the United States," continued under the Farm Credit Act of 1971 as permanent institutions similar to the other banks of the system.

Policies of each district bank are determined by the respective District Farm Credit Boards. The Central Bank for Cooperatives has its own board of directors, one elected by each of the 12 Farm Credit District Boards and a director-at-large, appointed by the governor. The directors of each bank employ a staff to carry on the affairs of the bank.

The Central Bank for Cooperatives does not have a counterpart in the Land Bank and Production Credit Systems. Its primary function is to participate with the district banks in financing large loans.

Ownership. The Banks for Cooperatives, organized and largely owned for many years by the federal government, are now owned by current and former borrowing cooperatives. In general, cooperatives borrowing from a Bank for Cooperatives are required to purchase voting stock in the bank in relationship to interest paid on their loans. Additional amounts of voting stock are issued to borrowers at the end of each year in distribution of patronage refunds. The stock thus acquired has voting rights as long as the cooperative continues as an eligible borrower, each borrower being entitled to one vote. Capital may also be raised by sale of nonvoting stock to investors.

In addition to capital acquired by issuance of stock, the Banks for Cooperatives have accumulated substantial amounts of surplus and reserves. A part of these funds are earnings on government capital accumulated until 1955 that were left in the banks when the government capital was retired.

Loan Funds. Banks for Cooperatives obtain the major part of their loan funds from sale of debentures in the national financial market. These are the joint obligations of all Banks for Cooperatives. Provisions for Banks for Cooperatives to borrow from each other, other banks of the system, and from other financial institutions are the same as for the FLBs and FICBs.

Debentures sold by Banks for Cooperatives are similar to debentures sold by FICBs. They usually have a term of 6 months to 3 years. Those with a term of 1 year or longer bear coupons, while those for shorter periods carry a stated rate of interest, are sold at par, and at maturity both the principal and accrued interest are paid to the investor.

Loans. Banks for Cooperatives make loans to eligible cooperatives that, in general terms, are farmer cooperatives and cooperatives composed of producers and harvesters of aquatic products. They also participate with commercial banks and other financial institutions in extending credit to eligible cooperative associations.

Banks for Cooperatives provide credit to meet all the needs of a cooperative to establish and maintain a modern, efficient operation of the size required to carry on the business of its members. Included is credit to buy, construct, or expand plant sites, buildings, and equipment, and to provide capital for operating the business. In addition, the banks provide credit for inventories of farm supply and service cooperatives and for storing and marketing commodities of farm marketing cooperatives. (Thus, in passing, it may be noted that the Banks for Cooperatives alone provide a credit service for cooperatives comparable to that which the FLBs and the FICBs combined provide for individual farmers through the local credit associations.) Inventory loans permit the cooperative to extend credit to members on supplies purchased. Commodity loans assist cooperatives in making immediate payments to members on commodities delivered to the association. Loans generally are secured by a first lien on items involved in the loan or on other acceptable collateral.

Repayment plans are adapted to the type and requirements of the cooperative financed. Loans to finance commodities in storage generally are repaid from sales proceeds of the collateral. Inventory loans are repaid when the supplies are sold, or when payment is received. Seasonal or short-term operating loans are payable during the year. Term loans to finance plant sites, buildings, and equipment generally are repaid in installments over a period of years, the period varying according to the type of collateral involved and the needs of the borrower. There is no legal limitation as to a maximum repayment period.

The same general type of information is needed in making a loan to a cooperative as in making a loan to an individual. However, in place of dealing with the farmer and his wife, the bank in making a loan to a cooperative deals with a corporation that operates under policies established by a board of directors elected by the members. In considering an application for a loan, the articles or certificate of incorporation, with all amendments thereto, certified by the secretary of state must be considered to make sure the cooperative is a legal entity. The bylaws also are considered. Among other things they provide a basis for determining the eligibility of the cooperative to borrow from the bank. Audit reports, balance sheets, and operating statements for recent years are analyzed to determine the trend and present financial status of the cooperative.

This type of information is considered in making new loans. Where the cooperative has been doing business with the bank, the bank already has much of this information either from direct contact or from reports in the files. In such cases, where the cooperative has developed a good credit rating, the credit transaction is relatively simple and can be handled with dispatch.

Interest Rates and Dividends. The policy in setting interest rates by the Banks for Cooperatives is the same as for other banks of the system. Rates are established by the Board of Directors of the bank, with the approval of the FCA. Rates charged by a bank vary somewhat, depending on the type and term of loan involved. The level of rates varies slightly among districts due to differences in cost of operation and earnings objectives.

Dividends not exceeding 8 percent per annum may be paid only on nonvoting investment stock. Dividends are noncumulative and may be paid only out of current earnings.

Taxation. Banks for Cooperatives are not exempt from income taxes, except when government capital is invested therein. Tax returns are filed like any other corporation operating on a cooperative basis. Banks for Cooperatives debentures and the income derived therefrom are exempt from state, municipal, and local taxation, except surtaxes, and estate, inheritance, and gift taxes. Interest on such obligations are subject to federal income taxes in the hands of the holder. Real and tangible personal property are subject to federal, state, territorial, and local taxation to the same extent that similar property is taxed.

QUESTIONS AND PROBLEMS

1. Outline the organization of the Farm Credit System.
2. Explain the ownership and control of each type of bank and association of the Farm Credit System. Do all those having a part in ownership have a voice in control? Explain.
3. What is the function of the Farm Credit Administration?
4. What is the function of the various banks and associations of the Farm Credit System?
5. What is the primary source of loan funds for the banks and associations?
6. What type of loans are made by the Federal Land Bank System? The Production Credit System? The Banks for Cooperatives?
7. Compile a list of Farm Credit System bonds and debentures that are outstanding. A good source is a current issue of the *Federal Reserve Bulletin*. Several financial newspapers also list these items. Classify the issues by length of term and then compare the term of the issues with the term of loans funded.
8. Outline the facilities and procedures that have been provided within the Farm Credit System for handling different types of large loans and for spreading the risk involved in extension of credit.
9. Explain what avenues have been provided whereby banks and associations of the system may aid in financing farmers through other lenders. What is your appraisal of these provisions?
10. What is the tax status of the banks and associations? How does their tax status affect their competitive position as lenders?
11. Commercial banks make all types of loans to farmers and cooperatives as well as to other sectors of the economy. Why, then,

should there be three types of banks in the Farm Credit System? Do you think it would be more efficient if the three types were consolidated into one?

12. The proportion of farm mortgage loans made by the FLBs has increased substantially in recent years, while the proportion made by insurance companies has declined. Some informed individuals feel that with the present tax status the land banks will drive the insurance companies out of the farm loan field. Do you think this would be desirable?

REFERENCES

Evans, Carson D. *An Analysis of Successful and Unsuccessful Farm Loans in South Dakota.* ERS, USDA, Feb. 1971.

"Farm Credit Administration-Administrative Provisions: Farm Credit System." *Federal Register,* vol. 37, no. 110, June 7, 1972.

Farm Credit Administration. *Annual Reports.*

————. *Publications on the Farm Credit System,* Circular A-29.

Federal Reserve Bank of Chicago. "The Farm Credit System." *Business Conditions,* Sept. 1972.

Herr, William McD. *New Borrowers in the Farmers Home Administration Operating Loan Program Compared with New Borrowers Obtaining Loans from Banks and Production Credit Associations.* ERS, USDA, Agr. Econ. Rept. 160, May 1969.

House of Representatives. *Farm Credit Act of 1971.*

Penson, John B., Jr., and Warren, Forest G. *Federal Land Bank Farm-Mortgage Loans: A Statistical Study of Loans Outstanding, September 30, 1966,* USDA, ERS-438, July 1970.

CHAPTER 25: **FARMERS HOME ADMINISTRATION**

THE FARMERS' CAMPAIGN for credit, extending from colonial time, called for low cost direct loans from the government. In response, the Farm Credit System was sponsored by the government. However, the demand for direct loans was not ignored. Government credit assistance was provided from time to time through temporary government agencies to meet emergency credit needs. The government also established the Farmers Home Administration (known formerly as the Farm Security Administration and, initially, as the Resettlement Administration) to help beginning farmers and other farmers with limited resources who were unable to obtain adequate credit from commercial lenders, including the Farm Credit System. In recent years the government has broadened the lending authority of the Farmers Home Administration to include the entire rural community.

The Farmers Home Administration (FHA) should not be confused with the Federal Housing Administration, also designated FHA. It is important to note, also, that there is no direct connection between the Farmers Home Administration and the Farm Credit System discussed in the preceding chapter.

ORGANIZATION. The organization of the Farmers Home Administration, an agency in the United States Department of Agriculture, is portrayed in Figure 25.1. The national office, under direction of an administrator, determines policies within the framework of laws established by Congress, issues procedures, controls budgets, and directs and gives technical training to field staffs. The national finance office handles the fiscal, business management, and accounting services. The state offices, each under a state director, serve all 50 states.

The state director has been delegated broad authority and responsibility by the administrator to carry out the loan program in his state. He and his staff direct and train county office staffs, analyze loan programs, and administer the budgets allotted to his state for loans and administrative expenses. He also approves certain types of loans, authority for which is not delegated to county supervisors. In most states the state director appoints selected leading farmers and businessmen interested in farmers' problems to a state advisory com-

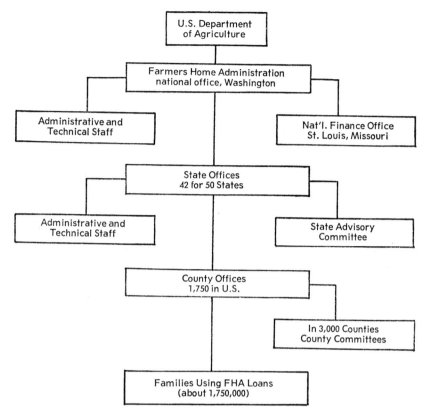

FIG. *25.1—Organization chart of the Farmers Home Administration. (Courtesy of Farmers Home Administration.)*

mittee. From time to time he consults with this committee on the credit needs in the state and on the adapting of national policies to state problems.

The 1,750 county offices strategically located throughout the country usually are in county seat towns, with some offices serving more than one county. All applications for loans are made through these county offices. The county supervisor in charge of each county office helps farm families prepare farm and home plans, approves most loans, gives technical advice to borrowers during on-the-farm visits, and accepts payments from borrowers. He also gives technical assistance, long-range development planning assistance, and general supervision in connection with other types of loans.

A Farmers Home Administration Committee, consisting of three members, is appointed by the state director for each county or county office area. At least two members of the committee must be farmers.

The third member may be a local businessman familiar with local farmers and their needs. These committees determine the eligibility of applicants, certify the value of farms where real estate loans are being made, review borrowers' progress, and make recommendations concerning certain loan approval and loan servicing actions.

OBJECTIVES. The lending authority of the Farmers Home Administration as it exists today involves two principal objectives, both of which are supplementary to the services of commercial lenders. The first objective is to strengthen the economic position of individual family farmers. Providing supervised credit to individual farmers who are unable to obtain adequate credit from commercial lenders at reasonable rates and terms continues as a major function of the agency. This objective includes extension of credit to eligible farmers for those things that will improve the level of agricultural income and living standards. We are primarily concerned with this objective in this chapter.

The second principal objective of FHA is to improve rural communities, defined as towns with as many as 50,000 people for certain business and industrial loans, but restricted to towns of not more than 10,000 for farm, housing, and certain community service loans. This objective has evolved in recent years as the scope of United States Department of Agriculture activities has broadened to include the entire rural community. Lending authority includes extension of credit and accompanying counsel and supervision for items such as business and industrial development, community facilities, rural housing (including individual dwellings, rental or cooperative units, and farm labor housing), resource conservation and development, rural community water and waste disposal systems, watershed protection, and development of recreation areas.

SOURCE OF LOAN FUNDS. Money that FHA lends comes from three sources:

1. A direct loan account provided by Congress. Collections of principal and interest on loans from this account are returned to the account and used for future loans. The amount that may be loaned each year is established by Congress and the Office of Management and Budget. Congressional appropriations constitute a minor source of loan funds at the present time.
2. Revolving funds for agriculture, emergency, housing, and business and industrial loans. These funds, initially established by Congress, are funded by the sale of "Farmers Home Insured Notes" in

the financial market; that is, as loans are made, the borrower's notes, fully insured by the FHA, are sold to investors, thereby providing funds for other loans. Principal and interest on the loans are paid to FHA and deposited in the appropriate revolving account, thereby providing funds for annual principal and interest payments to holders of the notes. The amount of loans that may be made from each of the revolving funds is specified by the Office of Management and Budget. Currently, practically all the funds loaned by FHA come from this source, but it is anticipated that when the guaranteed loan program, authorized by the Consolidated Farm and Rural Development Act of 1972, is developed and operating, it will provide a substantial part of the loan funds.

3. Funds furnished by commercial banks and other lenders. As indicated under (2), the 1972 act provides for a guaranteed loan program similar to that of the Federal Housing Administration, whereby certain business and industrial loans made by commercial lenders may be guaranteed by FHA up to 90 percent of the amount of the loan. Terms of the loan are negotiated by the borrower and the lender, and principal and interest payments are made directly to the lender.

In addition to loan funds, FHA has a certain amount of grant funds, or funds that may be used for making grants. Grant funds are appropriated annually by Congress.

SPECIAL FEATURES OF FHA LOANS. In addition to the features outlined in the preceding section, FHA financing has a number of other special features. The FHA is authorized by law to make loans only to those who are unable to obtain adequate credit from other sources on reasonable terms. Moreover, FHA borrowers agree to obtain their credit from other lenders when they reach or regain a position where they can do so. Every year thousands of borrowers "graduate" to other lenders. The FHA credit program is designed to supplement rather than compete with other sources of credit. One of its real values lies in the fact that it operates in all sections of the country, providing a dependable source of loans to qualified borrowers who have good character and experience but insufficient assets to qualify for adequate credit from commercial sources.

The FHA may make larger loans, relative to value of security, than commercial lenders. With farm ownership loans, for example, it may lend up to 100 percent of the value of the farm as determined by appraisers. This provision is essential to achieving the main objective of the agency—that of helping farmers and others in rural areas with limited means become established in business, or if already established, to enlarge, reorganize, or develop and improve their operations to enable them to continue on a sound basis. Thus FHA loans are made with the expectation that they will be repaid out of income to be produced rather than on the basis of the amount of security the borrower can provide. However, loans are secured by liens on real estate, livestock, machinery, crops, and other assets, depending upon the type of loan.

As one means of reducing the risk involved and to help borrowers become established on a sound basis as quickly as possible, credit extended by FHA is backed with advice and technical assistance. For example, farm ownership borrowers receive planning and supervisory assistance through a systematic five-step process. The county supervisor is primarily responsible for furnishing this advice and assistance.

First, the county supervisor helps the borrower and his wife develop a *long-time plan* showing the system of farming to be followed and the major adjustments and improvements to be put into effect on the farm and in the home over a period of years. They then develop an *annual* farm and home plan to guide the year's operations and to facilitate progress in achieving the long-time plan. Both the annual and long-time plans take into consideration the problems, needs, and resources of the family and the farm.

Second, the county supervisor periodically visits the farm during the year to provide the family with technical advice and encouragement in carrying out the adjustments, improvements, and practices laid out in the farm and home plans.

Third, the county supervisor assists the family in carrying out a good system of record keeping to help evaluate management practices and financial progress.

Fourth, at the end of the year he assists the family in analyzing the outcome of their farm and home operations. Strong and weak points are pointed out and suggestions made for improvement.

Fifth, the county supervisor assists the family in developing an annual farm and home plan for the new year. The new annual plan is based on the results of the past years' farm operations, points brought out in the year-end analysis, and the resources and marketing prospects.

Thus the FHA's supervised credit program consists of providing adequate credit and assisting the borrowers to make effective use of the credit.

Interest rates charged borrowers on loans made from the direct loan account and from the revolving funds are somewhat lower than prevailing market rates. This may also be the case with guaranteed loans made under the Consolidated Farm and Rural Development Act of 1972. In other words, the FHA provides interest supplements on these loans to reduce the interest rate charged borrowers. Since rates charged borrowers on the various types of loans are not changed very often, the amount of the reduction varies from time to time, depending on the level of interest rates in the financial markets. When rates are high, FHA interest supplements are relatively large, and vice versa. Interest supplements also vary from one type of loan to another. For example, the rate charged on farm ownership loans is 5 percent while the rate on emergency loans is 1 percent.

TYPES OF FHA LOANS. The FHA makes many different types of loans. Or, put another way, the FHA makes loans under a large number of authorizations. Some of the authorizations stem from specific legislation pertaining to FHA. For example, authorization to make farm ownership loans emanates from the Consolidated Farm and Rural Development Act of 1972, as amended, and earlier from the Farmers Home Administration Act of 1946. Other authorizations are derived from legislation that is broader in scope. For example, rural housing loans are made under provisions of Title V of the Housing Act of 1949. Since authorizations emanate from a number of different legislative acts passed by Congress over a period of years, some overlapping has occurred. This complicates classification and explanation of FHA loans. However, it is of minor significance in operations of the agency since loans can simply be made under the authority that is most convenient or appropriate.

Loans made by the FHA can be classified in five general groups. The major types of loans (and grants) in each group are indicated by the following outline.

1. Individual operating loans
   a. Farm operating loans
   b. Emergency credit loans
2. Individual real estate loans
   a. Farm ownership loans
   b. Soil and water loans
   c. Recreation loans
3. Rural housing loans
   a. Owner occupancy housing loans
   b. Rental housing loans
   c. Labor housing loans and grants
   d. Site loans
   e. Technical assistance grants
4. Rural development loans
   a. Loans to rural businesses
   b. Industrial development loans

    c. Pollution abatement grants
    d. Industrial development grants
    e. Planning grants
5. Community service loans
    a. Association loans
    b. Watershed loans
    c. Flood prevention loans
    d. Resource conservation and development loans
    e. Water system loans and grants
    f. Waste disposal system loans and grants
    g. Community facility loans and grants

All types of loans made by the FHA have a bearing on agriculture, particularly since they are made in rural areas. However, some of them have a direct bearing since they are made to farmers, to groups of farmers, or to groups including farmers. These types of loans are considered in the following sections.

Farm Operating Loans. Operating loans are made primarily to enable farmers to obtain chattel resources essential to successful farm operation. They are made largely to help family-type farmers improve the use of their land and labor resources by making needed changes in their farming systems and by adopting improved farm practices. Funds may be advanced to pay for other farm and home operating needs, to make minor real estate improvements, and to refinance chattel debts.

To qualify for an operating loan a farmer must have a *good* character rating. To go with the supplementary training and supervision provided by FHA, he must have the necessary experience, training, and managerial ability to operate a family-type farm. The income from his farming operations plus income from other sources must be sufficient to support his family and repay the loan. Both owners and tenants are eligible for these loans.

The size of operating loans depends upon the system of farming to be followed and the actual needs of the applicant, Loans range from a few thousand dollars up to $50,000. A borrower's total outstanding indebtedness for operating loans may not exceed $50,000.

The repayment period for operating loans depends upon the use made of the funds. Loan funds advanced to meet operating expenses during a crop year generally will be repaid when that year's income is received. Funds loaned to buy breeding livestock and equipment are repaid over a period of years. The repayment schedule for these loans is based on income available after reasonable expenses are met, and consideration is given to making payments on the borrower's other debts. These livestock and equipment loans qualify as intermediate-term credit since the repayment period can be extended up to 7 years. Where conditions warrant, deferments also can be granted, extending the period to a maximum of 12 years.

A cardinal principle in the operating loan program is that the farm and home plan must reflect enough income from the farm and other sources to provide an adequate living for the farm family, meet farm operating expenses, and enable the family to repay their debts and have a reasonable reserve to meet unforeseen emergencies.

Farm Ownership Loans. Farm ownership loans are for the purpose of helping farm families become successfully established on owner-operated farms. The standards of character, ability, and earning capacity required for operating loans are also applicable here.

Farm ownership loans may be used for a wide range of items:

1. Purchase and enlargement of farms
2. Development and improvement of farmland
3. Carrying out basic land treatment practices such as liming, fertilizing, and seeding
4. Construction, improvement, and repair of farm buildings and of the farm home
5. Drilling wells and otherwise improving water supply systems for home use, livestock, and irrigation
6. Providing drainage systems
7. Establishing and improving farm forests, including clearing and preparing land for planting, buying seed or seedlings, and establishing approved forestry practices
8. Providing facilities to produce fish under controlled conditions
9. Financing recreational enterprises that will supplement farm income, including purchase and development of land, construction of buildings and other facilities, and purchase of equipment. Recreational enterprises that may be financed on family farms include camping grounds, swimming facilities, tennis courts, riding stables, vacation cottages, lakes and ponds for boating, nature trails, and picnic grounds.
10. Refinancing debts

A unique feature of the farm ownership program is the provision allowing direct or insured loans up to the value of the farm as determined by trained appraisers of the FHA. However, a farm ownership loan may not exceed the appraised value of the farm and other security less any debts against the property.

A farm ownership loan, plus any other debts against the security, may not exceed $100,000. The maximum term is 40 years. When justified, the first payment of interest and principal on loans for approved forestry purposes may be deferred for up to 15 years. Loans are secured by a mortgage on the farm, including chattels and other suitable security. Just as with operating loans, supervision and assistance is provided by the FHA to help assure success of the loan.

Loan payments are due on January 1 each year. Borrowers are encouraged to build a reserve fund in years of good income to help keep the loan in good standing during low income years. This reserve fund plan has entirely replaced the variable payment plan formerly used.

The variable payment plan provided for payments to be based upon the amount of net cash income available after necessary living expenses were deducted. It was used on an optional basis for a period of years but was discontinued for a number of reasons. Among other things, it was hard to administer, and a fully satisfactory basis could seldom be determined for computing payments that should be made.

Housing Loans. Loans for housing may be made to farmers for owner occupancy and also for occupancy by tenants and employees. The farmer must have sufficient income to pay operating and living expenses and to meet principal and interest payments on debts, including the proposed housing loan. Funds may be used to finance building sites and to construct adequate economically designed homes and essential farm improvements. In addition to major construction, funds are available to modernize homes—add bathrooms, central heating, modern kitchens, and other home improvements—as well as to enlarge or remodel farm service buildings and related facilities such as yard fences and driveways. The maximum term of these loans is 33 years. Loans generally are secured by a mortgage on real estate or a lien on other suitable property.

The FHA also makes a number of other types of housing loans. Loans are made to residents in rural areas and communities with populations of up to 10,000 people. Conditions and terms of these loans are similar to those for farmers. Loans and grants are also made to individuals, partnerships, corporations (including municipal corporations and other corporate agencies of state or local governments), trusts, and associations for rental housing in rural communities. Applicants must demonstrate ability to incur and repay the loan, give adequate security, and have a plan for maintaining and operating the housing for rental purposes. The maximum term of these loans is 50 years or the life expectancy of the project, whichever is less.

Emergency Loans. Emergency loans are made by the FHA in designated areas where farmers and ranchers have suffered substantial production or housing losses and are temporarily unable to obtain needed credit from other sources. An area is designated eligible for emergency credit by the president or the secretary of agriculture when it is determined that a production disaster, such as a drouth or flood, creates in the area a widespread need for agricultural credit that cannot be met from private and cooperative lenders or the regular FHA lending program. Emergency loans may also be made to eligible farmers outside designated disaster areas.

Loans may be made for the purchase of feed, seed, fertilizer, replacement equipment, and livestock; for other essential farm and home operating expenses; and for the replacement or repair of housing, buildings, fences, and drainage and irrigation systems damaged or destroyed by a disaster. Loans may also be made for refinancing existing debts.

Repayment schedules for emergency loans depend upon the purposes for which funds are advanced and upon the estimated income of the applicant. For example, loans for crop production are usually scheduled for repayment when income from the crops is normally received. Loans for replacement of livestock and equipment are repayable over periods of 1 to 5 years, while loans for the repair of buildings and other improvements to real estate are usually repayable over periods of 1 to 10 years.

Recreation Loans. The FHA may finance recreational enterprises as a part of operating and farm ownership loans. The motivating thrust behind this loan authorization is to shift unneeded and marginal cropland into other more useful and more profitable purposes and to provide rural communities with needed recreation facilities. Loans may also be made to individual farmers to develop marshes and swamps into profitable wildlife hunting areas; to dam creeks and to enlarge ponds and small lakes into fishing and swimming facilities; and to transform woodlands into profitable campsites.

Association Loans. The FHA makes loans to various types of nonprofit associations of farmers that facilitate individual farm operations. For example, loans are made to grazing associations to purchase land; to secure grazing rights and leases; to construct necessary facilities; for water development; and for land and pasture improvement, including brush removal and necessary conservation programs. Shifting land and water resources to better uses, including the development of recreational areas and game and wildlife facilities, may also qualify for loans. The term of the loan may not exceed 40 years.

Loans may also be made to cooperatives to provide services, supplies, or facilities not otherwise available. These loans are scheduled for repayment over a period not to exceed 30 years.

Watershed Loans. Local organizations that are protecting and developing land and water resources in small watersheds can obtain loans from the FHA to help finance the projects. Eligible local organizations include soil conservation districts, irrigation districts, drainage districts, flood prevention or control districts, and similar organizations.

Loan funds may be used to install, repair, or improve facilities; store and convey irrigation water to farms; drain farm areas; stabilize annual stream flow; store water for such purposes as municipal water supply, recreation, fish and wildlife improvement, pollution abatement, and for similar purposes. Only watershed projects approved by the Soil Conservation Service are eligible for loans.

Loans are scheduled for repayment within the shortest period consistent with the borrowers' abilities to repay, but not to exceed 50 years.

QUESTIONS AND PROBLEMS
1. Outline the organization of the FHA.
2. What are the objectives of the FHA?
3. What are the sources of funds for FHA loans?
4. What are the special features of FHA loans?
5. Outline the types of loans that are made by the FHA. Are the various types necessary? Why not have just one broad type of loan that would include all the different types?
6. What are FHA operating loans? Discuss.
7. What are FHA farm ownership loans? What is their purpose? Discuss.
8. Compare farm ownership loans with insurance company and Federal Land Bank loans. Compare loan terms, payment plans, stock, availability, maximum loans, and loan procedure.
9. What are the dangers in making long-term loans for 100 percent of farm value? What are the advantages?
10. Would a program similar to the farm ownership program be practical and profitable for a private agency? Discuss.
11. What are the social gains in the farm ownership program?
12. How does the FHA insured loan program operate? The guaranteed loan program?
13. For your state and the nation, compare the percentage of farm debt outstanding held by the FHA and by the other institutional lenders. Data are available in the *Agricultural Finance Review* Supplement. Can you determine whether the share held by FHA has increased or decreased over the past 5 to 10 years?

REFERENCES
Acts of Congress Administered by or Affecting the Farmers Home Administration. Farmers Home Administration, USDA, Washington, D.C., revised 1972.

Administrator of the Farmers Home Administration. *Annual Reports.*

Building Rural America through Farmers Home Insured Notes. Farmers Home Administration, USDA, Washington, D.C., revised Jan. 1971.

Christiansen, R. A.; Staniforth, S. D.; and Walton, Richard. *Effectiveness of Development Credit in Facilitating Rural Adjustments.* Dept. Agr. Econ., Univ. of Wis. and Farm Prod. Econ. Div., ERS, USDA, cooperating, Agr. Econ. 45, Oct. 1965.

Collins, G. P.; Neufeld, G. H.; and Hunter, T. K. *Credit and Capital Growth: A Study of Farmers Home Administration Borrowers in Southeastern Oklahoma.* Okla. Exp. Sta., Processed Series P-490, Jan. 1965.

Herr, William McD. *Characteristics of New Borrowers Obtaining Farm Ownership Loans from the Farmers Home Administration—Fiscal 1966.* ERS, USDA, Agr. Econ. Rept. No. 184, May 1970.

APPENDIX

APPENDIX TABLE 1: Amount of 1 at Compound Interest

$$S = (1 + i)^n$$

n	1%	2%	3%	4%	5%	6%	n
1	1.0100	1.0200	1.0300	1.0400	1.0500	1.0600	1
2	1.0201	1.0404	1.0609	1.0816	1.1025	1.1236	2
3	1.0303	1.0612	1.0927	1.1249	1.1576	1.1910	3
4	1.0406	1.0824	1.1255	1.1699	1.2155	1.2625	4
5	1.0510	1.1041	1.1593	1.2167	1.2763	1.3382	5
6	1.0615	1.1262	1.1941	1.2653	1.3401	1.4185	6
7	1.0721	1.1487	1.2299	1.3159	1.4071	1.5036	7
8	1.0829	1.1717	1.2668	1.3686	1.4775	1.5938	8
9	1.0937	1.1951	1.3048	1.4233	1.5513	1.6895	9
10	1.1046	1.2190	1.3439	1.4802	1.6289	1.7908	10
11	1.1157	1.2434	1.3842	1.5395	1.7103	1.8983	11
12	1.1268	1.2682	1.4258	1.6010	1.7959	2.0122	12
13	1.1381	1.2936	1.4685	1.6651	1.8856	2.1329	13
14	1.1495	1.3195	1.5126	1.7317	1.9799	2.2609	14
15	1.1610	1.3459	1.5580	1.8009	2.0789	2.3966	15
16	1.1726	1.3728	1.6047	1.8730	2.1829	2.5404	16
17	1.1843	1.4002	1.6528	1.9479	2.2920	2.6928	17
18	1.1961	1.4282	1.7024	2.0258	2.4066	2.8543	18
19	1.2081	1.4568	1.7535	2.1068	2.5269	3.0256	19
20	1.2202	1.4859	1.8061	2.1911	2.6533	3.2071	20
21	1.2324	1.5157	1.8603	2.2788	2.7860	3.3996	21
22	1.2447	1.5460	1.9161	2.3699	2.9253	3.6035	22
23	1.2572	1.5769	1.9736	2.4647	3.0715	3.8197	23
24	1.2697	1.6084	2.0328	2.5633	3.2251	4.0489	24
25	1.2824	1.6406	2.0938	2.6658	3.3864	4.2919	25
26	1.2953	1.6734	2.1566	2.7725	3.5557	4.5494	26
27	1.3082	1.7069	2.2213	2.8834	3.7335	4.8223	27
28	1.3213	1.7410	2.2879	2.9987	3.9201	5.1117	28
29	1.3345	1.7758	2.3566	3.1187	4.1161	5.4184	29
30	1.3478	1.8114	2.4273	3.2434	4.3219	5.7435	30
31	1.3613	1.8476	2.5001	3.3731	4.5380	6.0881	31
32	1.3749	1.8845	2.5751	3.5081	4.7649	6.4534	32
33	1.3887	1.9222	2.6523	3.6484	5.0032	6.8406	33
34	1.4026	1.9607	2.7319	3.7943	5.2533	7.2510	34
35	1.4166	1.9999	2.8139	3.9461	5.5160	7.6861	35
40	1.4889	2.2080	3.2620	4.8010	7.0400	10.2857	40
45	1.5648	2.4379	3.7816	5.8412	8.9850	13.7646	45
50	1.6446	2.6916	4.3839	7.1067	11.4674	18.4201	50
55	1.7285	2.9717	5.0821	8.6464	14.6356	24.6503	55
60	1.8167	3.2810	5.8916	10.5196	18.6792	32.9877	60

APPENDIX TABLE 1 *(Continued)*: Amount of 1 at Compound Interest

$$S = (1 + i)^n$$

n	7%	8%	9%	10%	11%	12%	n
1	1.0700	1.0800	1.0900	1.1000	1.1100	1.1200	1
2	1.1449	1.1664	1.1881	1.2100	1.2321	1.2544	2
3	1.2250	1.2597	1.2950	1.3310	1.3676	1.4049	3
4	1.3108	1.3605	1.4116	1.4641	1.5181	1.5735	4
5	1.4026	1.4693	1.5386	1.6105	1.6851	1.7623	5
6	1.5007	1.5869	1.6771	1.7716	1.8704	1.9738	6
7	1.6058	1.7138	1.8280	1.9487	2.0762	2.2107	7
8	1.7182	1.8509	1.9926	2.1436	2.3045	2.4760	8
9	1.8385	1.9990	2.1719	2.3579	2.5580	2.7731	9
10	1.9672	2.1589	2.3674	2.5937	2.8394	3.1058	10
11	2.1049	2.3316	2.5804	2.8531	3.1518	3.4785	11
12	2.2522	2.5182	2.8127	3.1384	3.4984	3.8960	12
13	2.4098	2.7196	3.0658	3.4523	3.8833	4.3635	13
14	2.5785	2.9372	3.3417	3.7975	4.3104	4.8871	14
15	2.7590	3.1722	3.6425	4.1772	4.7846	5.4736	15
16	2.9522	3.4259	3.9703	4.5950	5.3109	6.1304	16
17	3.1588	3.7000	4.3276	5.0545	5.8951	6.8660	17
18	3.3799	3.9960	4.7171	5.5599	6.5435	7.6900	18
19	3.6165	4.3157	5.1417	6.1159	7.2633	8.6128	19
20	3.8697	4.6610	5.6044	6.7275	8.0623	9.6463	20
21	4.1406	5.0338	6.1088	7.4002	8.9492	10.8038	21
22	4.4304	5.4365	6.6586	8.1403	9.9336	12.1003	22
23	4.7405	5.8715	7.2579	8.9543	11.0263	13.5523	23
24	5.0724	6.3412	7.9111	9.8497	12.2391	15.1786	24
25	5.4274	6.8485	8.6231	10.8347	13.5855	17.0000	25
26	5.8074	7.3964	9.3992	11.9182	15.0799	19.0401	26
27	6.2139	7.9881	10.2451	13.1100	16.7386	21.3249	27
28	6.6488	8.6271	11.1671	14.4210	18.5799	23.8838	28
29	7.1143	9.3173	12.1722	15.8631	20.6237	26.7499	29
30	7.6123	10.0627	13.2677	17.4494	22.8923	29.9599	30
31	8.1451	10.8677	14.4618	19.1943	25.4104	33.5551	31
32	8.7153	11.7371	15.7633	21.1138	28.2056	37.5817	32
33	9.3253	12.6760	17.1820	23.2251	31.3082	42.0915	33
34	9.9781	13.6901	18.7284	25.5477	34.7521	47.1425	34
35	10.6766	14.7853	20.4140	28.1024	38.5748	52.7995	35
40	14.9745	21.7245	31.4094	45.2592	65.0008	93.0508	40
45	21.0024	31.9204	48.3273	72.8904	109.5301	163.9873	45
50	29.4570	46.9016	74.3575	117.3908	184.5645	289.0015	50
55	41.3150	68.9138	114.4082	189.0590	311.0017	509.3196	55
60	57.9464	101.2570	176.0312	304.4812	524.0562	897.5950	60

APPENDIX TABLE 2: Present Value of 1 at Compound Interest

$$v^n = \frac{1}{(1+i)^n}$$

n	1%	2%	3%	4%	5%	6%	n
1	0.9901	0.9804	0.9709	0.9615	0.9524	0.9434	1
2	0.9803	0.9612	0.9426	0.9246	0.9070	0.8900	2
3	0.9706	0.9423	0.9151	0.8890	0.8638	0.8396	3
4	0.9610	0.9238	0.8885	0.8548	0.8227	0.7921	4
5	0.9515	0.9057	0.8626	0.8219	0.7835	0.7473	5
6	0.9420	0.8880	0.8375	0.7903	0.7462	0.7050	6
7	0.9327	0.8706	0.8131	0.7599	0.7107	0.6651	7
8	0.9235	0.8535	0.7894	0.7307	0.6768	0.6274	8
9	0.9143	0.8368	0.7664	0.7026	0.6446	0.5919	9
10	0.9053	0.8203	0.7441	0.6756	0.6139	0.5584	10
11	0.8963	0.8043	0.7224	0.6496	0.5847	0.5268	11
12	0.8874	0.7885	0.7014	0.6246	0.5568	0.4970	12
13	0.8787	0.7730	0.6810	0.6006	0.5303	0.4688	13
14	0.8700	0.7579	0.6611	0.5775	0.5051	0.4423	14
15	0.8613	0.7430	0.6419	0.5553	0.4810	0.4173	15
16	0.8528	0.7284	0.6232	0.5339	0.4581	0.3936	16
17	0.8444	0.7142	0.6050	0.5134	0.4363	0.3714	17
18	0.8360	0.7002	0.5874	0.4936	0.4155	0.3503	18
19	0.8277	0.6864	0.5703	0.4746	0.3957	0.3305	19
20	0.8195	0.6730	0.5537	0.4564	0.3769	0.3118	20
21	0.8114	0.6598	0.5375	0.4388	0.3589	0.2942	21
22	0.8034	0.6468	0.5219	0.4220	0.3418	0.2775	22
23	0.7954	0.6342	0.5067	0.4057	0.3256	0.2618	23
24	0.7876	0.6217	0.4919	0.3901	0.3101	0.2470	24
25	0.7798	0.6095	0.4776	0.3751	0.2953	0.2330	25
26	0.7720	0.5976	0.4637	0.3607	0.2812	0.2198	26
27	0.7644	0.5859	0.4502	0.3468	0.2678	0.2074	27
28	0.7568	0.5744	0.4371	0.3335	0.2551	0.1956	28
29	0.7493	0.5631	0.4243	0.3207	0.2429	0.1846	29
30	0.7419	0.5521	0.4120	0.3083	0.2314	0.1741	30
31	0.7346	0.5412	0.4000	0.2965	0.2204	0.1643	31
32	0.7273	0.5306	0.3883	0.2851	0.2099	0.1550	32
33	0.7201	0.5202	0.3770	0.2741	0.1999	0.1462	33
34	0.7130	0.5100	0.3660	0.2636	0.1904	0.1379	34
35	0.7059	0.5000	0.3554	0.2534	0.1813	0.1301	35
40	0.6717	0.4529	0.3066	0.2083	0.1420	0.0972	40
45	0.6391	0.4102	0.2644	0.1712	0.1113	0.0727	45
50	0.6080	0.3715	0.2281	0.1407	0.0872	0.0543	50
55	0.5785	0.3365	0.1968	0.1157	0.0683	0.0406	55
60	0.5504	0.3048	0.1697	0.0951	0.0535	0.0303	60

APPENDIX TABLE 2 *(Continued):* Present Value of 1 at Compound Interest

$$V^n = \frac{1}{(1 + i)^n}$$

n	7%	8%	9%	10%	11%	12%	n
1	0.9346	0.9259	0.9174	0.9091	0.9009	0.8929	1
2	0.8734	0.8573	0.8417	0.8264	0.8116	0.7972	2
3	0.8163	0.7938	0.7722	0.7513	0.7312	0.7118	3
4	0.7629	0.7350	0.7084	0.6830	0.6587	0.6355	4
5	0.7130	0.6806	0.6499	0.6209	0.5935	0.5674	5
6	0.6663	0.6302	0.5963	0.5645	0.5346	0.5066	6
7	0.6227	0.5835	0.5470	0.5132	0.4817	0.4523	7
8	0.5820	0.5403	0.5019	0.4665	0.4339	0.4039	8
9	0.5439	0.5002	0.4604	0.4241	0.3909	0.3606	9
10	0.5083	0.4632	0.4224	0.3855	0.3522	0.3220	10
11	0.4751	0.4289	0.3875	0.3505	0.3173	0.2875	11
12	0.4440	0.3971	0.3555	0.3186	0.2858	0.2567	12
13	0.4150	0.3677	0.3262	0.2897	0.2575	0.2292	13
14	0.3878	0.3405	0.2992	0.2633	0.2320	0.2046	14
15	0.3624	0.3152	0.2745	0.2394	0.2090	0.1827	15
16	0.3387	0.2919	0.2519	0.2176	0.1883	0.1631	16
17	0.3166	0.2703	0.2311	0.1978	0.1696	0.1456	17
18	0.2959	0.2502	0.2120	0.1799	0.1528	0.1300	18
19	0.2765	0.2317	0.1945	0.1635	0.1377	0.1161	19
20	0.2584	0.2145	0.1784	0.1486	0.1240	0.1037	20
21	0.2415	0.1987	0.1637	0.1351	0.1117	0.0926	21
22	0.2257	0.1839	0.1502	0.1228	0.1007	0.0826	22
23	0.2109	0.1703	0.1378	0.1117	0.0907	0.0738	23
24	0.1971	0.1577	0.1264	0.1015	0.0817	0.0659	24
25	0.1842	0.1460	0.1160	0.0923	0.0736	0.0588	25
26	0.1722	0.1352	0.1064	0.0839	0.0663	0.0525	26
27	0.1609	0.1252	0.0976	0.0763	0.0597	0.0469	27
28	0.1504	0.1159	0.0895	0.0693	0.0538	0.0419	28
29	0.1406	0.1073	0.0822	0.0630	0.0485	0.0374	29
30	0.1314	0.0994	0.0754	0.0573	0.0437	0.0334	30
31	0.1228	0.0920	0.0691	0.0521	0.0394	0.0298	31
32	0.1147	0.0852	0.0634	0.0474	0.0355	0.0266	32
33	0.1072	0.0789	0.0582	0.0431	0.0319	0.0238	33
34	0.1002	0.0730	0.0534	0.0391	0.0288	0.0212	34
35	0.0937	0.0676	0.0490	0.0356	0.0259	0.0189	35
40	0.0668	0.0460	0.0318	0.0221	0.0154	0.0107	40
45	0.0476	0.0313	0.0207	0.0137	0.0091	0.0061	45
50	0.0339	0.0213	0.0134	0.0085	0.0054	0.0035	50
55	0.0242	0.0145	0.0087	0.0053	0.0032	0.0020	55
60	0.0173	0.0099	0.0057	0.0033	0.0019	0.0011	60

APPENDIX TABLE 2 *(Continued):* Present Value of 1 at Compound Interest

$$v^n = \frac{1}{(1 + i)^n}$$

n	13%	14%	15%	16%	18%	20%	n
1	0.8850	0.8772	0.8696	0.8621	0.8475	0.8333	1
2	0.7831	0.7695	0.7561	0.7432	0.7182	0.6944	2
3	0.6931	0.6750	0.6575	0.6407	0.6086	0.5787	3
4	0.6133	0.5921	0.5718	0.5523	0.5158	0.4823	4
5	0.5428	0.5194	0.4972	0.4761	0.4371	0.4019	5
6	0.4803	0.4556	0.4323	0.4104	0.3704	0.3349	6
7	0.4251	0.3996	0.3759	0.3538	0.3139	0.2791	7
8	0.3762	0.3506	0.3269	0.3050	0.2660	0.2326	8
9	0.3329	0.3075	0.2843	0.2630	0.2255	0.1938	9
10	0.2946	0.2697	0.2472	0.2267	0.1911	0.1615	10
11	0.2607	0.2366	0.2149	0.1954	0.1619	0.1346	11
12	0.2307	0.2076	0.1869	0.1685	0.1372	0.1122	12
13	0.2042	0.1821	0.1625	0.1452	0.1163	0.0935	13
14	0.1807	0.1597	0.1413	0.1252	0.0985	0.0779	14
15	0.1599	0.1401	0.1229	0.1079	0.0835	0.0649	15
16	0.1415	0.1229	0.1069	0.0930	0.0708	0.0541	16
17	0.1252	0.1078	0.0929	0.0802	0.0600	0.0451	17
18	0.1108	0.0946	0.0808	0.0691	0.0508	0.0376	18
19	0.0981	0.0829	0.0703	0.0596	0.0431	0.0313	19
20	0.0868	0.0728	0.0611	0.0514	0.0365	0.0261	20
21	0.0768	0.0638	0.0531	0.0443	0.0309	0.0217	21
22	0.0680	0.0560	0.0462	0.0382	0.0262	0.0181	22
23	0.0601	0.0491	0.0402	0.0329	0.0222	0.0151	23
24	0.0532	0.0431	0.0349	0.0284	0.0188	0.0126	24
25	0.0471	0.0378	0.0304	0.0245	0.0160	0.0105	25
26	0.0417	0.0331	0.0264	0.0211	0.0135	0.0087	26
27	0.0369	0.0291	0.0230	0.0182	0.0115	0.0073	27
28	0.0326	0.0255	0.0200	0.0157	0.0097	0.0061	28
29	0.0289	0.0224	0.0174	0.0135	0.0082	0.0051	29
30	0.0256	0.0196	0.0151	0.0116	0.0070	0.0042	30
31	0.0226	0.0172	0.0131	0.0100	0.0059	0.0035	31
32	0.0200	0.0151	0.0114	0.0087	0.0050	0.0029	32
33	0.0177	0.0132	0.0099	0.0075	0.0042	0.0024	33
34	0.0157	0.0116	0.0086	0.0064	0.0036	0.0020	34
35	0.0139	0.0102	0.0075	0.0055	0.0030	0.0017	35
40	0.0075	0.0053	0.0037	0.0026	0.0013	0.0007	40
45	0.0041	0.0027	0.0019	0.0013	0.0006	0.0003	45
50	0.0022	0.0014	0.0009	0.0006	0.0003	0.0001	50
55	0.0012	0.0007	0.0005	0.0003	0.0001	0.0000	55
60	0.0007	0.0004	0.0002	0.0001	0.0000	0.0000	60

$$v^n = \frac{1}{(1 + i)^n}$$

n	25%	30%	35%	40%	45%	50%	n
1	0.8000	0.7692	0.7407	0.7143	0.6897	0.6667	1
2	0.6400	0.5917	0.5487	0.5102	0.4756	0.4444	2
3	0.5120	0.4552	0.4064	0.3644	0.3280	0.2963	3
4	0.4096	0.3501	0.3011	0.2603	0.2262	0.1975	4
5	0.3277	0.2693	0.2230	0.1859	0.1560	0.1317	5
6	0.2621	0.2072	0.1652	0.1328	0.1076	0.0878	6
7	0.2097	0.1594	0.1224	0.0949	0.0742	0.0585	7
8	0.1678	0.1226	0.0906	0.0678	0.0512	0.0390	8
9	0.1342	0.0943	0.0671	0.0484	0.0353	0.0260	9
10	0.1074	0.0725	0.0497	0.0346	0.0243	0.0173	10
11	0.0859	0.0558	0.0368	0.0247	0.0168	0.0116	11
12	0.0687	0.0429	0.0273	0.0176	0.0116	0.0077	12
13	0.0550	0.0330	0.0202	0.0126	0.0080	0.0051	13
14	0.0440	0.0254	0.0150	0.0090	0.0055	0.0034	14
15	0.0352	0.0195	0.0111	0.0064	0.0038	0.0023	15
16	0.0281	0.0150	0.0082	0.0046	0.0026	0.0015	16
17	0.0225	0.0116	0.0061	0.0033	0.0018	0.0010	17
18	0.0180	0.0089	0.0045	0.0023	0.0012	0.0007	18
19	0.0144	0.0068	0.0033	0.0017	0.0009	0.0005	19
20	0.0115	0.0053	0.0025	0.0012	0.0006	0.0003	20
21	0.0092	0.0040	0.0018	0.0009	0.0004	0.0002	21
22	0.0074	0.0031	0.0014	0.0006	0.0003	0.0001	22
23	0.0059	0.0024	0.0010	0.0004	0.0002	0.0001	23
24	0.0047	0.0018	0.0007	0.0003	0.0001	0.0001	24
25	0.0038	0.0014	0.0006	0.0002	0.0001	0.0000	25
26	0.0030	0.0011	0.0004	0.0002	0.0001		26
27	0.0024	0.0008	0.0003	0.0001	0.0000		27
28	0.0019	0.0006	0.0002	0.0001			28
29	0.0015	0.0005	0.0002	0.0001			29
30	0.0012	0.0004	0.0001	0.0000			30
31	0.0010	0.0003	0.0001				31
32	0.0008	0.0002	0.0001				32
33	0.0006	0.0002	0.0001				33
34	0.0005	0.0001	0.0000				34
35	0.0004	0.0001					35
40	0.0001	0.0000					40
45	0.0000						45

APPENDIX TABLE 3: Annuity Which 1 Will Buy
(Annuity Whose Present Value at Compound Interest Is 1)

$$\frac{1}{a_{\overline{n}|i}} = \frac{i}{1 - (1 + i)^{-n}}$$

n	1%	2%	3%	4%	5%	6%	n
1	1.0100	1.0200	1.0300	1.0400	1.0500	1.0600	1
2	0.5075	0.5150	0.5226	0.5302	0.5378	0.5454	2
3	0.3400	0.3468	0.3535	0.3603	0.3672	0.3741	3
4	0.2563	0.2626	0.2690	0.2755	0.2820	0.2886	4
5	0.2060	0.2122	0.2184	0.2246	0.2310	0.2374	5
6	0.1725	0.1785	0.1846	0.1908	0.1970	0.2034	6
7	0.1486	0.1545	0.1605	0.1666	0.1728	0.1791	7
8	0.1307	0.1365	0.1425	0.1485	0.1547	0.1610	8
9	0.1167	0.1225	0.1284	0.1345	0.1407	0.1470	9
10	0.1056	0.1113	0.1172	0.1233	0.1295	0.1359	10
11	0.0965	0.1022	0.1081	0.1141	0.1204	0.1268	11
12	0.0888	0.0946	0.1005	0.1066	0.1128	0.1193	12
13	0.0824	0.0881	0.0940	0.1001	0.1065	0.1130	13
14	0.0769	0.0826	0.0885	0.0947	0.1010	0.1076	14
15	0.0721	0.0778	0.0838	0.0899	0.0963	0.1030	15
16	0.0679	0.0737	0.0796	0.0858	0.0923	0.0990	16
17	0.0643	0.0700	0.0760	0.0822	0.0887	0.0954	17
18	0.0610	0.0667	0.0727	0.0790	0.0855	0.0924	18
19	0.0581	0.0638	0.0698	0.0761	0.0827	0.0896	19
20	0.0554	0.0612	0.0672	0.0736	0.0802	0.0872	20
21	0.0530	0.0588	0.0649	0.0713	0.0780	0.0850	21
22	0.0509	0.0566	0.0627	0.0692	0.0760	0.0830	22
23	0.0489	0.0547	0.0608	0.0673	0.0741	0.0813	23
24	0.0471	0.0529	0.0590	0.0656	0.0725	0.0797	24
25	0.0454	0.0512	0.0574	0.0640	0.0710	0.0782	25
26	0.0439	0.0497	0.0559	0.0626	0.0696	0.0769	26
27	0.0424	0.0483	0.0546	0.0612	0.0683	0.0757	27
28	0.0411	0.0470	0.0533	0.0600	0.0671	0.0746	28
29	0.0399	0.0458	0.0521	0.0589	0.0660	0.0736	29
30	0.0387	0.0446	0.0510	0.0578	0.0651	0.0726	30
31	0.0377	0.0436	0.0500	0.0569	0.0641	0.0718	31
32	0.0367	0.0426	0.0490	0.0559	0.0633	0.0710	32
33	0.0357	0.0417	0.0482	0.0551	0.0625	0.0703	33
34	0.0348	0.0408	0.0473	0.0543	0.0618	0.0696	34
35	0.0340	0.0400	0.0465	0.0536	0.0611	0.0690	35
40	0.0305	0.0366	0.0433	0.0505	0.0583	0.0665	40
45	0.0277	0.0339	0.0408	0.0483	0.0563	0.0647	45
50	0.0255	0.0318	0.0389	0.0466	0.0548	0.0634	50
55	0.0237	0.0301	0.0373	0.0452	0.0537	0.0625	55
60	0.0222	0.0288	0.0361	0.0442	0.0528	0.0619	60

APPENDIX TABLE 3 *(Continued):* Annuity Which 1 Will Buy
(Annuity Whose Present Value at Compound Interest Is 1)

$$\frac{1}{a_{\overline{n}|i}} = \frac{i}{1 - (1 + i)^{-n}}$$

n	7%	8%	9%	10%	11%	12%	n
1	1.0700	1.0800	1.0900	1.1000	1.1100	1.1200	1
2	0.5531	0.5608	0.5685	·0.5762	0.5839	0.5917	2
3	0.3811	0.3880	0.3951	0.4021	0.4092	0.4163	3
4	0.2952	0.3019	0.3087	0.3155	0.3223	0.3292	4
5	0.2439	0.2505	0.2571	0.2638	0.2706	0.2774	5
6	0.2098	0.2163	0.2229	0.2296	0.2364	0.2432	6
7	0.1856	0.1921	0.1987	0.2054	0.2122	0.2191	7
8	0.1675	0.1740	0.1807	0.1874	0.1943	0.2013	8
9	0.1535	0.1601	0.1668	0.1736	0.1806	0.1877	9
10	0.1424	0.1490	0.1558	0.1627	0.1698	0.1770	10
11	0.1334	0.1401	0.1469	0.1540	0.1611	0.1684	11
12	0.1259	0.1327	0.1397	0.1468	0.1540	0.1614	12
13	0.1197	0.1265	0.1336	0.1408	0.1482	0.1557	13
14	0.1143	0.1213	0.1284	0.1357	0.1432	0.1509	14
15	0.1098	0.1168	0.1241	0.1315	0.1391	0.1468	15
16	0.1059	0.1130	0.1203	0.1278	0.1355	0.1434	16
17	0.1024	0.1096	0.1170	0.1247	0.1325	0.1405	17
18	0.0994	0.1067	0.1142	0.1219	0.1298	0.1379	18
19	0.0968	0.1041	0.1117	0.1195	0.1276	0.1358	19
20	0.0944	0.1019	0.1095	0.1175	0.1256	0.1339	20
21	0.0923	0.0998	0.1076	0.1156	0.1238	0.1322	21
22	0.0904	0.0980	0.1059	0.1140	0.1223	0.1308	22
23	0.0887	0.0964	0.1044	0.1126	0.1210	0.1296	23
24	0.0872	0.0950	0.1030	0.1113	0.1198	0.1285	24
25	0.0858	0.0937	0.1018	0.1102	0.1187	0.1275	25
26	0.0846	0.0925	0.1007	0.1092	0.1178	0.1267	26
27	0.0834	0.0914	0.0997	0.1083	0.1170	0.1259	27
28	0.0824	0.0905	0.0989	0.1075	0.1163	0.1252	28
29	0.0814	0.0896	0.0981	0.1067	0.1156	0.1247	29
30	0.0806	0.0888	0.0973	0.1061	0.1150	0.1241	30
31	0.0798	0.0881	0.0967	0.1055	0.1145	0.1237	31
32	0.0791	0.0875	0.0961	0.1050	0.1140	0.1233	32
33	0.0784	0.0869	0.0956	0.1045	0.1136	0.1229	33
34	0.0778	0.0863	0.0951	0.1041	0.1133	0.1226	34
35	0.0772	0.0858	0.0946	0.1037	0.1129	0.1223	35
40	0.0750	0.0839	0.0930	0.1023	0.1117	0.1213	40
45	0.0735	0.0826	0.0919	0.1014	0.1110	0.1207	45
50	0.0725	0.0817	0.0912	0.1009	0.1106	0.1204	50
55	0.0717	0.0812	0.0908	0.1005	0.1104	0.1202	55
60	0.0712	0.0808	0.0905	0.1003	0.1102	0.1201	60

$$\frac{1}{a_{\overline{n}|i}} = \frac{i}{1 - (1 + i)^{-n}}$$

n	13%	14%	15%	16%	17%	18%	n
1	1.1300	1.1400	1.1500	1.1600	1.1700	1.1800	1
2	0.5995	0.6073	0.6151	0.6230	0.6308	0.6387	2
3	0.4235	0.4307	0.4380	0.4453	0.4526	0.4599	3
4	0.3362	0.3432	0.3503	0.3574	0.3645	0.3717	4
5	0.2843	0.2913	0.2983	0.3054	0.3126	0.3198	5
6	0.2502	0.2572	0.2642	0.2714	0.2786	0.2859	6
7	0.2261	0.2332	0.2404	0.2476	0.2549	0.2624	7
8	0.2084	0.2156	0.2229	0.2302	0.2377	0.2452	8
9	0.1949	0.2022	0.2096	0.2171	0.2247	0.2324	9
10	0.1843	0.1917	0.1993	0.2069	0.2147	0.2225	10
11	0.1758	0.1834	0.1911	0.1989	0.2068	0.2148	11
12	0.1690	0.1767	0.1845	0.1924	0.2005	0.2086	12
13	0.1634	0.1712	0.1791	0.1872	0.1954	0.2037	13
14	0.1587	0.1666	0.1747	0.1829	0.1912	0.1997	14
15	0.1547	0.1628	0.1710	0.1794	0.1878	0.1964	15
16	0.1514	0.1596	0.1679	0.1764	0.1850	0.1937	16
17	0.1486	0.1569	0.1654	0.1740	0.1827	0.1915	17
18	0.1462	0.1546	0.1632	0.1719	0.1807	0.1896	18
19	0.1441	0.1527	0.1613	0.1701	0.1791	0.1881	19
20	0.1424	0.1510	0.1598	0.1687	0.1777	0.1868	20
21	0.1408	0.1495	0.1584	0.1674	0.1765	0.1857	21
22	0.1395	0.1483	0.1573	0.1664	0.1756	0.1848	22
23	0.1383	0.1472	0.1563	0.1654	0.1747	0.1841	23
24	0.1373	0.1463	0.1554	0.1647	0.1740	0.1835	24
25	0.1364	0.1455	0.1547	0.1640	0.1734	0.1829	25
26	0.1357	0.1448	0.1541	0.1634	0.1729	0.1825	26
27	0.1350	0.1442	0.1535	0.1630	0.1725	0.1821	27
28	0.1344	0.1437	0.1531	0.1625	0.1721	0.1818	28
29	0.1339	0.1432	0.1527	0.1622	0.1718	0.1815	29
30	0.1334	0.1428	0.1523	0.1619	0.1715	0.1813	30
31	0.1330	0.1425	0.1520	0.1616	0.1713	0.1811	31
32	0.1327	0.1421	0.1517	0.1614	0.1711	0.1809	32
33	0.1323	0.1419	0.1515	0.1612	0.1710	0.1808	33
34	0.1321	0.1416	0.1513	0.1610	0.1708	0.1806	34
35	0.1318	0.1414	0.1511	0.1609	0.1707	0.1806	35
40	0.1310	0.1407	0.1506	0.1604	0.1703	0.1802	40
45	0.1305	0.1404	0.1503	0.1602	0.1701	0.1801	45
50	0.1303	0.1402	0.1501	0.1601	0.1701	0.1800	50
55	0.1302	0.1401	0.1501	0.1600	0.1700	0.1800	55
60	0.1301	0.1401	0.1500	0.1600	0.1700	0.1800	60

$$\frac{1}{a_{\overline{n}|i}} = \frac{i}{1 - (1 + i)^{-n}}$$

n	19%	20%	21%	22%	23%	24%	n
1	1.1900	1.2000	1.2100	1.2200	1.2300	1.2400	1
2	0.6466	0.6545	0.6625	0.6705	0.6784	0.6864	2
3	0.4673	0.4747	0.4822	0.4897	0.4972	0.5047	3
4	0.3790	0.3863	0.3936	0.4010	0.4085	0.4159	4
5	0.3271	0.3344	0.3418	0.3492	0.3567	0.3642	5
6	0.2933	0.3007	0.3082	0.3158	0.3234	0.3311	6
7	0.2699	0.2774	0.2851	0.2928	0.3006	0.3084	7
8	0.2529	0.2606	0.2684	0.2763	0.2843	0.2923	8
9	0.2402	0.2481	0.2561	0.2641	0.2722	0.2805	9
10	0.2305	0.2385	0.2467	0.2549	0.2632	0.2716	10
11	0.2229	0.2311	0.2394	0.2478	0.2563	0.2649	11
12	0.2169	0.2253	0.2337	0.2423	0.2509	0.2596	12
13	0.2121	0.2206	0.2292	0.2379	0.2467	0.2556	13
14	0.2082	0.2169	0.2256	0.2345	0.2434	0.2524	14
15	0.2051	0.2139	0.2228	0.2317	0.2408	0.2499	15
16	0.2025	0.2114	0.2204	0.2295	0.2387	0.2479	16
17	0.2004	0.2094	0.2186	0.2278	0.2370	0.2464	17
18	0.1987	0.2078	0.2170	0.2263	0.2357	0.2451	18
19	0.1972	0.2065	0.2158	0.2251	0.2346	0.2441	19
20	0.1960	0.2054	0.2147	0.2242	0.2337	0.2433	20
21	0.1951	0.2044	0.2139	0.2234	0.2330	0.2426	21
22	0.1942	0.2037	0.2132	0.2228	0.2324	0.2421	22
23	0.1935	0.2031	0.2127	0.2223	0.2320	0.2417	23
24	0.1930	0.2025	0.2122	0.2219	0.2316	0.2414	24
25	0.1925	0.2021	0.2118	0.2215	0.2313	0.2411	25
26	0.1921	0.2018	0.2115	0.2213	0.2311	0.2409	26
27	0.1917	0.2015	0.2112	0.2210	0.2309	0.2407	27
28	0.1915	0.2012	0.2110	0.2208	0.2307	0.2406	28
29	0.1912	0.2010	0.2108	0.2207	0.2306	0.2405	29
30	0.1910	0.2008	0.2107	0.2206	0.2305	0.2404	30
31	0.1909	0.2007	0.2106	0.2205	0.2304	0.2403	31
32	0.1907	0.2006	0.2105	0.2204	0.2303	0.2402	32
33	0.1906	0.2005	0.2104	0.2203	0.2302	0.2402	33
34	0.1905	0.2004	0.2103	0.2203	0.2302	0.2402	34
35	0.1904	0.2003	0.2103	0.2202	0.2302	0.2401	35
40	0.1902	0.2001	0.2101	0.2201	0.2301	0.2400	40
45	0.1901	0.2001	0.2100	0.2200	0.2300	0.2400	45
50	0.1900	0.2000	0.2100	0.2200	0.2300	0.2400	50
55	0.1900	0.2000	0.2100	0.2200	0.2300	0.2400	55
60	0.1900	0.2000	0.2100	0.2200	0.2300	0.2400	60

APPENDIX TABLE 4: Present Value of 1 Per Annum at Compound Interest

$$a_{\overline{n}|i} = \frac{1 - (1 + i)^{-n}}{i}$$

n	1%	2%	3%	4%	5%	6%	n
1	0.9901	0.9804	0.9709	0.9615	0.9524	0.9434	1
2	1.9704	1.9416	1.9135	1.8861	1.8594	1.8334	2
3	2.9410	2.8839	2.8286	2.7751	2.7232	2.6730	3
4	3.9020	3.8077	3.7171	3.6299	3.5460	3.4651	4
5	4.8534	4.7135	4.5797	4.4518	4.3295	4.2124	5
6	5.7955	5.6014	5.4172	5.2421	5.0757	4.9173	6
7	6.7282	6.4720	6.2303	6.0021	5.7864	5.5824	7
8	7.6517	7.3255	7.0197	6.7327	6.4632	6.2098	8
9	8.5660	8.1622	7.7861	7.4353	7.1078	6.8017	9
10	9.4713	8.9826	8.5302	8.1109	7.7217	7.3601	10
11	10.3676	9.7868	9.2526	8.7605	8.3064	7.8869	11
12	11.2551	10.5753	9.9540	9.3851	8.8633	8.3838	12
13	12.1337	11.3484	10.6350	9.9856	9.3936	8.8527	13
14	13.0037	12.1062	11.2961	10.5631	9.8986	9.2950	14
15	13.8651	12.8493	11.9379	11.1184	10.3797	9.7122	15
16	14.7179	13.5777	12.5611	11.6523	10.8378	10.1059	16
17	15.5623	14.2919	13.1661	12.1657	11.2741	10.4773	17
18	16.3983	14.9920	13.7535	12.6593	11.6896	10.8276	18
19	17.2260	15.6785	14.3238	13.1339	12.0853	11.1581	19
20	18.0456	16.3514	14.8775	13.5903	12.4622	11.4699	20
21	18.8570	17.0112	15.4150	14.0292	12.8212	11.7641	21
22	19.6604	17.6580	15.9369	14.4511	13.1630	12.0416	22
23	20.4558	18.2922	16.4436	14.8568	13.4886	12.3034	23
24	21.2434	18.9139	16.9355	15.2470	13.7986	12.5504	24
25	22.0232	19.5235	17.4131	15.6221	14.0939	12.7834	25
26	22.7952	20.1210	17.8768	15.9828	14.3752	13.0032	26
27	23.5596	20.7069	18.3270	16.3296	14.6430	13.2105	27
28	24.3164	21.2813	18.7641	16.6631	14.8981	13.4062	28
29	25.0658	21.8444	19.1885	16.9837	15.1411	13.5907	29
30	25.8077	22.3965	19.6004	17.2920	15.3725	13.7648	30
31	26.5423	22.9377	20.0004	17.5885	15.5928	13.9291	31
32	27.2696	23.4683	20.3888	17.8736	15.8027	14.0840	32
33	27.9897	23.9886	20.7658	18.1476	16.0025	14.2302	33
34	28.7027	24.4986	21.1318	18.4112	16.1929	14.3681	34
35	29.4086	24.9986	21.4872	18.6646	16.3742	14.4982	35
40	32.8347	27.3555	23.1148	19.7928	17.1591	15.0463	40
45	36.0945	29.4902	24.5187	20.7200	17.7741	15.4558	45
50	39.1961	31.4236	25.7298	21.4822	18.2559	15.7619	50
55	42.1472	33.1748	26.7744	22.1086	18.6335	15.9905	55
60	44.9550	34.7609	27.6756	22.6235	18.9293	16.1614	60

APPENDIX TABLE 4 *(Continued)*: Present Value of 1 Per Annum at Compound Interest

$$a_{\overline{n}|i} = \frac{1 - (1 + i)^{-n}}{i}$$

n	7%	8%	9%	10%	11%	12%	n
1	0.9346	0.9259	0.9174	0.9091	0.9009	0.8929	1
2	1.8080	1.7833	1.7591	1.7355	1.7125	1.6901	2
3	2.6243	2.5771	2.5313	2.4869	2.4437	2.4018	3
4	3.3872	3.3121	3.2397	3.1699	3.1024	3.0373	4
5	4.1002	3.9927	3.8897	3.7908	3.6959	3.6048	5
6	4.7665	4.6229	4.4859	4.3553	4.2305	4.1114	6
7	5.3893	5.2064	5.0330	4.8684	4.7122	4.5638	7
8	5.9713	5.7466	5.5348	5.3349	5.1461	4.9676	8
9	6.5152	6.2469	5.9952	5.7590	5.5370	5.3282	9
10	7.0236	6.7101	6.4177	6.1446	5.8892	5.6502	10
11	7.4987	7.1390	6.8052	6.4951	6.2065	5.9377	11
12	7.9427	7.5361	7.1607	6.8137	6.4924	6.1944	12
13	8.3577	7.9038	7.4869	7.1034	6.7499	6.4235	13
14	8.7455	8.2442	7.7862	7.3667	6.9819	6.6282	14
15	9.1079	8.5595	8.0607	7.6061	7.1909	6.8109	15
16	9.4466	8.8514	8.3126	7.8237	7.3792	6.9740	16
17	9.7632	9.1216	8.5436	8.0216	7.5488	7.1196	17
18	10.0591	9.3719	8.7556	8.2014	7.7016	7.2497	18
19	10.3356	9.6036	8.9501	8.3649	7.8393	7.3658	19
20	10.5940	9.8181	9.1285	8.5136	7.9633	7.4694	20
21	10.8355	10.0168	9.2922	8.6487	8.0751	7.5620	21
22	11.0612	10.2007	9.4424	8.7715	8.1757	7.6446	22
23	11.2722	10.3711	9.5802	8.8832	8.2664	7.7184	23
24	11.4693	10.5288	9.7066	8.9847	8.3481	7.7843	24
25	11.6536	10.6748	9.8226	9.0770	8.4217	7.8431	25
26	11.8258	10.8100	9.9290	9.1609	8.4881	7.8957	26
27	11.9867	10.9352	10.0266	9.2372	8.5478	7.9426	27
28	12.1371	11.0511	10.1161	9.3066	8.6016	7.9844	28
29	12.2777	11.1584	10.1983	9.3696	8.6501	8.0218	29
30	12.4090	11.2578	10.2737	9.4269	8.6938	8.0552	30
31	12.5318	11.3498	10.3428	9.4790	8.7331	8.0850	31
32	12.6466	11.4350	10.4062	9.5264	8.7686	8.1116	32
33	12.7538	11.5139	10.4644	9.5694	8.8005	8.1354	33
34	12.8540	11.5869	10.5178	9.6086	8.8293	8.1566	34
35	12.9477	11.6546	10.5668	9.6442	8.8552	8.1755	35
40	13.3317	11.9246	10.7574	9.7791	8.9511	8.2438	40
45	13.6055	12.1084	10.8812	9.8628	9.0079	8.2825	45
50	13.8007	12.2335	10.9617	9.9148	9.0417	8.3045	50
55	13.9399	12.3186	11.0140	9.9471	9.0617	8.3170	55
60	14.0392	12.3766	11.0480	9.9672	9.0736	8.3240	60

$$a_{\overline{n}|i} = \frac{1 - (1 + i)^{-n}}{i}$$

n	13%	14%	15%	16%	18%	20%	n
1	0.8850	0.8772	0.8696	0.8621	0.8475	0.8333	1
2	1.6681	1.6467	1.6257	1.6052	1.5656	1.5278	2
3	2.3612	2.3216	2.2832	2.2459	2.1743	2.1065	3
4	2.9745	2.9137	2.8550	2.7982	2.6901	2.5887	4
5	3.5172	3.4331	3.3522	3.2743	3.1272	2.9906	5
6	3.9975	3.8887	3.7845	3.6847	3.4976	3.3255	6
7	4.4226	4.2883	4.1604	4.0386	3.8115	3.6046	7
8	4.7988	4.6389	4.4873	4.3436	4.0776	3.8372	8
9	5.1317	4.9464	4.7716	4.6065	4.3030	4.0310	9
10	5.4262	5.2161	5.0188	4.8332	4.4941	4.1925	10
11	5.6869	5.4527	5.2337	5.0286	4.6560	4.3271	11
12	5.9176	5.6603	5.4206	5.1971	4.7932	4.4392	12
13	6.1218	5.8424	5.5831	5.3423	4.9095	4.5327	13
14	6.3025	6.0021	5.7245	5.4675	5.0081	4.6106	14
15	6.4624	6.1422	5.8474	5.5755	5.0916	4.6755	15
16	6.6039	6.2651	5.9542	5.6685	5.1624	4.7296	16
17	6.7291	6.3729	6.0472	5.7487	5.2223	4.7746	17
18	6.8399	6.4674	6.1280	5.8178	5.2732	4.8122	18
19	6.9380	6.5504	6.1982	5.8775	5.3162	4.8435	19
20	7.0248	6.6231	6.2593	5.9288	5.3527	4.8696	20
21	7.1016	6.6870	6.3125	5.9731	5.3837	4.8913	21
22	7.1695	6.7429	6.3587	6.0113	5.4099	4.9094	22
23	7.2297	6.7921	6.3988	6.0442	5.4321	4.9245	23
24	7.2829	6.8351	6.4338	6.0726	5.4509	4.9371	24
25	7.3300	6.8729	6.4641	6.0971	5.4669	4.9476	25
26	7.3717	6.9061	6.4906	6.1182	5.4804	4.9563	26
27	7.4086	6.9352	6.5135	6.1364	5.4919	4.9636	27
28	7.4412	6.9607	6.5335	6.1520	5.5016	4.9697	28
29	7.4701	6.9830	6.5509	6.1656	5.5098	4.9747	29
30	7.4957	7.0027	6.5660	6.1772	6.6168	4.9789	30
31	7.5183	7.0199	6.5791	6.1872	5.5227	4.9824	31
32	7.5383	7.0350	6.5905	6.1959	5.5277	4.9854	32
33	7.5560	7.0482	6.6005	6.2034	5.5320	4.9878	33
34	7.5717	7.0599	6.6091	6.2098	5.5356	4.9898	34
35	7.5856	7.0700	6.6166	6.2153	5.5386	4.9915	35
40	7.6344	7.1050	6.6418	6.2335	5.5482	4.9966	40
45	7.6609	7.1232	6.6543	6.2421	5.5523	4.9986	45
50	7.6752	7.1327	6.6605	6.2463	5.5541	4.9995	50
55	7.6830	7.1376	6.6636	6.2482	5.5549	4.9998	55
60	7.6873	7.1401	6.6651	6.2492	5.5553	4.9999	60

APPENDIX TABLE 4 *(Continued):* Present Value of 1 Per Annum at Compound Interest

$$a_{\overline{n}|i} = \frac{1 - (1 + i)^{-n}}{i}$$

n	25%	30%	35%	40%	45%	50%	n
1	0.8000	0.7692	0.7407	0.7143	0.6897	0.6667	1
2	1.4400	1.3609	1.2894	1.2245	1.1653	1.1111	2
3	1.9520	1.8161	1.6959	1.5889	1.4933	1.4074	3
4	2.3616	2.1662	1.9969	1.8492	1.7195	1.6049	4
5	2.6893	2.4356	2.2200	2.0352	1.8755	1.7366	5
6	2.9514	2.6427	2.3852	2.1680	1.9831	1.8244	6
7	3.1611	2.8021	2.5075	2.2628	2.0573	1.8829	7
8	3.3289	2.9247	2.5982	2.3306	2.1085	1.9220	8
9	3.4631	3.0190	2.6653	2.3790	2.1438	1.9480	9
10	3.5705	3.0915	2.7150	2.4136	2.1681	1.9653	10
11	3.6564	3.1473	2.7519	2.4383	2.1849	1.9769	11
12	3.7251	3.1903	2.7792	2.4559	2.1965	1.9846	12
13	3.7801	3.2233	2.7994	2.4685	2.2045	1.9897	13
14	3.8241	3.2487	2.8144	2.4775	2.2100	1.9931	14
15	3.8593	3.2682	2.8255	2.4839	2.2138	1.9954	15
16	3.8874	3.2832	2.8337	2.4885	2.2164	1.9970	16
17	3.9099	3.2948	2.8398	2.4918	2.2182	1.9980	17
18	3.9279	3.3037	2.8443	2.4941	2.2195	1.9986	18
19	3.9424	3.3105	2.8476	2.4958	2.2203	1.9991	19
20	3.9539	3.3158	2.8501	2.4970	2.2209	1.9994	20
21	3.9631	3.3198	2.8519	2.4979	2.2213	1.9996	21
22	3.9705	3.3230	2.8533	2.4985	2.2216	1.9997	22
23	3.9764	3.3254	2.8543	2.4989	2.2218	1.9998	23
24	3.9811	3.3272	2.8550	2.4992	2.2219	1.9999	24
25	3.9849	3.3286	2.8556	2.4994	2.2220	1.9999	25
26	3.9879	3.3297	2.8560	2.4996	2.2221	1.9999	26
27	3.9903	3.3305	2.8563	2.4997	2.2221	2.0000	27
28	3.9923	3.3312	2.8565	2.4998	2.2222	2.0000	28
29	3.9938	3.3317	2.8567	2.4999	2.2222	2.0000	29
30	3.9950	3.3321	2.8568	2.4999	2.2222	2.0000	30
31	3.9960	3.3324	2.8569	2.4999	2.2222	2.0000	31
32	3.9968	3.3326	2.8569	2.4999	2.2222	2.0000	32
33	3.9975	3.3328	2.8570	2.5000	2.2222	2.0000	33
34	3.9980	3.3329	2.8570	2.5000	2.2222	2.0000	34
35	3.9984	3.3330	2.8571	2.5000	2.2222	2.0000	35
40	3.9995	3.3332	2.8571	2.5000	2.2222	2.0000	40
45	3.9998	3.3333	2.8571	2.5000	2.2222	2.0000	45
50	3.9999	3.3333	2.8571	2.5000	2.2222	2.0000	50
55	4.0000	3.3333	2.8571	2.5000	2.2222	2.0000	55
60	4.0000	3.3333	2.8571	2.5000	2.2222	2.0000	60

INDEX

Abstracts, 215, 225
Accrual method, 117
Actuarial rate of interest, 153
Add-on loans, 155. *See also* Interest rates
Administrator (of an estate), 263
Agricultural credit, amount outstanding, 7–9, 302–11
Agricultural finance
  definition, 3
  significance, 5–10
Agricultural lenders, relative importance of, 303–11. *See also* Lenders; *specific lending agency*
Agriculture, technological revolution of, 5–11
Alternative uses for money, 41–42
Amortized loans, 168–72. *See also* Loan repayment terms
Amount of 1 at compound interest, tables, 389–90
Annuities
  life annuities, 200, 259–60, 264–65
  present value of, 45
Annuity which 1 will buy, tables, 395–98
Aplin, Richard D., 41
Appraisal report, 242–43
Assets. *See also* Balance sheet
  in balance sheet, 101–6
  value in farming sector, 7–8
Assignments, 226
Automobile insurance. *See* Insurance

Bailey, Warren R., 196
Baker, C. B., 60
Balance sheet
  analysis, 101–15
  characteristics, 102
  examples, 102, 104, 108, 109, 237–39
  of farming sector, 7–8
  physical data, 104–5
  preparation, 102–5
  ratios, 110–14
    current, 110
    debt to equity, 113
    equity to value, 113
    intermediate, 112
    net capital, 112–13
    quick, 112
  trend analysis, 106–10
  valuation of assets, 105–6

Balloon payment, 167
Bank Holding Company Act, 322
Bankruptcy, 228–29
Banks. *See* Commercial banks
Banks for Cooperatives, 372–75
  interest rates on loans, 374–75
  loan policies, 373–74
  loan repayment terms, 374
  ownership, 372–73
  source of loan funds, 373
  taxation, 375
Benefit:cost ratio, 50
Benson, Richard A., 141
Bonds
  definition, 46
  investment characteristics, 254, 256–59
  valuation, 46–47
Book value, 8, 106
Borrowing. *See also* Credit; Farm loan volume; Loans
  advantages, 96–97
  definition, 91
  disadvantages, 97
  risk, 57–59, 62–65, 72–73, 92
Bradford, Lawrence A., 70
Bragg, Errol, 311
Brake, John R., 141, 150, 156, 157, 159, 250, 252
Branch banking, 319–20
Breeding herds
  leasing, 89
  public offerings, 312–13
Brokers, 254–55, 279, 284–85
Budgeting
  budgeted loans, 139–40
  cash flow budgeting, 139–42
  partial budgets, 21
Bunn, Charles, 218
Business failure, 228–29

Capacity, reserve of, 15
Capital
  acquisition, 4, 71–72, 78–99
  allocation to alternative uses, 4–5, 30–38, 73
  control of, 5, 72–73, 78–99
  definition, 3
  protection, 5, 73–74
  requirements in farming sector, 7–8
  sources of, 29–30, 72–73, 78–99
  supply and demand, 279–80